MW00476799

RED ROUND GLOBE HOT BURNING

RED ROUND GLOBE HOT BURNING

A TALE AT THE CROSSROADS OF COMMONS
AND CLOSURE, OF LOVE AND TERROR, OF RACE
AND CLASS, AND OF KATE AND NED DESPARD

Peter Linebaugh

UNIVERSITY OF CALIFORNIA PRESS

University of California Press, one of the most distinguished university presses in the United States, enriches lives around the world by advancing scholarship in the humanities, social sciences, and natural sciences. Its activities are supported by the UC Press Foundation and by philanthropic contributions from individuals and institutions. For more information, visit www.ucpress.edu.

University of California Press
Oakland, California

Library of Congress Cataloging-in-Publication Data

Names: Linebaugh, Peter, author.
Title: Red round globe hot burning : A tale at the crossroads of commons and
    closure, of love and terror, of race and class, and of Kate and Ned Despard.
Description: Oakland, California : University of California Press, [2019] |
    Includes bibliographical references and index. |
Identifiers: LCCN 2018028780 (print) | LCCN 2018032370 (ebook) |
    ISBN 9780520971189 (Epub) | ISBN 9780520299467 (cloth : alk. paper)
Subjects: LCSH: Commons—History—18th century. | Public lands—18th
    century. | Despard, Edward Marcus, 1751–1803. | Despard, Catherine.
Classification: LCC HD1286 (ebook) | LCC HD1286 .L56 2019 (print) |
    DDC 941.07/30922 [B] —dc23
LC record available at https://lccn.loc.gov/2018028780

28   27   26   25   24   23   22   21   20   19
10   9   8   7   6   5   4   3   2   1

To Michaela Brennan

Omnia Sunt Communia.

PEASANTS REVOLT, 1525

Let us haif the bukis necessare To commoun weill.

DAVID LYNDSAY, 1481–1555

Let us finally imagine, for a change, an association of free people, working with the means of production held in common.

KARL MARX, *Capital, 1867.*

It is already a big part of the earth and it will come. To own everything in common. That's what the Bible says. Common means all of us. This is old commonism.

WOODY GUTHRIE, 1941

CONTENTS

ACKNOWLEDGMENTS

This book has been the product of many years and many people. Looking back on its production, I am filled with gratitude for those who have helped it along. I cannot describe everything and everybody who made it possible, but it is with affection that I try to describe some. And it is with respect that I acknowledge the generosity implicit in this immense though imperfect commons of Truth.

Long ago, Edward Thompson gave me his copy of the *Trial of Despard,* and ever since it has been in my luggage—in South Africa, Ireland, India, Costa Rica, Europe, and New York. Dorothy Thompson gave me her husband's extensive typed transcripts from the English Home Office papers for the years 1802 and 1803, as well as notes from French archives which had been composed by Alfred Cobban. Well after I began work on this book, two biographies of Despard appeared. Their authors, Clifford Connor and Mike Jay, have been exceptionally generous.

Marcus Rediker and I wrote *The Many-Headed Hydra,* whose eighth chapter is the first approximation of the story told here. One day, looking at my photographs, which I had not yet provided words for, he let me know I was on a kind of quest. This insight led me to the quest for the commons and the quest for a woman who lived over two hundred years ago. Shipmate, thanks!

On May Day 2000, I asked my Irish colleagues at the Keough Centre at Notre Dame University how to say "workers of the world unite" in the Irish language. After a little effort, a literal rendition was offered, though it did not please everyone in the assembly. An old Irish saying was provided instead: *ar scáth a chéile a mhaireann na davine* (we live in the shadow of each other). So has it been with this book.

Kevin Whelan of the Keough Centre of Dublin and Notre Dame and his wife, Ann Kearney, offered unstinting hospitality in every respect, scholarly and otherwise. A remarkable 1798 conference held in Belfast, Dublin, and the train in between the two cities felt like an initiation into an international and ancient fraternity of scholars. It took place as the Good Friday Agreement was signed! Thanks to Luke Gibbons for his generous introductions to poetry, film, and social history, and to the Field Day tendency. Thanks to Louis Cullen and the graduate history seminar at Trinity College, Dublin, and to Patrick Bresnihan of Dublin's Provisional University, 2014.

I thank the ever-helpful staff of the National Library of Ireland, Mr. Gregory Connor of the National Archives of Ireland, the Royal Irish Academy, the Trinity College Library, the Rathmines Public Library, and the Friends Historical Library, Swanbrook House, Dublin.

I thank Dermit Ferriter and Daire Keogh of St. Patrick's College, Drumcondra; I thank Fidelma Maddock, who visited the source of the Nore and described the salmon run for me; and I thank Geraldine and Matthew Stout, who introduced me to the old earthen monuments of the Boyne Valley. Bill Jones accompanied me on a ramble in Upperwoods of county Laois. After I had jumped off a mossy slab of stone in an old graveyard, he rubbed it clean of moss and lichen to reveal aslant the chiseled letters of William Despard and his wife, Elizabeth: we had stumbled on the grave of Despard's grandfather and grandmother.

The quest was interrupted by a state of emergency, which in addition to the familiar combination of war and domestic repression propounded a discourse of empire and the "unitary executive" that swept all before it. This emergency required recovering the hidden traditions of the commons forgotten by the domineering effects of the twentieth-century Communist parties. So, in response, I wrote the *Magna Carta Manifesto*, along with studies of John Ball, Wat Tyler, Thomas Paine, William Morris, and the Luddites, whom I tried to reintroduce to a new generation. Later these were collected in my volume *Stop, Thief!*

I am grateful to my hosts at several universities that invited me to speak: the University of West England, November 2006; Duke University, 19 October 2001, and Yale University a week later; Sharzad Majab and David McNally of the University of Toronto; the Creative Destruction Conference, Graduate Center, CUNY, 17 April 2004; and John Roosa and Ayu of the University of British Columbia, Vancouver, 2013. I also thank Professor Nick Faraclas and his colleagues in the literature and linguistics department at the

University of Puerto Rico for wonderful discussions on these themes in March 2004; Barry Maxwell and Fouad Makki of the Terra Nullius Project at the Institute for Comparative Modernities, Cornell University; the National Lawyers Guild at the University of Seattle in 2009; Goldsmith's College, London, in 2014; Ruskin College, Oxford, in 2014; and the University of Cape Town in 2015.

Besides being supported by universities, this book has origins in many gatherings at locations outside the walls of universities: The May Day Rooms, 88 Fleet Street; the Blue Mountain Center (Adirondacks), for a week on the commons, 2010; the Andrew Kopkind Center, Vermont, for a week on the commons, summer 2014; the Marxist School of Sacramento; and the Marx Memorial Library, 2013. I am grateful to the Bristol Radical History Group's 2008 conference, Down with the Fences! The Struggle for the Global Commons; the Re-Thinking Marxism conference, Amherst, November 2003; Andre Grubacic of the California Institute of Integral Studies, San Francisco; Anarchist Bookfairs in London and San Francisco, 2014; the Liverpool Writing on the Wall conference, 2001; Sheila Rowbotham in Cork, Ireland, for her company on May Day; the Left Forum of New York City; and Boxcar Books, Indianapolis. I thank Tom Chisholm for a remarkable visit in 2003 to the Ojibway Reservation in the Upper Peninsula of the Great Lakes.

I have benefited from direct debates, on different occasions, with E. J. Hobsbawm and Perry Anderson, and arguments with Staughton Lynd and Marty Glaberman. Alexander Cockburn and Jeffery St. Clair offered Anglo-Irish American hospitality and complete support. Alan Haber and Joel Kovel were indispensable cornermen. Robin D. G. Kelley was ever ready to lay his own pen down and respond to various requests in the ever-going recovery of African American history. George Caffentzis and Silvia Federici have been like ancient oaks to this project.

I thank the indignados of Spain, particularly Ana Mendez, and those who invited me to deliver a 2013 lecture at the Museo Reina Sofia in Madrid. Gustavo Esteva of the University of the Earth in Oaxaca taught me about the *usos y costumbres* of Mexico. Scholars and translators in Istanbul, the homeland of Aesop, helped me to understand human history in the light of the wisdom of other creatures.

There have been many whose own work, thought, and example have been essential and valuable: Penelope Rosemont, Ruthie Gilmore, David Lloyd, Christine Heatherton, David McNally, Roxanne Dunbar-Ortiz, Michael Löwy, Henrietta Guest, John Barrel, Dan Coughlin, Massimo De Angelis,

Joanne Wypijewski, Amy Goodman, "Poetree," Laura Flanders, Astra Taylor, Mumia abu Jamal, Lucien van der Linden, Peter Alexander, Deborah Chasman, Peter Werbe, Bettina Berch, Forrest Hylton, Fran Shor, Michael West, Anthony Barnett, Justus Rosenberg, Cedric Robinson, and Richard Mabey.

Three companions in particular have accompanied me at different stages of this quest. Manuel Yang, who offered passionate responses to my own first and tentative drafts, and whose work on Yoshimoto Taka'aki was invaluable; David Riker, the filmmaker, whose encouragement was unfailing and whose own incomparable storytelling was always an example to follow; and Iain Boal, the anchor of the Retort Group of Arch Street, Berkeley, which published my *Ned Ludd and Queen Mab,* who was my companion on many trips and voyages, including two "tours de Albion" in 2015 and 2017. In Edinburgh, on the first of these tours, I came across a brick in the pavement inscribed with David Lindsay's words from the sixteenth century, which provide this book's epigraph and solemn hope: "Let us haif the bukis necessare to commoun weill."

One takes encouragement where one can, and for me Edinburgh wasn't the only place I found it underfoot. In Grahamstown, South Africa, I walked daily down Africa Street along the grassy verge, passing the grass playing fields of an expensive school. On either side of the high fences separating it from the road, I observed little hills built by moles tunneling underground. At the end of the day, they would be flattened out by groundskeepers or the pair of donkeys who treated the roadside verge as a commons of herbage. But every day, especially after it rained, new evidence of their persistence would appear. Spending time in a country of miners, I was reminded of the Marikana massacre (2012) and the fable of Hamlet, Hegel, and Marx—well said, old mole!

Phil Bonner and Noor Nieftagodien of the History Workshop at Witswatersrand welcomed me to Johannesburg. Nicole Ulrich, Lucien van der Walt, and Richard Pithouse welcomed me to Rhodes University in Grahamstown. There I composed a first draft in 2015, even as the students sought to baptize the university anew. Varieties of commoning, whether a spring of fresh water from the hillside or cattle grazing in the suburbs, were invisible in plain sight. A loose assemblage of readers of my drafts from Palestine, Namibia, Libya, and South Africa met weekly as the "Pig Club," named for a nineteenth-century Lincolnshire cooperative's curious democratic rules of conduct ("only one person shall speak at a time, and be upstanding").

A second draft was produced in 2017, in Ann Arbor, Michigan. I thank the Eisenberg Institute at the University of Michigan for access to library-lending privileges and the staff at the Clements Library for their help. This was made possible by Professor Ronald Suny's innumerable courtesies, as well as his convening of the MSG Group. I thank Julie Herrada, director of the Joseph A. Labadie Collection, with its labor and anarchist archive. At Eastern Michigan University in Ypsilanti, I thank Christine Hume, poet; Jeff Clark, artist; and Ruth Martusewicz for the Ecology and Activism conference of 2016.

I especially thank Megan Blackshear of the friendly bookshop Bookbound in Ann Arbor and her friendly editorial word—"Go big or go home!" We met weekly for a year going over chapters. Our work seemed a reversion to a time when production and distribution were not so separate, a cellular instance of the commons. The draft was completed during the revival of opposition to racist violence by police. The killing in Ann Arbor of Aura Rosser in 2014 brought together scholars, artists, and activists, who inspired me to see the quest described in this book as also a story of origins.

Niels Hooper has been a splendid editor of encouragement, patience, and insight. Ann Donahue was immensely helpful in the production of a third draft, and then copyedited a manuscript whose references were gathered over three decades, spanning two centuries and three continents during the major transition to the electronic and digital tools of writing. She battled carefully against the inconsistencies and confusions of such itinerant scholarship. I alone am responsible for resulting errors.

Riley Linebaugh accompanied these subjects from a Dublin childhood to graduate school discussions at Café Ambrosia to attendance in 2014 at the Zapatista's *escuelita*. Animated by outrage at the police shootings in Ferguson, Missouri, and skilled in her own craft, she both located important documents from the Place manuscripts at the British Library (among other searches) and provided me with ongoing sharp and sympathetic commentary.

Michaela Brennan, a public health nurse and activist, has accompanied me on this quest every step of the way, bringing to it not only the bump of irreverence but the flame of righteous anger. So with all kinds of love (eros, philia, and agape!) I dedicate *Red Round Globe Hot Burning* to her.

FOREWORD

Only that historian will have the gift of fanning the spark of hope in the past who is firmly convinced that even the dead will not be safe from the enemy if he wins. And the enemy has not ceased to be victorious.

WALTER BENJAMIN, *"THESES ON THE PHILOSOPHY OF HISTORY"*

Anyone who has read Peter Linebaugh's magnificent *The Many-Headed Hydra,* coauthored with Marcus Rediker in 2000, will be somewhat familiar with the principal story told in *Red Round Globe Hot Burning,* that of Edward "Ned" Despard and his partner, Catherine, or "Kate." As quite briefly told in that book's final chapter, the story is that of an Anglo-Irish son of a minor landed family, who in the late eighteenth century served as an engineer in the British army, primarily in the Caribbean and Central America, and eventually became an administrator in Honduras and Belize. He there met and married a creole woman, Catherine, who accompanied him on his return to London after his ouster by plantation and logging interests for his defense of commoning rights. In London, he was imprisoned, first for debt and eventually for his revolutionary activities, and was executed in 1803 for plotting to assassinate the king. Catherine, during this period, became a tireless prison reformer, though considerably less is documented about her life before and after her association with Despard.

As the subtitle suggests, the current book is even less a biography in any usual sense than was the earlier chapter. The Despards' story stands, rather, as a single node, if an organizing one, in an extraordinary network of narratives that in their ensemble tell not just a life story but the history of a crucial episode in the long struggle between the suppressors and defenders of the commons. This history of the commons and its struggle to survive the depredations of capital and empire has been for some decades Linebaugh's main preoccupation, recounted in several books and articles that include not only *The Many-Headed Hydra* but also *The London Hanged* (1991), *Magna Carta Manifesto* (2008), and a series of shorter articles and pamphlets. *Red Round Globe Hot Burning* is the culmination of what is by now a considerable and respected body of work, both in terms of its content and especially in its quite innovative form. As a work it is sui generis and could only have been written by Peter Linebaugh.

Readers of his previous works will recognize here Linebaugh's remarkable abilities as a historian who continually deciphers in the official archives of the police, or of the Admiralty, or in the records of landholding and property deeds, the stories of those that such archives were intended to silence. Linebaugh is also familiar as a tremendous spinner of yarns out of those gapped and reluctant archives. To spin a yarn demands the winding together of numerous strands, sometimes of quite different provenance or dye, in order to weave into one complex thread the materials that will compose its peculiar texture and its feel between finger and thumb. Likewise, the good storyteller—such as the Irish shanachie invoked in the chapters on Despard's boyhood in what was then known as Queen's County—moves by digression and apparent indirection, often defying the listener to decipher how it all hangs together till, after hours maybe, the multiple threads come together in a fantastic weave. This is not, of course, the approach of standard historiography, which prefers the apparently greater clarity of a linear narrative, the concatenation of cause and effect, the distinction of major and minor events and personages, or the triumphal progress of the forms of state and civil society.

Reader's seeking such a linear narrative may well be startled (but never disappointed) by the very different approach that Linebaugh takes in *Red Round Globe Hot Burning* to historical events and the personages that lived them. The book is a complexly articulated work that brings together the findings of many decades of research and weaves them into a constantly shifting and moving fabric. Since his early work *The London Hanged* Linebaugh has been a critic of the nation-based approach to historical studies, with its propensity to isolate the narrative of individual states and their emergence, and has been rather a practitioner of "history from below" in the tradition of the radical English historian of the working class and its "moral economies," E. P. Thompson. His work in this vein is augmented by his acute understanding of the necessity to grasp the circulation of radical ideas, both among an international proletariat and through its contacts with indigenous societies that had yet to be fully incorporated into a rapidly rising colonial capitalism. In this respect, Linebaugh has been a pioneer of Atlantic Studies, and this book brilliantly expands not only the archive of that field but also its imaginative possibilities. It documents the circulation of people, things, and ideas through the Atlantic World, as capitalism engaged in the violent business of enclosing the commons, expropriating native peoples, trading in enslavement, and exploiting and impressing the poor.

Linebaugh's corresponding achievement has been to find a form in which to render the ways in which people who have engaged in dispersed struggles against their dispossession and displacement, against the decimation of their lifeways and means of survival, have forged connections with one another, momentary or enduring, in their very circulation through the constantly shifting and diverging routes that capitalism followed. Capitalism was not only the fiery forge, the "Red Round Globe Hot Burning," in which labor was coerced and exploited, mines and forests were plundered for fuel and materials, or indigenous peoples were slaughtered and dispossessed. It simultaneously created the conditions and the necessity for countercultures of resistance, whose ideologies might be as disparate as their activists were dispersed but which came together around the unyielding and perennial demand to shape, in place of capitalism's violent drive to enclosure and monopoly, the conditions for life in common. As Linebaugh shows, the forms of such a life in common, cultural and material, were as various as the multiple histories and ecologies of a richly varied human and natural life could support. Even as capitalism and empire sought to draw the world's resources into their furious, all-consuming orbits, resistance to them remained—to its peril and to its advantage—decentered and multiple, a "many-headed hydra." Various in its forms and sometimes fleeting in its insurgent manifestations, what Linebaugh encapsulates as the "commons" had and continues to have a real material existence that, however threatened, underpins a vital repertoire of alternative possibilities and imaginations, whose potentials remain unexhausted.

Linebaugh's remarkable breadth and variety of historical erudition match the rich diversity of the forms of life that he assembles in *Red Round Globe Hot Burning*. Their copiousness can only be sketched by a selective list of the issues he gathers in the shimmering net of his narrative: Irish agrarian struggles and the 1798 uprising; the lifecycle of the eel; the Haitian revolution; the story of the Phrygian Cap of Liberty and its relation to revolutionary coinage and medals; Native American culture and social values; military engineering techniques; commodity culture in the Atlantic World, from sugar to mahogany; the history of prisons and executions in Britain and the United States; smog; William Blake and British Romanticism—the list could be extended indefinitely. But it is not an arbitrary assemblage of fascinating facts any more than it ever gets confined to a cute biography of a single commodity. On the contrary, both the diverse array of topics and their formal organization represent an impressive solution to the difficulty posed by seeking to tell the history of a capitalism in which things, persons, and ideas are whirled together and apart and in which the life story of any individual or community is necessarily impacted by the intricate weave of encounters and vectors of change that—accelerating in the rapid forces of change that capitalism notoriously spawns—determine their movements, associations, and ideas. Linebaugh calls these "vectors of transmission" and has been documenting them for several decades now. They might include the colonial service of administrators better known for their domestic innovations, like Patrick Colquhoun, founder of the London police, or the background of radicals like the great Thomas Spence, whose mother was from the Orkneys. But they would also include the circulation of radical ideas in below-deck conversations or within the highly multicultural grounds of the prison yard that already furnished some of the "yarns" that Linebaugh and Rediker brought together in *The Many-Headed Hydra*.

In that respect, *Red Round Globe Hot Burning* represents a culmination of Linebaugh's work to date, precisely in offering his formal solution to the problems posed by this kind of "history from below." Necessarily devoted not to great events or "great men" but to the blurred traces of the silenced, lacking in official archives that represent the perspective of the poor, and devoted to reading them against their grain, such history cannot tell the kind of continuous stories that narrative history and biography generally seek to relate. Linebaugh's contribution to radical historiography is exemplary, insisting on certain counterdisciplinary strategies, such as the importance for the historian-from-below of speculation in the absence of archives or the necessity for shedding a "Satanic light" on the sources, so that "a glimmer of the commons shines through them." The book is constructed accordingly in a series of episodes that disperse the lives of its two protagonists among the web of their connections and associations. But it is not only disjunctive and episodic chapter by chapter. Within each episode, Linebaugh sets up a principle of digression that links together in often highly surprising ways, and often through historical coincidence and a good salting of necessary speculation that bridges the fragmentary or missing archives, a cast of radical and indigenous personages, who either actually did encounter one another or may be imagined to have intersected in the Atlantic World. Sometimes this is a matter of assembling the historical density of a location, whether Despard's rural neighborhood in Queen's County (which turns out to have been an unexpected ferment of ideas and connections, from folklore to United Irish radicalism) or the Miskito Indian coast of Central America. But it is also a matter of following through the *dislocations* that people, things, and ideas alike undergo in the circulating spheres of a capitalist economy. The latter both displaces and brings people together, often in what Angela Davis once termed "unlikely coalitions," *and* furnishes the means to distribute ideas. Such ideas circulate not only in the form of writings but also through symbolic artifacts, folkloric or commodified. These in turn get refunctioned in and by different communities that preserve through them the memory and values of the commons.

In this respect, Linebaugh seems to emulate not only the digressive manner of literary works from the period he is most devoted to, from Laurence Sterne to Thomas De Quincey, but also the manner of the Irish storytellers he invokes in Despard's childhood region. Doubtless he would regard this analogy as a compliment. The formal qualities of the work do, however, pose some potential difficulty to the reader: it's easy to lose sight of the narrative of the Despards, enthralled as one is by the intricate pattern of other tales. But, like the eager listener to the shanachie or the Native American storyteller, it is for the readers to suspend their impatience, to find a forward-moving thread, and to dwell with the shifting perspectives and the interwoven narratives— animal, vegetable, and mineral, as well as human—that Linebaugh orchestrates. As he reminds us, "These stories, from nations of storytellers, were means of making sense of historical defeats." But the manner in which Linebaugh, learning from them, tells such stories is also the means of recounting the possibilities that survive historical defeat: defeat, we learn from *Red Round Globe Hot Burning* is never absolute, never the end of the story. Rather, the continuous tale of the destruction, in one place or another, of some actual indigenous alternative to capitalism, or of some revolutionary initiative that sought to overthrow it, is counterpointed always by the emergence elsewhere, out of the fugitive assemblages of the impoverished and displaced, of new imaginaries in which the promise of the ravaged commons is renewed.

These are lessons with which we cannot and never should dispense. In the first decades of another century, the new modes of enclosure and theft that go by the name of neoliberalism aim to seize from us once again all that multiple social struggles managed to preserve of the commons in the form of public goods. In the face of this new wave of expropriation, the question as to how we can imagine and shape, in keeping with the traditions of the oppressed, new practices of life in common faces us with peculiar urgency. In Peter Linebaugh's narrative of another era's defenders of the commons and their imagination of alternatives to the still-emerging and nakedly brutal nightmare of global capitalism, we may find the indispensable reminders that, despite the "aura of inevitability" that accompanied neoliberalism's development, the possibilities that the past knew or imagined are not lost to history. It is for us to fan the spark that Linebaugh has here so lovingly brought to life.

David Lloyd
Los Angeles, 2018

Introduction

GLOBAL PHENOMENA OF RESISTANCE TO ENCLOSURES have been led by the Zapatistas in Mexico (1994), the antiglobalizers of intellectual property at the "battle of Seattle" (1999), the women of the Via Campesino against the corporate seizure of the planetary germplasm, the shack dwellers from Durban to Cape Town, the women of the Niger River delta protesting naked against the oil spillers, the indigenous peoples of the Andes Mountains against the water takers, the seed preservers of Bangladesh, the tree huggers of the Himalayas, the movement of "the circles and the squares" in the hundreds of municipal Occupys (2011), and the thousands of water protectors at Standing Rock (2017). Inspired by these phenomena, revisions of the meaning of "the commons," and its relationship to communism, socialism, anarchism, and utopianism, have become part of the worldwide discourse against the effort to shut it down or enclose it. In general the story is a couple hundred years old.

In 1793, William Blake, the London artist, poet, and prophet, came to the conclusion that Enclosure = Death. Two of his contemporaries decided to do something about it. This book tells a love story between an Irishman and an African American woman, Ned and Kate, two revolutionaries, who yearned for another world and tried to bring it about. Their love for each other and their longing for the commons point us to a new world and a new heart.

This is what Blake wrote:

> They told me that I had five senses to inclose me up,
> And they inclos'd my infinite brain into a narrow circle,
> And sunk my heart into the Abyss, a red round globe hot burning
> Till all from life I was obliterated and erased.[1]

1 *Visions of the Daughters*, 196.

Blake had the prophetic power to imagine a different world, and a different heart. That single phrase, "a red round globe hot burning," might refer to the war between England and France, or to the struggle for freedom among the Haitian slaves, or to the fires making steam for the new engines of the time—war, revolution, and work—but it is even deeper than that. It concerns the planet itself. Blake's geology anticipates the planetary Anthropocene, the "red round globe hot burning." As for the five senses that close up his heart and brain, they refer to the dominant philosophy of the time—secular, empirical, utilitarian—and the resulting political economy. How else might knowledge be obtained?

Edward Marcus Despard and Catharine Despard were comrades seeking to change the world of enclosure and exploitation. For their pains, he was hanged and beheaded in February 1803 in England, while she escaped to Ireland. Colonel Edward Marcus Despard, an Anglo-Irish imperialist who became an Irish freedom fighter, was called Ned as a child.[2] Since I am writing a kind of family history, I call him Ned to make him more familiar. His wife, Catherine, the "poor black woman, who called herself his wife," I treat with similar familiarity. Hence, Kate.

The overall arc of their story is consonant with the three parts of this book. It begins with my search for Ned and Kate and for the commons ("The Quest"), which in turn led me to what the poet William Blake called the "Atlantic Mountains." Their American experiences beyond and beneath the seas are described in the second part of this book. When they returned to England from the Caribbean in the year 1790, the French Revolution had already begun and the signs of the commons—*liberté, égalité,* and *fraternité*—had set fire to the epoch, a second meaning of "red round globe hot burning." The third part of this book, "Love and Struggle," shows how Ned and Kate's love for each other expressed itself through resistance to the English advocacy of King, God, and Property to justify wars against equality and wars of imperial conquest.

War between France and England began in 1793 and did not conclude until 1815. There is a story of possible republics—France, England, Scotland, Ireland, Haiti, and the United States—but each fell short of equality or of any real notion of commonwealth. France became an empire under Napoleon. England became an empire as the United Kingdom. One island disappeared as an independent polity (Ireland), while another's independence actually

2. E. Despard, "Recollections," 22. See also J. Despard, "Memoranda."

began to appear (Haiti). The United States consolidated itself as a white, settler-property regime with Jefferson's election (1800) and more than tripled its size with the Louisiana Purchase (1803).

The North American continent was taken, surveyed into squares, and sold.[3] In England, thousands of individual parliamentary acts of enclosure closed the country, parish by parish. The United States (1789) and the United Kingdom (1801) were new political entities devoted to the enclosure of the commons. They became deeply entangled as plantation production shifted from Caribbean sugar to mainland cotton, destroying cotton production in India and the Ottoman Empire. Cotton imports rose from £32 million in 1798 to £60,500,000 in 1802, while the value of exported English manufactures went from £2 million in 1792 to £7,800,000 in 1802.[4] Edmund Cartwright's steam-powered loom was adopted in 1801. Eli Whitney's cotton gin was at work by 1793, and cotton production had tripled by 1800. It was the machine, particularly the steam engine and the cotton gin, that economically connected the other two structures, Enclosure and Slavery. The Ship connected them geographically.[5]

Enclosure refers to *land,* where most people worked. Its enclosure was their loss. No longer able to subsist on land, people were dispossessed, and in a literal painful way they became rootless. Arnold Toynbee, the originator of the phrase "industrial revolution," in his lectures of 1888 showed that it was preceded by the enclosures of the commons. Karl Marx understood this, making it the theme of the origin of capitalism.

Besides land, enclosure may refer to the *hand.* Handicrafts and manufactures were enclosed into factories, where entrance and egress were closely watched, and women and children replaced adult men. Allied with enclosure in the factory was the enclosure of punishment in the *prison* or penitentiary.

Besides land, hand, and prison, enclosure may refer to the *sea.* Those who have read Marcus Rediker's book *The Slave Ship* or have acquainted themselves with the infamous "Middle Passage" by reading early abolitionists like Thomas Clarkson or Olaudah Equiano, or by visiting the museums in Detroit; Washington, DC; Liverpool; or Elmina that are devoted to the African American experience, will at once be overcome by the stench, cruelty, claustrophobia, and attempted dehumanization enclosed within "the wooden walls."

3. Linklater, *Measuring America.*
4. Mantoux, *Industrial Revolution,* 252.
5. Beckert, *Empire of Cotton*; Baptist, *Half*; Frykman, "Wooden World."

For Marx, capitalism's "original sin" was written "in letters of blood and fire." The dwellings of Armagh, the slave quarters of the Caribbean plantations, the longhouses of the Iroquois, the giant prison of Newgate, and the Albion mill in London were set on fire. Coal replaced wood as fuel for fires, the fires burned to produce steam, and the steam-powered machines spelled the ruin of a whole mode of life. This occurred during war, when the ground of Europe was drenched in blood, and the blood of the chained bodies of the slaves colored the Atlantic crimson. The blood has not ceased to flow nor the fire to burn, red round globe hot burning.

Actually there was one year of peace, when the guns fell silent, the Peace of Amiens between 1802 and 1803. This was decisive to Despard's insurrectionary attempt. Napoleon consolidated his dictatorship, uniting church and state. Jacques-Louis David in 1802 painted the first consul, soon to be emperor, crossing the Alps, clothed in a billowing scarlet cape trimmed with gold and mounted on a rearing white steed. It was the picture of empire expressing its pompous grandiosity of domination. (Actually, he crossed on a mule!) In the same year, just as Despard and his forty companions at the Oakley Arms were arrested, Beethoven published his piano fantasia the *Moonlight Sonata,* whose arpeggios, at first dreamy then tempestuous, perfectly convey the spirit of hope and struggle.

The *commons* is an omnibus term carrying a lot of freight and covering a lot of territory. The commons refers both to an idea and to a practice. As a general idea the commons means equality of economic conditions. As a particular practice the commons refers to forms of both collective labor and communal distribution. The term suggests alternatives to patriarchy, to private property, to capitalism, and to competition. Elinor Ostrom, Maria Mies, Veronika Bennholdt-Thomsen, Naomi Klein, Silvia Federici, Silke Helfrich, Leigh Brownhill, Rebecca Solnit, Vandana Shiva, and J. M. Neeson are noted scholars who have written about the commons.[6] Not that the subject has been ignored by men. Gustavo Esteva, George Caffentzis, Michael Hardt, Antonio Negri, David Graeber, Lewis Hyde, David Bollier, Raj Patel, Herbert Reid, Betsy Taylor, Michael Watts, Iain Boal, Janferie Stone, and

6. Ostrom, *Governing the Commons*; Bollier, Helfrich, and Heinrich Böll Foundation, *Wealth of the Commons*; Mies and Bennholdt-Thomsen, *Subsistence Perspective*; Brownhill, *Land, Food, Freedom*; Federici, *Caliban and the Witch*; Federici, "Feminism"; Solnit, *Paradise Built in Hell*; Klein, "Reclaiming the Commons"; Shiva, *Violence*; Neeson, *Commoners*.

Massimo De Angelis have contributed to the planetary discussion.[7] Historically, the commons has been friendlier to women (and children) than the factory, mine, or plantation. This book is about the commons, whose meanings gradually emerge through the history recounted here. The following summaries can help that understanding. The three parts of this book are divided into ten sections.

1. Love is the beginning of the commons and the reason this Anglo-Irish renegade died for "the human race," in the words Ned and Kate composed together and Ned delivered on 21 February 1803 as he stood on the gallows. "The Quest" for the grave of Catherine Despard and the quest for the commons are joined. One chapter introduces an unknown but extraordinary African American woman and the part that Irish revolutionaries played in protecting her after her husband was executed as a traitor to the English crown. This is a story both of a couple and of the commons. Doubtless eros was part of their love—Ned and Kate had a son—and so was philia, or that egalitarian love of comrades and friends. The love of the commons was akin to that love the Greeks called agape, the creative and redemptive love of justice, with its sacred connotations. Silvia Federici has expressed agape this way: "No common is possible unless we refuse to base our life, our reproduction on the suffering of others, unless we refuse to see ourselves as separate from them. Indeed if 'commoning' has any meaning, it must be the production of ourselves as a common subject."[8] The human race as understood by Ned and Kate was a collective subject. They were not in it for riches or fame but for freedom and equality. The commons was both a goal and a means to attain them. Henry Mayhew, the Victorian investigator of the urban proletariat and Karl Marx's contemporary, described two means of equalizing wealth, communism and agapism.[9] Were we not to neglect the commons and their enclosures we might find that it—the commons—is the bridge linking romanticism and radicalism, philia with agape. That is the project of this book, that is, to walk that bridge, hand in hand with Ned and Kate. "The Quest for the Commons" places the notion of the commons within a specific location—Ireland—and a specific time in Irish history, by referring to Robert

7. Esteva and Prakash, *Grassroots Post-Modernism;* Patel, *Value;* Hyde, *Common as Air;* Hardt and Negri, *Commonwealth;* Graeber, *Debt;* Reid and Taylor, *Recovering the Commons;* Bollier, *Silent Theft;* Boal, Stone, and Winslow, *West of Eden;* De Angelis, *Omnia Sunt Communia;* Caffentzis, "On the Scottish Origin."

8. Federici, *Re-enchanting the Commons.*

9. Mayhew, *London Life,* 2:256.

Emmet's revolt of 1803 and the Gothic and Romantic treatments of the commons.

2. Two obstacles troubled our quest. The gallows was one, killing and thus silencing those who knew, and the underground was the other, where those who knew covered their tracks. *Thanatocracy* means government by death. Three chapters explore state hangings. The first ("Despard at the Gallows") was on 21 February 1803, when Colonel Edward Marcus Despard with six others were executed as traitors in London.

The Despard story is told often in the empirical mode of a whodunit, or, rather, a did he or didn't he? After he with forty others were apprehended at the Oakley Arms in November 1802, he was found guilty of treason for conspiring to destroy the king; subvert the constitution; and seize the tower, the bank, and the palace. The capitalist class distills financial, economic, military, political, and cultural power in centralized establishments of the state, which in Despard's day included the Crown, the armory, the mint, and the church. These became the targets of the conspiracy bearing his name. Several skilled historians have dealt with the conspiracy (E. P. Thompson, David Worrall, Ann Hone, Malcolm Chase, Iain McCalman, Marianne Elliott, Roger Wells) and two biographers (Clifford Conner and Mike Jay) have put him in Irish and Atlantic settings.[10] My approach replaces the question of whodunit with why bother, which is answered by shifting perspectives on the commons, from the local, to the national, to the imperial, to the terraqueous, to the transatlantic, to the red round globe.

Ned's "last dying words" ("Despard at the Gallows") express Ned and Kate's vision of the commons. "Gibbets of Civilization" shows how the development of gallows humor began to undermine the repressive effects of hanging. It takes significant examples from the major components of the proletariat, namely, servants, artisans, slaves, and sailors. These can become political divisions within the working class. "Apples from the Green Tree of Liberty" ends with the "last words" of other Irish revolutionaries who were martyred during the Rebellion of 1798. Their words evince both colonial liberation and the commons. Irish freedom fighters transformed the gallows from a stage of terror to a platform of resistance.

3. The first of two chapters in "The Underground" concerns the geological strata lying beneath the ground ("The Anthropocene and the Stages of

10. Thompson, *Making*; Worrall, *Radical Culture*; McCalman, *Radical Underworld*; Elliott, "'Despard Conspiracy' Reconsidered"; Hone, *For the Cause*; Chase, "*People's Farm*"; Conner, *Colonel Despard*; Jay, *Unfortunate Colonel Despard*; Wells, *Wretched Faces*.

History"). The human race was changing, and so was planet Earth. Enclosure, slavery, steam power, and coal, the latter with unintended chthonic consequences, were upon us. The International Commission on Stratigraphy of the International Union of Geological Sciences has taken the term *Anthropocene* under consideration to designate a new epoch said to have commenced at this time with its "human perturbations of the earth system."[11]

Rather than being associated with the dire connotations of the Anthropocene, the epoch has traditionally been connected to the progressive connotations of the Industrial Revolution. Its factory-housed, steam-powered machinery together formed an automatic system that inverted the relation between human labor and tools, removing intelligence, depriving interest, forbidding play, and consuming the life and body parts of humans. A flaw in some current thinking jumps from our era of Internet commoning to the agricultural commons of medieval Europe, omitting the period when "mechanization took command,"[12] when the archipelago of prisons began to overspread the world, and when the death ships (Middle Passage) and the death camps (plantations) became the engines of accumulation. This oversight prevents analysis of the struggle between those who lost commons and the landlords, bankers, and industrialists, who were responsible for the "human perturbations of the earth system" and who turned the world upside down by inverting the lithosphere and the stratosphere.

The historian describing the origins of capitalism looks skeptically at the aura of inevitability that accompanied it, because in their victory parade history's rulers not only trampled on the losers, as Walter Benjamin pointed out, but claimed that there was no alternative. History became a machine with laws, determinations, and inevitabilities called "improvement," "development," or "progress." Ned and Kate provide an antidote to such determinism. Ned and Kate were revolutionaries, a man and a woman consciously working with others to change the course of history to obtain specific goals.

"E. P. Thompson and the Irish Commons" is about the necessity of clandestine organizing when the repressive apparatus of the ruling class pushes the opposition into exile, silence, or cunning. Taking their cue from *Hamlet,* historians from Hegel to Marx have likened this underground to the mole. Others link the underground to hell, "the belly of the beast." The commons persisted underground. On the one hand, its radicalism, from the cognate

11. Zalasiewica et al., "Response to Austin," e21–22.
12. Giedion, *Mechanization Takes Command.*

roots, developed a vast mycelium. The geological, political, and mythic meanings, on the other hand, are applied to a false philosophy of history and to a startling omission in historiography. Coincidences abound at the time of Despard's arrest in November 1802—scientific socialism (Engels), the theory of the earth (Hutton), coal as industrial energy, and finally the Anthropocene itself. One of the themes of this story is the "underground," so to think of mountains beneath the sea is no more weird than finding evidence of the sea among the mountains, as the fossil hunters of the epoch so often did.

4. The five chapters in "Ireland" find meanings of the commons through biographical facts in the life and family of Edward Marcus Despard.

The "commons," expresses first, that which the working class lost when subsistence resources were taken away, and second, "the commons" expresses idealized visions of *liberté, égalité,* and *fraternité.* As a term, *commons* is indispensable despite its complex associations with Romanticism and communism. We can think of the commons as negation, that is, as the opposite of privatization, conquest, commodification, and individualism. This, however, is to put the cart before the horse. If the commons is too general a category because it is susceptible to idealizing misuse, the remedy is not to discard it but rather to begin the analysis by means of historical induction. When Tacitus, the Roman historian of the first century, described it among the Germanic tribes, it became a linguistic and economic puzzle to generations upon generations of scholars of the commons.

We're inclined to put the commons in the Middle Ages, as a habit of mind or a habit of being—even a longing for habitus or home—that originates in the stages theory of history known as stadialism. For modern history, the antagonistic dynamic between the state and the commons began in the sixteenth century. In its Renaissance origins, the state was against the commons. On the eve of Henry VIII's 1536 dissolution of the monasteries, the single largest state land grab in British history, Thomas Elyot, Henry VIII's advisor, wrote the *Book Named the Governor* (1531). Elyot begins by distinguishing *res publica* from *res communis,* defining the latter as "every thing should be to all men in common." He asserts it was advocated by the plebeians, and was without order, estate, or hierarchy. This distinction between the public, or the realm of the state, and the commons, or the realm of the common people, became the essence of statecraft.

The planetary conception of the commons refers to the idealized one developed in Christianity, the Enlightenment, and Romanticism. The radical Digger of the English Revolution Gerrard Winstanley, for instance, said that the earth is a common treasury for all, while Jean Jacques Rousseau, the Swiss philosophe, took the commons as his starting point in the story of man.[13] The Romantic poets expanded the notion in the 1790s, helped by Thomas Spence, the humble, tireless advocate of the agrarian commons.

Despard was a minor part of the Anglo-Irish Ascendancy, that is, the ruling class of Protestant, English-language speakers, in contrast to the Catholic, Irish-language-speaking peasantry ("Habendum" and "Hotchpot"). His ancestors came to Ireland at the time of Queen Elizabeth, when one of its conquerors—John Harington (1560–1612)—quipped, "Treason doth never prosper. What's the reason? Why if it prosper, none dare call it treason," indirectly linking colonial liberation to revolutionary change in the metropolis. Irish storytelling remained unenclosed; it retained and expressed miraculous relations ("'That's True Anyhow'"). Ned himself prospered more by talent than property and was able to escape the Irish Whiteboy agrarian war against enclosures by a commission in the British army, which led to his assignment in the Caribbean ("A Boy amid the Whiteboys").

5. In the five chapters making up "America," Kate and the meaning of "love" in a slave society are introduced ("America! Utopia! Equality! Crap."). As the Irishman Lawrence Sterne wrote to the African Ignatio Sancho, "'tis no uncommon thing, my good Sancho, for one half of the world to use the other half of it like brutes, & then endeavor to make 'em so." The relationship of male master to female slave was vile and violent. Two political meanings of *America* are described: one led to the creation of the United States, which was deliberately and consciously opposed to the commons, while the other exalted the commons. "Cooperation and Survival in Jamaica" relates how Despard's career as an artillery officer took him to successes in Jamaica after Tacky's slave revolt (1760). The chapter on "Nicaragua and the Miskito Commons" describes the disastrous military expedition of 1780, the results of which almost saved Despard's neck twenty-three years later. He befriended, among others, the Miskito Indians, and that friendship formed part of his policy, described in "Honduras and the Mayan Commons." He bucked imperial policy and rejected white racial supremacy. His sympathetic understanding of indigenous practices strengthened his commitment to the commons, causing the colonial planters to have him removed.

Three kinds of commons have emerged from this quest—subsistence, ideal, and American. The subsistence commons embraces mutuality, or

13. Rousseau, *Discourse on Inequality*.

working together. You *practice* the commons, you *common*: "So much of the land was in some way shared."[14] Enclosure is a dis-commoning. Of course there are ecologies—woodland, highland, wetland, and sea—other than the arable field, with its grasses of wheat (bread) and barley (beer). In these ecologies, foraging prevailed over millennia, providing the basis of that "barbarian" commons described by James C. Scott.[15] Still the classical commons has classical roots in the *ager publicus* that Spartacus fought for. What was called "The Agrarian Law" of equal land distribution was advocated by the Gracchi brothers, Tiberius and Gaius.

Common right is a power of direct, mutual appropriation, in contrast to the exclusivity of private property that goes one way—from "ours" to "mine." It bypasses the commodity form and commodity exchange by meeting human needs directly, usually in the form of housework or domestic subsistence, as is the case with wood for cooking fuel or pasturage for cow's milk. The commons as a social relationship is related to the commons as a natural resource, but they are not the same. The two meanings of the *commons* were suggested in Dr. Johnson's *Dictionary* (1755): 1) "one of the common people; a man [*sic!*] of low rank; of mean condition," and 2) "an open ground equally used by many persons."[16]

The second type is the ideal commons. "The Whole Business of Man is the Arts & All Things in Common," wrote William Blake, etching in copper. The early Christians were enjoined to have "all things common" (Acts 2:44, 4:32). From "the Golden Age" of Greek and Roman antiquity to the medieval "Land of Cockaigne" (where there are no lice, flies, or fleas, and monks actually fly), you read about the ideal commons, or you might dream it. These ideas were not restricted to the commons of property; they described general conditions of mutuality and happiness for all. It is also important to see that these states of perfection arose in historical conditions that were more or less understood but that nevertheless happened in *this* world and not in the hereafter. These are stirring notions, able to excite the idealism of young and old. Ever since the rainbow sign of the Peasant's Revolt of 1525 called for all things in common, *omnia sunt communia* has been the program of those opposing state-backed privatization.

14. Neeson, *Commoners: Common Right*, 3.
15. Scott, *Against the Grain*.
16. *A Dictionary of the English Language* (London, 1755).

The third type of commons is observed (not dreamt), and it applies to the whole society (not dropouts). I call it the American commons because of a powerful and dangerous ambivalence at its heart: it is neither wholly real nor wholly imaginary. Like "America," it was a European name whose referent was to the indigenous people in contrast to European settlers. Europeans mixed travelers' observations with projected fantasies, hopes and fears of their own. The commons became literally utopian, a neologism derived from two Greek words meaning good place or no place and the title of the 1516 book by Thomas More.[17] In Utopia, an island commonwealth off the coast of South America, "all things being there common, every man hath abundance of everything." This commons could be an aspect of the early days of the settler colony with its theft of indigenous common land.

"In the beginning all the world was America," wrote John Locke, "and more so than is now; for no such thing as money was any where known."[18] The ambivalence of the American commons is found in the influential anthropological theory of "primitive communism" developed by Lewis Henry Morgan, whose studies of the Iroquois peoples (and advocacy of their lands) directly influenced Marx and Engels, as well as in the anthropological notion of "primitive communism"—a condition of mutual aid, simplicity of tools, and group ownership of resources.

Ned and Kate experienced all three kinds of commons—the subsistence, the ideal, and the American. They were not alone. People with experience in all three began to encounter one another during the 1790s. Because of the revolutionary promise of such encounters, the rulers attempted to obliterate and erase the commons with the enclosures of prison, land, factory, and plantation: Blake's abyss—the "red round globe hot burning." The red round globe hot burning might refer either to what we would call the Anthropocene, with its planetary warming, or to the revolutionary struggles of the era and the fires on the slave plantations.

6. "Haiti" shows that there is no understanding either modern Europe or America unless the Haitian Revolution is placed squarely in the middle.[19] It commenced on a commons, the Bois des Caïmen, in August 1791, and lasted until independence was won more than a decade later, at the time of Despard's

17. *Utopia*, 43–44.
18. Locke, *Two Treatises of Government*, 145.
19. Scott, *Common Wind*.

plot and execution in 1803. Susan Buck-Morss says of 1802 and Hegel's simultaneous engagement with Adam Smith and the Haitian revolt that "theory and reality converged at this historical moment."[20] None personified that convergence as fully as the couple Edward and Catherine Despard.

"Thelwall and Haiti" introduces a leading reformer in England who opposed enclosure. The government mobbed John Thelwall when he was speaking and locked him up in prison. His reactions to the Haitian revolt reveal the historic separation between the practical revolutionary and the poetic idealist. Constance Volney, an aristocratic philosophe and revolutionary, is described in "Volney in Ireland." His work, translated into English by Jefferson, influenced both Haitian and Irish militants by its secular critique of religion and class analysis of political power. The thinking of the ruling class asserted that the "splits" between man and woman, patrician and plebeian, black people and white, and poor folk and rich were "natural" and "eternal." By bringing temporal exactitude to the political origins of these divisions, the chapter "A Spot in Time" shows them to be otherwise. What did *race* mean and how were its meanings changing with the expansion of racial slavery? Ned and Kate had a child, a mixed-race boy named John Edward, who rebuts one of those splits.

7. "England" follows Ireland, America, and Haiti as the fourth peak among the Atlantic mountains. Ned and Kate embarked on their revolutionary project with its woeful termination. England was ruled by landlords, of both an aristocratic militarist kind and a bourgeois kind intent on high rents. To advance their causes of conquest and profit, the enclosure of land and the abolition of commons at home became part and parcel with war on colonial subjects and their commons. "The System of Man Eaters" describes the systematic worldwide violence led by the prime minister William Pitt and the opposition in England that included direct action by Despard against that system. "Goose and Commons" takes its inspiration from the folkloric by approaching the commons from the standpoint of a little poetic koan about a goose. A "Den of Thieves" examines a single act of enclosure in Enfield that transpired at the time of Despard's plot. With "Commons or True Commons," the section on England concludes by directly exploring what the commons meant during the 1790s, when actual commons were destroyed by landlords' law, but virtual commons were elevated as revolutionary ideals.

20. Buck-Morss, *Hegel, Haiti*, 60.

8. "The Business" is a euphemism that Despard and his coconspirators used to refer to their insurrectionary conspiracy and revolutionary intentions. Their "business" was necessarily clandestine, and the popular forces to which it appealed were necessarily underground. The euphemism covers an indeterminate group of forces, some of which are described in part two ("Atlantic Mountains"), where the struggles for the commons in Ireland, in the Caribbean, in central America, and in England are taken up. In London Despard and his coconspirators met a proletariat of exiled Irish revolutionaries—veterans of war, sailors, servants, and craftsmen facing machine degradation—influenced by ideas of the London democrats. In parallel to the enclosure of land, they found their labor in handicraft and manufactures either enclosed in the factory or criminalized by the police authorities, as described in "Criminalization and the Labor Process." Artisan, servant, and laborer were alienated from the means and materials of production, as well as from its products. As products became commodities, custom became crime. Ned and Kate may be understood as colonial personifications of volcanic energies—"hot burning" from below. The "business" of the day was the commons, understood as both a *description* of healthy subsistence practices and as a revolutionary *aspiration* of human freedom. Thermodynamic forces became essential to the struggle as shown in "Irish Labor, England Coal." The cough became a sign of the times.

9. The section called "Prison" consists of four chapters, each touching on Despard's incarceration and the closing of the commons in England. Prison "reform" at the end of the eighteenth century sought 1) to protect private property and 2) to establish social discipline and a compliant subject to the economic, social, and racial hierarchies. "In Debt in Prison" began to replace the gallows, reaching a culmination in the panopticon named and elaborated by Jeremy Bentham, a utopian architect of enclosure in its broad sense. Arthur Young, the agronomist, meanwhile, was its practical advocate in the narrow sense. Young concentrated on the agrarian field as Bentham focused on manufacturers in his advocacy of social enclosure. Despard was imprisoned in King's Bench Prison for debt. In Cold Bath Fields Prison, he suffered extreme deprivation and was quite literally "In Prison without a Spoon." Also in King's Bench he dwelt in a porous environment where sport ("Rackets in Prison") was practiced in a common space. The last chapter, "Kate Confronts the Penitentiary," brings *Red Round Globe Hot Burning* to its climax. The prison was a crossroads among countries and among ideas. Neither gallows, fences, high walls, war, nor exile could obliterate or erase the

commons. Kate, the fearless abolitionist, the tireless prison reformer, the United Irish woman, is the hero of this story.

10. "Two Stories" has four chapters. "The Whole Business of Man" concerns Blake and Despard—neighbors and contemporaries of each other. They summarized this epoch in the history of mankind, the former with the poetry of prophecy and the other by prophetic deeds In so doing, they pointed to roads not taken. The following two chapters tell actual stories. The first ("The Red Cap of Liberty") is a ghost story from famine times that recollects the revolutionary times of Despard's era of the '98. It is a tale in which hopefulness is firmly footed in county Laois, Ned's Irish birthplace. The second is an animal story ("Red Crested Bird and Black Duck) that arose in the Great Lakes of North America and was retold in 1802 among Dublin's antiquaries, who compared it to Homer. These stories, from nations of storytellers, make sense of historical defeats. *Red Round Globe Hot Burning* concludes with a question. "What Is the Human Race?" starts with Ned and Kate's gallows speech. To ask the question reasserts the power of human agency, of freedom.

Contemporary forms of commoning (Zapatistas, Occupy, Standing Rock, and their like) inspired the renewed discourse of the commons, and they also inspired me to investigate its history and to discover that the ideas were not pie in the sky, though of course the ruling class and its chroniclers will say otherwise. If knowledge of the commons when it was actually produced was suppressed, this suppression was related, I thought, to the suppression of women's history in social reproduction. Professor Neeson taught us in the 1990s that commons regimes were friendlier to women than the economic and social regimes based on private property.

Ned and Kate were colonial subjects who lost their bid to put humankind on a different path, a road not taken. Their love for each other was part of their love of the commons. Eros, philia, and agape met their downfall in the Malthusian love of calculated breeding, or *ektrophe,* which serves the state and capital. If to remember Ned and Kate is to say that the Blakean equation, Enclosure = Death, need not rule and if their memory helps us affirm the association between our love of one another and the project of commoning, then surely, I thought, my investigation should begin with Kate's remains.

PART ONE

THE QUEST

FIGURES 1 AND 2. "Before the Revolution" and "After the Revolution." Two trade tokens struck by Thomas Spence.

A

THE QUEST

ONE

———

The Grave of a Woman

ON A BLUSTERY AUTUMN SUNDAY afternoon in the year 2000, I went
for a stroll with family and friends on the towpath of the Grand Canal outside Dublin. We were taking a weekend break from archival work in the
records of the Irish Rebellion of 1798. The '98 was at the crux of that revolutionary epoch. The idea was to combine a pleasant excursion with a prelimi-
nary reconnoitering. On the towpath, I stopped at a rose bush growing wild.
A single red rose was still in bloom, its petals glistening in the afternoon
sunlight with droplets from a recent shower. Besides being part of a revolutionary epoch, the '98 took place during the age of Romanticism, and this
rose, at this place, at that time, seemed to me an encouraging sign.

I was searching for the remains of Catherine Despard. After her husband,
Colonel Edward Marcus Despard, was hanged and beheaded in London on
21 February 1803, as a traitor to the Crown, his widow, Catherine, the
intrepid African American revolutionary, after doing what she could to
ensure his decent burial, disappeared, it seems, from the archival record into
historical silence.[1]

Was I to think of her as a slave woman or as an African American
woman—lost now and far from her ethnic culture—who had been emancipated from the Atlantic slave plantation, whose terrors were the basis of
European riches? Or were there other ways to think about her—as a prison
reformer; as a helpmeet and comrade; as a figure of London's West End, bustling under the recently (1789) planted plane trees of Berkeley Square, where

1. *Jackson's Oxford Journal,* 16 September 1815, reported that Mrs. Despard died in
Somers Town in London, a report also reported five months later across the Atlantic in the
New England Palladium. These references were found by Bernadette M. Gillis, "A Caribbean
Coupling beyond Black and White (MA thesis, Duke University, 2014), 54.

Charles James Fox, the great reform politician, was her neighbor? She had led an effort to limit the enclosing instincts of the elite, the lords of empire. Are we, therefore, to thank her for making sure that Jeremy Bentham's panopticon remained only a dystopian idea of the totalitarian imaginary? Was I to think of her as an acquaintance of Lord Horatio Nelson, already the nation's hero? She who could so disturb the chief magistrate of the new London police force that he was reduced to whinging pathetically to the home secretary, wishing that she'd simply go away?

One on one, a woman to a man, a descendant of slaves to a lord of the realm, Catherine Despard expressed truth to power. Experienced on two or three continents, she was a revolutionary of the time. Her story is that of the working class at a time when women, like African American slaves, generated the wealth of Europe and, so it was intended, also reproduced that impossible commodity, future workers. In the context of Irish history, she should be compared to Anne Devlin, the faithful comrade of Robert Emmet, himself hanged and decapitated in September 1803, six months after Despard. Devlin, who led a clandestine, revolutionary life, lived long until 1851 but was unremembered. Women were couriers of revolutionary ideals. In faraway Saint Domingue, soon to be the independent republic of Haiti, Rochambeau, Napoleon's commander against the former slaves, ordered Cap-Français (Haiti) in February 1803 "to force all women back in their houses, especially *négresses*."[2] Catherine could not be "forced back."

A tantalizing allusion to Catherine in the *Recollections* of Valentine Lawless, the second Lord Cloncurry, notes that she had left London after her husband Edward's dreadful death, to be looked after at Lyons—a reference not to the second city of France but to one of those magnificent mansions, like Jefferson's Monticello or the English country estates of the Whig ruling class, this one built and inhabited by Cloncurry on the border between counties Dublin and Kildare. "We became a sort of centre of refuge for the hosts of poor people driven from their homes by the atrocious deeds of an army," he wrote. A half century later he wrote, "She lived in my family at Lyons for some years."[3] Here he was able to offer her "an asylum from destitution." Lyons is adjacent to the Grand Canal in county Kildare. The Grand Canal was completed in 1803, the same year that Catherine fled to Lyons. If this is where her life ended, perhaps we could find her remains?

2. Girard, *Slaves Who Defeated Napoleon*, 288.
3. Lawless, *Personal Recollections*, 48; Jay, *Unfortunate Colonel Despard*, 310.

The following themes did not vanish with Edward's death or Catherine's disappearance. The abolition of slavery, the independence of Ireland, the amelioration of the prison, and the emancipation of women had been the causes of her day, and they were nearly extinguished by instruments of counterrevolution—the hangman's rope and executioner's blade. Would I find evidence of her remains in the actual dust caked on the coffins in the sarcophagus of Valentine Lawless, Lord Cloncurry? (And even if I did find her remains, what then?)

Lyons is a mansion with a private lake, whose construction began in 1785. On the death of his father in 1799, Cloncurry came into its possession. "I created a fine place, and employed an army of men" to improve his property.[4] Its shallow bows on either side of the central building consist of granite, rusticated ashlars. The grand, pedimented entranceway is topped by a granite sculpture of bull and ram and a coat-of-arms with badge and coronet. Doric colonnades on either side of the main building join the two wings, in themselves ample as any palace. He hired skilled craftsmen like Gaspare Gabrielli to do the frescoes and the roundels. Pope Pius VII gave him a marble stoup for the entrance. That was 1801, the year the Act of Union abolishing the Irish Parliament came into force and when this pope concluded the concordat with Napoleon. Usually a stoup holding holy water was just inside the door of a church. Pope, Napoleon, Cloncurry: all hostile to the English Crown.

Born in 1773, Valentine Lawless was younger than Despard but Portarlington, county Laois, was the place of his birth, so he would have at least known the name Despard. Friendship, however, was based not on their proximity as countrymen; they were both United Irishmen, that is, revolutionary comrades. Lawless joined the United Irishmen in 1793. Like Robert Emmet, who came after him, he dressed in green and remained close to the leadership. He was arrested, along with Despard, as part of the 1798 roundup of radicals in London and committed to the Tower of London for six weeks. He was arrested again in April 1799 and remained in the Tower until 1801. In September 1802, a rumor reached the Privy Council that Cloncurry had advanced £700 to Despard.[5]

Upon his release, Cloncurry went to live in Rome. This was the time when Britain and France fought for control of Egypt and the eastern Mediterranean, pillaging whenever possible. Lord Elgin began the systematic plunder of the

4. *Lyons Demesne.*
5. NA, PC 1/3117.

marble sculptures of the Parthenon and Erechtheum on the Greek acropolis.[6] Cloncurry also "collected" ancient sculptures and furniture: twelve-foot columns of Egyptian granite, a statue of Venus excavated from Ostia (Rome's port), three red granite pillars from the Golden House of Nero, another pillar from the baths of Titus, sculptures from the Temple Fortuna Virilis, three boatloads of plunder that he shipped back to be freighted up the Grand Canal to Lyons, and one boatload that sank in a storm in Wicklow Bay. The revolutionary bourgeoisie venerated Greece and Rome and surrounded themselves in the classical style of stately architecture in Whitehall; Monticello; Washington, DC; Dublin; or Lyons.

As Catherine gazed at this booty from Africa and Rome, what were her thoughts? She may have shared the Irish revolutionary's regret that in 1798 Napoleon decided to invade Egypt rather than Ireland. Years later (c. 1850). the American former slave Wells Brown experienced an epiphany in Paris while beholding the obelisk from the Nile: the greatness of the builders of Egypt suggested the priority of African to European civilization. This was common knowledge in Catherine's time, because it was the theme of the most popular radical book of the time, Constantine Volney's *Ruins,* which provided evidence of the African origin of civilization. Thus it refuted the emerging doctrine of white supremacy with its corollary, the innate inferiority of Africans.

In the National Gallery of Ireland, there is a marble sculpture. A female figure, "Lady Liberty," rests her left arm around the shoulder of a marble bust of Cloncurry. The marble of the statue expresses the contradictory nature of Cloncurry, his house, and his cause: the bourgeois revolution proclaims universal liberty in terms only white rich people could afford.

Before they built railways, steamships, automobiles, or jets, the bourgeoisie built canals.[7] The two great canals that spread out to the west from Dublin—the Royal Canal north of the river Liffey, built between 1790 and 1817, and the Grand Canal south of the river, built between 1756 and 1803—provided a clandestine milieu for the conduit of revolutionary ideas as well as commerce. The Grand Canal went eighty-two miles to the river Shannon. These were the waterways that drained the wealth of central Ireland, its wheat and potatoes, for instance, into the "'world system" of commerce. They helped put an end

6. Elgin had them transported to Britain to decorate his mansion in Scotland before selling them to the British Museum.

7. Way, *Common Labour.*

to local subsistence production. While subsequent historians are inclined to see in them the infrastructure of progress, not all contemporaries could afford such a view. On the one hand, great wealth arose from the grain *trade;* on the other hand, famine awaited the grain *producers.*

The construction of canals was gang work—digging with shovels and hauling by barrow. Thousands were employed in dirty, dangerous conditions. The unskilled laborers were known as "navvies," shortened from navigators. Rebels and fugitives lifted a spade among them. Richard Griffith joined the board of the Grand Canal in 1784, bringing a West Indian fortune accumulated from the gang labor of slaves. In summer 1798, the military used the canal to transport troops out of Dublin and prisoners to the city. The canal masons combined for higher wages in the winter Despard was hanged. A report referred to the "unchecked spirit of combination among the artificers and workmen of every denomination." In 1803, advertisements appeared in Irish newspapers offering workers six shillings a day to cut canals in England, double the rate for workers in Ireland.[8]

Lyons is named for the hill behind it, with a rath on top, *Cnoch Liamhna* in Irish, or for Liamhain, the name of the territory, including the house, its demesne, and most of the parish of Newcastle, county Dublin. The hill was a medieval inauguration and assembly site. Celtic kings had resided there. Here Brian Boru obtained a victory. The story of the place's name is recorded in twenty-eight verses of the twelfth-century Book of Leinster, written in the Irish language.[9] The canal navvies spoke Irish. The heroic tales of Gaelic history that arose in pastoral periods of what James Connolly called "Celtic communism" were preserved by the scholars and bards among them who were Irish speakers.[10] In Connolly's day, the countryside still seethed with grief, defeat, and loss, and not for the first time either. "Many were the tales of bravery and indomitable daring of repulse and defeat did he hear in his boyhood from his father's workmen as they ploughed and harrowed up the ancient demesne around the old ruins of the lordly O'Byrne."[11] The stories belonged to the land; they were of it and in it. Was Catherine aware that Liamuin disobeyed a king? Were the servants, craftsmen, navvies, and tillers

---

8. Delany, *Grand Canal,* 44.
9. Gwynn, *Metrical Dindshenchas.*
10. Connolly, *Labour in Irish History.* See also D. Lloyd, "Rethinking National Marxism: James Connolly and 'Celtic Communism,'," in *Irish Times.*
11. Connolly, *Labour in Irish History.*

of the soil aware of her and her story? The lore of location contributed to the revolutionary conspiracy developed in Ireland in spring and summer 1803.

The story told in the Book of Leinster is about the disobedience of a king's four daughters. One, Liamuin, was a warrior and is buried on the hill of the Lyons demesne—"the woman with marital array is killed, so that her name clave to the hill." The hill takes its name from the burial of this legendary woman who disobeyed her father, the king. "Liamuin is slain, perfect of temper, thick-haired, skillful in defense; she met death through her peculiar prowess, wherefore Liamuin is full famous." Unlike Catherine, Liamuin was buried with her husband, "the white-haired soldier-pair, alike are the lovers twain." Catherine Despard also challenged royal authority, George III. The verses commence as follows: "The notable place of Leinster—wealth of valour do the historians declare them the notable places, and next the raths, many are the causes when they are named."[12]

We are dealing with what has been called "the hidden Ireland."[13] Yet we can easily name Catherine's causes—abolition, independence, emancipation, amelioration. Altogether they might be summarized, as this book shall argue, as the commons. There is romantic beauty in this idea, which is why the rose on the towpath at Lyons so struck me when I went looking for Catherine's grave.

12. "Book of Leinster," MS H 2.18, cat. 1339, Trinity College Dublin. See also O'Sullivan, *Newcastle Lyons*.
13. Corkery, *Hidden Ireland*.

TWO

Quest for the Commons

IN 1807, ROBERT EMMET'S COLLEGE FRIEND the Romantic poet Thomas Moore also expressed the longing and the loneliness after the failure of Emmet's revolutionary project with the metaphor of the rose:

> 'Tis the last rose of summer
> Left blooming alone;
> All her lovely companions
> Are faded and gone;
> No flower of her kindred,
> No rose-bud is nigh,
> To reflect back her blushes,
> Or give sigh for sigh.[1]

The feeling is strong and the grief palpable. Emmet is a flower. The aesthetic expression of history can be a problem. The symbol, the rose, does not lead us on to the principles he died for. The poetic effect is powered by silence or isolation. Contemplating the poem, the deaths of Despard and Emmet in 1803, and the appearance of the rose on the towpath in 2000, I could only blush myself, sigh, and return to my quest, no longer conflated with the rose in the towpath.

Though he was not a United Irishman, Moore became the Romantic, national poet who translated the Irish songs of the Belfast Harp Festival of 1793 into the English language, in the process turning what was indigenous and wild in spirit into urbane literary elegance. He wrote directly of Emmet,

1. "The Last Rose of Summer," in *Poetical Works*.

25

Oh! breathe not his name, let it sleep in the shade,
Where cold and unhonour'd his relics are laid:
Sad, silent, and dark, be the tears that we shed,
As the night-dew that falls on the grass o'er his head.[2]

Silence persists. In words that were memorized by the young Abraham Lincoln, were sympathetic to the plight of the Irish, and were commemorated by W. B. Yeats and in the hearts of Irish people, Robert Emmet spoke at the conclusion of his trial over the hectoring interruptions of the judge,

> I am now going to my cold and silent grave, my lamp of life is nearly extinguished, my race is finished, the grave opens to receive me and I sink into its bosom. I have but one request at my departure from the World. It is the charity of its Silence, let no man write my Epitaph, for as no man who knows my motives dare vindicate them, let not prejudice or ignorance asperse them, let them and me repose in obscurity and peace and my tomb remain uninscribed, till other times and other men can do justice to my Character; when my Country takes her place amongst the nations of the Earth, then, and then only may my Epitaph be written.[3]

There are two kinds of silence. There is the actual silence that befell Catherine, the hundreds who perished with Emmet in Dublin, and the seven who perished with Despard in London. It is the silence, the uninscribed tomb, the unknown relics that Catherine shares with Robert Emmet. Then there is a second kind of silence—the cunning silence of Emmet that eloquently sings across the abyss of time.

Cloncurry settled into Lyons. He became an improving landlord, a magistrate, and a director of the Grand Canal, serving three times as chairman of its board. He was a paternalist landlord extending hospitality. He was never idle with the draining, building, planting, and cultivating of the demesne.

Newcastle was a troubled parish. The strips of medieval farming were consolidated and the fields enclosed under an Enclosure Act of 1818, thus commencing "the reign of the bullock." To this day, several fields are still labeled "common" on the ordnance survey map. Writing his recollections in 1848, the most devastating year of disease and starvation in Ireland's history, Cloncurry could not look back to the revolutionary principles of 1798 with triumph.

2. "Oh! Breathe Not His Name," in *Poetical Works*.
3. The speech with a full description of its published origins is reprinted in Deane, Carpenter, and Williams, *Field Day Anthology*, 1:933–39.

Canal locks were flash points, where tensions could easily ignite over, for example, cattle grazing on the towpath or a tree cut for a Maypole. Lockkeepers were armed. Double lock number 13 on the canal at Lyons was such a flash point. The canal was the target of nocturnal attack by country people, who feared the export of their foodstuffs into Dublin.[4] High prices, shortages, and eventually famine were associated with the canal. Malicious breachings of the canal occurred in 1812. In 1814, flour boats were plundered by a "fellow stiling himself Captain Fearnought or Firebrand."[5] The ordnance survey map of 1838 shows a cornmill had been built there (evidence of it remains), and a police station is noted on the map.

In 1803, the year of Despard's death, Lyons House was invaded and ransacked. One of the tenants led a large military force to search the house for a cache of arms or to capture those wounded in Emmet's July insurrection. "The house was, at the time, in the hands of workmen, and every room open except the library, which he forced, and robbed of a quantity of papers, three or four fowling pieces, some curious ancient armour, and a silver tea-urn." Years later Cloncurry minimized the violence as "perpetuated by a squireen in pursuit of Castle favour. . . ." Felix Rourke, one of Emmet's lieutenants, was hanged in Rathcoole, his birthplace, on 12 September 1803.[6]

Lyons is adjacent to the Newcastle demesne that borders Rathcoole on the south. It was from here that on 19 February 1804, nearly the anniversary of Despard's execution, Captain Clinch rode with two soldiers to attack the house of Darby Doyle in Athgoe, the hill adjoining Lyons, and arrest his sons and a sailor working at the house. Leading the local yeomanry with a company of foot, Clinch arrested all but Doyle himself, who ran naked to Lyons, scaled the wall, and passed the night in the snow without shoe or stocking. The next night he found refuge at a friend's. It is people like him, fugitives, who will later join insurgents in the Wicklow Mountains under Michael Dwyer in the aftermath of the 1798 rebellion.[7] As for Clinch, years later he came before Cloncurry as a magistrate in a wage dispute for failure to pay the mower's wages.

A village here was burnt a century and a half earlier during the wars of 1641. The Catholic church was destroyed, only to be rebuilt on a smaller scale as a church of Ireland, St. Finian's. Jim Tancred showed me Cloncurry's family pew: "This is where Catherine would have sat," he said. In the vestry book

4. E. Thompson, "The Moral Economy of the English Crowd," in *Customs in Common*.
5. Delany, *Grand Canal of Ireland*, 77.
6. O'Donnell, *Robert Emmet*, 151.
7. O'Donnell, *Insurgent Wicklow 1798*.

we learned that in 1800, a surplice was stolen, value 1 pound, 2 shillings, and ninepence, its fabric perhaps retailored for a uniform of a United Irishman. Sitting in his pew looking past the red candles and Christmas holly to see out the window behind the altar, you can observe the arches that once supported the roof of the Catholic church. The geographer E. Estyn Evans described the culture of the Irish townland as "throughother." The historian Robert Scally applied the concept "throughother" to the conflict between a geometrics of land as privatized, numbered, and graphic and the oral, moral economy among people, who were often strangers to either shoes or hats and who lived in dwellings "dripping soot from above and oozings from below," to quote Brian Merriman, the county Clare hedge school poet. They measured land by human uses, such as "a cow's grass."[8] Staring at the very stones, evidence of the victory of Anglo-Protestantism, and looking long enough through the window, you can find granite evidence of the Catholic Church.

When I visited the ruins of an old castle and the decrepit parish church, the nave and chancel overgrown with ivy, it looked like rubble, this bricolage of past ages—Victorian iron railing; wooden tree trunks; stones from Reformation, Old English, and Gaelic castles—had become the family burial vault (fig. 3). Jim Tancred was my guide to the Cloncurry family vault. Needing both keys and hammer to unlock the padlocked gate and bang its rusted hinges loose, he laughed at some macabre joke just before it opened. It was definitely a "gothic" experience and my guide was fully alive to the situation. Was Catherine about to become a ghost story?

Gothic was the mode of Catherine's era, not the medievalism extolled by William Morris but the art born of submerged, unconscious forces, the acknowledgment of the unknown, the sense that death was not the end of the story. Hers was an age of terrors. While Edmund Burke might have found them "sublime," they were murderous—genocidal—giving rise to the Gothic imagination.[9] The Gothic mode dominated the London stage during the 1790s. Foreboding and fear were the moods; the uncanny and the unconscious were the energy; the specter and ghost were the devices; and the prison or the castle were the scenes. It was the art form of repression par excellence. Jim Tancred's laughter helped to discharge our fears, so brushing cobwebs from my face and letting my eyes adjust to the dim light, I entered the tomb. Coffins, inscriptions, and dust there were aplenty but no physical evidence of

8. Scally, *End of Hidden Ireland*, 13–16; Evans, *Personality of Ireland*.
9. Burke, *Philosophical Enquiry*.

FIGURE 3. Inside the Cloncurry Mausoleum at Lyons, county Kildare. Photo by the author.

Catherine Despard. Had my search been in vain? Historical memory may begin with relics and bones, but it is not a mortuarial science.

United Irishmen of the parish fought and suffered: John Clinch was hanged in Dublin in 1798; Felix Rourke, a shoemaker and associate of Edward Fitzgerald, was hanged in September 1803; and James Harold fled in '98, part of the planetary diaspora that in his case included Australia, Rio de Janiero, and Philadelphia A few miles from Lyons in Rathcoffey, Hamilton Rowan had a printing press that put out the first United Irish leaflet on May Day 1793. It was against the war declared on the French Revolution. Let the lords be the first to suffer, but "Alas my poor Countrymen, how many years calamity awaits you before a single dish or a glass of wine will be withdrawn from the tables of opulence?" It continues,

> Let others talk of glory. Let others celebrate Heroes who are to deluge the world with blood: the words of the poor manufacturers still resound in my ears.
>
> We do not want Charity.
> We do want work.
> We are starving. For what? A War?[10]

10. Whelan, "Events and Personalities."

A modern-day, local historian writes, "The Lyons crossroads was one of the haunts of the Black Dog who seems to have been related to the dog of Greek mythology who guarded the underworld."[11] Catherine entered a kind of underworld: not quite criminal, not quite guerrilla war. She became part of the clandestine network of support for Robert Emmet's plans. In July 1803, a shoemaker named Lyons, related to Cloncurry, was accused of bringing ten people to Dublin to support Emmet's rebellion. He was to have stopped the mail coach from passing through Kildare.[12] The signal to the country was the stopped coach. Despard's plan in London was the same as Emmet's in summer 1803.

As I strolled along in the demesne of Lyons House, at the time owned by the CEO of Ryan Air, it was not easy to find evidence of the commons of two hundred years earlier. In the 1790s, the privatization of property intensified, becoming a matter of life and death. The Defenders were Catholic peasants, whose insurgence in 1795 sought to defend land, commons, and community against marauders and death squads promoted by the imperializing gentry in alliance with the Orange Order. One such Defender was Lawrence O'Connor, a schoolmaster in the neighborhood of Lyons. Found guilty of administering an oath with a soldier, he was hanged in 1795. He explained the meaning of three terms in this oath—*love, liberty,* and *loyalty*—as follows:

> By *Love* was to be understood that affection which the rich ought to shew [*sic*] the poor in their distress and need, but which they withheld from them.... *Liberty* meant that liberty which every poor man had a right to use when oppressed by the rich, in laying before them and expostulating with them on their sufferings—but the poor man in this country had no such liberty.... *Loyalty* he defined as meaning that union which subsisted among the poor—he would die in that loyalty—it meant that the poor who formed the fraternity to which he belonged would stand by each other.[13]

All the stones in the graveyard could not prove more durable, I thought, than these words. The chief secretary of Ireland, William Wickham (1802–4), confirmed this definition of working-class solidarity as "loyalty" when he

---

11. Kelly, "History of Lyons Estate."

12. This was the sworn statement of Carter Connolly, a teacher at Maynooth. Rebellion Papers, 620/11/129/5, National Archives of Ireland.

13. John Brady, "Lawrence O'Connor: A Meath Schoolmaster," *Irish Ecclesiastical Record,* vol. 49 (1937), 281–87.

wrote of the Emmet insurrection that its leading activists were "all mechanical operatives, or working people of the low order of society . . . that if any or a number of the higher orders of society, had been connected they would divulge the plot for the sake of gain."[14] As for liberty its meaning here is closely related to the right of resistance to class injustice. *Love* means that justice itself in action. We might call it restorative justice or reparations.

I do not counterpose a materialist, archaeological interpretation of history against an idealist, documentary interpretation. Each has its aesthetics as well as its truth. My search for Catherine's grave led me to the continuity of ideas rather than to a dead-end. Although I did not find her grave, I found some expressions of the causes for which she lived. The silence was broken. These meanings to the words *love, liberty,* and *loyalty* express ideals of equality in a revolutionary epoch that arose from actual practices. They help explain how the relationship between Ned and Kate was a love story. To develop these ideas, indeed to understand the revolutions and counterrevolutions of the 1790s with their origins of racism, their imposition of enclosures, and the genesis of communism out of the commons, we must turn to the story of Catherine's husband, Edward.

14. O'Donnell, *Robert Emmet*, 169.

B

THANATOCRACY

THREE

Despard at the Gallows

ON MONDAY, 21 FEBRUARY 1803, with the hangman's noose loosely around his neck, Edward Marcus Despard stepped to the edge of the platform, high up on the roof of Horsemonger Gaol, south of the river Thames in Surrey. He addressed the crowd, estimated at twenty thousand, that had been gathering from all over London since early morning. At four o'clock, drums called the Horse Guards to assemble; they rode sentinel at the bridges and principal roads. At five o'clock, the bell of St. George's began to sound and tolled for an hour. Sir Richard Ford, the chief magistrate of London, had an uneasy night sleeping next to the jail. Leaflets had been circulated calling for an uprising to halt the executions. It had been difficult to find carpenters willing to build the scaffold. Constables were ordered to watch "all the public houses and other places of resort for the disaffected."[1] The jail keeper had been issued a rocket to launch as a signal to the military in the event of trouble. It was a tense moment when Despard stepped forward to speak:

> Fellow Citizens, I come here, as you see, after having served my Country faithfully, honourably and usefully, for thirty years and upwards, to suffer death upon a scaffold for a crime which I protest I am not guilty. I solemnly declare that I am no more guilty of it than any of you who may be now hearing me. But though His Majesty's Ministers know as well as I do that I am not guilty, yet they avail themselves of a legal pretext to destroy a man, because he has been a friend to truth, to liberty, and to justice

1. NA, HO 42/70, 20 February 1803. Because Despard was a prisoner of state and a convicted traitor, the state archives contain much material about the case. A full discussion of these sources can be found in the twentieth-century biographies on Despard by Clifford D. Conner and Jay Mike.

[a considerable huzzah from the crowd]

because he has been a friend to the poor and to the oppressed. But, Citizens, I hope and trust, notwithstanding my fate, and the fate of those who no doubt will soon follow me, that the principles of freedom, of humanity, and of justice, will finally triumph over falsehood, tyranny and delusion, and every principle inimical to the interests of the human race.

[a warning from the Sheriff]

I have little more to add, except to wish you all health, happiness and freedom, which I have endeavoured, as far as was in my power, to procure for you, and for mankind in general.[2]

The speech was a joint production with Catherine, who had been in and out of his cell for days, carrying papers and helping him with the writing of his petition of mercy. Despard spent his time writing, at one point asking for an amanuensis. The attorney general, Percival (a future prime minister), wrote Lord Pelham, the home secretary, "that so intensive and voluminous a correspondence cannot be upon his own private business." Despard would have known, Percival wrote, that "he cannot be certain that she will not be searched any day and have the papers taken from her." He concluded, "His past Habits have been such as fully to justify any suspicion of mischievous intention and plotting on his part, and therefore . . . he shall not be permitted to send any more papers out of prison by his wife or by anyone else unless he shall submit them to the Inspection of some person who may be trusted." Sir Richard Ford, the evening before the hangings, wrote to Pelham that "the crowd is now dispersed, but I have ordered all my men, a hundred in number, to stay up all night. Mrs. Despard has been very troublesome, but at last she has gone away."[3]

The government was afraid of "equalization." To prevent oratory on its behalf the sheriff interrupted, demanding that inflammatory words not be used. What else might he have said? This is the link to the revolutionary commons. It is the combination from the famous triad of two of its elements, equality and fraternity, which compose one meaning of the commons.

As it was, the speech was quickly reproduced: in *The Times* the next day, which is one thing, but also in leaflet form in Wolverhampton, which is quite another. Its printer, an Irishman named John English, was arrested. Despard's

2. NA, HO 42/70, 20 February 1803.
3. NA, HO 42/70, 20 February 1803.

is a carefully wrought speech in a tradition developed by the United Irish, who whenever possible turned the tables on their prosecutors.

The Gentleman's Magazine published a different version, including a statement veering on a claim of innocence: "I know that from having been inimical to the bloody, cruel, coercive, and unconstitutional measures of Ministers, they have determined to sacrifice me under what they are pleased to term a legal pretext." The conclusion is also different: "Although I shall not live to experience the blessings of the godlike change, be assured, Citizens, that the period will come, and that *speedily*, when the glorious cause of Liberty shall effectually triumph."

We can make four observations about the speech. First, the speech is a continuation of the struggle, with active participation by the multitudes, who crammed the lanes and avenues to bear witness. Second, he twice addresses the crowd as "citizens," the egalitarian and revolutionary mode of address that levels the distinctions of "Sir," "My Lady," "Your Majesty," "Madame," "Your Excellency," and so on. Originating among the French Jacobins, the word had by this time become international. It is both egalitarian and democratic in that it also lays claim to self-government. Citizenship did not mean loyalty to the state per se; it had two other meanings—allegiance to humanity and to the revolutionary project. Third, it is a rhetorical production relying heavily on triads: a triad of accomplishments ("served my Country faithfully, honourably and usefully"), a triad of vices ("triumph over falsehood, tyranny and delusion"), and three triads of virtues ("the principles of freedom, of humanity, and of justice," "a friend to truth, to liberty, and to justice," and "health, happiness and freedom"). These last remind us of the triad that rang through the epoch beginning in 1789, namely, *fraternité, égalité,* and *liberté.* Constantin Volney explained in his revolutionary manifesto *The Ruins of Empire* (1790) that *égalité* ought to precede *liberté,* since the former is the basis for the latter, and from "the minutest and most remote branches of government [*égalité*] ought to proceed in an uninterrupted series of inferences."[4] These triads of oral knowledge were prompts for debate and discussion. Years later, when Frederick Engels identified this year as the one when the division, as he saw it, between utopian and scientific socialism occurred, he fell into a similar triad. For him, love, liberty, and loyalty were a triad implying classless and mutual commons.

For most of his life as a soldier, Despard had enjoyed a robust life outdoors. He had known moments of *happiness* and *freedom* —during an Irish boyhood

4. Volney, *Ruins,* 70.

in the hills of the Slieve Bloom among his healthy family, while on an expedition up the San Juan River in Nicaragua, and doubtless with Catherine in Jamaica or Belize. By 1803, however, the fifty-two-year-old Despard's health had been compromised by frequent spells in many English prisons, including Cold Bath Fields in Clerkenwell, where the prisoners were kept in deliberately terrible conditions and which was known as the "Steel," or "Bastille," in the political slang of the common people.

He had served the Crown *usefully* in Ireland, Jamaica, Ruatan, and Honduras: *faithfully* in refraining from mutiny or disobedience and in keeping faith with the big planters, rather than bending to the money of shipowners or cowering before the "baymen"; and *honorably* in the sense of sobriety and sanity of mind. Francis Place, his colleague among the revolutionary democrats in London during the 1790s remembered that "Colonel Despard was a singularly mild gentlemanly person, a singularly good hearted man as I well know."[5] It is important to emphasize this, because soon after his death, the opinion was circulated that he had been mad or insane, a view that stuck for a hundred years.[6] Only two years earlier, the father of psychiatry, Philippe Pinel, the man who famously took off the shackles of the inmates in insane asylums, published a treatise on mental alienation that adopted the novel method of listening, comforting, and reassuring to explore the confusion that arises, in times of revolution, between losing one's head by decapitation and losing one's mind by illness.[7] In England, meanwhile, the 1800 attempted assassination of King George III by James Hadfield, a wounded and heavily scared veteran of the Flanders Campaign and an admirer of Tom Paine's *Rights of Man,* led to the passage of the Criminal Lunatics Act, which made it possible to confine a person indefinitely without trial. In 1802, Hadfield escaped but was recaptured and spent the next twenty-five years in a stone cell in Newgate, painting watercolors, writing poetry, and prophesizing.[8] So it is that the calumny against Despard as insane was a structural effect of the counter-revolution's making life sentences without trial possible.

5. Francis Place Papers, BL, Add MSS 27808/224, British Library.

6. Jay, *Unfortunate Colonel Despard*; Conner, *Colonel Despard*; and Linebaugh and Rediker, *Many-Headed Hydra* emphasize the Atlantic dimension, or the Irish dimension, of Despard. In this they depart from E. P. Thompson's classic study *The Making of the English Working Class.*

7. Pinel, *Medico-Philosophical Treatise.*

8. Moran, "Origin of Insanity," 487–519.

The last of the four points in the speech marks a moment of solidarity with the others on the scaffold, by asserting they are also innocent. There were six of them. John Francis, a shoemaker and a soldier; John Wood, a laborer and a soldier; James Sedgwick Wratten, a Flemish shoemaker; Thomas Broughton, a Lincolnshire carpenter; Arthur Graham, a fifty-three-year-old Westminster slater; and John Macnamara, a middle-aged carpenter and a United Irishman. They were all family men, whose hangings widowed wives and orphaned children.[9]

The prosecutor, Lord Ellenborough, intervened with the home secretary to deny the jury's recommendation of mercy for Despard. He was informed on 20 February, the day before the execution, that his petition for clemency had been denied. As reflected in the sheriff's interruption of Despard's speech, the government feared equalization. Lord Ellenborough charged in his speech after the guilty verdict, "And instead of the ancient limited monarchy of this Realm, its established, free, and wholesome laws, its approved usages, its useful gradations of rank, its natural and inevitable, as well as desirable inequalities of property, to substitute *a wild scheme of impracticable equality* [my emphasis], holding out for the purpose of carrying this scheme into effect, a vain and delusive promise of provision for the families of the *heroes. . . .*" This was the hope expressed in a slip of paper passed hand to hand across England: "Constitution—the independence of Great Britain and Ireland—An equalization of civil, political, and religious rights—An ample provision for the families of the heroes who shall fall in the contest—A liberal reward for distinguished merit—These are the objects for which we contend, and to obtain these objects we swear to be united." The prosecutor inferred that "it seems to me to be clear, that an annihilation of all distinctions and inequalities in rank, property, or political right whatever, is the fair, the reasonable, and necessary interpretation of them; and, indeed, that any other interpretation cannot be the meaning of this paper is obvious to demonstration."[10]

Lord Ellenborough charged in his summing up to the jury, "Equalization . . . seems clearly to mean, *the forcible reduction to one common level* of all the advantages of property, of all civil and political rights whatsoever, and, in short, introducing amongst us that mischievous equality, which, as far as it is attainable at all, has been considered, and, perhaps, very justly, as the bane and

9. In 1802, Amelia Alderson Opie wrote a powerful poem called "Address of a Felon to His Child on the Morning of His Execution." Is shame the only legacy of crimes committed from want? she asked.

10. *Trial of Edward Marcus Despard,* 36–37, 220, 265.

destruction of those, who have endeavoured to establish it in another Country." Ellenborough combines two of the most significantly egalitarian words in the English political vocabulary—common and level. The first goes back at least to the Charters of English liberty and the other refers to the Levelers of the seventeenth-century English Revolution

The Reverend Mr. Winkworth ministered to the condemned under instructions to wheedle confessions from them. He gave the following account of his conversations with Despard:

> I asked him whether being an Irishman, he had not been educated in the Roman Catholic Religion, in which case he might have a priest to attend him, and otherwise I had come to tender my services. He replied he had sometimes been at eight different places of worship on the same day, that he believed in a Deity, and that outward forms of worship were useful for political purposes; otherwise he thought the opinions of Churchmen, Dissenters, Quakers, Methodists, Catholics, Savages, or even Atheists, were equally indifferent. I then presented Dr. Dodderidge's *Evidences of Christianity,* and begged as a favour that he would read it. He then requested that I would not "attempt to put shackles on his mind," as on his body (pointing to the iron on his leg) . . . and said that he had as much right to ask me to read the book he had in his hand (a treatise on Logic) as I had to ask him to read mine.

Despard gracefully refused to take divine service. Despard was a seeker as well as a soldier: a friend, as he said, of truth. As for confessing to Winkworth, Despard shot back, "Me—no never—I'll divulge nothing. No, not for all the treasure the King is worth."[11]

Winkworth suggested that Despard was familiar with Thomas Paine's *Age of Reason: Being an Investigation of True and Fabulous Religion,* which was published in 1794–95 but was conceived while Paine was imprisoned during the French revolutionary terror. He dedicated it to his "Fellow Citizens of the United States of America." At first it was well received as a revolutionary, deistic challenge to orthodox Christianity, but with counter-revolution, it was greeted with accelerating opprobrium. So much, in fact, that in September 1802, when Paine returned to the United States (which he had named!) after many years in England and France, he was rejected by every lodging house and innkeeper at the port of entry, Baltimore, until he met an "honest Hibernian," who took him in.

Paine was not the only one to question established religion. He was preceded by Constantin Volney, whose materialist and historical anthropology

11. "Chaplain's Letters and Notes," MS, Mr. and Mrs. M. H. Despard.

of religion *Ruins of Empire* had first appeared in 1792 and now, ten years later, was being freshly translated by Joel Barlow and Thomas Jefferson. This death row dialogue, as it were, between logic and religion was an attempt to shackle the mind as well as the legs of Despard. With William Blake's "London," we also hear of the "mind-forg'd manacles." Only in 1803, the manacles of the mind were not on "Man"—a universal and revolutionary subject—but were imposed by Reverend Winkworth, an established churchman under direction by government, on Edward Despard, an Irish revolutionary soldier, whose living moral, spiritual, and political solidarity with a freedom movement was about to be extinguished.

Napoleon agreed to an 1801 concordat with the pope, and in April 1802, according to one of its provisions, the revolutionary calendar was abolished and the Sunday sabbath was restored. The revolutionary hopes of the year 1 were concluded with this return to the Christian calendar and its Caesarian names of the months. The battle of ideas corresponded to battles between countries and battles between classes.

Despard was hanged, then decapitated. It could have been worse. The actual sentence was a sanguinary piece of traditional butchery. He and the others were to be drawn in a hurdle to the gallows, "where you are to be hanged by the neck, but not until you are dead; for while you are still living, your bodies are to be taken down, your bowels torn out and burnt before your faces; your heads and quarters to be then at the King's disposal; and may the Almighty God have mercy on your souls."

Disemboweling and quartering were avoided, thanks to Catherine Despard and her tireless protests. The execution was part of that transition described by Michel Foucault from the public punishment on the body to the imprisoned punishment of the soul.[12] Alluding to an old kind of street theater performed in England and Ireland on Plough Monday (6 January), in which the villain of the piece was named Slasher, Despard called the gruesome elaboration of the death sentence "mummery." The *Dublin Evening Post* reported on 1 March 1803 that as the decapitated heads "were exhibiting the populace took off their hats."

Nelson dined with Lord Minto, or Gilbert Elliot, a Scottish diplomat and colonial administrator, who had been viceroy of Corsica in the years of the enclosure of its commons (1793–96) and later became a governor-general of India (1807–13). He wrote, "My dinner at Nelson's was entertaining enough.

12. Foucault, *Discipline and Punish*.

A great deal of talk about Despard. Nelson read us a letter written to him by Despard . . . extremely well written and it would have been affecting from any other pen . . . . He enclosed a petition for pardon, but said hardly anything on the subject." Nelson passed the letter and petition on to the prime minister, Henry Addington, who told Nelson "that he and his family had sat up after supper, weeping over the letter." Nelson also told Minto that "Mrs. Despard was violently in love with her husband." It is a powerful phrase. We get some notion of its meaning as Lord Minto continued, "Lord Nelson solicited a pension, or some provision for her, and the Government was well disposed to grant it; but the last act on the scaffold may have defeated any chance of indulgence to any member of his family."[13] These words cost more than the lives lost on the scaffold.

Despard was one of seven who suffered a traitor's death on the gallows. The others represent the struggling working people in various parts of England and Ireland: the textile workers of the western counties; the degraded artisans of London; the dockers, lumpers, and soldiers of London; the spalpeens of Ireland, the orphans in the factory mills. In the first census of 1800, they had become numbers, whose dwellings were identified and enumerated in Horwood's great map of 1799 London. Looking back from 1827, William Blake wrote, "Since the French Revolution Englishmen are all intermeasurable by one another: certainly a happy state of agreement, in which I for one do not agree."

Within days of the mass execution a single-sheet broadside costing two pence was broadcast about London's streets and chapels. It is confused, ambiguous, and pretentious in the way that unconventional literary efforts may seem to be; nevertheless, amid its apparent incoherence is a powerful subtext. A torn and soiled copy is preserved in the National Archives, having been scooped up by authorities at the time for study. Presented in a jumble of type sizes and littered with typographical doodads, it was called "A Christian Effort to Exalt the Goodness of the Divine Majesty, even in a Memento, on Edward Marcus Despard, Esq. and Six other Citizens undoubtedly now with God in Glory." With its declaration of "citizens" resting in "glory," the title mixes revolutionary and Christian phraseology. It begins by citing the Oakley Oath to form a new constitution; it alludes to Ireland and to George Washington; it stresses the butchery of the decapitation; it compares Despard to Job, to St. Stephen (stoned by Paul), and to Uriah (slain by King David);

13. Farington, *Farington Diary,* 83.

it characterizes England's wars as wars against republics. Subtitled "An Heroic Poem: in Six Parts," it is formally heroic in its use of poetic couplets and in its content. The second half presents an astonishing and nearly incoherent cry against enclosures and cattlemen before concluding with hints that the evidences at the trial were purchased with government money. A prose footnote quotes the political agronomist and encloser Arthur Young and implies that the landed gentry deny cottagers even a cow or a pig. The fifth part of the poem is a commentary on Oliver Goldsmith's "Deserted Village," the most well-known poem against enclosure of the commons produced in the eighteenth century. Written by an Irishman, it teaches that colonial policy prefigures domestic policy. So with an air of the sacred, the broadside connects the Despard insurgency with the struggle for the commons. We can understand why government took an interest in it.

When I described Catherine's role in mercifully mollifying Despard's death sentence to the labor history seminar at the University of Pittsburgh, Dennis Brutus, the South African poet, was moved to write a poem.

> "For Catherine Despard, 'the Mysterious Wife,' on the
> Signing of the Crime Bill, September 1994"
>
> Hanged yes, but not quartered,
> Not that, not that horror,
> Spare him that agony,
> Let him be condemned as a traitor,
> Yes, yes, let that stand
> For he made his choice
> And would want the world to know,
> He would want it said of him
> That he was a friend to justice
> That he was on the side of truth
> That he was of the common man.
> He will die, not anxious to end his life
> But not unwilling to assert beliefs
> And thinking that his death
> And news of the cause for which he died
> Will light a fire in the hearts of men
> And women nurture flames with their clustered hands:
> Many will look up to the scaffold and his dangling corps
> And walk away with their heads held high.

FOUR

Gallows Humor and the Gibbets
of Civilization

AMONG THOSE IN THE CROWD departing the gallows with their heads held high was a thirteen or fourteen year old boy named Jeremy Brandreth, who fourteen years later, in 1817, would himself be hanged as a Luddite and leader of the Pentrich Uprising, "a wholly proletarian insurrection."[1] Brandreth remembered Despard's project and his death, so when he came to his own, he met it with peace and generosity. "God bless you all," he said.

The extreme class division between rich and poor was maintained by the last resort, that is, public hanging, which was actually often the first resort. The cynical, brutalized, and bloody-minded aspects of the English proletariat, especially in London, were created by these frequent, atrocious acts of state terror. Tyburn, the "fatal tree," was the altar of this thanatocracy. In 1794, John Binns, a Dublin radical in London, attended the hanging of twenty-three men and women. "They were all apparently in full health, praying, trembling, and expecting death. At an unexpected moment, the drop suddenly fell from under their feet, and their lifeless bodies in a few minutes were the sport of the wind, moving hither and thither, more like the empty garments in front of a tailor's ready-made clothing store, than the remains of what, but an instant before, were human beings animated by the breath of life."[2]

This means of disciplining the class relations was severely tested by the Gordon Riots of June 1780 at the height of the American War of Independence. A march to petition Parliament against permitting Roman

---

1. Shelley wrote magnificently about him in a new kind of prose, no longer ironic but strictly conscious of the class basis of capital punishment. The essay's title, *We Pity the Plumage but Forget the Dying Bird,* is a quote from Tom Paine's devastating charge against Edmund Burke.

2. Binns, *Recollections,* 280.

Catholics from entering the armed forces ignited class anger, which suddenly and furiously turned into the most dangerous urban insurrection of the century. The Bank of England was attacked, and hundreds of prisoners were released. In response, the soldiery shot and killed several hundred, London became an armed camp, and thirty or forty people were hanged at sites scattered about town.

Enclosure and mechanization affected hanging, as they affected everything else in that era. In London after the Gordon Riots (1780), the administration of capital punishment underwent a number of changes. For one thing, the three-mile procession across the city from Newgate Prison to Tyburn was abolished and hangings were enclosed in the prison. For another thing, the mechanization of death was advanced by the introduction of the "new drop," whereby a trap on the scaffold was sprung open from beneath the feet of the condemned, whose death was caused by a broken neck, rather than by strangulation that resulted when the cart or ladder under the condemned's feet was removed.[3]

The first biographer of Edward Marcus Despard was James Bannantine, who had been his secretary in the Bay of Honduras. Bannantine published a joke book in 1800, when Despard was imprisoned, with subsequent editions appearing the year Despard was arrested for treason (1802) and the year after his execution (1804). It contains nearly two thousand jokes. The two men shared jests. We begin by telling two of them, both about hanging.[4] So, Bannantine tells us, "A man having been capitally convicted at the Old Bailey, was, as usual, asked what he had to say why judgment of death should not pass against him. 'Say!' replied he, 'why, I think the joke has been carried far enough already, and the less said about it the better—if you please, sir, we'll drop the subject.'" "Dropping the subject" refers to the new scaffold technology, as well as to the opportunity to answer the judge's sentence. These were years when a person could be jailed for saying the wrong thing in his front garden, as happened in 1803, to the poet William Blake. The joke reverses the correlation between politeness and social class, with the condemned criminal here assuming airs of insulted refinement.

3. Gatrell, *Hanging Tree*, 51. The new drop was installed by two evangelical sheriffs. It was described with clinical precision in *Gentleman's Magazine* 2, 1783, 991.

4. On 14 July 1800, James Ridgway published Bannantine's *New Joe Miller; Or, the Tickler, Containing Five Hundred Good Things,* which was a jest book full of anecdotes, satires, jokes, and Irish bulls. I am informed by a scholar in Cape Town that "Bannantine's joke book" still circulates in Mauritius.

The other joke was told of John "Walking" Stewart (1747–1822). This philosopher, friend of Thomas Paine and William Wordsworth, had walked from Madras, across India, Persia, Arabia, Abyssinia, and Africa, to Europe before settling in London in 1803. He is credited with the famous ironic deduction that, having been shipwrecked, he spied a man hanging on a gibbet and concluded that "we were in a civilized society." The joke was that while most of the world did not hang or exhibit the corpses of its wrongdoers, England felt superior because it did.

Indeed, "civilization" was undergoing mighty changes. It instituted structures that deeply damaged both human societies worldwide and the geology of the whole earth. Three of these structures—enclosure, slavery, and mechanization— proved to be as dynamic as they were oppressive. "When, in countries that are called civilized, we see age going to the workhouse and youth to the gallows, something must be wrong in the system of government," wrote Thomas Paine.[5] In England and Wales, these magnitudes exceeded the victims of the French revolutionary terror. Thirty-five thousand people were condemned to death between 1770 and 1830, and perhaps seven thousand were actually put to death.[6] In Ireland, thirty thousand people were put to violent death in the repression of the Rebellion of 1798.

"Gibbet" could refer to the gallows or to an upright post with a projecting arm from which the bodies of executed criminals were hung in chains, as carrion for the birds and as a warning to others (fig. 4).[7] This "civilization" was supported by a proletariat whose morbidity was of as much interest to the state as its generation or "making." Hanging provided the spectacle of thanatocracy. Gallows humor helped turn the tables.

Servants, artisans, sailors, and slaves were major components of the proletariat, corresponding to capitalism in its financial, manufacturing, agrarian, and mercantile modes, respectively. It was to these kinds of workers, like the men who accompanied Despard to the gallows, that Despard appealed, hoping by word or example to find those who preferred to risk insurgence than suffer degradation. A few examples from each show how the process of hanging was beginning to backfire. They may also suggest who stood for the commons.

In a population of about nine million, nine hundred thousand were servants, eight hundred thousand of which were female. The modern historian of

5. Paine, *Rights of Man,* pt. 2, 225, 240.
6. Gatrell, *Hanging Tree.*
7. This was done despite the prohibition in Deuteronomy 21:23 against leaving the condemned hanging all night.

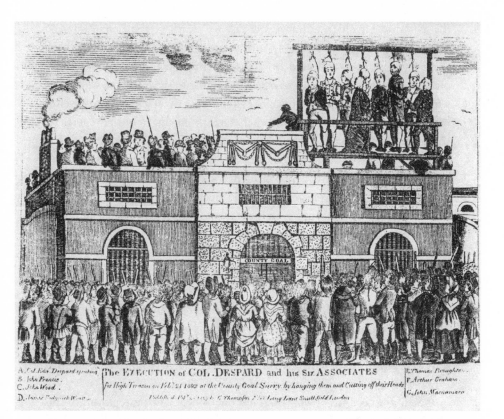

FIGURE 4. The mass hanging atop the Horsemonger Lane Gaol of Edward Marcus Despard, John Francis, John Wood, James Sedgwick Wratten, Thomas Broughton, Arthur Graham, and John Macnamara. *Morning Chronicle,* 22 February 1803.

these workers observes that "domestic servants constituted a kind of first modern labour force through the sheer weight of their numbers and the amount of 'contract' spoken by them and about them."[8] Lifestyles of both the upper and middle classes depended on her labors: she mopped floors, washed linens, emptied chamber pots, cleaned necessary closets, cooked and served dinners, lit fires and removed ashes, dusted rooms, swept stairs, made beds, milked cows, weeded vegetable gardens, changed clouts (nappies), kept secrets, comforted children, peeled potatoes, and on and on.

The Waltham Black Act of 1723—the "bloody code"—defined hundreds of offences as capital. Among them was setting fire to a haystack, and it was

8. Steedman, *Labours Lost,* 44.

for this that Elizabeth Salmon was cast for death at the Lent Assize at Thetford in 1802.[9] The stack contained gleanings she had gathered. Some of them had also been collected from a neighboring commons, without the owners' leave. She set fire to a haystack belonging to the man who was living with her. He, however, abandoned her after selling the stack to someone else, who brought an indictment against her. After promising to burn the stack to the ground rather than let it be sold, she called some neighbors out to watch as she used burning coals, encouraged by her bellows, to incinerate it. The neighbors did not interfere. The incident took place in broad daylight. The judges stated that "the property was not precisely ascertained."[10] Whether they referred to the types of hay in the stack, to the varieties of its appropriation, or to multiple claims of ownership is not entirely clear. Whatever they meant, the statement might stand for the epoch. Despite the ambiguity of ascertainment, the criminalization and the hangings proceeded apace.

Thomas Paine grew up in Thetford, when harvesting was a collective, community labor. In England in 1802, respect for Thomas Paine could be expressed only in jest. Bannantine tells a joke that depends on the difference between a book and a birthright. A country gentlemen, upon hearing that several persons were punished for selling *Rights of Man,* protested that he knew no punishment too great for those who dared to SELL the rights of man.

One of the customs of women, if not one of her rights, was gleaning. The great gleaning case of 1788 arose only a few miles from Thetford, when General Cornwallis, the loser at Yorktown, the victor in Ireland, the privatizer of Bengal, attempted to deny this ancient common right to the harvest laborers, Mary Houghton in particular, in the rich agricultural lands of East Anglia. The court ruled that gleaning was not a right of common law.

On the evening of Despard's execution, his body was removed for burial by his friends. The same evening, the Pantheon opened for a masked ball, but the critic was disappointed that the dancers were mirthless, and the costumes insipid, consisting of "the usual number of unmeaning Characters," such as housemaids and a "host of sailors who had never been at sea."[11] Yet these were precisely the categories of workers who were most numerous in England at the time. Far from being "unmeaning characters," they gave England its rec-

9. Her name does not appear among the Home Office petitions for pardons, so it seems that besides being sentenced to hang she was actually hanged. NA, HO 47.

10. E. Thompson, *Whigs and Hunters,* 256; 168 Eng. Rep. 665 (1743–1865).

11. *Times,* 23 February 1803.

ognizable meanings, the goods from overseas and the upstairs-downstairs hierarchy—say the cup of tea and its service at teatime.

Sarah Lloyd, a nineteen-year-old servant maid, was hanged in the rain at Bury St. Edmunds in 1800. She had stolen a watch from her mistress the year before. She was defended by Capel Lofft, a member of the Anti-Slavery Society, a prison reformer, and in 1789 a subscriber to the Revolution Society declaration, "That all civil and political authority is derived from the people; That the abuse of power justifies resistance." On a rainy day Lofft and the pregnant Lloyd trundled to the gallows in the same cart, he holding the umbrella.[12] He mounted the scaffold with her. She held back her hair when the hangman faltered, while he denounced the government: "The rich have everything, the poor nothing." In consequence of pointing out this obvious truth, he was removed from the bench of justices of the peace.

Class inequality had been palliated by the moral economy. At fifty-four years old, Hannah Smith "headed up a mob" in Manchester, which brought down the prices of potatoes, butter, and milk, and boasted that she could raise a crowd in a minute.[13] She was convicted of highway robbery for selling butter cheaply to the crowd and was hanged for it in 1812.

Acts like Hannah Smith's were called *taxation populaire* in France and the "moral economy" in Ireland. They were performed in opposition to the economy of laissez-faire, which won its first victories in repealing the legislation against forestalling, that is, refusing to bring food to market in order to force a price rise. The repeal was the background to the intellectual victory of liberalism, with Adam Smith leading the triumphal march. We call them food riots. At the time, they were called "risings of the people" or "insurrections," and they took place in England in 1709, 1740, 1756–57, 1766–67, 1773, 1782, 1795, and 1800–1801. The 1795 riots were widespread. Barbara and J. L. Hammond called them "the revolt of the housewives," because of the conspicuous part taken by women.[14]

In December 1800, the Brown Bread Act (41 George III, c. 16) prohibited millers from grinding anything except whole wheat flour called "mealie." The poor called it the "Poison Act." James Bannantine had a joke for the perfection of English law: "the poor man is hanged for taking a loaf from a baker's shop to satisfy the cravings of nature—the baker, who cheats a whole parish

12. Gatrell, *Hanging Tree*, 339–43.
13. E. Thompson, "Moral Economy Reviewed," in *Customs in Common*, 330.
14. Hammond and Hammond, *Village Labourer*.

is fined a few shillings—and the great man, who plundered the nation of thousands, goes unpunished."[15]

Man does not live by bread alone, but he is ruled by it. "It is the quantity of food which regulates the number of the human species," wrote Reverend Joseph Townsend a dozen years before Reverend Malthus came to the same conclusion. He continued in a terrifying passage:

> Hunger will tame the fiercest animals, it will teach decency and civility, obedience and subjection, to the most perverse. In general it is only hunger which can spur and goad [the poor] on to labor; yet our laws have said they shall never hunger. The laws, it must be confessed, have likewise said, they shall be compelled to work. But then legal constraint is attended with much trouble, violence, and noise; creates ill will, and never can be productive of good and acceptable service: whereas hunger is not only peaceable, silent, unremitting pressure, but, as the most natural motive to industry and labor, it calls forth the most powerful exertions; and, when satisfied by the free bounty of another, lays lasting and sure foundations for good will and gratitude. The slave must be compelled to work but the free man should be left to his own judgment, and discretion; should be protected in the full enjoyment of his own, be it much or little; and punished when he invades his neighbor's property.[16]

The artisans and the craftsmen of England suffered disaster as a result of mechanization, urbanization, dispossession, and the utter loss of traditional protections of standards and apprenticeship. With young women and children they were consigned to factories, without protection of unions, and with a growing class-consciousness. The textile trades (silk, cotton, wool, worsteds) suffered as a result of the invention of machines, first for spinning and then for weaving, with the steam engine to follow.[17] The direct action against the gig mill and a shearing frame machinery (which raised the nap on woven cloths in preparation for the work of the shearmen or croppers) followed the formation of a committee of the workers, coordination with similar skilled workers in other parts of England and Ireland, the petitioning of Parliament, and the documentation of legal and customary prohibitions of the offensive machines.[18] Thomas Helliker refused to give evidence against the other Trowbridge shearmen who had burned the Littleton mill in summer 1802. In Salisbury, Wiltshire, Thomas

---

15. Bannington, *New Joe Miller.*

16. *Dissertation.*

17. See Mantoux, *Industrial Revolution*; or Hammond and Hammond, *Skilled Labourer.*

18. E. P. Thompson's *The Making of the English Working Class* depended especially on evidence of such workers.

Helliker was hanged for machine-breaking just three weeks after Despard was executed. The previous summer, he had participated in the destruction of a textile mill containing a gig mill and a shearing frame. His face was blackened in disguise, a violation of the 1723 Black Act. His body was pulled in procession by thousands of mourners, despite the presence of dragoons, cavalry, and the chief London police officer's apparatus of informers.[19]

Soldiers and sailors returned with the Peace of Amiens, only to find no paying work. A number of workmen, having been dismissed from their employment at a great Manchester manufactory soon after the war commenced, were at the same time told that the want of trade that occasioned this step did not proceed from the war—"Now to me," said one of them bluffly, "the case appears directly contrary; are we not at the moment employed in *shooting our customers?*" The joke would not have been lost on Tom Paine who had written, "Nothing can appear more ridiculous and absurd, exclusive of all moral reflections, than to be at the expense of building navies, filling them with men, and then hauling them into the ocean, to try which can sink the other fastest."[20]

Richard Parker, "well educated and the bravest of the brave," was chosen to be president of the mutinous fleet of the Royal Navy, the "floating republic." The mutiny began in April 1797 at Spithead and continued in May at the Nore in the mouth of the river Thames. Twenty-four vessels hoisted the red flag of the mutineers. Each ship governed itself and elected delegates to represent the whole. The historian of the mutiny concludes, "They established the first government based on universal male suffrage the world had ever seen."[21] The Royal Navy totaled 100,000 men and boys. Perhaps 11,500 of them were Irish. One third of the mutineers had Irish names. Valentine Joyce, United Irishman from Belfast, drafted this March petition: "We are now obliged to think for ourselves, for there are many (nay, most of us) in the Fleet who have been prisoners since the commencement of the War, without receiving a single farthing." The United Irishmen petitioned, "First, That our provisions be raised to the weight of sixteen ounces to the pound . . . Secondly, that there might be granted a sufficient quantity of vegetables of such kind as may be the most plentiful in the ports to which we go . . ., third, that the sick be better attended to, Fourthly, . . . that we may in somewise have grant and opportunity to taste the sweets of liberty on shore."[22]

19. Randall, *Before the Luddites*, 171ff; Ponting, *Woollen Industry*, 103.
20. Bannantine, *New Joe Miller*; Paine, *Rights of Man*, pt. 2, chapter 5, 289.
21. Dugan, *Great Mutiny*, 36.
22. Dugan, *Great Mutiny*, 64. See Wells, *Insurrection*, 90–91, 96–97, 102–3, 145–51.

Richard Parker was to be hanged on 30 June 1797. He was the president of the General Committee of Delegates at the Nore. In his cell in the orlop he wrote a childhood friend, "By the Laws of War I acknowledge myself to be legally convicted, but by the Laws of Humanity, which should be the basis of all laws, I die illegally." He consoled himself and his friend writing, "I am to die a Martyr to the cause of humanity."[23] This was also the cause of Despard, who died in "the interests of the human race."

From the mainmast yardarm, Parker leapt to his death, denying his enemies the gratification of killing him and absolving his messmates of the deed. Altogether fifty-nine were sentenced to death, and at least thirty-six were executed. Parker's funeral nearly caused a massive riot in London. Dozens of mutineers were later imprisoned in Coldbath Fields Prison, where they crossed paths with Despard, whose cell was adjacent to theirs. In prison, suicide, starvation, pneumonia, or "visitation from god" awaited them.[24]

Slaves from the western coast of Africa, who had undergone the infamous Middle Passage, provided the labor for the plantations of the Caribbean and mainland America. Sugar, tobacco, coffee, and indigo were the main commodities produced by their collective labor. Commencing on 21 August 1791 in San Domingue, they led the Atlantic freedom struggle against slavery, achieving victory as the independent black Republic of Haiti at the end of 1803. This is the period when the slave plantation underwent the economic and geographic transition from sugar to cotton.

Gabriel Prosser was a magnificent man—over six foot, and the leader of a revolt of enslaved Africans in Virginia—whose goal was to attack Richmond up the river James from Chesapeake Bay, capture arms, burn the warehouses, and take the governor hostage. "The negroes are about to rise, and fight the white people for our freedom."[25] Estimates as to the number involved in the plot vary from one to fifty thousand. They planned to attack the city under the flag "Death or Liberty," the battle cry of San Domingo. The plot was foiled on 30 August 1800. Thirty-five were executed. Gabriel was confronted by Governor James Monroe, one of the "Founding Fathers" of the United States of America, but Gabriel refused to confess. He went to his hanging without flinching. When a rebel asked what he had to say for himself, he replied, "I have nothing more to offer than what General Washington would

23. Dugan, *Great Mutiny,* 356.
24. Frykman, "Wooden World," 250ff.
25. Harding, *There Is a River,* 55–58.

have had to offer, had he been taken by the British officers and put to trial by them. I have ventured my life in endeavouring to obtain the liberty of my countrymen, and am a willing sacrifice to their cause; and I beg, as a favour, that I may be immediately led to execution. I know that you have predetermined to shed my blood, why then all this mockery of a trial?"[26]

Governor Picton began to supervise Trinidad when the British took it in 1797. By 1801, at the peak of imports of slave labor from Africa, he had become governor. He had a large personal stake in the plantation economy. He ruled by means of torture, hangings, and pimping slave women. In 1801, he tortured the young domestic servant and concubine Louisa Calderon by the picquet, a torture first used on British soldiers, before it was applied to slaves. Her case was brought to King's Bench in 1804 and became a cause célèbre in the abolitionist movement in England.[27]

Picton was accused of brutally executing slaves, whom he accused of practicing the black art necromancy, burning them alive or decapitating them. They were executed without trial and detained in a jail without light or air. The most vivid witness to these proceedings was Pierre Franc McCallum, originally from Ayrshire in Scotland—an Atlantic radical, or "a free-born Briton."[28] He was accused of editing a London newspaper that had supported the mutinies of 1797. He was a friend of Toussaint L'Ouverture and joined him when Leclerc invaded Haiti in 1802. His thirteenth letter describes twenty-six victims of Picton's 1801 inquisitorial commission against sorcery, divination, poisoning by means of charms, and converse with the devil.

In December 1801, Pierre François, despite protestations of innocence, was ordered to his knees and sentenced to be burnt alive. Thisbe was a servant, whose husband was accused of sorcery by "this diabolical tribunal." She confessed under "the agony of excruciating torture," saying on the way to the gallows "that it is but a drink of water to what I have already suffered." Her husband was ordered to accompany her to the gallows and attend the burning. She suffered in February 1802.[29]

Significantly, the earliest cruelty practiced by Picton was not on African American slaves but on Irishmen in the island military corps. In 1797, Hugh Gallagher was hanged without trial, and three other Irishmen received a

26. Aptheker, *American Negro Slave Revolts*, 223–24.
27. Epstein, "Politics of Colonial Sensation."
28. M'Callum, *Travels in Trinidad*. See also Epstein, "Radical Underworld Goes Colonial."
29. Fullarton, *Statement, Letters, and Documents*.

sentence of fifteen hundred lashes each, a sentence tantamount to a death sentence.

In looking at servants, slaves, a craftsman, and a sailor, we have found individuals from major sectors of the proletariat at the time—that is, those whose service helped produce the personages of the "quality," those whose collective labor produced the sweetness of life (sugar), those whose work on machines in factories produced the warm softness of life (cotton), and finally the mariners who carried the sugar and cotton to the Quality. Together they formed the class of people who did *without* and who *labored,* or who *wanted* and *worked.* Gallows humor kept terror at bay, it toughened the hoi polloi, it prepared the downtrodden to turn the tables. The class consciousness of these members of the proletariat, however, was not such that it included the historical duty to terminate social inequalities. Despard did not know this. His conspiracy, or insurrectionary bid, failed.

A reason for this failure, doubtless, was the character of the class composition itself. Both racism and nationalism become major dividers of the Atlantic working class. This is an economic way of understanding Atlantic labor power. There is also a political way, inasmuch as the new nations of the period defined themselves partly by who they hanged. Hangings taught lessons, and one of these was racial.

The hanging in June 1790 of Thomas Bird, a forty-year-old English sailor, was the first execution by the newly constituted federal government of the United States. As a sailor aboard slavers, Bird had first hung his hammock before the American war of independence. He was impressed; he was imprisoned; he escaped. In short, he was a typical picaresque proletarian. He was hanged for murdering the captain of a slave ship in 1787 near the Bight of Benin ("where few come out though many go in"). The circumstances were that Bird and black crewmen had escaped a drunken captain, only to be returned by "local natives." The captain resumed his abuse, reducing their rations and stealing their cloth. In January 1787, Bird murdered him and dropped the corpse into the bottomless pit (200 fathoms deep) off the coast of Cape Lahou (Ivory Coast). George Washington could find no "palliating circumstance" to pardon him.[30] Thus was a race traitor the first victim of capital punishment in the new slave republic. The race doctrine of white supremacy received its imprint from the new sovereignty, the white republic.

30. Genesio, *Portland Neck.*

FIVE

Apples from the Green Tree of Liberty

DURING THE REVOLUTIONARY EPOCH OF THE LONG 1790S, Despard had good examples of how to die at the gallows without shame—Wolfe Tone, Thomas Russell, William Orr, and Robert Emmet all died in autumn at apple harvest time. It is said that by their fruits you shall know them. These are just a few of the revolutionary Irishmen who forfeited their lives for the liberation of Ireland in the Rebellion of 1798. In addition to them I add a rotten apple, Joseph Wall, from Despard's home county, Laois.

The doctrine of popular sovereignty, in contrast to monarchy, expressed its constitutional form as the republic. *Res publica* is the Latin cognate. It means things of the public in contrast to *res communa,* or things of the commonalty belonging to plebeians. To quote a Renaissance manual of political science, *res plebeia* "signfieth only the multitude wherein be contained the base and vulgar inhabitants."[1] It is a crucial distinction. Politically the epoch was one of sprouting republics and failing monarchies. Republics succeeded in Haiti (1804), France (1792), and the United States (1789) but failed in Ireland (1798), Scotland (1794), and England (1803), where monarchy prevailed. Economically, the epoch was one of enclosure, before which subsistence commons and ideal commons alike vanished, and the inhabitants were compelled to become that multitude of the base and the vulgar. The meaning of commons changed accordingly. Despard's effort, his conspiracy of 1802, was caught in this dilemma and crumbled before it. Ireland was both a colony and a place of commons. Despard became part of the United Irishmen, whose military leader was "Citizen" Edward Fitzgerald.

1. Elyot, *Book Called the Governor.*

Fitzgerald was a scion of the most privileged strata of aristocracy. As a soldier, he survived battle owing to the ministrations of Tony Small, the former African American slave, who saved his life at the battle of Eutaw Springs. They trekked by snowshoe and canoe from the coast of Maine to Detroit, where Fitzgerald was inducted into the Seneca Nation with the name of Egnidal, before he advanced to Michalmackinac and boated the length of the Mississippi to New Orleans. Upon returning to Ireland to form and command the army of the United Irishmen, Fitzgerald was assassinated on 4 June 1798.

Helots were the class of agricultural workers of the ancient Spartan constitution. Slaves to the land, they gave up their product to the state and were required to be soldiers. *Helot* was the term used by William Drennan to describe the mass of the Irish population.[2] Irishmen and women brought in the grain during labor-intensive seasons of agriculture in England. Irishmen and women provided the navvies who dug out the canals. Irishmen supplied cannon fodder for army and navy. Drennan (1754–1820) was a poet (he coined Ireland as "the emerald isle"), an architect of the United Irish (he composed its oath), and an obstetrician who assisted Irishwomen giving birth.

On 19 November 1798, the prison surgeon (a French émigré) whispered over the severely weakened body of Wolfe Tone that, should he attempt to move or speak, death would arrive instantly. Having already written farewell to his wife and children, Tone simply asked, "What should I wish to live for?" Thus did the first, paramount leader of the struggle for an independent Irish Republic duly expire, denying his enemies, as Richard Parker had done, the gratification of hanging him.

Since the defeat of the Irish Rebellion of 1798, during which as many as thirty thousand were punished or killed, life had become meaningless. Tone's death prepared for the Act of Union of summer 1800, which extinguished the name of Ireland as a nation and formed the United Kingdom in 1801.[3] His son describes the subsequent mood: "The apparatus of military and despotic authority was every where displayed; no man dared to trust his next neighbor, nor one of the pale citizens to betray, by look or word, his feelings or sympathy."[4] Ten years earlier, the mood had been far different.

In August 1791, as the slaves in Haiti took the oath of the Bois Caïman and revolted, Wolfe Tone published *An Argument on Behalf of the Catholics*

2. William Drennan wrote *Letters to Orellana, an Irish Helot* in 1784.
3. Bartlett, Dickson, Keogh, and Whelan, *1798—A Bicentenary Perspective*.
4. Tone, *Life of Theobald Wolfe Tone*, 879.

of Ireland, which joined others in the age of manifestoes— by Paine, Sièyes, Equiano, Volney, Wollstonecraft, Oswald, Spence, and Thelwall—expressing a new prose, new politics, new class, and new way of thinking with a lucidity arising from its purpose, which was the destruction of odious government and iniquitous civilization. *Rights of Man,* Tom Paine's manifesto defending the revolutionary republic of France appeared in Dublin in March 1791, and in eight months it sold forty thousand copies, twice the sales in England.

"Hath not a Catholic hands; hath not a Catholic eyes, dimensions, organs, passions? Fed with the same food, hurt by the same weapons, healed by the same means, warmed and cooled by the same summer and winter, as a Protestant is. If ye prick us, do we not bleed? If ye tickle us, do we not laugh? If you poison us do we not die? And if ye injure us, *shall we not revenge?*"[5] wrote Tone.

On a clear day, Tone ascended Cave Hill with its spectacular views over Belfast and much of Ulster and swore with his comrades of the United Irishmen "never to desist in our efforts until we had subverted the authority of England over our country, and asserted our independence." Within two years, with England's declaration of war against France, Wolfe Tone and family went into exile, sailing to America. There he loathed the greed and complained against the "mercantile aristocracy," stating "I bless God I am no American." He stayed in West Chester between Philadelphia and Wilmington, Delaware, where he might have read *The Delaware Gazette,* which was edited by the former prisoner of war Robert Coram, a noted democrat. In 1791, Coram published *Political Inquiries.* It contained a critique of the law of private property and equally extolled Native American practices of the commons.

> In the comparative view of the civilized man and the savage, the most striking contrast is the division of property. To the one, it is the source of all his happiness; to the other, the fountain of all his misery.
>
> . . . with the sword of violence and the pen of sophistry, a few had plundered or cheated the bulk of their rights, the few became ennobled and the many were reduced from mere animals of prey to beasts of burden.
>
> . . . men have been butchered for crimes occasioned by the laws and which they never would have committed, had they not been deprived of their natural means of subsistence.[6]

5. Bartlett, *Life of Wolfe Tone,* 294.
6. Coram, *Political Inquiries,* 21, 47, 53.

The land question was raised in practice before it was raised in utopian, Celtic, or communist theory. It was raised in opposition to tithes to an alien church, it was raised in opposition to Church lands, and it was raised in opposition to landlordism pure and simple. The propertyless increased dramatically. Tone believed that 150,000 Irish served in the imperial army and navy. On New Year's 1796, he sailed from New York for France. He told the French that "the revolution was not to be made for the people of property." "If the men of property will not support us, they must fall; we can support ourselves by the aid of that numerous and respectable class of the community, *the men of no property.*"[7]

The Dublin Society of the United Irish addressed the people of Ireland in 1794, in a sheet intended to hang in cabins. It called for "pure Democracy," and rights for the poorest class of people, against whom the doors of justice had been shut. The poorest man owns "a property in his Labour" and the value it brings to field and manufactory. In fact, the address argued, property itself is "merely the collection of Labour." To stigmatize the poor as "*Swine, Wretches and Rabble*" inverts the true situation because only they, "the mass of Living Labour," can prevent aristocratic despotism. The same year, William Drennan composed a defense against the charge of sedition, in which he says it is "the very time for men to popularize themselves," to assert the common rights of humanity against the claim of the propertied "to dominion and ascendancy." Legislators have been turned into "land-measurers, and land-measurers into legislators; extending lines of demarcation on the one side of which privilege is heaped up, and on the other, common right trodden down."[8]

In 1798 the United Irish published in a widely distributed pamphlet *The Union Doctrine or Poor Man's Catechism:*

> It is not possible that God can be pleased to see a whole nation depending on the caprice and pride of a small faction, who can deny the common property in the land to his people, or at least tell them, how much they shall eat, and what kind; and how much they shall wear, and what kind. As we every day experience from the hands of these cruel usurpers, who have formed themselves into a corporation of lawmakers, and are constantly exporting our provisions, or curtailing its growth, on the horrid policy of preserving subordination, by degrading our characters, and forcing on us every servile occupation to earn a scanty livelihood in a country capable to the greatest plenty.

7. Smyth, *Men of No Property.*
8. Drennan, "Intended Defence," 324–26.

William Wickham, secretary of state for Ireland, intended "to make the leaders contemptible and to represent them to the people as traitors to the cause and [as] sacrificing the lower orders by their own falsehood." On 7 June 1798, Coigly peeled an orange on the Guildford gallows while waiting for the executioner to get on with his work, cocking his snoot at the Orange Order formed, three years earlier with the connivance of the government, to rape, pillage, and burn Catholic homes in county Armagh.[9]

Thomas Russell wrote *An Address to the People of Ireland* in 1796: "It is well known that the traveller will receive in the most wretched cabin in the wildest parts of Ireland all the hospitality that the circumstances of the owner can afford: he will get his share of the milk, if there is any, and of the potatoes; and if he has lost his way he will be guided to the road for miles, and all this without expectation of wish for reward."[10] Lewis Henry Morgan, the nineteenth-century American anthropologist and scholar of the Iroquois people, stated unequivocally that "the law of hospitality tended to the final equalization of subsistence," and testimony after testimony speaks of this "law" among indigenous people.[11] Jonathan Carver found "a community of goods" among the Ojibwas of the Upper Peninsula of Michigan; James Adair found the rule of hospitality among the Cherokee, Choctaw, Chickasaw, and Creek in the American south; John Heckewelder found the rule of hospitality among the Delaware, Cayuhoga, Tuscarora, and Muskingum of Pennsylvania. Some United Irishmen (Tone, Hope, Russell, Nielson) sought to stimulate mass mobilization regardless of religion by explicitly urging social radicalism with respect to rents, wages, and tithes. John Citizen Burk wrote *The Cry of the Poor for Bread,* which does its utmost to avoid abstract hypocritical appeals. It was written in the radical Liberties of Dublin, a working-class district, in the year 1795, an exceptionally hard year for food.

> OH! Lords of Manors, and other men of landed property, as you have monopolized to yourselves the land, its vegetables, and its game, the fish of rivers, and the fowls of Heaven, can you afford no more than 1lb. 12oz. of very bad, wet, musty, and adulterated bread for 4d? and butter, cheese, and flesh proportionably dear....

9. Keogh, *Patriot Priest.*
10. Russell, *Address to the People.*
11. Morgan, *Houses and House-Life,* chapter 2.

AND will you do more, will you hunt, will you kill, and will you destroy with the sword, as well as with hunger, your thus degraded and miserable brothers if they cry to you for bread. . . .

CITIZENS, Soldiers, Militia, Fencibles, Countrymen, and Kindred Blood, will you kill your brothers from whose bowels and rags, hitherto the principal part of your miserable pay has been extorted?

OH! Ireland, if thy rulers are deaf to thy cry for bread, despair not, neither destroy thyself by party or intestine divisions! . . . Will thy freedom. And speak thy will with one voice, and his irresistable power to affect it, may be on the wings of the wind![12]

A large crowd gathered at Downpatrick, county Down, Ireland, for the hanging of Thomas Russell on the morning of 21 October 1803. He was the quintessential United Irishman, from its foundation in 1791 to its last stand in 1803.[13] Tall, handsome, poetic, spiritual, athletic, Russell possessed powers of remarkable mobility: between Belfast and Dublin, between Protestant and Catholic, between urban proletarians and country peasants, between town and country, between England and Ireland, between bourgeois and plebeian, between Europe and Asia. Like Oswald or Stewart, Thomas Russell was one of the great pedestrians of the decade. He was a roving emissary, covering immense distances, spreading the gospel of republicanism by peregrination of propaganda, newspapers, pamphlets, broadsheets, handbills. According to his nephew, as he stepped out onto the scaffold, he said, "Is this the place?" This sense of uncertain geographical coordinates is conveyed in the ballad about him, "The Man from God Knows Where."[14]

Russell also swore the Dublin oath of the United Irish—"I shall do whatever lies in my power to forward a brotherhood of affection, an identity of interests, a communion of rights, and a union of power among Irishmen of all religious persuasions, without which every reform must be partial, not national, inadequate to the wants, delusive to the wishes and insufficient for the freedom and happiness of this country"—so striking if its phrases are taken politically, to die for Russell inveighed against the unwholesome conditions of the factories or cotton mills and praised combinations of workmen. "Poverty is a sort of crime," he said. He felt disgraced by the Act of Union and

12. John Citizen Burk, *The Cry of the Poor for Bread* (Dublin, n.d.).
13. Whelan, *Fellowship of Freedom*, 34.
14. Quinn, *Soul on Fire*.

the conversion of the building of the Irish Parliament into a bank, "a temple of mammon." He was an abolitionist and wrote poems against slavery.[15]

"I am no traitor! I die a persecuted man for a persecuted country." So protested William Orr—a prosperous young farmer of county Antrim, a Presbyterian, and a United Irishman—who was hanged on 14 October 1797. Orr was arrested while sowing flax, the basis of the celebrated Irish linens. For being in violation of the recent Insurrection Act, he was hanged for swearing an oath with two soldiers of the Fifeshire fencibles to "persevere in endeavoring to form a brotherhood of affection amongst Irishmen of every religious persuasion."[16] The soldiers were part of the British army of occupation and, unbeknown to Orr, informants. Orr was taken from Carrickfergus courthouse to the Gallows Green. The silent and sullen people refused to attend the hanging, although for the funeral thousands crowded the roads and adjacent hills. He left a pregnant widow, Isabella, and their five children. The next year, the redcoats put her house to flame, leaving her "with only God's earth beneath her feet and His sky overhead."[17] "Remember Orr!" became the rallying cry of the United Irish before they commenced the rising of '98 and was their watchword once it began. "Remember Orr!" was written on the walls and on the pavements. Trade tokens bore the words. It was engraved on pike handles. Printers produced cards for his cause, "the injur'd RIGHTS OF MAN." Remember Orr.

A witness at the hanging noticed, "A poor man who was his tenant, stood weeping by his side, to whom he stretched out his hat, which he presented to him as a token of friendship and remembrance." At the beginning of the twentieth century, Francis Joseph Bigger, a Presbyterian lawyer and Ulster scholar, accessed Antrim oral tradition. Although buried as a Presbyterian, the "poor man" was doubtless of Catholic stock, "a remnant of the 'mere Irish' left after the plantation had swept over the country, and that they clung to their old patrimony, even as under-tenants." Far from "poor" they had once been lords of Rathmore. The gesture of passing the hat was a symbol for sharing the hegemony in the land as well as solidarity from the "underground gentry."[18] Thus we remember Orr, because he provides a window to the underground gentry and the underground landscape before the property

15. Carroll, *Man from God Knows*.
16. Bigger, *William Orr*, 9.
17. Bigger, *William Orr*, 21.
18. Whelan, *Tree of Liberty*, 3–59.

dispensation of the Anglo Ascendancy. A theme of this book is the widespread possibility in 1802 of a multiethnic, nonsectarian, transatlantic project of a republic composed of citizens and commoners, the people of no property, sharing common things—the *res plebeia*. Often we find it in practice. While Orr was imprisoned, a neighbor organized the corn and potato diggings and the ploughing for his widow. Hundreds came to help.[19]

For the rule of law to be effective as an ideology, gaining the consent of the Many to be governed by the Few, prosecutions of individuals of the ruling class are required at carefully considered times. Joseph Wall, who was hanged one year before Despard, was one such individual. Like Edward Despard, Joseph Wall (1737–1802) was Anglo-Irish, born, like Despard, in county Laois. Furthermore, as governor of Senegambia, he was, also like Despard an agent of empire. But there the similarities end. Governor Joseph Wall was tried and convicted on 20 January 1802 for the murder in 1782 of a soldier, Benjamin Armstrong, on the island of Goree in the mouth of the Gambia River. West African slave-trading culture on the island goes back to the mid-seventeenth century. It was the source of gold, "Old Mr. Gory," the provenance of the almighty English fetish. But it was also the source of a far more valuable resource, human labor power.

In 1780, when Wall was lieutenant governor of Goree, a discontented garrison threatened mutiny over the maladministration of the subsistence stores. Wall had three soldiers flogged, whom he conceived to be ringleaders. He ordered the executioner not to spare himself in his work, and the three died in consequence, while Wall himself stood by. Upon his return to England, an indictment for murder was preferred against him, but he made his escape to Naples, where he lingered for twenty years. At Newgate Prison, he was hanged before a howling mob, chiefly soldiers and sailors, "every one of whom felt it as his own personal cause." "Their joy at seeing him appear upon the scaffold was so great, that they set up three huzzas,—an instance of ferocity which had never occurred before." Wall begged the hangman to hasten his work. "The Irish basket-women who sold fruit under the gallows were drinking his damnation in a mixture of gin and brimstone!" The hangman was drunk and did not adjust the rope properly, so Wall hung slowly for eleven minutes before somebody took pity and pulled on his feet.[20] The hanging was intended to show that the law was impartial, in that it punished the powerful as well as the poor.

19. Whelan, *Tree of Liberty*.
20. Bigger, *William Orr*.

Robert Emmet's revolt of July 1803 and Despard's conspiracy of November 1802 shared significant similarities. They both had the same goal, the independence of Ireland, yet one depended on a configuration of alliances based in Dublin, the other in London. They specifically sought to wrest independence without the aid of the French. They were both egalitarians, who were regarded as class traitors or renegades to democracy by their judges; they relied on helots, or men of no property. They each advocated social justice, including redistribution of land or preservation of commons. Both were "nipped in the bud," testimony to superior British intelligence gathering, and lacked the historic element of surprise.

Emmet was well practiced as an orator from years in college debating such questions as these: Was the discovery of America of more advantage than injury to the human race? Was the peasant a more useful member of society than the soldier? Was it a good law of Solon's that declared neutrality in an insurrection infamous? Is a soldier bound on all occasions to obey orders of a commanding officer? In Emmet's speech from the dock, he spoke of "the emancipation of my country from the superinhuman oppression under which she has so long and too patiently travailed." Robert composed an allegorical poem of "Two Ships."

> I know I have on board some men,
> That seem rebellious now and then,
> But what's the cause? You know full well –
> Allowance short—makes men rebel;
> And you have many a hand of mine
> That on my crew's provision dine;
> Each day on biscuit we must work,
> Forsooth to send you beef and pork.[21]

In Dublin itself, the Belfast weaver James Hope was to lead the workers of the south Dublin Liberties. He had a long talk with Robert Emmet, saying that there could be no peace in Ireland until "the rights of the people in relation to the soil ... were recognized." Emmet's Proclamation of the Provisional Government stated in the first of its thirty provisions, "Tithes are for ever abolished, and church lands are the property of the nation." Its second provision prohibited the transfer of land until "the national will [is] declared." The third said the same for bonds, debentures, and public

21. Emmet, *Memoire of Thomas Addis*, 2:13–15.

FIGURE 5. Statue of Robert Emmet at St. Stephen's Green, Dublin. Photo by the author.

securities. It abolished flogging, torture, and capital punishment, and generally abjured the English "system of terror."[22]

Emmet's proclamation of a provisional government promised to "take the property of the country under its protection." It stated simply, "We war not against property—We war against no religious sect—We war not against past opinions or prejudices—We war against English dominion." But what was meant by property? To William Blackstone, the grand Oxford jurist, it meant exclusive, "despotic dominion." But the first decree of Emmet's

22. Emmet, *Memoire of Thomas Addis*, 2:547–52.

proclamation was the abolition of tithes and the confiscation of church lands. A second qualification arose from the appropriation of English military stores and "all English property in ships or otherwise," whose value was "to be divided equally without respect of rank" except that widows, orphans, and parents of the war dead were entitled to "a double share." Of the thirty articles in this decree, many deal with the county committees, which were to appropriate "all state and church lands, parochial estates, and all public lands and edifices."[23] Commons here means a power of the whole people to confiscate land.

The English romantic poet, Samuel Coleridge, was "extremely affected by the death of young Emmett." Only days after Emmet's hanging Coleridge wrote his aristocratic patrons that he no longer shared the vision of an "amelioration of the human race," as once he had in advocating equality and the commons. That had been a wanton, juvenile vison. The apostate made timely excuses. But not Emmett.[24]

"Not yet," replied Robert Emmet, when the executioner afforded the Irish patriot a last courtesy on the scaffold, asking the twenty-five year old whether he was ready to be hanged. After a pause he asked again, "Are you ready, sir?" and again Emmet replied, "Not yet." The third time, the hangman became impatient and let the weight of the law swing into awful action, launching Robert Emmet into eternity. "Behold, the head of a traitor!" the hangman held up the severed head of Robert Emmet dripping with blood for the dogs to lap up from the cobblestones of Thomas Street.

"Not yet," then, are words that apply both to the man's hunger for life and to his yearning for the revolutionary project. Despard and Emmet were silent before the law itself. It is not known where either Emmet or Despard is buried. This book in its quest for Edward and Catherine Despard, and in its quest for the meaning of Despard's last words, proposes to vindicate his motives and bring their project, shared with Emmet, out of its uninscribed obscurity. The Helots, the people of England's first colony, triggered the formation of the United Kingdom in 1801; mobilized the Atlantic (the sailors, the lumpers, the dockers, the navvies); constituted the vanguard of the proletariat pertaining to mercantile capitalism; and were unique in languages, religions, and lore. They provided the fire for the volcanic eruptions of the era.

23. Proclamation reprinted in O'Donnell, *Robert Emmet*, 303–13.

24. Letter to Sir George and Lady Beaumont, 1 October 1803, 402394, MA 1581 (Coleridge) 4, Morgan Library and Museum, New York.

C

UNDERGROUND

SIX

The Anthropocene and the Stages of History

HISTORIANS HAVE CALLED THE ERA the great transformation, the industrial revolution, the great divergence, the age of democratic revolutions, the age of Napoleon, the age of Paine, or the age of revolution. They write with a sense of continuity with our time; their themes are ours; we are part of the same epoch. Sometimes their titles express the action rather than the period: thus "mechanization takes command" or "the making of the English working-class."[1] The machine is applied to many human endeavors and is used as a metaphor; likewise, "making" applies both to production and to interpretation, or to the base and the superstructure. The "machine" suggests predictability and determinism; "making" suggests surprises and voluntarism.

In *The Prelude* (1805), Wordsworth's powerful lines about the French revolution, when "human nature seeming born again," refer to the whole world, and to its remaking:

> ... the meek and lofty
> Did both find helpers to their hearts' desire,
> And stuff at hand, plastic as they could wish, —
> Were called upon to exercise their skill,
> Not in Utopia, subterranean fields,
> Or on some secret island, Heaven knows where!
> But in the very world, which is the world
> Of all of us, the place where in the end
> We find our happiness or not at all![2]

1. Polanyi, *Great Transformation*; Pomeranz, *Great Divergence*; Palmer, *Age of Democratic Revolutions*; Hobsbawm, *Age of Revolution*; Giedion, *Mechanization Takes Command*.

2. Bk. 6, lines 341, 701–2, 720–28.

To apply "lofty" to Despard, descendant of landowners, and "meek" to Catherine, descendant of slaves, is to accept stereotypes of the masculine soldier and the feminine helpmeet. Still we shall find that Wordsworth's lines aptly describe their project.

Edward and Catherine Despard conspired in the belly of the beast of the newly named United Kingdom. The beast they were in the belly of was imperial, hungry for the world. Yet already the world was hitting back. He, an Irishman, was hanged and decapitated as a traitor on 21 February 1803, and she, an African American woman, disappeared into the United Irish underground in county Kildare. Though their conspiracy is of real significance to British history, as forming the underground or illegal tradition, and though he was a prominent leader among the revolutionary United Irishmen, the last words on his lips expressed sentiments of neither Irish patriotism nor English class struggle but of solidarity with the oppressed for the sake of "the human race."

The *Anthropocene* is a technical geological term that calls attention to a certain spot in time, the turn of the eighteenth to the nineteenth century. The term combines a new chronological unit, whose dreaded effects in the twenty-first century include species extinction, ocean acidification, desertification, and planetary warming. We learn from glaciological evidence that concentrations of atmospheric "greenhouse gasses," such as CO_2 or CH_4, began to appear in 1800. A group of geologists wrote, "We thus suggest that the year AD 1800 could reasonably be chosen as the beginning of the Anthropocene."[3] These changes commenced with the industrial revolution. In some ways the term *Anthropocene* is parallel to, if not synonymous with, that earlier one, but where *industrial revolution* was a term from a broader discursive field of progress, the *Anthropocene* portends catastrophe.

From the standpoint of geopolitics, the year 1802 saw a conjuncture of events that included 1) the defeat of an independent Irish republic with the formation of the United Kingdom in 1801; 2) the victory of the armies of the Haitian slaves and the independence of the black republic in 1804; 3) the disputed "Negro election" of 1800 in the United States, which resulted in Jefferson's presidency and the "termination" of Indian history; and 4) a temporary lull in the imperial rivalry between England and France in 1802–3.[4]

3. Steffen, Grinevald, Crutzen, and McNeill, "Anthropocene," 849. See also Zalasiewicz et al., "Stratigraphy of the Anthropocene," 1050.
4. Wills, *"Negro President."*

From Port-au-Prince to Naples; from Jamestown, Virginia, to Paris; and from Cape Town to Seringapatam, everything seemed to be, to use Frederick Engels' phrase, "Sturm und Drang"—coups d'état, rigged elections, *complot aristocratique,* plots, whiffs of grapeshot, insurrections, revolutionary *journées,* riot, revolt, revolution. Only England seemed immune, apart from Despard.

Two millennia of human mechanics had undergone a fundamental change by 1802, just a year before Despard's death, with the development of the "fire engine," as the steam engine was first called. Its development in the eighteenth century helped the transition from wood to coal as a source of energy. Coal mining, iron smelting, and cotton and wool textile production in spinning, carding, combing, weaving, and dyeing were transformed. The factory became the location of production. Colliers (as the ships were called), canals, and then rails became the means of transporting grain to feed the population and coal to fuel its engines.

James Hutton's *Theory of the Earth* was published in 1795. In 1802, John Playfair's *Illustrations of the Huttonian Theory of the Earth* put the theory on the map, so to speak, of public knowledge.[5] The peasantry of the lowlands, the pastoralists of the Highlands, and the proletariat of the towns played parts in the development of Hutton's theory of the earth. Hutton learned from the workers who ploughed, delved, harrowed, climbed, roamed, and moved the earth. The Highlanders of Scotland knew in their bones the height, slope, outcrops, grass, and stones. People noticed erosion of the streams. The navvies were familiar with the structure, weight, and solidity of dirt. In Scotland, Hutton enclosed his sloping fields with stone walls, abandoning the runrig method of farming. Drainage ditches were dug under the supervision of specialist agrarian technicians from Suffolk. In 1764, less than twenty years after the defeat of the Highland Scots at the Battle of Culloden, Hutton accompanied George Clerk-Maxwell of the Commission for Forfeited Annexed Estates on a tour of the Highlands to assess and sell lands. He thus had hands-on knowledge of the relation of conquest to the commodity. Hutton became a wealthy man as a director of the Forth and Clyde Canal that connected Glasgow and Edinburgh. For him the theory of the earth and earthly accumulation were integral.

The first section of the first chapter of the first volume of Hutton's book refers to the earth as a machine: "When we trace the parts of which this terrestrial system is composed, and when we view the general connection of

5. Repcheck, *Man Who Found Time.*

those several parts, the whole presents a machine of a peculiar construction by which it is adapted to a certain end." The mechanism of the globe consists of parts, connections, and powers. His purpose was "to see if there be, in the constitution of the world, a reproductive operation, by which a ruined constitution may be again repaired, and a duration or stability thus procured to the machine, considered as a world sustaining plants and animals." A geological epoch commenced with a machine, the steam engine, at the same historical moment that the study of the earth, or the science of geology, conceived of the earth as a machine with heat energy at its heart.[6]

In the paper "Concerning the System of the Earth," which he gave to the Royal Society of Edinburgh in 1785, Hutton developed the concept of subterranean heat. This opposed the concept of the universal ocean as the principal force of the mineralizing process (lithification) that makes rocks from sediments. Hutton writes that he wants "to look for active powers or efficient causes, in that part of the earth which has been commonly considered as passive and inert, but which will be found extremely active, and the source of mighty revolutions in the fate of land."[7] That J. M. W. Turner had a similar idea is shown by his paintings of Newcastle colliers, which remove the certainty demarking the three forms of matter—gas, liquid, solid—by means of the central energy of fire. Each sedimented strata was compressed over many hundreds of thousands, or millions, of years, and the energy of those distant strata was not inaccessible: on the contrary, as petroleum or as coal, the social thirst for the energy underneath the surface was insatiable.

The concatenation of coal went like this: coal led to the burning of coal; the burning of coal heated the steam engine; the coal-fired steam engine enabled water to be pumped from flooded coal mines to obtain more coal; the coal-fired steam engine powered bellows that blew in the iron foundry to make iron for rails, allowing coal to be carried in greater volume and more quickly from the mine face to the shaft; the burning of coal heated the steam engine to pump the water in the canals, which carried the barges that conveyed the coal to sale. Everything seemed to begin and end with coal through a gigantic feedback loop.

Technical innovations replaced horsepower.[8] The network of inland navigation provided the infrastructure in the home market for staple commodi-

6. Hutton, *Theory of the Earth*, 1:35.
7. Hutton, "Concerning the System of the Earth, in *Theory of the Earth*, 1:35.
8. Curr, *Coal*.

ties. Coal carriage was the purpose of most of the canal acts passed between 1760 and 1801. The Regent's Canal in London, with its culverts, bridges, tunnels, locks, channels, reservoirs, basins, aqueducts, inclined planes, and towpaths, was the site of immense engineering works. The Grand Junction Canal connecting the English midlands to the port of London originated in 1792 and opened successively between 1796 and 1800.[9] The engineers—Telford, Brindley, Trevithick—are celebrated; the navvies are forgotten.

By 1803, Richard Trevithick (1771–1833), the Cornish mining engineer, was building a steam locomotive to run on iron rails. One year to the day after Despard's beheading, the world's first locomotive-hauled railway journey took place along the tramway of Perrydarren ironworks in Merthyr Tydvill, Wales. In 1803, he built a steam-powered road vehicle, which drove from Holborn to Paddington and back. The steam tugboat the *Charlotte Dundas* tested on the Clyde in 1801. In 1803, the Swede Erik Svedenstjerna toured Wales, the English midlands, and the Scottish lowlands, noting that steam engines were everywhere.[10] That same year, one of Trevithick's stationary pumping engines exploded in Greenwich, killing four workmen.

According to its own chroniclers, the story of coal is a happy one. Erasmus Darwin was already imagining the horseless carriage, or steam-powered automobile. His *Phytologia* took coal and limestone, not as materials arduously and dangerously produced by workers underground, but as "monuments of the past felicity of organized Nature!" since eons earlier they had consisted of lifeforms—biota; and where life is, happiness had been![11]

The energy from those far off geological horizons functioned in the historical moment of 1802, at the commencement of the Anthropocene, namely, as thermodynamic energy for machines, as illumination of the commodity spectacle, and as warmth against winter's cold. The story of coal is usually told through the lens of political economy as an essential part of the modern saga of progress. Ten million tons of coal were produced in England and Wales in 1800, up from two million in 1660. Its geography changed. The infrastructure of its transportation changed. All of these changes—mining, canal digging, engineering—required a new understanding of the earth and its crust and a new understanding of energy—thermodynamics.

9. Priestley, *Historical Account*, 570.
10. Cited by Mantoux, *Industrial Revolution*, 335.
11. *Phytologia*, section 19.8, 560.

Adam Smith defined the division of labor as division of labor in the workshop, where machines replaced skills, and as division of labor in society, where geographic specialization organized production. The latter changed the infrastructure of transportation, while the former increased the productivity of hand workers. Canals, roads, and railroads connected the divisions of labor in the latter case; connections in the former case were made by trenels, and screws. Heterogenous manufacture required assembly of component parts. This accounts for the importance of Henry Maudsley's invention of the slide-rest lathe in 1800, which enabled standardization of screw threads and other precision parts, allowing interchangeability of nuts and bolts.

For the design and building of steam engines, the inventor James Watt and the entrepreneur Matthew Boulton formed a company outside Birmingham—the Soho Works, which employed more than a thousand workers. Among its mechanical productions was the coining of money, particularly the pennies, halfpennies, and farthings for workers' purchases. Between 1797 and 1806, it consumed four thousand tons of copper, which became payment (wages) for untold lives. The factories devoured people as surely as the engines devoured coal.[12] Erasmus Darwin extravagantly praised the steam-powered coining machine at Soho in terms that clearly revealed the master's preference for child labor and his worry about theft. The machine, he claimed, reduced both pilfering and hangings.[13] It reduced the number of counterfeiters, and thus the work of the executioner, and "by this machinery four boys of ten or twelve years old are capable of striking thirty thousand guineas in an hour, and the machine itself keeps an unerring account of the pieces struck."[14]

According to Patrick Colquhoun, the Scotsman who transformed the London police, opulence grew in tandem with the growth of its opposite, misery, and thus it was with the Soho Works. On Christmas Eve 1800, William Fouldes, a disgruntled employee and father of four, along with several others, robbed the famous factory. With the collusion of the watchmen, they broke down the door of the wall and took fifty or sixty guineas from the watchhouse. Fouldes took a bad fall escaping over the walls enclosing the

12. The consumption of body parts was integral to this mode of production. The founder of the factory system, Richard Arkwright, began his career buying the hair of village girls to sell to the peruke-makers.

13. Darwin, *Economy of Vegetation*, canto 1, section 6.

14. Darwin, *Botanic Garden*, 18.

works and was run over by the Wolverhampton coach, breaking his arm. A doctor set it for ten shillings six pence, and turned him in.[15]

The Battle of Culloden (1746) was the culmination of a violent expropriation of the Scottish Highlands and one factor in the termination of its culture. William Robertson, Adam Smith, Adam Ferguson, and John Millar explained it as a historical inevitability, because it conformed to history's stages. According to them, these stages were fourfold, viz., savagery (based on hunting and gathering), barbarism (based on pastoralism), feudalism (based on agriculture), and commercial civilization (based on the commodity). Not only were these four stages distinct, they followed one another in strict succession. They had an economic base to which corresponded distinct social relations of government, language, arts, and culture. Together they amounted to a theory of history called "stadialism," which has influenced evolutionary models of human progress ever since.[16] In the new United States, the stadial theory anticipated extirpation.[17]

The hidden hand of Adam Smith and the division of labor in both its senses, that is, the globalization of the market and the fractionation of labor, molded the fourth stage by manufacture (de-skilling the hand). In *The Wealth of Nations* (1776), he described the productivity of the division of labor in his famous example of pin-making, in which different workers specialized in drawing out, cutting, straightening, pointing, head-making, and so on, thus increasing the productivity of one worker doing all the operations. The hidden hand of allocating resources by the expansion of the market and the fractionation of labor destroyed the domestic economy, whereby an unmonetized, self-provisioning, subsistence economy provided a gender regime in which women had independent access to common resources. They had not yet become those "housewives" of patriarchal capitalism, whose monetary value was represented at best by "pin money."[18]

In contrast to the storm and stress of geopolitics, the standpoint of political economy seems to provide an interpretation of rock-solid inevitability and historical determinism. Historical materialism, as defined by Engels, "seeks the ultimate cause and the great moving power of all important

15. County of Stafford, "The Examination of William Fouldes," Boulton and Watt MSS, 10 April 1801, Birmingham Central Reference Library.

16. Caffentzis, "On the Scottish Origin."

17. Wood, *Thought*.

18. Valenze, *First Industrial Woman*; Bennholdt-Thomsen and Mies, *Subsistence Perspective*.

historical events in the economic development of society—the changes in the modes of production and exchange, the consequent division of society into distinct classes, and the struggles of these classes against one another."[19] Historical determinism is the law of empire: knowledge of the future is gained by its stadial methods, and its signs are the machines of social production. The steam hammer, the spinning machine, the power loom, the cotton gin, and so on, are instruments of production that seem to transform the activity of labor with the resources of nature. The signs have become inanimate objects, and history has been objectified. Engels said that we owe to Marx the conception that class struggle and production by surplus value are the discoveries of scientific socialism.[20]

Johannes Fabian has argued that temporal distance is used to attain objectivity, or the creation of the Other. It thus is a methodological principle in the science of "discovery," in that the colonial subject inhabits a different temporality than the scientist or historian of the imperial power. Stadialism denies coevality, or equality— the sense of being involved in the same project, belonging to the same age—between empire and colony. It places the rulers and the ruled in different temporalities. Indigenous people live in a history of near timelessness formed in a mythopoeic past.[21] In contrast, civilization is in a hurry, in an endless rush. By this logic, Ireland was doomed.

In 1788, three men—James Hutton, John Playfair, and John Hall—set out in a boat. Their goal was to examine the outcrops along the cliffs where the North Sea pounded the rugged Scottish coastline. At Siccar Point, the action of the sea revealed strata of Old Red (Devonian age) and Greywacke (Silurian age) sandstones, which were not layered horizontally. "They were vertical, standing straight up, like a row of books on a shelf."[22] This was a eureka moment. History became, as it were, vertical. All its horizons were simultaneously available. "Eternity is in love with the productions of time," said Blake. "There is not in nature any appearance more distinct than this of perpendicular fissures and separations in strata. These are generally known to workmen by the terms of veins or backs and cutters."[23] *Backs* is a miner's term that refers to a diagonal parting in coal. *Cutter* is a crack or fissure intersect-

19. Engels, *Socialism: Utopian and Scientific.*
20. Engels, *Socialism: Utopian and Scientific,* 50, 53.
21. Fabian, *Time and the Other.*
22. Repcheck, *Man Who Found Time,* 21.
23. Hutton, *Theory of the Earth,* 51.

ing the bedding or the lines of stratification. Perpendicular or vertical strata prove that some other force than sedimentation formed them.

Subterraneous fire causes oceans to subside or lands to elevate. The observed vertical strata result from such previous outbursts and uplifts. "The bowels of the earth [are] the place of power and expansion."[24] The convulsions, fractures, and dislocations renovate the earth's constitution. The sedimented weight of ages seems to be lifted, overturned, buckled about, wrinkled. These geological observations occurred at the same time as William Blake's prophetic reconstitution of the earth's constitution, and the "Atlantic mountains." Despard's army was composed of men and women who were products of the same social forces that produced these insights into geology—the canal builders (Regent's Canal, Paddington Canal), those vanquished from colonial conquests, and the displaced former occupiers of common lands. Despard attempted to form a revolutionary army led by Irish veterans, metal workers in the new engineering trades, navvies, dispossessed textile workers in the north of England, and veterans among the soldiers and sailors.

In September 1802, the croppers of the largest woolen mill in Leeds struck against the employment of two boys who were older than the recognized age for apprenticeship. It was a pretext for a showdown between Benjamin Gott and the croppers and the whole West Riding on the question of apprenticeship. If the workers lost that fight, the circumstances would be ripe for de-skilling, for child labor, and for the creation of that capitalist fantasy, the imagined anticommunity of the labor market.[25]

According to Frederick Engels, 1802 was a crucial year in the development of socialism, when the utopian socialists Saint Simon, Charles Fourier, and Robert Owen enunciated theories intended to be the culmination of the Age of Reason. The demand for equality was no longer restricted to the political franchise but extended to the social condition of individuals—men and women, bourgeois and proletarian. They sought to reorganize society and emancipate humanity. Engels writes that to the utopians, "socialism is the expression of absolute truth, reason, and justice, and has only to be discovered to conquer all the world by virtue of its own power. And as absolute truth is independent of time, space, and of historical development of man, it is a mere accident when and where it is discovered."[26] He might be

24. Hutton, *Theory of the Earth*, 51.
25. Polanyi, *Great Transformation*.
26. Engels, *Socialism*, 43.

paraphrasing Despard. Compare Engels's triad "truth, reason, justice" to Despard's "truth, liberty, justice."

Frederick Engels's 1880 book *Socialism: Utopian and Scientific with the Essay on "The Mark"* was part of those debates about socialism that gave him the opportunity to make his and Marx's views more connected than ever before.[27] Utopian socialism and scientific socialism share an understanding of class struggle. They also are alike inasmuch as they both propose abolishing private property and social classes. But what differentiates them, according to Engels, is first, scientific socialists adhere to the materialist conception of history, and second, they understand that the secret of capitalist production is surplus value, or the appropriation of unpaid labor. The cause of the transformation of utopian to scientific socialism was the development of the capitalist mode of production itself, in particular the application of machinery (Engels stresses steam power and tool-making machinery) at one pole of development and the accumulation of proletarians at the other.

Criminalization of the workers' appropriation of the materials of production is essential to the separation, alienation, and expropriation of the worker, and thus to the making of the proletariat. This is why Engels wrote of "the unwritten law of the mark."[28] The workers cultivated the lands in common by strip and redistributed the strips by lot. The advent of private property in forest and field had met fierce opposition going back to the Peasant's Revolt of 1526. What artisans had owned or used at will mutated into perquisites, or customary appropriations, that were criminalized in community-destroying transformations.

Engels's book has special interest for us because he places the origin of utopian socialism in 1802, the year of the Despard conspiracy. He names three utopian socialists: Robert Owen, whose New Lanark Mill opened in 1800; Charles Fourier, the groundwork for whose theory was laid in 1799; and Saint Simon, whose *Geneva Letters* was published in 1802. But the puzzle in Engels's thinking comes with the essay on the "mark," the remnant of the German commons, whose intricacy he traces in this essay and whose origin is partly described by the evidence the Roman historian Tacitus provides in his *Germania*. The separation Engels makes between socialism of either kind and the mark may help us think about communism and the commons. He puts the mark in the past.

27. Engels, *Socialism*, 43.
28. Engels, *Socialism*, 84

The fundamental fact that governs "the primitive history of all, or almost all, nations" wrote Frederick Engels, is "common property in the soil."[29] Land is at the root of the commons. The roots are tangled, deep, or shallow. The field, the forest, the uplands, and the coast are the landscapes of the commons. "England is not a free people, till the poor that have no land, have a free allowance to dig and labour the commons," quoth Winstanley in 1649.[30] "As late as 1800 much of the world's grassland—the North American prairies, the south American pampas, the Australian outback, the African savannahs—was still communally owned by indigenous people."[31]

Adam and Eve were expelled from the Garden of Eden, an expropriation from the commons, and ever since the commons has been treated mainly as an agrarian or horticultural phenomenon. It is true that Adam and Eve were not thrown out of the wheelwright's shop or the handloom weaver's shed or the mariner's cabin. But others were, and they originated not in Eden but in Ireland, Atlantis, Iroquoia, Scotland, and Albion.

Engels bluntly raises the question of agency: who has the capability of bringing about the communist revolution? In actual practice there were many other forces practicing commoning, including the slaves of the Caribbean, the Indians of North America, the Irish of Ireland, and the peasantry of England—even the urban mob, as Gracchus Babeuf realized. But "the Negro is not capable of becoming as intelligent as the European," wrote the utopian socialist Saint Simon at the time of Despard's plot.[32] Racism and stadialism were congruent. By ignoring slavery and its power in the freedom struggle, the stadial, or economic determinist interpretation of history, seemed to be a lock and geology superseded history.

The ghost of Hamlet's murdered father called from the grave for revenge, and Hamlet, surprised, answered, "Well said, old mole! canst work i' the earth so fast?—A worthy pioneer!" In 1805, in his Jena lectures, Hegel recalls Hamlet's words: "Spirit often seems to have forgotten and lost itself, but inwardly opposed to itself, it is inwardly working ever forward (as when Hamlet says of the ghost of his father, 'Well said, old mole! canst work i' the ground so fast?') until grown strong in itself it bursts asunder the crust of earth which divided it from the sun, its Notion, so that the earth crumbles

29. Engels, *Socialism*, 77.
30. Winstanley, *True Levellers Standard Advanced*, 249.
31. Linklater, *Owning the Earth*, 5. He might have added the jungle of the Indian subcontinent.
32. Saint-Simon, *Selected Writings on Science*, 77.

away." Half a century later, Marx remembers them too: "we do recognize our brave friend Robin Goodfellow, the old mole that can work in the earth so fast, that worthy pioneer—the Revolution." Shakespeare's ghost calls for legitimacy, Hegel's spirit calls for truth, and Marx's revolution demands justice. Whether in open-field commons or enclosed by fences, the mole tunnels on. To Marx, the proletarian revolution is "our brave friend Robin Goodfellow," a figure from the folklore of commoners. To Shakespeare, "There are more things in heaven and earth, Horatio, / Than are dreamt of in your philosophy," a rebuke to conventional knowledge.[33]

We conclude these reflections on nature's underground with the long filamentous structure called the mycelium, which supports the unpredictable appearance of toadstools from the underground. The English mycologist Alan Rayner writes,

> I have increasingly come to regard the mycelium as a heterogeneous army of hyphal troops, variously equipped for different roles and in varying degrees of communication with one another. Without a commander, other than the dictates of their environmental circumstances, these troops organize themselves into a beautifully open-ended or indeterminate dynamic structure that can continually respond to changing demands. Recall that during its potentially indefinite life, a mycelial army may migrate between energy depots; absorb easily assimilable resources such as sugars; digest refractory resources such as lignocellulose, mate, compete and do battle with neighbours; adjust to changing microclimatic conditions; and reproduce.[34]

33. *Hamlet,* act 1, scene 5; Hegel, *Hegel's Lectures;* Marx, speech at a dinner celebrating the founding of the *People's Paper,* London, 14 April 1856.

34. Rayner, "Conflicting Flows," 24–35.

SEVEN

E. P. Thompson and the Irish Commons

AN IMPORTANT COINCIDENCE CAN ADVANCE THE DISCUSSION. "Strata" Smith was the first to map the underground of England.[1] In 1801, he finished drawing and coloring "the map that changed the world." The son of a blacksmith, he was born in 1769, the year of Richard Arkwright's water frame, James Watt's condensing steam engine, and Josiah Wedgwood's pottery factory. He was eighteen when his Oxford village birthplace, Churchill, was enclosed by act of Parliament. He studied the art of surveying with the man who enclosed his village. Steel chain, dividers, theodolite, and pantograph became the instruments to measure enclosure, conquest, and canal building. In 1794, he was made surveyor of the Somerset Canal Company. The miners taught him and named the seams. The workmen identified twenty-three strata down the Somerset coal mine.

In April 1803, Strata Smith took lodgings in London off the Strand at 16 Charing Cross Road. He shared these costly lodgings with another upwardly mobile man, Francis Place—tailor, lobbyist, friend of Jeremy Bentham, and proponent of utilitarianism. Smith and Place had gone underground and climbed out to say what they saw. Francis Place, archivist of the early English working class, was a member of the London Corresponding Society. He was the prime witness and remains the prime source for historians of the English artisan. The coincidence of the first map of the geological underground being presented in 1802, at the time the working-class movement in England was forced underground, is of importance. The two developments are related.

At the end of *The Making of the English Working Class*, E. P. Thompson writes, "These years appear at times to display, not a revolutionary challenge,

1. Winchester, *Map*.

but a resistance movement, in which both the Romantics and the Radical craftsmen opposed the annunciation of Acquisitive Man. In the failure of the two traditions to come to a point of junction, something was lost."[2] I am going to try to describe that junction point with the purpose of finding that lost "something."

In 1963, Edward Thompson proposed a crucial phase between 1803 and 1822, when the working-class movement went underground. The Despard conspiracy inaugurated what Thompson called the "illegal tradition." This began to occur in 1795, with the passage of the Two Acts. The Treasonable Practices Act made it a crime punishable by death to say or write anything that might incite contempt for the king, constitution, or government. The Seditious Meetings Act banned all meetings of more than fifty people that lacked permission of the local magistrates.

Members of the London Corresponding Society, including Francis Place, archivist of the early English working class and friend of Despard, "were forced to go underground and to adopt the organizational methods of a secret society."[3] Place resigned from the London Corresponding Society in 1797. He described Edward Despard as one of three "extraordinary men, to each of whom I was indebted for some portion of the knowledge I possess and for whom I shall always entertain strong feelings of regard." Few people who were "well off in the world and well instructed condescended to visit me at all," he wrote of 1795. Nevertheless "some remarkable men visited me frequently, and frequently conversed with me for considerable period . . . and those visits were very advantageous to me in intellectual and moral points of view."[4]

The Combination Acts were directed particularly against makers of engines or engineers. The Combination Acts of 1799 and 1800 "forced the trade unions into an illegal world in which secrecy and hostility to the authorities were intrinsic to their very existence."[5] The government thereby "unwittingly brought the Jacobin tradition into association with the illegal unions. . . . The act jolted the Jacobins and trade unionists into a widespread secret combination." Jacobins and Spenceans, feminists and republicans, were driven to silence. The political and social underground was a defense against the terror.

Thompson put the change into geological time by comparing it to "the great plain of Gwaelod," which lies twenty miles west into Cardigan Bay.

2. E. Thompson, *Making*, 832.
3. E. Thompson, *Making*, 181.
4. Place, *Autobiography of Francis Place*, 181.
5. E. Thompson, *Making*, 500.

Seven millennia ago, according to Welsh folklore, the sluice gates failed to open, a drunken gatekeeper was distracted by a fair maiden, the icecap melted, the sea level rose a few hundred meters, and the forested, inhabited land was drowned. From the hills above the coast, the great plain of Gwaelod is there to be seen. In similar fashion, we see Place and Despard in the political underground.

Thompson gives us "the working class" without the commons. Although the components of the working class have been considerably enlarged since 1963, to include enslaved people, servants, sailors, miners, prisoners, housewives, and the criminalized, the historical energy Thompson gave to the dynamics of the working class has persisted. The omission of the commons has had an unforeseen consequence. When the commons returned as a notion of inquiry in the twenty-first century, as it did after the collapse of the USSR and with the expropriation of villages in China, Africa, Southern Asia, and Iberian America, it lacked *any* notion of the working class.

David Bollier and Lewis Hyde give profound accounts of the cultural commons, but when they reach back in history, they go to the agricultural commons of feudal times.[6] Further, they move from the agricultural commons to the cultural and informational commons without considering what took place culturally and agriculturally in the intervening period of history when manufacturing and mechanization became the dominant forms of production. Manufacture promoted the division of labor. We can also follow the division of labor in the field, with the shepherd, the thatcher, the wheelwright, and the hayward. Historically, however, the division plays out most significantly with slavery— on the plantation, sometimes called "factories in the field." In omitting manufacture, Bollier and Hyde also omit *class,* or the origin of the proletariat. This is why it is necessary to turn to E. P. Thompson.

Thompson mentions the commons once, not in his own words but in the words of the Chartist leader Feargus O'Connor (1794–1855), the charismatic, redheaded Irish orator and editor. As the nephew of Arthur O'Connor and the son of Roger O'Connor, Feargus O'Connor was the heir of the Rebellion of 1798 and the descendant of Irish kings. At the time Despard suffered, he was being schooled in Portarlington, in the same county Despard was from.

6. David Bollier, *Silent Theft: The Private Plunder of Our Common Wealth* (London: Routledge, 2002); Bollier, *Think Like a Commoner: A Short Introduction to the Life of the Commons* (British Columbia: New Society, 2014); Lewis Hyde, *Common as Air: Revolution, Art, and Ownership* (New York: Farrar, Straus and Giroux, 2010); Hyde, *The Gift: Creativity and the Artist in the Modern World* (New York: Vintage, 2007).

His brother fought with Bolivar. Unlike Despard the insurrectionist, O'Connor advocated mass meetings and huge petitions. While in prison (1840–41), O'Connor elaborated his theories of land. Though he might have boasted, "I have levelled all those pygmy fences," his land plan was a failure. In 1843, he published *The Employer and the Employed*, a fictional dialogue between a millowner and old Robin, and it is from this that Thompson quotes.

Feargus O'Connor begins *The Employer and the Employed* with lines from Goldsmith's "The Deserted Village": "Ill fares the land—to hastening ills a prey, / Where wealth accumulates, and men decay." Goldsmith's poem was published in 1760, just in advance of the Whiteboy uprising, among the Irish peasantry, against the enclosure of their commons. Like Goldsmith, Feargus was also raised in county Meath, though his family was made up of powerful landlords of county Cork. Goldsmith visited Ireland just before writing "The Deserted Village." We may see it as the result of actual investigation on the eve of the volcanic eruption of the Whiteboys. If English colonization of Ireland included "plantation," when the empire struck back, one of the ways it did so was as "transplantation." "Ill fares the land" when "land" is without nationality; this was England and Ireland. O'Connor builds a national story: "Here's that we may live to see restoration of Old English times, old English fare, old English holidays, and old English justice, and every man live by the sweat of his brow; when the gaol was a terror to the wicked, instead of a refuge for the destitute, when her hardy honest peasantry were their country's pride, when the weaver worked at his own loom, and stretched his limbs in his own field, when the laws recognized the poor man's right to an abundance of everything."[7]

In O'Connor's vision, the commons included owning the means of production; owning a bit of land; owning justice, health, and food. The vision was based on abundance, not scarcity. The poor folk were bundled out. And now? "There's police barrack, bank, church, lock-up, session house, beer shop, billiard table, and brothel, all standing on my acre of ground." Here the corruption which follows enclosure is contrasted not with the common but with "my acre of ground." Where was the "common"! the millowner asks:

"Why bless my life here, here Maister Smith, here, where thou callest 'Shoddy Hall.' Doesn't know 'common.' Why, I thought every child in Riding knew

7. Thompson, *Making*, 230. Thompson selectively quotes from Feargus O'Connor's pamphlet, 15, 41–42, 56.

'common.' All reet and left, up away to bastille and barracks was all common. And all folk in Devil's Dust would have a cow, or donkey, or horse on common, and they'd play cricket, and have running matches, and wrestling, and all sorts of games in summer time. Ay, bless my old limbs, I remember when lads and lasses would 'loose' work in evening and meet at market-house to run up the common."[8]

Shoddy Hall is where Smith lives. The barracks were built in Despard's time as enclosures to sever the connection between the soldiery and the people. The "bastille" was slang for any prison or workhouse. Despard in fact was imprisoned in the first prison bearing the revolutionary name. Shoddy refers to the deterioration of standards brought on by mechanization and to the consequent enclosure of handicrafts. The village name, Devil's Dust, refers to the dust raised up by mechanical spinning, the cause of brown lung disease. O'Connor is writing an allegory. The commons is now posted: "beware of dogs," or "man-traps and spring-guns set here," or "any person trespassing on these premises will be prosecuted according to law." Sport or play is now firmly opposed to the new types of exploitation; the lads and lasses would "loose" work to play on the commons, which was a location of subsistence too.

Robin walks to Mr. Smith's, Shoddy Hall: "I haven't been as far as 'common' for now two-score years." That would put the scene in 1803, the year of Despard's death. "Aye, it's more than that. Let me see," Robin continues, "it was time when rich folk frightened poor folk out of their senses with 'He's a-cooming' and 'they're a-cooming.'" And who's that, Smith asks, forgetting the resumption of war with Bonaparte in 1803 after the Peace of Amiens.

"Why, God bless thy life, don't thou know? Why, Boney and the French, to be sure. Well, that time when rich folk frightened poor folk and stole all the land. 'Ecod, much the same as mesmerized like, and folk were expecting to be eat up every minute, but they let the Lords and Squires take the land, but 'ecod, they'll na give it back again. This was all common then, Mr. Smith. Common for poor folk y' Devil's dust, to keep a cow on; but 'ecod, Squire Gambler represent Riding then, and Billy Pitt was hard pushed to keep in, and Squire a good dodger, and folks say, that when minister axed Squire for vote, Squire axed minister for 'common;' and 'ecod, sure enough, minister got vote, and Squire got common, and poor folk's cow got road, and poor folk got bag. But ay, Mr. Smith, it would take too long to tell thee all about the rows and riots about inclosure of common.

8. F. O'Connor, *Employer and the Employed*, 42.

"Aye, dearee me, many's the honest man was hung [*sic*] and transported over ould common."[9]

It is a surprisingly precise account, not at all mythic. It is not blood and fire but legal chicanery and a ruling-class hocus-pocus that causes the loss of commons. From O'Connor and Goldsmith, we have allegorical and poetic summaries of enclosure. It is significant that they are both Irish voices.

The phrase the "moral economy" itself derives from Bronterre O'Brien, the Irish leader of the English Chartists:

> True political economy is like true domestic economy; it does not consist solely in slaving and saving; there is a moral economy as well as political . . . these quacks would make wreck of the affections, in exchange for incessant production and accumulation. . . . It is indeed the moral economy that they always keep out of sight. When they talk about the tendency of large masses of capital, and the division of labour, to increase production and cheapen commodities, they do not tell us of the inferior human being which a single and fixed occupation must necessarily produce.[10]

The Making of the English Working Class largely ignored Irish workers, whether in England, in Ireland, or in between (ships), so it is remarkable that two of the ideas that are significant to Thompson's arguments—one negatively (the commons) and the other positively (the moral economy)—came to him from Irishmen, Feargus O'Conner and Bronterre O'Brien. The fact is that both were leading organizers, journalists, and speakers of the working-class and trade union movement *in England* during the second quarter of the nineteenth century. In fact they were leaders of the revolutionary working-class movement of Chartism.

He treats it as "moral economy." The food riot was legitimized "by the assumption of an older moral economy," which taught that it was unfair to profit from the necessities of the people. "These popular actions were legitimized by the old paternalist moral economy." Why did he turn to "custom" rather than the "commons"?

The Luddites were part of the struggle against the centripetal force of capitalism—its tendency to intensify exploitation. The Haitians were the strongest part of the struggle against the centrifugal force of capitalism, with its tendency to extend expropriation. When E. P. Thompson wrote that the

9. F. O'Connor, 42.
10. E. Thompson, *Customs in Common*, 337; Plummer, *Bronterre*, 77.

years of the underground were "of a richness at which we can only guess," we need to add to that wealth not only such commoning experiences as those of "the wuthering heights" of Yorkshire or the Luddite country but also those of the "Atlantic mountains" of William Blake that Edward and Catherine Despard knew so well. Stadialist habits of mind obliterate the memory of commoning economies.

The concept of the "commons" is related to the dream, the gothic, the surreal, the hidden, and the mythic. It is related to the "underground," and this is the junction point, the "something," where the Romantic and working-class traditions met, as the story of the Despards can teach us once their context is fully drawn. John Clare, former agricultural man whose commons had been enclosed, closing him out, refers several times in his poetry to those underground creatures, moles:

> While I see the little mouldywharps hang sweeing to the wind
> On the only aged willow that in all the field remains
> And nature hides her face where theyre sweeing in their chains
> And in a silent murmuring complains
> Here was commons for their hills where they seek for freedom still
> Though every commons gone and though traps are set to kill
> The little homeless miners.[11]

They became metaphors for history's surprises.

A local historian of county Kildare wrote, "The Lyons crossroads was one of the haunts of the Black Dog who seems to have been related to the dog of Greek mythology who guarded the underworld."[12] Catherine entered an underground if not an underworld. In the history of the underground, there are mythic, geological, and political moments that are coeval with the Despard plot of 1802–3.

The twentieth-century Cuban Marxist Che Guevara and the nineteenth-century Cuban nationalist José Martí referred to the revolutionary project by alluding to what Jesus said about Jonah. Che told a visiting American student to return to the belly of the beast. Martí wrote before he died, "I have lived in the monster and I know its entrails."[13] When asked for a sign, Jesus answered, "It is a wicked generation that asks for a sign; and the only sign that will be given it is the sign of Jonah" (Matt. 16:4). Exterior forces alone

11. Clare, "Remembrances," p. 259, lines 37–43
12. Kelly, "History of Lyons Estate."
13. Martí, *José Martí Reader*, 234.

will not reveal the just society: freedom of action can alone perform the ideal commons. In secular terms, the economic determinism of stadialism opposes the power of human freedom.

However, "For as Jonah was three days and three nights in the whale's belly; so shall the son of man be three days and three nights in the heart of the earth" (Matt. 12:40). Between crucifixion and resurrection, Jesus descended into hell, "the heart of the earth." The episode is known as the harrowing of hell. In English plebeian tradition, Hell is this Earth: Hell is the Law: Hell is the Commodity. From Milton's *Paradise Lost* to Blake's *The Marriage of Heaven and Hell,* this tradition provided the underground horizon of class war. Jonah was part of a crew, Jesus part of the salt of the earth, the Despards part of the Atlantic proletariat. All suffered hell in the belly of the beast.

Subterranean fields, the bowels of the earth, or the heart of the earth are parallel to both "the belly of the great fish," or "entrails of the monster," and to "history from below." "The heart of the earth" can have these three meanings: 1) the location of dark energies like the "thesterness" of coal and petroleum; 2) the inferno, the place of great heat, and thus of diastrophic change causing the twisted inequalities of rich and poor on the earth's crust; and 3) the several horizons of the geological commons. I suggest that the meanings of "underground"—mythic, geological, and political—are interrelated and that they concern meanings of the commons. Before we return to England, our quest for Catherine Despard and for the commons requires us to broaden our gaze, first to Ireland and then to America, to what Blake called "the Atlantic mountains."

PART TWO

ATLANTIC MOUNTAINS

FIGURES 6 AND 7. "One Only Master Grasps the Whole Domain" and "The End of Oppression." Two trade tokens struck by Thomas Spence.

D

IRELAND

EIGHT

Habendum and the Anglo-Irish Ascendancy

EDWARD MARCUS DESPARD WAS BORN IN 1751, in county Laois—called Queen's County in Despard's time after Queen Mary (1516–58)—when it was the westernmost limit of the Pale.[1] Born in the middle of the century, born in the middle of Ireland, and born in the middle of the elevation between sea level and "the height of Ireland" (as the Slieve Bloom Mountains were locally known), Despard was born in the thick of the geography, the history, and the struggle of Ireland. Born sixty years after the settlement of King William and forty years before the formation of the United Irishmen (1791), Despard knew of the repression of the county rulers and the rebellion of the county ruled.

Elizabeth Despard, Edward's niece, was the family historian. She was born in 1770 and died in England ninety-six years later. Her recollections (supplemented by the memoirs of her sister, Jane) are the principal source of knowledge of Edward's early life, and it is from them that we learn he was called Ned.[2] When Elizabeth was six (1776), six families of Despards lived within six miles of each other. The family historians wrote with pride and resentment about Irish identity. Jane spoke proudly of "a drop of the real old Irish blood." Elizabeth explained the malice toward Edward: "the English press always malicious when an Irishman is in the case."

Elizabeth's family recollections begin, "As I ever had my ears open to tales and traditions, since I heard my good mother check her good mother for something not to be talked of in my presence, because little pitchers had wide ears, so her remark is verified by my gathering up a great many such things in

1. Bannantine, *Memoirs.*
2. E. Despard, "Recollections." See also J. Despard, "Memoranda."

my memory, as well as the many facts which poor Father was fond of telling (who had the most capacious memory to the last hour of his life) while we sat so much together in his latter years." She combines "tales and traditions" from her mother with "many facts" from her father in a familiar epistemology based on gender.[3]

This chapter emphasizes the "facts" of family history, which were violent in themselves, rigid, apparently unassailable, recognized in law, and preserved in the hefty volumes in the Registry of Deeds in Henrietta Street, Dublin. It is concerned with the authoritarian structure of the property settlement underlying the imperial conquest. The next chapter, on the other hand, starts with the "tales and traditions" of family lore, which were unsteady, oral, and sometimes subversive, and discusses the widespread resistance that was the cultural result of that property settlement.

William Petty (1623–87) surveyed and mapped the country in the Down Survey, published in 1659, which shows that the possessions of the Despard family in county Laois already existed in 1640. Petty contrived to "help himself to one hundred thousand a year in poor plundered Ireland," writes Elizabeth. Petty famously stated in *Political Arithmetic* (1690), "Now the Observations or Positions expressed by Number, Weight, and Measure, upon which I bottom the ensuing Discourses, are either true, or not apparently false, and which if they are not already true, certain, and evident, yet may be made so by the Sovereign Power."[4] Yes, coercion cooked as well as backed facts.

There were three phases in the conquest and settlement of Ireland: Elizabethan, Cromwellian, and Williamite. Mountrath, a town in county Laois, lay within the Pale, one of the first Tudor plantations. Philip Despard was sent to Ireland by Queen Elizabeth I to superintend the partitioning of lands; hence it is "still called the Despards county by the lower class." The organizers of the Massachusetts Bay Colony, Emanuel Downing and John Winthrop Sr., attempted to settle Mountrath before moving across the Atlantic.[5] They sold out to Charles Coote, the ruthless soldier and entrepreneur, who aggressively dominated the plantation against the claims of the Fitzpatrick sept. He was earl of Mountrath and owned twenty thousand acres in the county, later acquiring Ballyfin, which commanded the county beneath spectacular views.

3. Quoted in Poovey, *History.*
4. Preface to *Political Arithmetick.*
5. Loeber, "Preliminaries."

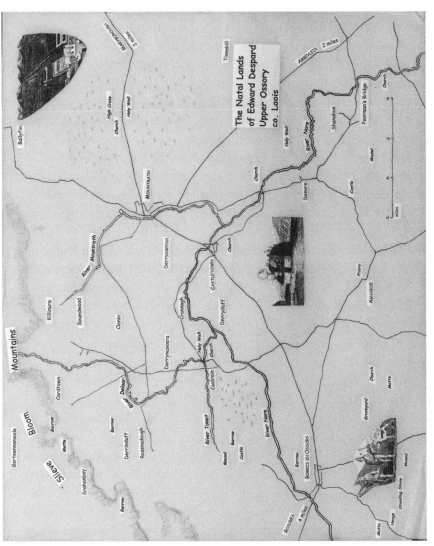

FIGURE 8.   The natal lands of Edward Despard, Upper Ossory, county Laois. Map drawn by the author.

By the eighteenth century, one might find the conquest, the plantation, and the conveyancing of land distilled in the powerful legal expression "to have and to hold," in the landlord's lease to the tenant. Here were facts backed and cooked by sovereign power. Lawyers referred in Latin to the clause as the "habendum clause." It is also the binding clause in the reigning marriage vow: "to have and to hold for better for worse, for richer for poorer, in sickness and health, until death do us part." Edward Ledwich (1738–1823) was the vicar of Aghaboe, a few miles south of Donore. He quoted the opinion of an English ruler, John Davies (1570–1626), about Irish tenures "the uncertainty of the possession was the very cause that no civil habitations were erected, no inclosure or improvement was made in the lands of the Irish countries," and that "bastards had their portions with the legitimate."[6]

The habendum of private property and patriarchy could be found in nationalism. James Fintan Lalor (also from Queen's county and a neighbor of the Despard family holdings) brought the habendum clause from the realms of private property and marriage to revolutionary nationalism: "Ireland her own—Ireland her own, and all therein, from the sod to the sky. The soil of Ireland for the people of Ireland, to have and to hold from God alone who gave it—to have and to hold to them and their heirs for ever, without suit or service, faith or fealty, rent or render, to any power under Heaven."[7]

Edward Marcus Despard lived when private property, agrarian infrastructure, and commercial development seemed secure to the Anglo-Irish Ascendancy. The genealogy of the family and the prosopography of Despard's brothers and sisters mirror the militarism of the Anglo-Irish; the several ties with North America and the Caribbean; the integration with an Atlantic economy; and the classical education and athletic formation of this powerful cultural, political, and economic fraction of the British ruling class. Despard's childhood was passed in the tension between two economies.

An inventory of Despard properties in county Laois reveals the incomplete nature of conquest; the survival of "the hidden Ireland" and the variety of ecology (mountain, bog, river, and woods); and the residuum of the commons evidenced even in the leases and deeds of lands. Maps of eighteenth-century Mountrath and vicinity clearly contrast retrenched lands for tillage

---

6. *Antiquities of Ireland* (1790). Ledwich is quoting John Davies, *Discovery of the True Causes Why Ireland Was Never Entirely Subdued* (1612), published in Deane, Carpenter, and Williams, *Field Day Anthology*, 1:217.

7. Lalor, *Irish Felon*, 172.

and individual tenancies from other types of uses and tenure—"Redd Bogg in Comon," "Mountain in Comon," "Commons of Sconce," they will say.[8]

Passing from the summit of the mountains to the bog beneath and thence to the tributaries of the river Nore, one of the "three sisters" of the Irish midlands, one passes distinct ecological zones that determined the conditions of life: mountain, plain, and river. Along with these were their corresponding types of commons—pasturage, tillage, and fishing. The southern side of the mountains faces mainly heath and bog, branches of the central bog of Allen, and the turf yields both white and red. William King published an essay in 1685, expressing the wish that the bogs would sink forever. They caused roads to be crooked, they destroyed the cattle, they sheltered thieves and tories, and they corrupted the air and water. Nevertheless, he added, the natives had "some advantage by the woods and bogs; by them they were preserved from the conquest of the English."[9] As late as 1801, Sir Charles Coote described this part of county Laois as "by no means populous, but wild." At that date two-thirds were pasture, and one-third was arable. Most of the county was either upland or bogland.

"The real destroyer of the woods was agriculture."[10] Leases in county Laois contained vexatious provisions requiring that so much timber be cut and destroyed per annum, while another clause forbade the tenant to use turf or peat for fuel. Another required him to make ditches and plant hedges. The last of the derries were grubbed out. Every bit of land was tilled or grazed. In the mid-seventeenth century, county Laois had been more extensively cleared of woodland than any other Irish county, except for some at the five hundred-foot level of the Slieve Bloom Mountains, owing to the voracious appetite for wood of the Coote's ironworks in Mountrath. Elizabeth attributed much of the initial wealth of the family to "immense iron mines on their properties."[11] Extracted in the mountains, the iron was floated down the Nore to Kilkenny, where it was hammered and manufactured. Mountrath was a small protoindustrial town.

For seven decades of peace (1690–1760), 230 families ruled the county, and of these, forty to eighty played a conspicuous role. While they were "lean years for the great mass of the population," rents steadily rose. The characteristic

8. Hogan, *Book of Maps, Earl of Mountrath's Estate,* 1740, National Library of Ireland.
9. *Philosophical Transactions,* 15, repr. in Deane, Carpenter, and Williams, *Field Day Anthology,* 1:969.
10. Rackham, *History of the Countryside,* 116.
11. E. Despard, "Recollections."

landscape of agrarian capitalism was formed—roads, bridges, improved fields, estate villages, churches, country houses, demesne walls, plantation.[12] Credit, banking, and capital easily flowed in. Enclosure was well underway by the middle of the century, and with it graveling, marling, and liming. By the 1730s, county Laois had become part of the Dublin provisioning zone. The universalization of a potato diet was accomplished by 1740.

Despard grew up on land that contained constant reminders of embattled conquest. Describing one way the Cromwellian phase of conquest was represented, Elizabeth wrote "a great tree which stood on the hill overlooking Donore when I was a child was the gallows for the Protestants of 1641."[13] Like settler's children everywhere, she grew up with stories of native atrocity, in this case rooted in the landscape itself. The "improvements" of eighteenth-century Ascendancy agriculture took place within a rich and layered archaeological record. In county Laois, these were monuments of Gaelic, Christian, Celtic, and Norman pasts: the inauguration sites of the local Gaelic kings, stone chairs, or sacred trees, unassuming among the low hills; the remains of ringforts, the enclosed single farmsteads of the early Christian period; the round towers and high crosses of the Celtic Christian past from the end of the first millennium; the mottes or defensive earthworks of the twelfth-century Normans; the tower houses of the Gaelic lords and Old English lords.

The third phase of modern English settlement of Ireland, the Williamite, followed the defeats at the Boyne (1690) and Aughrim (1691) and the betrayal of the Treaty of Limerick (1691). James Bannantine believed that Despard had an ancestor who was an engineer at the Battle of the Boyne.[14] In Upper Ossory alone, there were seventeen hundred forfeitures that predominated in clusters on the Slieve Bloom Mountains. The barony of Upperwoods was parceled out to officers and soldiers, who, not wanting to reside in Ireland, often sold the land to the Hollow Sword Blade Company. In 1709, the Hollow Sword Blade Company bought the townlands of Derrycanton "together with all Castle, Houses, Messuages, Edifices, woods, underwoods, water, watercourses, bog commons, common of pasture, [and] fishing rights."[15] Founded in 1691, with imported German (Solingen) sword smiths,

12. Beaumont, "Gentry."
13. E. Despard, "Recollections," 4.
14. Bannantine, *Memoirs*.
15. Collis and Ward, Despard Estate, National Archives of Ireland.

FIGURE 9. The hollow remains of Despard's ancestral home at Donore, county Laois. Photo by the author.

who crafted an improved design with a sharper edge, by 1703, its directors ("a true triumvirate of modern thieving," wrote Defoe[16]) had transformed it into a moneymaking enterprise combining government debt, insider trading, and military technology. It then took to land speculation in estates acquired by conquest, whose rental yield was double that of prime English land.

Daniel Beaumont, the historian of the county gentry, wrote that by 1690, the landowners lived in castles or fortified houses; fifty years later this was no longer the case. Residential architecture of the big house under the Ascendancy, with broad lawns and ample fenestration, indicates a confident class unconcerned with peasant uprisings or military sieges, though danger from bandits, tories, and raparees, as well as cattle stealing, remained a problem for them in the 1740s.

Ned's grandfather William drove six horses in his carriage, and Elizabeth dates the beginning of the family misfortunes with his early death in 1720. "He left as little behind as he could . . . except, generations of sorrow." He "brought many settlers and servants from this country and laboured hard to

16. Daniel Defoe, *Anatomy of Exchange Alley* (1719), quoted in M. E. Novak, *Daniel Defoe*, 571.

civilize the neighbourhood." When his portrait at Donore fell apart the eyes were picked out by pigeons, says Elizabeth, an apt symbol she implies.[17]

Despard's seven brothers and two sisters were the children of Jane Walsh and William Despard. At Eton, William dressed as a running footman so that he could run back and forth to London. Jane was the sister of Counsellor Walsh, solicitor general of Ireland, who gave his name to the "Walsh Hills" of Laois and Kilkenny. Edward's eldest sister, Catherine, sowed a thimbleful of larch seed from the Alps on the stone wall surrounding Coolrain. Jonah Barrington (1760–1834) of Abbeyleix in county Laois described how "the common people of co. Laois divided this gentry into three: *Half-mounted* gentlemen, Gentlemen every *inch of them, and* Gentlemen to the *backbone*."[18] Ned's eldest brother, William, inherited the Coolrain estate. He lived seventy-eight years. Raising the Coolrain Yeomanry against Irish independence from English rule during the '98 uprising, he was a gentleman to the backbone. Edward's next oldest brother was Philip, who lived to 1817. He served in Gibraltar for seven years under General Marcus Smith, who married a Pole of Ballyfin. Ned carried his name. Philip married Letitia Croasdaile, and they had five children, two girls: Elizabeth (1770–1866) and Jane (1773–1857), the historians of the family, and three boys, two who became army officers and a third who perished in the West Indies. Letitia Croasdaile's father was obliged to leave Ireland and was appointed chief justice of Barbados. Of the children, one was arrested for a three-thousand-pound debt and was "obliged to go abroad"; another married a New Yorker; a third started a starch manufactory in Dublin; a fourth owned a mill in Offlay; a fifth held "a good situation in the National Bank"; and a sixth was known as "the wild man of the woods." Philip "despised money except to throw it away." He could not avoid "sharing a shilling with anyone who wanted it." The laundress of the Monaghan barracks pined away after his death. His lavender-colored wedding coat, with buttonholes embroidered with silver thread, and his buff-colored silk waistcoat, with pockets embroidered in the pattern of a moss rose found their way to the children's dollhouse. A gentleman every inch of him.

Edward's third brother, Cateret, was named after his father's tutor at Eton College, who happened to be visiting Coolrain at the time of his birth. Dr. Cateret gave them books, including "a universal and ancient history," which remained a family treasure. Cateret died young.

17. E. Despard, "Recollections."
18. Barrington, *Personal Sketches*, 1:22.

His fourth brother, the "naval Uncle," was named Green. He lived in Larch Hill, a neighbor to Coolrain, where he built a "wigwam" to quote his nieces. They crouched "on their hams like Indians, around the big turf fire."[19] Bishop Berkeley queried of the Irish, "whether they are not yet civilized and whether their habitations and furniture are not more sordid than those of the savage Americans?"[20] Although he remained unmarried, Green had a child by his housekeeper. The tenantry was "to a man papist and at that time nearly in a state of slavery." A half-mounted gentleman.

Edward's fifth brother, John ("the General") was born in 1745 and died in 1829. Gazetted as an ensign in 1760, he had a distinguished military career in Quebec in 1773, in New York with Howe, and at the siege of Charleston in 1779. He was three times shipwrecked, thrice taken prisoner, and twice had horses shot from beneath him. An adjutant to General Cornwallis, he was part of the surrender at Yorktown (1783). "The three brothers were all in America together."

The sixth brother, Andrew, was born in 1745. He rose to be an army major and was "the pattern officer in the 59th Regiment."[21] He sponsored the Ballyfin Cavalry Yeomen formed in the '98 rebellion. He had two natural sons: one went to America and the other, a Papist, remained as steward on one of his farms. Alone among the brothers, Andrew retained contact with Edward after his change in politics. We will learn more about the family's feelings regarding Edward's politics in later chapters. Elizabeth concluded about the family as a whole, that "No Despard wife ever has pains in her lying in," and all in all, there were few drunkards in the family.[22]

Government was physical. Sport and war were not quite as separate as they are today. They knocked heads, broke bones. Wielding cudgel, sword, or whip they jabbed, they poked, they thwacked, they tripped. Jonah Barrington again: "The riders . . . carried long thong whips heavily loaded with lead at the butt-end, so that they were always prepared either to horsewhip a man or knock his brains out, as circumstances might dictate. These half-mounted gentlemen exercised the hereditary authority of keeping the ground clear at horse races, hurlings. . . . A shout of merriment was always set up when a half-mounted gentleman knocked down an interloper and some of the poets present, if they had opportunity, roared out their verses by way of a song to

19. Barrington, *Personal Sketches*, 1:28.
20. Barrington, *Personal Sketches*, 2:184.
21. E. Despard, "Recollections."
22. E. Despard, "Recollections."

encourage the gentlemen." One sang aloud "as he himself lay sprawling on the grass, after having been knocked down and ridden over by old Squire Flood, who showed no mercy in the 'execution of his duty.'"

> There was Despard so brave,
> That son of the wave,
> And Tom Conway, the pride of the bower;
> But noble Squire Flood
> Swore, G-d d-n his blood!
> But he'd drown them all in the Delower

That was the river running by Coolrain.[23]

Of Henry, her ancestor and Despard's contemporary, Elizabeth Bowen writes, "Education is not so important as people think," calling attention to his flair for living.[24] As with Henry, so with the Despards. Despard's oldest brother, William, was the first boy to leap the great dyke in Trinity College Park in a standing leap. His brother John, the general, as a young man "used to ride about standing in his saddle." "Sport and death are the two great socializing factors in Ireland," writes Elizabeth Bowen.[25] Sport indeed requires a field, if not a commons.

Still, education was not unimportant to the Despards. Ned's brothers John and Andrew were enrolled at the Quaker school in Ballitore in 1754.[26] Jane wrote that John's younger brothers— plural—attended the school, though there is no record that Edward was enrolled. Scholars boarded from France, England, Norway, and Jamaica. Quick-tempered and generous Richard Shackleton, was "desirous above all things," his daughter wrote, "to promote the cause of truth and righteousness." A passionate, energetic teacher, he helped to form a generation of patriots: his curriculum was modern—history and math, Greek and Latin. He stripped off his coat and worked with his men during the summer harvest.[27]

Elizabeth tells a story of her father and young Ned that illustrates his family loyalty and an early acquaintance with the "the moment of force": "A sergeant came to Colruane one day on business to our father, when Ned who

---

23. Barrington, *Personal Sketches*. The poem is by a poet named Daniel Bram, whom Barrington quotes.

24. Bowen, *Bowen's Court*, 124.

25. Bowen, 126.

26. McAuliffe, *An Irish Genealogical Source*, 8.

27. Leadbetter, *Annals of Ballitore*, 75.

was standing at the door asked what did he want and the sergeant replied that he was come to take his brother to jail. Upon which Ned ran in to warn Phil of the terrible intent of the sergeant and urged him to come and hide. And then hid himself. The sergeant had been fooling. The older brothers learned strict morals and the Bible from the old grandmother (she lived to be a hundred) at Coolrain. Edward detested the old woman, the Bible, and the coffee. Elizabeth understood "that from a boy he was of exceeding gravity of manners" as were his brothers. Elsewhere she says "he was of a remarkably mild temper and mild manners."[28]

Jane called Edward, "the youngest and most talented of the whole family." He was placed as a page to the countess of Hertford, whose husband was the lord lieutenant of Ireland: "the proudest and least moral family of any in the British dominions then as now," reported Elizabeth. There he learned to serve wine, attend on the coach-and-six, and run messages. Eyes open and mouth shut, he absorbed what was around him, thus receiving an education in corruption and an intimate understanding of all that is hollow in pomp and circumstance.

Oppressive exploitation and parasitic luxury, on the one hand, and defeat, degradation, and despair, on the other. These were the facts. The times were changing literally. In 1751, an act was passed abolishing the Julian calendar and bringing in the Gregorian, so along with everyone else in the British dominions, the young Edward became eleven days older one day than he was the day before. In fact, he may have been born eleven days old!

28. E. Despard, "Recollections."

———

NINE

Hotchpot, or Celtic Communism

THE REGISTRY OF DEEDS IN DUBLIN preserves copious records of Irish land transfers. They are indexed by surname. They form a "bleak house" of private property and *meum et tuum*. I have studied 69 of the 165 deeds concerning Despard over the fifty-five years from 1730 to 1785.

Elizabeth Bowen imagines her ancestor, Ned's contemporary, come to full bloom and by holding in 1750, "a metaphorical fistful of Kilbolane, Ballymackey or Farahy earth, [and] was prepared to flatten his hand and say, 'This is mine.'"[1] With private property came commerce. Between June 1746 and February 1758, William Despard of Coolrain "granted, demised, let, and farmed" fourteen deeds. Between 1749 and 1753 Richard Despard of Cranna entered into five, and Richard Despard of Donore entered into three.[2]

Meanwhile, the money economy was being introduced. In 1738, Charles Pim, a Quaker, leased a premise in Mountrath from Richard Despard of Crannagh, in which the rents of three fat pullets and three days work were commuted to seven shillings sixpence and one shilling, respectively. The undertenants were required to grind their grain and malt on the premises. And the boundaries of the land itself? No more description than this: what was "formerly in possession of William Borris. A second lease of 1756 to Charles Pim was made over by Lambert Despard, Gent., at one peppercorn a year of "the Waste Plot of Ground formerly held by William Despard and Alexander Thompson."[3] While these leases look to the future, with the growth of commerce and the monetization of exchanges, they also look to

---

1. Bowen, *Bowen's Court,* 145.
2. Index of Surnames, Registry of Deeds, Dublin.
3. Friends Historical Library, deed box 2, folder 4/1.

the past, in that they depend on knowledge of the boundaries known only to the defeated.

As the vicar of Aghaboe, Edward Ledwich (1738–1823), antiquarian and advocate of privatization and the Anglo-Irish Ascendancy, was a neighbor of the Despard family in county Laois. As a scholar in the culture wars, he is a valuable witness: "Ireland, the seat of turbulence and discord for five centuries, and attached to barbarous . . . laws and usages, which occasioned a perpetual fluctuation of property."[4] The implied equivalence of "property" and "Ireland" is characteristic of a privatized version of the nation. "Barbarous municipal laws and usages" referred to the Brehon Law, or local custom. Here was preserved a cultural substratum of Irish civilization with deeply different conceptions of "property." While Elizabeth Bowen's ancestral forbear might have asserted, "This is mine!," letting that fistful of earth fall to the ground like Cadmus's dragon's teeth, there were myriads of others arising out of the ground as armed men. Robert Scally wrote, "Divergent mental geographies, one graphic and the other oral, governed the use of land simultaneously. One, embodied in the landowner's survey, was upheld by the law and the other by deeply embedded custom, a moral economy that was inextricable from peasant family and kinship systems but had no legal standing."[5]

According to Ledwich and Anglo-Irish historiography, the two causes of Irish barbarism were tanistry and gavelkind. Tanistry was the Irish system of life tenure, whereby the succession to an estate was conferred by election among the surviving kinsman. Gavelkind was a system of tribal succession, in which the land of the deceased occupant was thrown into the common stock and the whole area redivided among members of the sept. The clachan was a small settlement of kin, in which material resources of stock and land were shared. The members of the sept, or clan, "having thrown all their possession into hotchpot, made a new partition of all," as Ledwich put it.[6] *Hotchpot* was a term in English common law meaning the blending of properties to ensure that they were divided equally.

Disputes were settled by native Irish law called Brehon law (the Irish word for judges). Ledwich wrote, "One of these ancient judgment-seats is on the hill of Kyle, in the Queen's County," not very far indeed from the Aghaboe

4. Grose, *Antiquities of Ireland*, 1:ii.
5. Scally, *End of Hidden Ireland*, 14–15.
6. Ledwich, *Antiquities of Ireland*, 306, 316.

priory.[7] A few miles from Despard's Coolrain, south of Burrows-in-Ossory, was a rude red stone on Kyle Hill "called by the common people the Fairy Chair which is supposed to be the ancient judgment seat of the Brehons."[8] "Traditions of hospitality are a common accompaniment of pastoral life," wrote Estyn Evans.[9] The Brehon laws had a well-defined code of hospitality.[10] Edward's cousin, George Despard of Donore, "used to blow a horn at his door at dinner for any stranger passing the high road."[11]

Can we describe agrarian social relations from below as Celtic communism? "These self-sufficient communities were held together by blood ties and by the exchange of services under the Irish open-field or 'rundale' system of cultivation. Around the house-clusters were small walled gardens and haggards, but the arable land was an unenclosed open field in which each holder had his scattered patches, averaging perhaps a quarter of an acre in area." This was the Gaelic pattern of impermanent strips: the open field system of tillage was swept aside with the reconquest. Unenclosed strip fields survive "in small isolated pockets."[12]

The identification of common land and rights of commonage were explicit interests of official surveys from Cromwellian conquest to the Irish Free State. William Petty's surveyors were explicitly instructed that "in all common land, whether profitable or unprofitable, you are to mention the names of such places or persons as have commonage in the same with the proportion belong unto each of them," though they seldom carried this out.[13]

The second of the seven hundred pages of *A Handbook of Irish Folklore* (1942) instructs collectors to consider the commons: "Did all the local people or the people of a townland or even a group of families hold land in common down to comparatively recent times? ... Did several families own livestock in common, plant crops in the same field, and sub-divide the produce among themselves at any time? ... Did the herding of cattle and other farm or domestic activities rotate among the joint owners? ... Was (is) it common for

7. Ledwich provides a picture of the judges posed in ridiculous postures and dressed in absurd costume. His goal was to show that the hidden Ireland was actually gone and might now fall under the scholarly gaze.

8. Lewis, *Topographical Dictionary*, 2:18.

9. E. Evans, *Irish Heritage*, 52.

10. Feehan, *Landscape of Slieve Bloom*, 259.

11. E. Despard, "Recollections."

12. Feehan, *Landscape of Slieve Bloom*, 253.

13. Larcom, *History of the Survey*.

landless families to plant crops in land belonging to their neighbours?"[14] The *Handbook* notes five types of commoning. The first was the townland, according to which land was held in common (Ledwich called it "hotchpot"). The townland consisted of clusters of cabins, often without chimneys or windows, that were semiunderground, where building materials consisted of turf and thatch, "dripping soot from above and oozings from below." Outsiders "viewed the townland and their settlements as merely another obstinate obstacle to any rational management of the land and the people, an occult device that muddled responsibilities between master and tenant, perpetuated the old listless ways, and bred conspiracy."[15] As to writing down the names of the townlands, this was a source of mirth and tragedy, as Brian Friel shows in his play *Translations*. The clerks or solicitors of William Despard spelled Coolrain variously as Coolroane, Colerain, Collrain, Coolraine, Cloran. The hedges and ditches, not to mention fences or imagined surveyor's lines, were features of the future that were imposed on an extant system of property. The townland names preserve suggestions of older human ecology—town commons, bog commons, woods.

Despard was born in Coolrain, and his ancestors are buried in the protestant church there in a locality called Anatrim. It was deserted even by 1838, and now it remains in roofless ruin; nevertheless its tower continues to dominate the lands around. Great slabs of granite lie in the wet grass of the graveyard next to the ruin, one with the letters forming "Despard" cut into the hardness and lichen adorning its edges. "Numerous are the tombstones of that family," Elizabeth wrote.[16] Outside the churchyard is a well and "a large flat stone called St Kevin's Stone with a ring three feet in diameter cut on it and two hollows above said to be the impression of the Saint's tears, and two marks (hollows-like) said to be the marks of his feet." The sixth-century saint provided a basis of vernacular worship during the penal times. Beggars, cripples, the "dark people," assembled at the sacred fountain, where miracles of healing were performed: sight restored, broken bones mended, fever lifted, and motion restored to the paralyzed.

A comparison of the townlands described in 1709, and restated in an indenture of 1865, reveals that the following list of townlands were included in the various property deeds of Despards: Rosnacrina, Derryduff, Derrinduff,

14. Súilleabháin, *Handbook of Irish Folklore*, index.
15. Súilleabháin, *Handbook of Irish Folklore*, index.
16. E. Despard, "Recollections."

Laurel Hill, Killaghy, Cromogue, Derrycrag, Clonin, Moncknew, Killahy, Raheen, Ballentegort, Balaclough, Shraghanard, Tinnakill, Shanboe, Minoge, Minough, Moynoge, Derrycanton, Killenure, Lough, Lackagh, Condiglas, Cardstown, Rossendough, Gurteenmallagh, Monakeeba, Shranaboy, Lack-along, Cappagh, Cullenmule, Comer, Clanfadda, Ballynakill, Ballynoughy, Glankill, Glanamoon, Gliarndine, and Cargeen. And this does not mention the family seat at Donore or Coolrain or Crannagh, Shanderry.[17] The total Despard acreage fell between a thousand and two thousand, much of which was upland on the slopes of the mountain, where limekilns—a sure indication of agrarian productivity—were not present even by the 1830s. A good many of these townlands thus fell outside the ambit of commercial agriculture: they remained part of the subsistence economy.

The second type of commons named in *A Handbook of Irish Folklore* was hill pastures. These were still held in common and were reckoned in sums, lumps, or collops, or units of mountain grazing of different stock. Between St. Patrick's Day and Halloween, the animals were taken to mountain pastures, the booley, where "The cows are fed by a field being assigned for all the cottars of the farm."[18] The Celtic festival of Lughnasa is still celebrated in Slieve Bloom by the eating of bilberries and nocturnal merrymaking among abundant stills and shebeens.[19] The townlands belonging to Despard's family included steep and rugged pastureland in the Slieve Bloom Mountains. Centuries of human capital were embedded in the stock-proof, drystone walling of upland Laois. Here the mythic Fionn MacCumhaill ran down two deer. The family owned less elevated lands suitable to the "improvements," or the acts of privatization that destroyed communal or rundale forms of agriculture. Tithes were levied on corn, potatoes, flax, and meadow—for every churning, a hand of butter, and for every plough, a sheaf of corn.

17. As for the grant of lands to Despard, I would not claim that my list is comprehensive. Quite apart from mistakes of transcription, the nature of the problem is that complete accuracy is impossible. I have studied four groups of eighteenth-century property records concerning the Despard lands in county Laois. The four groups are: 1) a sample from the transcribed deeds preserved at the Registry of Deeds, Henrietta Street, Dublin; 2) some actual deeds among the Collis and Ward papers in the National Archives of Ireland; 3) six Despard family wills in *Betham's Abstracts*; and 4) a few Mountrath indentures preserved in the Swanbook House, Friends Historical Library, Dublin. My purpose was to estimate roughly the extent of Despard family lands in order to classify the family's power and status within the county. Ffolliott, "Registry of Deeds," 156.

18. A. Young, *Tour in Ireland* (1776–1779), ii, 428.

19. Evans, *Irish Heritage*.

In 1746, Ned's father let 68 acres of Baunavrona for £18; 714 acres of Killenure; 186 acres of Lough and Lackagh; 243 acres of Gurteenmallagh and Condiglas; acreage in Rossendou, otherwise Derry Duffe; and 30 acres commons in Killarmough, called Monekaba. He let 297 acres of Straugh and Moynouth, except for "the liberty of Hunting, Hawking, Fishing and Fowling." He let 231 acres of Raheen and Ballentegort, and 179 acres of Monicknew, "with all Commons & Privileges thereto belonging." Income amounted to over £626 a year.[20] Over time, the leases grow more interesting. A deed of 1753 shows William Despard demising to Richard Despard those parts of Derrynaseery called Cloran. Included in this deed was the right to cut turf on the bog of Derrynaseery, as well as timber for building houses, for *Fledge Boot,* and for *Plow Boot,* to use the terms for customary usufructs. Similarly arcane words like "hedgebole," "ploughbole," and "firebole" referred to common rights in the woods.

In a William Despard lease of 1778, we can read a hint of native land customs in the arable and pasture townlands of Derrynaseere "and the Subdenominations thereunto belonging." It was still difficult to measure the area of land and even difficult to name its units. In a different lease in the same year, when William Despard leased his dwelling house in Coolrain and "three acres profitable Land together with a supply of Turf Bank for sd. Trench and his Tennants residing on sd. Lands on that part of the Bogg of Coolrain aforesd called the Cow pasture with full liberty of cutting sawing and drawing away the same."

Even in the leases of an alien conquest to which the law of property conveyancing is at once its secretive and characteristic activity, the Gaelic order could not be completely absent. Private property as Ledwich understood it depended on primogeniture and patriarchy. Arthur O'Connor in *The State of Ireland* (1798) wrote, "We must look to those laws of primogeniture, entails and settlements which have been set up to secure and perpetuate the despotism of the few, and to ensure and perpetuate the exclusion of the many."[21]

In 1714, when John Despard of Cordstown conveyed to William Despard of Killagh "the lands of Ballyloughlin," the terms were described as "together with the Comons [*sic*] and all other rights Members and Appurtenances therein belonging in as large and ample manner as Florence Fitzpatrick did lately." The former regime could not be totally erased: the Fitzpatricks held

20. Collis and Ward, Despard Estate, 2/463/26, National Archive of Ireland.
21. A. O'Connor, *State of Ireland*, 45.

the ancient or traditional sept. These were part of the estates forfeited in county Laois to Charles Coote by Florence Fitzpatrick. Land delimitation, or the drawing of boundaries in the soil, was inevitably a negotiation with those who had made the land with their own previous labors (graveling, liming). Henry Bowen litigated a land dispute with a neighbor that lasted five years (1759–64). "Armies of country people, old employees and servants, children of employees and servants to both families were brought in as deponents" to depose what they had known since their cradles.

In uniting the land with the sea, the river connects agriculture with trade. The mercantile or commercial bourgeoisie settles on the rivers in order to increase this traffic, which originates in the surplus production of enclosed agriculture or in the raw materials extracted from mines or forests or in the partially refined productions of the protoindustries of the countryside. The hydrographic system becomes more efficient to this traffic as the rivers are traversed (bridges) or augmented (canals) or deepened (ports). The tendency is to speed the traffic; the trajectory tends downward toward the sea. The river Nore, one of the three sisters, along with the rivers Suir and Barrow, draining the Irish midlands, formed the eastern border of the Despard family estate at Donore. To landed people, it was an obstacle to local transportation— stepping stones, footbridge, fords, and "footsticks" are indicated on the Ordnance Survey map—but to people on the river, it was a source of livelihood, a resource of usufructs, such as reeds or salmon. While admitting that the banks of the Nore were "picturesque and well-wooded," Sir Charles Coote complained of its want of navigation: "nor is there any established fishery, except eel weirs, which many have usurped along the river, to the great detriment of the meadows lying on its banks." Piscary was a contested right. The old leases, including an early eighteenth-century Despard lease, preserved to the landlord the right "to hunt, hawk, fish, and fowl. Charles Coote describes one of these without qualification: the river may "improve" commerce, and obstacles to that improvement—increased inland trade—are usurpations or thefts. He found the women's character "extreme in idleness and sloth"; "they are much addicted to theft, which it is no disgrace with them to be detected in." It was no disgrace because it was not theft but custom.[22] As I noted in my discussion of the hanging of Hannah Smith for her part in an

22. Lease for Three Lives from John Despard of Cordstown to William Despard of Killaghy (1714), National Archives of Ireland; Collis and Ward, Despard Estate, 2/463/26, National Archives of Ireland.

English food riot and of the gleaners' case involving Mary Houghton, the association of women to commons rights contrasts with gender relations in privatization (see chapter 4). Here we see it again.

William Tighe, writing of the lower Nore in county Kilkenny, states unequivocally, "The fishing of these rivers is free by custom to the inhabitants of the shores."[23] The fishing territories were bounded by gashes and riffles. Their modern historian, Fidelma Maddock, writes that "fishing rights [were] harvested by common weir of the tribe and a common net to fish the pools."[24] The maintenance and repair of nets was one of the several skills required by river people. Another was the building of the river craft or "cots." Tighe describes the method of fishing: "with a snap net suspended between two cots, which are small boats, flat-bottomed, narrow, equal at both ends and governed by paddles; two men are in each boat, one of whom conducts it: when the fishermen feel the net drawn, the boats are closed immediately." Further, "An innate sense of rhythm is required and a facility of hands that allows two people to work together with elegant dexterity in the nocturnal hours." The fishermen had minute knowledge of the tides and the moons for their catch depended on it. It is the thread that links them to "their remote Mesolithic predecessors."[25] Thus the labor was characterized not only by physical dexterity or silent teamwork but by knowledge of the salmon, the river, and the heavens. In the stories of the people, the salmon conferred wisdom. The Nore fishermen shared "the feed" with their neighbors in the mid-August festivals. Slipping their cots into the coursing water as soon as the first star appeared in the night sky, "they would bless themselves, saying 'let's go in the name of God.'"[26] The labor process linked the commons with the sacred.

The third type of commoning was a commons of habitation, or squatting: "They provided themselves with two Caddows, a small Pot, two woodden Platters, two Trenchers, one Knife, and two Horn Spoons . . . and to save as much as would build a Cabin by the Road Side, on the Common."[27] The roadside verge became disputed territory.

The fourth type was that provided by the potato wage, which brought with it some common rights and was often accompanied by rights of pasture,

23. Tighe, *Statistical Observations*, 1:150.
24. Maddock, "Cot Fishermen," 542–54.
25. Tighe, *Statistical Observations*.
26. Maddock, "Cot Fishermen," 542–54.
27. Chaigneau, *History of Jack Connor*.

turbary, or estovers. The potato wage was not completely separated from the means of life, entailing as it did a relation to the potato plot, potato culture, the lazy bed, other potato cultivators, and a community of townland. Potatoes were the mainstay:

> Respecting the labour of a farm, the standing business is done by cottars; a cottar is one who has a cabbin, and an acre and a half of garden, charged at 30s., and the grass of one or two cows, at 25s. each, and the daily pay 6d. the year through, the account being kept by tallies, and those charges deducted; the years' labor amounts to about £6 after the cottar's time for his potatoes and turf is deducted; the remaining 40s. is paid in money, hay, or any thing else the man wants.

> Frequently large tenancies were held by cooperation, 'knots' of poor men combining to bid for them, and managing them in common, and frequently too labour was exacted in addition to a money rent. The purely labouring class were generally cottiers—paid for their labour not by money, but by small potato plots, and by the grazing of one or two cows, and they worked out these things for their employers usually at the rate of 6 1/2d. a day.[28]

For the fifth type of commoning, there was common labor as well, not mentioned in the *Handbook*. Anne O'Dowd, the historian of *meitheal* (the participation in cooperative labor) explains that by its nature cooperation is a hidden phenomenon. Preparing the land, sowing the crops, cutting the turf, harvesting, drawing home, threshing, taking to market, fishing and river work, and home industries were cooperative. Some labor was festive, some was based on exchange, or direct reciprocity. Technically this reciprocity was called "helping" or "joining," also "morrowing" or "neighbouring," the swap, the boon, the camp. It belonged to both potato, fish, and corn culture. When two or more joined together to plough, it was called a *coar* Teams of spade men might have replaced the plough, using the wooden *feac*, which was in fact a hand-plough rather than a spade. "There were certain men in each locality [of county Laois] who were superior to others in the making of the stacks or ricks in the haggard," so sturdy and tight, that not a drop of rain would come in.[29]

Specific lacks produced incentives to pool equipment and draught animals. Arthur Young described partnership farming on the rundale pattern in 1776. *Rundale* refers to the periodic redistribution of farming strips. It was

28. Salaman, *History and Social Influence*, 248, 259.
29. A. O'Dowd, *Meitheal*.

new rather than traditional, a means of dealing with particular shortages while other inputs, such as labor, were in abundant supply. Sir Charles Coote, whose *General View of the Agriculture and Manufacturers of the Queen's County* was published in 1801, noted the propensity of the peasantry to hire or lend each other the plough, to hold small farms in partnership, to enjoy "the usual privileges" of pig and poultry rearing and the "strong attachment to old customs." Sources such as Charles Coote or James Cotterel stress what is negative, quarrelsome, or stubborn in partnership leases. The complications of partnership pose "a constant bar to improvement," difficulty of receiving rents, or calculating them. The townland might be divided in 132 divisions, separated by strips of waste. The partners make swaps and barter the less good on the hills with the good of the lowlands. The commons "divided by mutual consent." Cotterel's 1812 survey of Kilcross, bounded on the south by the River Nore, shows how the land was partitioned at marriages of sons and daughters, and by "encouraging strangers" (a few rent-free cabins were permitted on the commons). The proportions held by each man determined "the number of beasts which each partner was to put on ground grazed in Common."[30]

Neither the "public" nor the "commons" quite hits the nail on the head, though both have been employed separately, and recently together, in generalizing eighteenth-century agrarian life in Ireland. Andrews notes the economically and morally inferior subculture associated with common lands. His evidence from county Laois notes that the commons of Fossy was "the resort of the principal robbers and rebels" during the '98.[31]

Maria Edgeworth in *Castle Rackrent* (1800) describes a materialism from below when she writes of "the most minute facts relative to the domestic lives, not only of the great and good, but even of the worthless and insignificant."[32] In the novel the steward, Thady Quirk, gives witness to the transition from customary perquisites to monetary wages when he says that "the tenants even were sent away without their whiskey—I was ashamed of myself and knew not what to say for the honor of the family." Edgeworth provides a footnote to explain the transformation of a gift into a right. "Thady calls it *their* whiskey; not that the whiskey is actually the property of the tenants, but that it becomes their *right*, after it has been often given to them. In this general

30. Coote, *General View.*
31. Andrews, "Struggle."
32. All quotations from the Macmillan edition published in 1895, Project Gutenberg, n.p.

mode of reasoning respecting *rights,* the lower Irish are not singular, but they are peculiarly quick and tenacious in claiming these rights. 'Last year your honor gave me some straw for the roof of my house, and I *expect* your honor will be after doing the same this year.'"

The economy of duties—turf cut, hay brought home, potatoes dug—"in short all the work about his house done for nothing"; "for my lady—eggs—honey—butter—meal—fish—game, growse, and herrings, fresh or salt—all went for something." Edgeworth explains that "in many leases in Ireland, tenants were formerly bound to supply an inordinate quantity of poultry to their landlords." The "clear perquisite" of my lady or the farmer's wife were the weed ashes. Edgeworth also explains that the great demand for alkaline salts—lime—rendered these ashes "no inconsiderable perquisite."

Maria Edgeworth describes "minute facts"—not the facts of state importance that Petty had in mind when he instructed his surveyors. Nevertheless, it was precisely in these minute facts that questions of crime, right, custom, theft, and honor arose. Colonialism denies the oppressed their own past history, precisely to close off the future. Custom, perquisites, hospitality, commons, clachan, rundale, piscary were all elements of eighteenth-century Irish commoning. They were destroyed, degraded, and criminalized by colonialism with its ideologies of improvement and modernity.

Lands within such commonages were distributed by lottery. This was of paramount importance to the later career of Ned Despard; indeed it provided a turning point to it as we shall see. The casting of lots was how Jonah singled out members of the crew for sacrifice. As a method of dividing land, the practice has precursors going back to Aeschylus and Moses and throughout European history. As a randomizer in distribution practices, it obviates permanent hierarchy and solves some aspects of "the tragedy of the commons." In Irish history, it was used by both the conqueror and the conquered. Edmund Ludlow, the Cromwellian conqueror, wrote, "Accordingly, the soldiers drew lots for their several portions, and in that manner all the forfeited lands were divided up among the conquerors and adventurers for money."[33] Some of "the farms under the landlord," Estyn Evans asserts, "are held in common, as respects both tillage and pasturage. In the land appropriated to tillage, each head of a family casts lots every year for the number of ridges he is entitled to.... The head of the village ... makes the division as equal as

33. Ludlow, *Memoirs.*

possible, requiring each man to cast lots for his ridge, one in a good field, another in an inferior, and another in a worse."[34]

Despite the land transfers that followed the conquests by Cromwell and William III, commoning retained its existence in Ireland. Despard grew up with it. Typical of the eighteenth century was the rundale-and-clachan pattern of settlement in the west and in the uplands of Ireland. Tenants holding partnership leases and inhabiting housing clusters regulated communal grazing (*buaile* or "booley") in the uplands, turbary rights in the bogland, and foreshore rights (*cearta trá,* or seaweed rights) by the strand. The strips of communal infield were rotated annually (rundale) to ensure ecological egalitarianism of all types of soil—deep, shallow, sandy, dry. This form of commoning, therefore, was a response to commercial expansion in the lowlands and should be seen as part of "modernism," rather than as a vestige from a mythic past.[35]

34. Evans, *Irish Heritage,* 50.
35. Aalen, Whelan, and Stout, 86–91.

TEN

"That's True Anyhow"

ON HOLY DAYS, AS AT SPORTING EVENTS, the Anglo-Irish and the indigenous people or the "mere" Irish, did not live in cultural apartheid, though in the case of Jonah Barrington's family, they nearly did. "The chase, and the bottle, and the piper were the enjoyments of winter, and nothing could recompense a suspension of these enjoyments." For Christmas, Barrington's brothers planned some "hard-going" deliberate dissipation, shutting themselves up in the hunting lodge with a piper, a jester, and fiddler. For the native Irish, candles lit all over the countryside, the wren-boys, and the chirping cricket the king of luck, while for the Barrington boys in Abbeyleix, it was drunken tallyho![1]

In Elizabeth's family history, she recounts that at Christmas "the story teller of the County was sent for to remain for the evening amusement of the young gentlemen and whenever he concluded one of a peculiarly miraculous nature and said 'that's true anyhow' the boys were quite certain it was a lie."[2] What sorts of stories did the young Ned Despard hear? Some perhaps were the legends of fairies, ghosts, and hobgoblins that inhabited the nursery.[3] Some may have been "tales of bravery and indomitable daring of repulse and defeat," such as those James Doyle learned in Wicklow from "his father's workmen as they ploughed and harrowed up the ancient demesne."[4] Edward's niece Jane records that "in the summer the huntsman and his assistants supplied the story teller's place." Indeed, they hunted in the Slieve Bloom Mountains, said to be the haunt of the fairies of mid-Leinster. "It is resorted

1. Barrington, *Personal Sketches and Recollections.*
2. E. Despard, "Recollections"; J. Despard, "Memoranda," 48.
3. Rawson, *Statistical Survey,* 200.
4. O'Donnell, *Insurgent Wicklow 1798.*

to by a famous piper, a fairy piper too, to whose all-potent music rocks, stones, trees, aye, the Slievebloom hills themselves are often caught dancing," wrote John Keegan.[5]

Oliver Goldsmith visited the Irish midlands and published an account in 1759 that describes the borderland, the edge of the Pale.

> When I had got about forty miles from the capital, I found the country begin to wear a different appearance from what it before appeared to me in. The neat inclosures, the warm and well built houses, the fine cultivated grounds, were no more to be seen, the prospect now changed into, here and there a gentleman's seat, grounds ill cultivated, though seemingly capable of cultivation, little irregular fences made of turf, and topped with brush wood, cut from some neighbouring shrub, and the peasants houses, wearing all the appearance of indigence and misery.

Goldsmith went in to visit. Despite the smoke, he saw the cow and admired the daughter. He stayed for potatoes and milk, and he was honored with a "print of butter." After supper, he supplied beer but then disappointed the host with his stories: "they wanted something *strange* and I had only *news* to tell them."[6] It's the distinction between Ascendancy empiricism and that miraculous history of possibilities. British philosophy at the time, not to mention the "modern fact," developed emerging protocols of verification that contrasted explicitly with the strange, the wonderful, and the miraculous.

After the Jacobite rising of 1745, the miracle bordered on treason, inasmuch as Protestant loyalists in Ireland swore an oath against belief in transubstantiation. David Hume, the Scottish philosopher, had recently published his *Enquiry concerning Human Understanding* (1748), with its controversial tenth chapter on miracles. His essay begins by arguing against the theological doctrine known as the Real Presence. He says that belief in miracles chiefly abounds "among ignorant and barbarous nations." Hence, the love of wonder was suspect on both religious and historical grounds. "A miracle may be accurately defined, as a transgression of a law of nature by a particular volition of the Deity, or by the interposition of some invisible agent."[7]

Thus, returning from the day's hunt in the woods and slopes of the Slieve Bloom, or during a gathering on the holy day of the nativity, the storyteller

---

5. J. Despard, "Memoranda"; O'Hanlon's introduction to Keegan, *Legends and Tales*.

6. "A Description of the Manners and Customs of the Native Irish," *Weekley Magazine,* December 1759; repr. in Deane, Carpenter, and Williams, *Field Day Anthology,* 665–66.

7. Mossner, *Life of David Hume,* 286–87; Hume, *Enquiry,* chapter 10.

in asserting "that's true anyhow" acknowledged the limits of hegemonic skeptical epistemology. "Anyhow" may indicate the priority of experience over method or it may indicate defiance overcoming doubt. One meaning points to the past, the other to the future. It is an assertion of dialectics. A technical rhetorical term, *antiperistasis,* expresses the attitude of opposition to existing circumstances.

When Elizabeth writes of "*the* story teller of the County" and Jane refers to those who took "the storyteller's place," they suggest that there was one such person, serving, as it were, a singular and representative, if informal, office. Such a person would have had mnemonic and perhaps bardic powers. It is tempting to speculate about who the person might have been. At the time, Elizabeth and Jane were writing, John O'Donovan (1806–61), the Irish scholar of antiquities and toponymy, who accompanied the mapmakers of the Ordnance Survey, visited just such a person in county Laois: "Old Laurence died soon after my visit to him and with him died all the Irish language and traditions of the Queen's county."[8]

One of the Despard family seats—Donore, by the river Nore—lies midway between Aghaboe and Shanahoe, from which hailed two powerful voices of the Irish cultural wars: Edward Ledwich, the vicar of Aghaboe, held an aggressive view of Anglo-Irish culture, and John Keegan, an Irish peasant of the townland of Shanahoe, recorded aspects of the recalcitrant and downpressed Gaelic culture.

John Keegan was a fiddler and stammerer, a crossroads dancer, a teacher of the catechism to the poor, and a little-known poet. He was born near Shanahoe, county Laois, a few years after Despard was executed, in a townland adjacent to Despard's house of Donore. He clung to this locale, bearing witness to the sorrows and struggles of its people. His father married Bridget Maloney, whose brother Thomas "had a great reputation for learning among the people of the neighborhood." Keegan grew up in fact with his uncle, a hedge schoolmaster, whose brother was a coachman for Despard! That the Parliamentary Committee on Irish Disturbances (1824) learned "much Agitation is caused by these Vagrants going about, and carrying extraordinary Stories among the People" helps to explain Keegan's insistence that "I am an Irish peasant, born and reared in an Irish cabin, and educated in an Irish hedge-school."[9] He died in the cholera sheds of Kilmainham in 1849.

8. *Letters Containing Information.*
9. O'Hanlon's introduction to Keegan, *Legends and Tales.*

John Keegan tells a story, "St. Kevin's Bush," about the Laurence of county Laois mentioned by O'Donovan. In 1836, to escape a sudden summer shower, a collection of country people—spademen, field laborers, wayfarers, and such—sought shelter under an old white thorn. Old Larry Cunningham told how the bush grew from the old bishop who buried St. Kenny. This was the saint who was schooled in Rome, who transcribed the four gospels, and who founded the neighboring monastery at Aghaboe.

The culture wars of Ireland of the mid-eighteenth century developed into full-scale opposition between two Anglo-Irish versions of the past—Edward Ledwich argued that England brought civilization to a barbaric people, while Charles O'Conor argued that the English invasions destroyed a Gaelic culture of "saints and scholars." The conflict had several methodological corollaries, one being the relative merits of the English and Irish languages, and another being the value of printed and oral evidence.

Old Larry continues in "St. Kevin's Bush," that "there was no oppression ov the poor in them times, no taxes, nor tithes, nor peelers, or land jobbers, to harriss the unforthunate people, but every one was happy an' continted, an' shure 'twas no wondher that people could lay their minds to their souls, an' so they did." The presence of miracles, or wonders, thus had a material precondition in the absence of police, tithes, taxes, and landlords. Gaelic history was politicized. The narrative of "'saints and scholars" implicitly opposed the master's narrative, which robbed the land and degraded the people. For a moment in the midst of a summer rain, the day's labors and sorrows were interrupted by the idea of a time without oppression. It was not a dream or a miracle or a wonder but a memory to which both Old Larry and the old white thorn attested: here is where the bishop was buried, and from his blood grew this tree. Keegan, speaking of the Nore peasantry, affirmed "their extreme love of the wild and visionary."[10] The miracle was a wonder rooted in the land.

Angela Bourke says that storytelling was a form of symbolic capital: "often it has stood in explicit opposition to material wealth, the most fervent tellers of stories about fairies being people whose worldly goods are modest, while their stories typically celebrate the virtues of cooperation and generosity, denigrating avarice and greed."[11] She stresses the theme of resistance to the dominant culture. The repertoire of the storyteller depended on the imagery

10. "The Midnight Mass—A Legend of Cromogue," in Keegan, *Legends and Tales*.
11. Bourke, *Burning of Bridget Cleary*, 55.

of the local landscape, implying that the land did not belong to human land-owners but was somehow vested in other beings. This was the view of a fairy folklorist of the Irish midlands who worked with Jenny McGlynn, a twentieth-century storyteller of Mountmellick, count Laois. The attitude of the storyteller was skeptical. Jenny McGlynn summarizes this aspect of her art, which might be applied to the storyteller of the Despards' Christmas two hundred years earlier: "Keep them in doubt; it keeps the stories going; it keeps the old traditions alive."[12]

The hunt or the holy day brought the subjugated culture right to the hearth of the provincial rulers. Miracles could be told. Young Ned preferred such stories to the Bible, which his grandmother made him read, and they contrasted with the stories he heard as a pageboy in Dublin Castle, from the least moral family of the English aristocracy. John O'Donovan lamented the fact that the language disappeared with the stories. Would Despard have learned the Irish language? Certainly he heard it. In 1801, Coote reported that "the English language is most generally spoken, except towards the mountains; but indeed, throughout, they all can converse in both tongues, with equal fluency."[13] Ned spoke Irish, and that's true anyhow.

12. Lysaght, "Fairylore from the Midlands," 31, 38.
13. Coote, *General View,* 67.

ELEVEN

A Boy amid the Whiteboys

Here is an anonymous letter from 1762:

> We, levellers and avengers for the wrongs done to the poor, have unanimously
> assembled to raze walls and ditches that have been made to inclose the com-
> mons. Gentlemen now of late have learned to grind the face of the poor so
> that it is impossible for them to live. They cannot even keep a pig or a hen at
> their doors. We warn them not to raise again either walls or ditches in the
> place of those we destroy, nor even to inquire about the destroyers of them. If
> they do, their cattle shall be houghed and their sheep laid open in the fields.
> Gentlemen, we beg you will consider the case of the poor nowadays. You that
> live on the fat of the land consider poor creatures whom you harass without
> means of proper subsistence.[1]

The enclosure of commonage and oppression of tithe farmers were grievances against the cattlemen, be they Catholic or Protestant. The Whiteboys
were also called Levelers for destroying fences, filling ditches, knocking
down walls, and houghing, or maiming, cattle. White-smocked insurgents
devoted to the worship of Queen Sive held nighttime meetings and rose in
direct action to abolish tithes; restore commonages; attack proctors, cantors,
and farmers of an alien agricultural settlement; and rescue prisoners.[2]
Turnpike booths were targeted for destruction. They held "fielden nights," in
a carnival atmosphere, with music, and in close association with the Celtic
calendar of festivals and feasts.

Whiteboys were widespread in Cork, Limerick, Waterford, Kilkenny,
Tipperary, and Laois. Country house gates, those grandiose symbols of the

---

1. Froude, *English in Ireland*, 2:24.
2. Curry, *Candid Enquiry*; Keegan, *Legends and Tales*, 2:594.

pride of private property, were particularly hated. Whiteboys liberated debtors from jail, and Whiteboys ordered magistrates to reduce the price of provisions. Mounted on horses and armed with guns, they were capable of mobilizing large numbers, of acting swiftly, of eluding capture, and of striking deep roots. Arthur Young wrote, "They began in Tipperary, and where owing to some inclosures of commons, which they threw down, levelling the ditches; and were first known by the name of Levellers."[3] The name was later applied to Despard.

In 1766, the sixteen-year-old Despard left Ireland at the zenith of what Edmund Burke, who was there, called a "savage period." The war for the land was murderous, and Edward's life, toward its beginning as toward its end, was marked by arson, death, and nocturnal peasant insurgence. They were hungry, violent times. That year "several towns were in great distress for corn; and by the humanity of the Lord Lieutenant Lord Hertford, money was issued out of the Treasury to buy corn for such places as applied to his Lordship for that relief."[4] The pageboy attended these petitions and observed Hertford's "humanity," if it were such. Edward was already familiar, at least indirectly, with famine.

In 1739–40, a murrain appeared in horned cattle, and the disease spread to England, so the Cattle Acts were abolished, allowing duty-free export of salted beef and butter into England. Though not the only cause, it contributed to the coming crisis of the land—enclosures, dispossession, ranching replacing tillage. A hard frost destroyed the potatoes. "The very birds of the air . . . perished," and people died in the roads and ditches. Dr William Wilde noted that dysenteries spread from the poor to the rich, followed by fever, influenza, scurvy, and smallpox. "Mankind [was] of the colour of the weeds and nettles on which they feed." People ate dogs and vice versa.[5] Of the famine of 1741, modern authorities conclude, "the twenty-one month crisis seems to have killed between 250,000 and 400,000 people, thus implying a higher death rate and proportionately greater impact than the Great Famine itself."[6]

When Despard's brother Philip was two years old, his house in Cartown was burnt to the ground, "his Mother gathering him and Aunt Kitty up in

3. A. Young, *Tour in Ireland.*
4. Crawford, "William Wilde's Table."
5. J.H. Hutchinson, *The Commercial Restraints of Ireland* (Dublin, 1779), quoted in Crawford, "William Wilde's Table."
6. Dickson, "Gap in Famines," 97.

her legs out of their beds to save them from the flames."[7] Elizabeth believed that he "built that frightful place Culruane" as a result, but she does not explain what frightened her about it. This occurred in the early 1740s. Her father, Philip, remembered the famine of 1741, accompanied as it was by daily flights of locusts, occasioned when the huntsman shook the willow tree and the locusts would fall out to be devoured by the hounds. Jane Despard recorded a second attack:

> My father [Ned's older brother] once more returned to a house in the country from whence, it is enough to say, that, living one Winter in terror, we were driven away by rebel whitefeet or blackfeet; lost all our plate, chiefly our mother's which had been placed in a neighbouring town for safety; the house we lived in set fire to and burnt with all the furniture, and my poor father received only £50 damages from the country. We were moved then to Mountmellick for protection and afterwards to Mountrath, where my dear mother breathed her last after years of bad health and suffering. This is the period of our lives, the particulars of which I must pass over.[8]

The term *whitefeet* retained a generic meaning for peasant resistance. She is expressing the terror—plunder, arson, flight, death, followed by silence. Such terror unnerved the placid surface of Elizabeth Bowen's gay recollections of the eighteenth century big house: "And all the night, while the parties were going on, Mallow was locked in the unknowing silence of fields."[9]

Kevin Whelan writes of moments of high intensity, such as the 1760s and 1790s, when through the interstices of the brittle land settlement "poured forth a scalding surge of energy, erupting from a pent-up reservoir of memory. . . . " He quotes Arthur Browne in 1787: "Property in Ireland resembled the thin soil of volcanic countries spread lightly over subterranean fires."[10] Thomas Moore continues the underground metaphor: "All this time the Catholic 'enemy' went on increasing in silence and darkness, like that fire which some French philosophers suppose to exist at the centre of the earth—working its way upward in secret, till it will at last make the surface too hot to hold us." Edmund Burke reverts to the comparison, writing to his son in 1792 that "the igneous fluid has its Lodging in a solid mass."[11] The "colonial sublime" represented an

7. E. Despard, "Recollections," 7.
8. J. Despard, "Memoranda," 40.
9. *Bowen's Court*, 144.
10. Whelan, *Tree of Liberty*, 56.
11. Gibbons, *Edmund Burke and Ireland*, 163.

unpredictable irruption in the continuum of history, resisting clarity and representation but animated by huge energy of historical solidarity.

The people of the improving silent fields, like the sugarcane workers in the Caribbean or the peasantry among the Tiers État in France or the serfs under Catherine the Great or the hired hands of Robert Frost's New England, might have harbored a desire for bloody murther. Owen of the Sweet Mouth (Eoghan Ruadh ó Súilleabháin, 1748–84), the celebrated farm laborer of Munster and the author of visionary aislings, wrote a poem for his friend James Fitzgerald, who was to put a handle on the spade. In this poem, with the delicate aid of Homer, he expresses the same wish with elegant insolence:

> At the close of day, should my limbs be tired or sore,
> And the steward give that my spade-work is nothing worth,
> Gently I'll speak of Death's adventurous ways
> Or of Grecian battles in Troy, where princes fell.[12]

" O sweet Mother Mary who keeps my rough hand from red murder but thee?" was Keegan's prayer.[13] The war for the land was indeed murderous.

Arthur Young says the intelligence of the Whiteboys was "universal, and almost instantaneous: the numerous bodies of them, at whatever distance from each other, seemed animated with one soul; and not an instance was known in that long course of time of a single individual betraying the cause; the severest threats, and the most splendid promises of reward, had no other effect but to draw closer the bands which connected a multitude, to all appearance so desultory."[14] The previous year the Dublin Parliament passed the Tumultuous Risings Act, which according to its penultimate article had to be read aloud in open court in every Irish county. It applied death to those who were found guilty of committing assault, imposing oaths, breaking open jails, rescuing prisoners, or—"killing, maiming, or worrying their cattle, or by destroying or spoiling their house or houses, barns, mills, milldams, hay, corn, or grain, or potatoes, whether the same be growing, standing, or lying in the field or haggard, or maliciously digging up ground, that all and every persons or persons so offending, and being thereof found guilty, shall suffer death, as in cases of felony without benefit of clergy." The Tumultuous

---

12. Quoted in Corkery, *Hidden Ireland.*
13. "The Irish Reaper's Harvest Hymn to the Virgin," in Keegan, *Legends and Tales.*
14. A. Young, *Tour in Ireland,* 2:64.

Risings Act provided the basis for the Whiteboy Acts, which only added more crimes, such as signaling by sound of drum, horn, musick, fire, or shouting; sending anonymous threatening letters; destroying corn granaries; and obstructing the exportation of corn, grain, meal, malt, and flour.[15] So blood thirsty and pompous was the legislation that it became a mockery.

The Jacobite poet Aodhagán Ó Rathaille (1670–1728) mocked the powers that be in "The Acts of the Parliament of Clan Thomas," turning the world upside down and expressing the repertoire of resistance of wage laborer and landless peasant alike. Items of the standard of living, and seasonally adjusted wage rates,

> We enact, in the time of reaping,
> Butter, cheese, and a piece of meat;
> Five pence without doubt
> In the time of fallow and turf.

Are followed by a lawyerly enactment of the restoration of the land,

> We enact that we meet together
> At Michaelmas and Easter Tuesday,
> That we may put down the deeds
> Of this set who have been oppressing us.

Accompanied by an explanation of sabotage,

> In the time of grubbing for your lords,
> Let your implements be broken,
> Your tackling and your plough
> And your traces in bits.

The poem concludes with a poetic enactment of the expropriation of the expropriators,

> We enact every thing
> According to prudence and wisdom,
> That our lords be tied down
> And we let loose.[16]

15. Further Whiteboy Acts were passed, viz., 17 and 18 George III, c. 36; 19 and 20 George III, c. 14; 21 and 22 George III, c. 40; 30 George III, c. 45; 34 George III, c. 23. Whiteboy Act 40 George III, c. 96 made it perpetual, Registry of Deeds, Dublin.

16. O'Rahilly, *Poems*, 3:174–75.

These were "parliamentary enactments" on paper or in poetry. The actual actions of the Whiteboy movement were nocturnal, secretive, anonymous, and collective, appearing, as we can say with Hume's understanding of miracles, as "some invisible agent."

The Whiteboy movement of the early 1760s coincided with relative agricultural prosperity, resulting in rising prices for pastoral commodities. Provision merchants found new markets in North America, the West Indies, and the British army and navy. Then the Seven Years' War added new economic demands for cattle products, inducing a conversion from tillage to pastoral farming.[17] Huge ranches, made up of thousands of acres, emerged in the grazing lands of Tipperary and Limerick, outbidding small-tillage farmers, who often rented on partnership leases that protected common rights.

In county Laois, weavers, schoolmasters, blacksmiths, and craftspeople, as well as peasants, joined. Partnership tenancy, prevalent in upland and mountainous areas, was the basis for Whiteboy organization. In Kilkenny, they are first heard of in March 1763. Jack Burtchel and Daniel Dowling write, "Pasture had spread rapidly in the early 1760s in response to increased overseas demand for beef and dairy products. This in turn increased the rent per acre on all land including tillage land and the plots of potatoes raised by agricultural labourers. Larger graziers and landlords sought to maximize grazing by enclosing former commonages thereby putting extra pressure or cottiers and labourers."[18] John Feehan, a historian of county Laois, refers to "the agony of mind of the labourers in Laois."[19] Despard was an impressionable boy.

17. Bric, "Whiteboy Movement in Tipperary," 151.
18. Burtchaell and Dowling, "Social and Economic Conflict, 267–68.
19. Feehan, *Landscape of Slieve Bloom*, 261.

TWELVE

The Same Cont.

THE SOCIETY OF UNITED IRISHMEN was founded in Belfast in October 1791. It was in sympathy with the great slave revolts of the epoch in Jamaica (1760), Tupac Amaru (1780), and San Domingue (1791–1803). The Irish notion of the republic was influenced by the Atlantic experience of both the slaves and the slavers. The American War of Independence provided an example of a bourgeois anticolonial revolt. It led to the arming of the propertied Volunteers, to Grattan's parliament, and to the organization of the Catholic Committee, all middle-class accomplishments. Victory would require an expanded strategy and outreach to the peasantry and urban working class, which in turn had demands of its own. The survival of the Irish commons would depend on the struggle of the Whiteboys and the Defenders, whose land was subject to the shocks of arson, terror, and conquest. Both clachan and rundale (forms of land tenure and forms of cooperative tillage and pasturage) were specifically Irish.

The Irish revolution drew on French ideas—*liberté, égalité, fraternité*—and on diplomatic and military alliance with France. The Irish term *saoirse* emerged as an abstraction corresponding to the English *freedom* or the French *liberté*. It also retained materialist and millennial associations in the Irish language. Jacobite poetry, characterized by prophecy, vision, and allegory, easily included the abolition of tithes, taxes, rents, and landlordism and the return of confiscated, ancestral lands. Such poetry was "a central and ubiquitous element in popular culture." "We have lived long enough upon potatoes and salt; it is our turn now to eat meat and mutton."[1]

---

1. Ó Buachalla, "From Jacobite to Jacobin," 75, 79ff.

Ireland was like a laboratory for experiments of rule, which could later be applied in England. Similarly, influential writers in England were often Irish. So it was with the Irishman Oliver Goldsmith, who wrote the great poem against English enclosures, "The Deserted Village," a village he called "sweet Auburn." He went to England in 1758, two years before the first signs of the Whiteboys. He completed "The Deserted Village in 1769," having collected materials for it over four or five years and then spending another two years composing it. It describes a general experience of depopulation and enclosure in the early 1760s, when the Whiteboys erupted: "Those fenceless fields the sons of wealth divide / And even the bare-worn common is denied."[2] Oliver Goldsmith's father was the curate, whose successor identified "Auburn" as the village of Lissoy in county Meath. Thus the great poem against the enclosure of common lands in England was based on the author's prior experience of the colonial conquest in Ireland. Auburn is not quite completely deserted:

> All but you widow'd, solitary thing,
> That feebly bends beside the plashy spring,
> She, wretched matron, forc'd in age, for bread,
> To strip the brook with mantling cresses spread,
> To pick her wintry faggot from the thorn,
> To seek her nightly shed, and weep till morn;
> She only left of all the harmless train,
> The sad historian of the pensive plain.[3]

In 1808, the widow was identified as Catherine Geraghty, known to Goldsmith from his Lissoy childhood. Nearly fifty years later, the brook and ditches near her cabin still abounded with water cress.[4] While the passivity and victimization of the inhabitants are emphasized in this poem, Catherine Geraghty bears witness.

Darby Brown was hanged in July 1762. He said, "By Sive we meant a distressed, harmless old woman, blind in one eye, who still lives at the foot of a mountain in the neighborhood."[5] In the next decade, other aliases, Calfskin, Cropper, Echo, Madcap, Setfire, Slasher, and Thumper, appear for the protagonists of revolt. John Wesley was told in June 1762 that Levelers "compelled everyone they met to take an oath to be true to Queen Sive." Luke

2. Goldsmith, *Collected Works*, 277.
3. Goldsmith, *Collected Works*, 277.
4. Gorster, *Life and Time*, 2:140–43.
5. Donnelly, "Whiteboy Movement."

Gibbons writes, "They owed their allegiance to a series of enigmatic female figures who hovered between the otherworld and everyday life in the imagination of the peasantry."[6] The Captain Rock of Thomas Moore's *Memoirs of Captain Rock* dies in defense of a poor woman, whose cow was taken by parish officers. The association of the female with the Irish commonages characterized the precapitalist, precolonial commons.

The intractability of the Irish situation released illicit energies of utopian, fanatic, and abstract visionaries, which uprooted the established order so often figured as female. The Stuart pretender's being sighted "disguised in woman's apparel" frightened the Whigs, or Hanoverians. Whiteboys were heirs to the Gaelic literary tradition—millenarian and Jacobite. The aisling, or vision poem, described a radiant woman, who personified Ireland. Brendan Ó Buachalla shows that this tradition praised outlaws, threatened the Church establishment, questioned the land settlement, and defied the social hierarchy. The Whiteboys preserved a vision, and they enacted a fantastic revolt.[7]

The fear expressed in 1787 by Dominick Trant of Dingle, county Kerry, was that the Whiteboys intended to "determine and limit the rent, value, and mode of taking lands, in short to level all those distinctions which have ever been established in all states, and, by a sort of Agrarian law, to reduce the nobility of the land, the ecclesiastical establishment, the opulent representatives of the property of this kingdom in its parliament, and every other proprietor of land and possessor of wealth, to a degrading subjection to the will of the lowest order of the state, the mere popish peasantry of this country."[8] In 1766, Catholics outnumbered the rest of the population by thirty to one. While the reference to the Agrarian Law calls attention to both a seventeenth-century debate about the modern state and the brothers Gracchi and their proposal for land redistribution under the Roman republic, the comparison is misleading if we take it to imply that the Whiteboys themselves had designs to take over the state. Subsequent generations of state engineers and political scientists of revolution thus find little in the Whiteboys and tend to demean them as "prepolitical."

If Goldsmith's "The Deserted Village" is the classic long poem against enclosures, the shortest had Irish inspiration

6. Gibbons, *Edmund Burke and Ireland*, 141.
7. Ó Buachalla, "From Jacobite to Jacobin."
8. Trant, *Considerations*.

The law locks up the man or woman
Who steals the goose from off the common
But lets the greater villain loose
Who steals the common from the goose.

In the last instance, the King was savior and fount of justice. Dr. John Curry described the crisis when the commons economy met the monetary economy.

A commotion was stirred up by some commoners, against engrossing their ground, when the king chanced to be invited, in his hunting journey, to dine with Sir Thomas—and turning short at the corner of a common, happened near to a countryman sitting by the heels in the stocks, who cried *Hossanna!* to his majesty; which invited the king to ask the reason of his restraint. Sir Thomas said, it was for stealing geese from the common: the fellow replied, I beseech your majesty, who is the greatest thief, I, for stealing the geese from the common; or, his worship, for stealing the common from the geese?—The king immediately ordered the common to be restored to the poor, and the witty fellow to be released; and care was taken to quiet the commotions.[9]

Suppose a laborer worked 300 days at a wage of 4p a day. This amounted to 100s. a year. Since rent for an acre of potato ground was 91s., the tithe was 9s., hearth money was 5s., and cabin rent was 2s., no money was left for seed, salt, clothes, firing, the priest, or "patron."[10]

In September 1764, the battle of Newmarket, the single most notorious incident in the Whiteboy movement, occurred. A long slow march of prisoners through the Walsh mountains on their way to Kilkenny jail set out from Pilltown. When a crowd of three hundred people armed with slanes (a spade with a wing on one side of the blade for cutting turf), pitchforks, and cudgels attempted to free them, a battle ensued in the road between Newmarket and Sheepstown, and many were killed. It was preceded by the 1762 arrest of Garret Nagle for assisting "the clan called White Boys." In 1763, Edmund Burke was shocked by the hanging of John Dwyer at Clonmel. "For Gods sake," he wrote his lawyer in Dublin, "let me know a little of this matter, and of the history of these new levellers. I see that you have but one way of relieving the poor in Ireland. They call for bread, and you give them 'not a Stone,' but the Gallows."[11]

In April 1765, six were hanged in Kilkenny, their breasts scored and their heads struck off. One of the Whiteboys, John Brennan, proclaimed his inno-

9. Curry, *Candid Enquiry.*
10. Curry, *Candid Enquiry,* 36–37.
11. As quoted by Gibbon, *Edmund Burke and Ireland,* 21.

cence, and his wife used his skull as a bowl to collect money for his funeral. Before preaching in Mountmellick market in county Laois, John Wesley described a multiple hanging in Waterford on 7 July 1762. "Two or three of them laid fast hold on the ladder and could not be persuaded to let it go. One in particular gave such violent shrieks as might be heard near a mile off."[12] Jonah Barrington, remembering the custom in county Laois, said, "The common people believed that the lord of Cullenaghmore had a right to save a man's life every summer assizes at Maryborough; and it did frequently so happen, within my recollection, that my father's intercession in favour of some poor deluded creatures (when the White Boy system was in activity), was kindly attended to by the Government...." Many of his tenants owed their lives to him for such intercession: it "enabled him to preserve his tenantry in perfect tranquillity, whilst those surrounding were in a constant state of insubordination to all law whatever."[13]

Nicholas Sheehy was hanged, drawn, and quartered on 15 March 1766. He was a Catholic priest, who was acquitted in Dublin on the charge of inciting to riot and rebellion but was then found guilty at a trial in Clonmel ("the most scandalous ever known") of being an instigator to murder. Edmund Burke was in Ireland at the time assisting the chief secretary for Ireland. He wrote of "an infinity of outrages and oppression" and excoriated "the inhuman proceedings." After Sheehy was hanged, Burke returned to England. As a boy, William Duane, the radical journalist of Calcutta, London, and Philadelphia, lived in Clonmel, where his daily path to school led him past the prison where Sheehy's skull was still displayed as a warning to others.[14] "This execution of Father Sheehy was one of those coups d'état of the Irish authorities, which they use to perform at stated intervals, and which saved them the trouble of further atrocities for some time to come."[15]

Between 1762 and 1765, twenty-six Whiteboys were sentenced to death. Between 1770 and 1776, the number rose to forty-eight. The disruption of the Whiteboys could not be easily repressed with selective terror or easily mollified by reform. They did not accept the breakup of a type of agriculture, the rundale system, or the attacks on a type of community, the clachan. This was the conjuncture of circumstances out of which Edmund Burke developed the notion of the sublime. Bringing them together, Luke Gibbons in

12. Wesley, *Works*, 128.
13. Barrington, "Patricians and Plebeians," in *Personal Sketches*.
14. Little, *Transoceanic Radical*, 22.
15. Moore, *Memoirs of Captain Rock*, 21.

Edmund Burke and Ireland identifies "the colonial sublime," as the mixture of mystery, fear, and terror that in this era took the aesthetic form of the Gothic. It was here near Roscrea that Thomas Moore in his fictional tale, *Memoirs of Captain Rock* (1824), places the confrontation between a naive English traveler and the nocturnal, recalcitrant, and dangerous force of the county Laois peasantry loyal to Roger O'Connor, King (ROCK). In fact, in 1802 as a mature revolutionary temporarily released from prison in England, Despard visited with the actual O'Connor at Bandon.

In Thomas Moore's anonymously published *Memoirs of Captain Rock the Celebrated Irish Chieftain* (1823), the purported narrator travels to convert the Irish "savages" and the peasant Whiteboys. He leaves Dublin on the Limerick coach, which passes through county Laois at the foot of the Slieve Bloom Mountains, a stone's throw from Despard's birthplace. "From Roscrea I turned off the main road to pay a visit to an old friend," who was "obliged to barricade his home of an evening, and having little embrasures in his hall-door, to fire through at unwelcome visitors." It is a moonlit night. He strolls out to observe the ruins of a nearby abbey. There he comes upon "some hundreds of awful-looking persons—all arrayed in white shirts." From one of them, Captain Rock, he receives the manuscript of the memoirs.[16]

Captain Rock was born in 1763, and his Irish-speaking father was beggared, then brutalized, and finally obliged "to sink into that class of wretched cottiers who then, as now, occupied the very nadir of human existence." He held "evening conversaziones round our small turf fire." Moore explains the imaginative dish, potatoes and point as follows: "when there is but a small portion of salt left, the potato, instead of being dipped into by the guests, is merely, as a sort of indulgence to the fancy, *pointed* at it."[17] The Rocks are of great antiquity, indeed nobility. The family embodies the spirit of resistance and rebellion throughout history. The family crest bears the motto, "Worse and Worse."

An economy of human subsistence was overthrown for the lowing herds that were slaughtered to become "the roast beef of old England." Salt beef and salted butter became staples of the imperial war economy. The cattle economy depended on the grass, which itself was a product of social labor, the clearing of forests, the draining of wetlands, the management of bogs, the liming of the earth, and the manuring of soil. The Whiteboys had another conception

16. *Memoirs of Captain Rock,* 4–5.
17. *Memoirs of Captain Rock,* 126.

of human development, one that depended on local needs and was often expressed in mixed Christian and pagan ways. It opposed the infrastructure of transportation (roads and bridges) because these entailed forced labor, because they benefited only a few, and because they conveyed wealth away. Faceless and nameless, the Whiteboys were part of the dispossessed, deracinated, and migrating people.

Kevin Whelan provides this summary: "The great redresser movements, the Whiteboys and Rightboys, sought a return to the days when the moral economy blunted the impact of the real one, and when the yawning chasm between rich and poor Catholics had not been so wide."[18] It is a double movement: economic and religious. The moral economy contrasts with the "free trade" that Adam Smith advocated. In 1766, he recommended it as colonial policy to Lord Shelburne, secretary of state for both domestic and Irish affairs. Adam Smith argued that Ireland had little coal or wood, "two articles essentially necessary to the progress of Great Manufactures. It wants order, police, and a regular administration of justice both to protect and to restrain the inferior ranks of people, articles more essential to the progress of Industry than both coal and wood put together. . . ."[19] Free trade was for the middle class, who owned something to trade, not for dispossessed cottiers, who wanted for something to subsist.

The Whiteboys mobilized Catholics, lower-class Presbyterians, and Anglicans, representing the small farmer and weaver. An observer wrote in 1786, "The luxurious parson drowned in the riot of his table the bitter groans of those wretches that his proctor fleeced and the poor remnant of the proctor's rapine was sure to be gleaned by the rapacious priest; but it was blasphemy to complain to him; Heaven, we thought, would wing its lightening to blast the wretch who grudged the Holy Father's share. Thus plundered by either clergy, we had reason to wish for our simple Druids again."[20]

At sixteen, young Ned Despard had a commission in the Fiftieth Regiment as an ensign, once the standard bearer, the lowest grade of commissioned officers.[21] The army, as were manufacturers, was beginning to bear the effects of the division of labor: "The genius of the master is cultivated, while . . . the soldier is confined to a few motions of the hand and foot." The vicar of

18. Whelan, *Tree of Liberty*, 26.
19. Rae, *Life of Adam Smith*, 351.
20. *Letter Addressed to Munster Peasantry* (1786), 61.
21. *Memoirs of the Life of Colonel E.M. Despard.* See also *An Authentic Narrative of the Life of Colonel Despard.*

Aghaboe Edward Ledwich was a staunch ally of Charles Coote. He argued against traditional Irish soldiering as described by seventeenth-century scholar Geoffrey Keating, who wrote, "no soldier was to be received who had not a poetical genius, and was well acquainted with the twelve books of poetry: that he was to be so swift and light of foot, as not to break a rotten stick by treading on it; that he was to leap over a tree as high as his forehead, and to stoop under one as low as his knees." Such passages received the full measure of Ledwich's scorn. Adam Ferguson did not reckon on such as Despard, who was constitutionally unable to treat the army "as an engine, the parts of which are men."[22]

Despard, in the wake of the Whiteboys, was part of a much larger migration from Ireland to America. Ireland was not merely a colonial island to the west of Great Britain but a global hub radiating 360 degrees to the North and South Atlantic from Newfoundland to Cape Town.[23] Like the little elvers that swam down the river Nore into the North Atlantic Ocean, making their way to the Sargasso Sea and returning as full grown eels, Despard belonged to Atlantic currents and to other unknown forces.

22. Ferguson, *Essay on the History,* 4:1, 183.
23. See for instance Ulrich, "International Radicalism."

E

AMERICA

———

THIRTEEN

America! Utopia! Equality! Crap.

DESPARD SPENT THE FIRST TWENTY-ONE YEARS OF HIS LIFE, from 1751 to 1772, in Ireland. He passed the next eighteen years in America, and spent the final thirteen years of his life in London. At first he worked *for* empire as a military engineer, and then he worked *against* empire as a radical renegade.

Ireland, America, London: his was a North Atlantic life. Ireland was the first colony of England, and Despard grew up Anglo-Irish, a descendant of settlers. Jamaica as an English colony dated back to Oliver Cromwell's "Western Design" of 1655, and British Honduras (now Belize) was being formed as a colonial plantation of England under (or despite of) the superintendence of Despard. It was there he began to turn. Most of his London years were spent in prisons with the subalterns of empire—in a city built by Irish people (maids, brickies, cleaners, lumpers, navvies, streetwalkers, hod carriers), a city that contained vast wealth from African American labor taken in the form of money.

The next chapters are about America.[1] Just as the previous chapters on Ireland and its various forms of the commons introduced Edward Marcus Despard, or Ned, so these chapters on America and its various types of commons introduce Catherine, or Kate. Little direct documentary evidence about Kate exists, so if we want to understand her, fully we must find other methodologies than the paper of archives. Historians contemporary to Ned and Kate developed historical "conjecture" as a kind of deductive principle; historians faced with a similar problem with the relation of Thomas Jefferson

1. Brandon, *New Worlds for Old*.

to his slave Sally Hemings find themselves falling back on imaginative fiction, such as Faulkner's *Absalom, Absalom* (1936).

Similar to the eel of the river Nore, one of the "three sisters" (the Suir and the Barrow being the other two), Despard set out on the long journey across the Atlantic. The Danish oceanographer Johannes Schmidt studied the length of larvae found in plankton hauls across the Atlantic. Discovering that the smallest came from the Sargasso Sea, he concluded that this must be the eel's breeding ground. He estimated that it took two and a half years to cross the Atlantic. These eel return to the Nore, which drains the Irish midlands. The little elvers arrive in the spring and swim up the Nore in lazy sinuations to nocturnal growth. They can live thirty years. As mature silver eels, they return to the Sargasso Sea, steering by the stars or magnetic influences, or by electrical patterns in the currents. It takes eighty days, and there they spawn. The Irish expert on eels Christopher Moriarty states that "the urge to press forward is remarkably strong."[2] The novelist Jean Rhys made the width of the Sargasso Sea a metaphor for the "hybrid" people of Atlantic slaving culture. It was the site of reproduction.

These were slave societies, where human beings were worked to death. The societies would have died with them, had not the slaveowners turned to migration and reproduction to ensure their survival. As the abolition of the Atlantic slave trade increased in likelihood, the demographic emphasis on "breeding" increased in importance. The slave society required reproduction on a daily basis as well; its male rulers were incapacitated unless nurtured, cleaned, fed, and tended to by others—generally by women though not always. Lord Edward Fitzgerald, for example, the future commander in chief of the underground army of the United Irishmen, nearly lost his life at the battle of Eutaw Springs (South Carolina) in 1781. Instead, he was saved by an African American slave named Tony Small, who accompanied the famous aristocrat and revolutionary Irishman known as "Citizen Edward" until his assassination, which happened on the eve of the 1798 rising. On the whole, however, and especially in tropical America, the rulers were served by women, usually slave women, sometimes African slave women, more often African American or "creole" slave women.

We know that Ned and Kate met in America. Since Ned's direct American experience included Jamaica, Nicaragua, and Honduras, our quest for the commons and for knowledge of Kate must be organized by his experiences in those

2. Schmidt, "Breeding Place," 179–208; Moriarty, *Eels.*

three colonies. It might be said that he had indirect experience of the mainland through the military service of his brothers during the American war. It is quite possible that Kate was among the tens of thousands of mainland African Americans who fled during the evacuation of Charlestown in 1782.

But what is America? It is two continents named after an Italian explorer. Yet Humboldt, the German explorer of the continents, who was carried around on men's backs and whose personal narrative was published in the year of Despard's conspiracy, regarded the great *S* formed by the North Atlantic littoral—from Virginia, the Carolinas, and Florida, through the greater and lesser Antilles of the Caribbean, across the northeastern part of South America, Surinam, Venezuela, Guiana, all the way to Bahia—as a single, African American geographical unit. One imagines a rhythmic sway to his arm as General Dalling lightly describes this *S* with his finger over Thomas Jefferys's *Atlas of the West Indies,* with Lawrie of the Mosquito Shore keenly looking on.

The English design was to cut this unity in half, into North and South America, by a combined military and naval expedition up the San Juan River to Lake Nicaragua, and from thence to the Pacific, ocean of the greater half of the world. Such an expedition had to rely on a base of provision, a depot of arms, a headquarters of command, and a port of communication. That was Jamaica. From the standpoint of geopolitics, such an adventure compensated for the loss of mainland American colonies and the diaspora of emancipated slave laborers out of Charleston. The expedition up the San Juan River occurred amid two upheavals on the American continents. The first was the revolt of indigenous peoples in South America led by Tupac Amaru. It began in November 1780 and ended six months later in May 1781. The second was the War of Independence of the North American colonies. Both of these were also wars against slavery, principally African slavery. As such they were precursors of the revolutionary war against slavery in Haiti that began on the night of 14 August 1791, in the Bois de Caïman.

America should not be mistaken for the United States, for in the continents of America there were many human settlements based on various forms of commons. The United States formed at a constitutional convention in 1787 was a settler-slave society based on private property or the extirpation of commons. The two most erudite contributors at that convention were James Madison and James Wilson.

In the famous *Federalist Paper* number ten Madison wrote, "the most common and durable source of factions has been the various and unequal distribution of property. Those who hold and those who are without property have ever formed distinct interests in society. Those who are creditors, and those who are debtors, fall under a like discrimination." The propertied class is divided into landed, manufacturing, mercantile, and moneyed interests. The unpropertied class he excludes from consideration, although "Theoretic politicians ... have erroneously supposed, that by reducing mankind to a perfect equality in their political rights, they would, at the same time, be perfectly equalized and assimilated in their possessions, their opinions, and their passions."[3] To the four "interests" that he names—the landed, manufacturing, mercantile, and monied—we might consider four economic moments of capital to which correspond four elements in the composition of the proletariat—the slave, the artisan, the sailor, and the servant. He does not name the "theoretic politicians," but we shall find them in all sectors over the following decade. The discussion of both class antagonism and communist approaches to property was central to the formation of the United States.

James Wilson's role at the constitutional convention stands out for an infamous fraction, for he is the one who found a solution to the otherwise intractable conflict between the representation in Congress of the expanding slave regimes of the South and the republican, even democratic political demands of the North. For the purposes of determining the size of the population on which depended the number of representatives, Wilson proposed that the slave be counted as three-fifths of a person, thereby recognizing but not enfranchising the slave—the body but not the voice was acknowledged. In this way political representation and economic exploitation were made to jive, the person of the slave producing both the wealth and the power of the master class.

George Washington appointed this fractionator to the first Supreme Court. Wilson became a professor at the first law school, the University of Pennsylvania, where in April 1791 he delivered a course of lectures "On the History of Property." Actually his lecture is a history of *private* property, "exclusive" or "separate" property as he calls it, from Noah's flood through the Scythians and Tartars, to the German tribes (Tacitus), to Greece and Rome, to the Saxons, to the Highlanders of Scotland, to the Indians of Peru. The "superiority of separate over common property has not always been admitted," he says and cites the experiences of settlers in Virginia and Massachusetts, who attempted common property regimes. The second half of his history presents arguments against the commons. "Exclusive property

3. *Federalist Papers,* ed. Lawrence Goldman (Oxford: Oxford University Press, 2008), no. 10.

multiplies the productions of the earth, and the means of subsistence. Who would cultivate the soil, and sow the grain if he had no peculiar interest in the harvest?" Anticipating almost word for word the arguments of the twentieth-century privatizer Garret Hardin, Wilson states, "What belongs to no one is wasted by everyone." Exchanges in the division of labor depend on private property. It prevents disorder and promotes peace. Otherwise, "the tranquility of society would be perpetually disturbed by fierce and ungovernable competition for the possession and enjoyment of *things insufficient to satisfy all*" (my emphasis)." Exclusive and separate property is especially necessary with land because it is the "principal source of attachment to the country in which one resides." In these arguments we see origins of nationalism, competitive individualism, and economic scarcity.[4]

Madison believed that communism was advocated by "theoretic politicians." But the commons was not only theoretical. At its origin and during the first decade of its existence, the United States aggressively attacked the commons of the indigenous peoples of the Ohio Valley. Similarly aggressive acts established an industrial-level slave society based on cotton in the slave South. Robert Coram, the Delaware antifederalist, journalist, abolitionist, and schoolmaster, who had sailed with John Paul Jones in Atlantic and Caribbean waters, was one such "theoretic politician," whose praise of the Indian commons had practical implications. He wrote a pamphlet called *Political Inquiries* in March 1791, just as Wilson was praising private property. Native people are "strangers to all distinction of property"; "their equality of condition, manners, and privileges" animates a "patriotic spirit" that encourages "the general good." "They esteem it irrational that one man should be possessed of a greater quantity than another and are amazed that any honor should be annexed to the possession of it." He sent copies to Washington and Jefferson. He aimed at leveling invidious social distinctions and advocated an equal distribution of property.[5]

While these arguments were being made, Despard was involving himself in constitutional and property arguments in another part of America. Despard's policy of egalitarianism arose from Irish sympathy, from Afro-American acquaintance, and from human compassion. It was encouraged by knowledge of recent European debates about the commons. We know this to have certainly been the case with his countryman and neighbor Thomas

4. Wilson, *Collected Works*, 1:387–98.
5. Coram, *Political Enquiries*, chapter 1. See also Cotlar, *Tom Paine's America*.

Russell. Russell lived in Durrow, county Laois, not far from Despard's neighborhood, though he was ten years younger and moved to county Laois after Edward had left. Russell, like Despard, had been a soldier and became a revolutionary United Irishman. Again, like Despard, he was hanged in 1803 for attempting to liberate Ireland. In September 1796, Thomas Russell published *A Letter to the People of Ireland on the Present Situation of the Country.* He was certainly ready to challenge privatization of land. In a beautiful tribute to the hospitality and rundale of the Irish peasantry, Russell sings out,

> The golden age will yet revive
> Each man will be a brother
> In harmony we all shall live
> And share the earth together

He followed his brother into the army, and was commissioned an ensign in the Fifty-Second Regiment of Foot in July 1783. His regiment was sent to relieve Mangalore on the Malabar coast, a royal port that was first seized, raped, and plundered and then lost to Tipu Sultan, who imprisoned the town's Christian population.

In 1797, a Jacobin club was established in Seringapatnam, a tree of liberty was planted, and *liberté, égalité,* and *fraternité* were declared for the first time on Indian soil. James Bristow, the son of a Norwich blacksmith, arrived in India at the age of fourteen. A year later, he was imprisoned. Bristow of the Bengal Artillery tells us of poor O'Bryan, "compelled to perform the office of common coolie and to carry dirt in the streets of Seringapatnam."[6]

Among the songs Russell sang in the cabins of counties Antrim, Armagh, and Down were "The Negro's Lament" and "The Captive Negro." He wrote, "There is perhaps no part of the earth where beasts of burden are so much oppressed as the negroes are in the sugar plantations. They are sixteen hours in the service of cruel masters; and the shouts of their drivers, and the cracks of the whip on their naked bodies, which cuts out small pieces of flesh at almost every stroke are heard all day in the fields."[7] In the early months of 1791, Russell read the history of Paraguay by the Jesuit of Pierre-François-Xavier de Charlevoix, published in English in 1769. Russell considered the "thirty towns" as "beyond compare the best, the happiest, that ever has been

6. *Narrative of Suffering,* 83.
7. "Enslavement of the African," *Northern Star,* 11 February 1792.

instituted."[8] It taught him that Christianity need not be reactionary. The "thirty cities" or missions that the Jesuits successfully established among the indigenous people of South America were populated by 150,000 Guaraní people and inspired by Guaraní practices of common land and by Christian ideas of all things in common. The common land was called God's property, or *tupambaé*. The people lived in communal houses and did not hold slaves. These communist communities lasted more than a century before kings and pope expelled the Jesuits in the 1760s.

Montesquieu in *The Spirit of the Laws* (1748) praised the thirty towns for bringing happiness to the indigenous people, in contrast to the conquistadors, who brought blood and fire. The former established a community of goods, a community-based commerce, and they proscribed money. Voltaire mocked them in *Candide* (1759). William Robertson (1721–93), the Scottish historiographer royale to George III, praised the towns as a "benefit of the human species." "They maintained a perfect equality among all the members of the community." "The produce of their fields, together with the fruits of their industry of every species, was deposited in common storehouses, from which each individual received everything necessary for the supply of his wants."[9]

Modern scholarship is more informative but no less contentious. Philip Caraman seems to agree with the nineteenth-century view that the thirty towns exemplified "the ideal of a Christian communist community in which everything was held in joint ownership for the equal benefit of all." The *tupambaé* supported widows, orphans, and the sick. Barbara Ganson, on the other hand, locates the origin of communal landholding in pre-Columbian agriculture, whereas the Jesuits introduced individual family plots. She says that "European literature has shown a tendency to romanticize these missions and their native people."[10] This is an important caution. Has scholarship fallen victim to the myth of "the noble savage"?

The phrase is a sly slur and has been endlessly used to dismiss indigenous experience. In English the phrase "noble savage" first appeared in the poet Dryden's play *The Conquest of Granada* (1672), in which a Spanish Muslim says,

8. Carroll, *Man from God*, 32.
9. Robertson, *History of the Reign,* bk. 6.
10. Caraman, *Lost Paradise*, 116; Ganson, *Guaraní under Spanish Rule*, 62. See also Reiter, *They Built Utopia.*

> I am as free as nature first made man,
> Ere the base laws of servitude began,
> When wild in woods the noble savage ran.

The expression originated in the French explorer Marc Lescarbot's 1609 travelogue that includes a chapter with the heading, "The Savages Are Truly Noble." By this, he meant simply that they enjoyed the right to hunt game, a privilege in France granted only to the nobility.[11] Thus, historically, it would be just to refer to the European aristocracy as "savage nobles," for the hated game laws prohibited anyone else from "the chase."

The leading Protestant antinomian and Romantic poetic prophet William Blake called his 1794 prophesy *The Book of Urizen*. The embodiment of reason, rule, and order, Urizen is devoid of imagination, which shriveled under the net of religion. Blake writes in the penultimate plate of this illuminated book,

> And their thirty cities divided
> In form of a human heart
> No more could they rise at will
> In the infinite void but, bound down
> To earth by their narrowing perceptions
> They lived a period of years,
> Then left a noisom body
> To the jaws of devouring darkness.

Blake is able to look back at the municipal commons of the thirty towns of the Guaraní with the distance of defeat and resurgence because he himself is living in London at a time of revolutionary upsurge and demise. Narrowing perceptions and the jaws of devouring darkness were closing around those who fought to keep their commons. The heavens, if not offering all things in common, at least permitted the random action of a lottery in the distribution of some among the human hearts:

> And their children wept, & built
> Tombs in the desolate places,
> And form'd laws of prudence, and call'd them
> The eternal laws of God

---

11. Ellingson, *Myth*; Dryden, *Conquest of Grenada*, pt. I, act 1, scene 1.

And the thirty cities remaind
Surrounded by salt floods, now call'd
Africa: its name was then Egypt.[12]

The antinomian revolutionary condenses knowledge of the Guaraní with his own Old Testament knowledge in order to describe allegorically the Atlantic transition to child labor and slavery. These lines are accompanied by an illustration of an infant falling headlong legs and arms outstretched, into the inferno with bright orange, yellow, and red tongues of fire surrounding the child. Here is the "underground" again, this time combining the mythic (hell) with the historical, as the political entity of the United States becomes an inveterate antagonist to the commons in its myriad forms.

12. Blake, *Complete Poetry and Prose*, p. 83, lines 7–10.

FOURTEEN

Cooperation and Survival in Jamaica

WHEN DESPARD ARRIVED IN JAMAICA—England's sweetest, bloodiest sugar island—about one half of all Britain's overseas trade consisted of sugar or tobacco. These commodities, drugs actually, were produced by an African slave population on plantations of great size and complex organization. Slave traders profited at a rate of 9.5 percent, a return way higher than that produced by land mortgages or government consols. The sugar boom rescued English (and European) economic development from the stagnation of the seventeenth century and prepared the foundation for industrial investment of the nineteenth century. England traded perhaps 2.5 million Africans into slavery during the eighteenth century, and slaves worked between seventy and eighty hours a week.[1] Other European powers, particularly France and Spain, were jealous of English success and looked hungrily on Jamaica—enemy number one. Its slave population struggled heroically against its condition—enemy number two.

Empires were acquired and maintained by a military caste, the leading expense of the state, and changing in numbers and weaponry. Despard was a soldier, which meant that he was prepared to kill and to die and willing to send others to kill or to die. At the outbreak of the American War of Independence, Despard was sent back to England to raise troops for the 79th Regiment, the Liverpool Blues. As quartermaster of a recruiting party working the midlands of England, he would have been familiar with the rough and ready needs of young men thrown off their land owing to acts of enclosure and willing to accept "the King's shilling." In the summer of 1778, in Great Warley in Essex, just east of London, Despard killed a man, Rowland

---

1. See chapters 9 and 10 of Blackburn, *Making of New World*.

Rochford, in a duel. Despard surrendered himself voluntarily to justice, and the court quashed the indictment, adding that the death of his antagonist was unregretted.[2] The code of honor with its homicidal potential was particularly active at this time of history, when the "gentleman" as a social hybrid of aristocratic (military) and bourgeois (commerce) types was being formed.[3] Despard was a man of his time and his caste, a soldier. He served his imperial masters with "honor."

Two words summarize Despard's experiences in Jamaica: cooperation and survival. Both pertain to commoning but not in the usual way. He learned to lead motley crews in unprecedented, cooperative, production efforts. Second, to be reproduced, or to survive, he relied on the skills of Catherine or people like her. In Jamaica, Despard's *aptitude* as an engineer was recognized and in Jamaica his *achievement* as an engineer was realized. "The unfortunate Edward," his niece wrote years after his death, "was an accomplished draughtsman, mathematician and engineer, and it was a great mistake that he was not placed where those qualifications could have been brought into more conspicuous utility, but it was by Engineering that Jamaica was [not] taken in the American War."[4]

He understood ballistics. He was accustomed to concussion and explosion. To him, the materiality of things was temporary. Thermodynamics was the most advanced technology of the period. For a person like Despard, taking a city was a technical problem. What was Napoleon's "the whiff of grapeshot" (1795), which defeated a royalist bid to take Paris, if not the application of artillery to politics? Many London radicals had direct experience with artillery—Thomas Hardy, the founder of the London Corresponding Society, had worked in the Carron armaments factory in Falkirk, Scotland. Olaudah Equiano, the abolitionist, had been a powder monkey between decks of a man-of-war. Richard Brothers, the millenarian, had been an artillery officer in the navy. And the man whose name is often given to the epoch was also an artillery man—Napoleon Bonaparte.

The engineer's labor was twofold, working with material and working with men. He supervised the labor that built roads and bridges. He conducted sieges, maintained fortifications, prepared maps and sketches, and

2. *Chelmsford Chronicle*, 12 March 1779; NA, ASS 35.219/1. I am grateful to Peter King for calling this to my attention.

3. Pocock, *Young Nelson*, 41; Oman, *Unfortunate Colonel Despard*; Kelly, "*That Damn'd Thing.*"

4. E. Despard, "Recollections," 22.

kept financial accounts. Jamaica was Britain's headquarters in the Caribbean; Kingston was its leading port. Altogether the tracery, hornwork, redoubts, or glacis in twenty-one locations required the attention of an engineer. These military improvements were remarked on forty years later by Tom Cringle, who admired the raking fire of Fort Augusta, the strong works at Port Royal, and the crossfire from the heavy metal of the Apostles Battery.[5] "It was here in these material arrangements" where "the white contribution to the island's cultural development lay," said E. K. Brathwaite, referring to the roads, bridges, aqueducts, churches, burial grounds, great houses, and forts erected in the last quarter of the eighteenth century.[6] This was architecture, "invented," said John Ruskin, to make "slaves of its workmen, and sybarites of its inhabitants," to which we must add its military function without which the other two could not exist.[7]

Theories of defense and the practice of engineering were thus twofold. "My dispositions must necessarily extend, to two essential objects. The internal and external security of the island. For this purpose one half of the Militia, with one Battalion of Regulars were appropriated to the internal security." As part of the policy of dividing the black population, freedom was promised to the slaves who joined the militia. Fifty twelve-pounder carronades with swivels were provided for service in the mountains, "so fitted as to render them portable by the Negroes to the summit of the highest Cliffs." The pioneers in each parish were to have been employed in erecting redoubts with ditches and abatis within the entrance to the defiles.[8]

Many thousands of men and women were mobilized to move dirt. The labor was as ancient as Aesop and as modern as the canals of industrialization.[9] Sappers, miners, pioneers did the pick and shovel work. Fatigue, with its double meaning as punishment for military misdemeanors and as physical exhaustion, enters the English vocabulary at this point. According to a nineteenth-century engineer, a pickaxe breaks the ground, two shovels following throw the earth towards the scarp whence two other shovels throw it up the berm; from thence again two shovels throw it upon the profile.[10] In

5. Cringle, *Tom Cringle's Log*, 181.

6. Braithwaite, *Development of Creole Society*, 126–29.

7. *Stones of Florence*, 244–45.

8. Campbell, *Memoir*, 214; "Observations on the Fortifying of Jamaica, 1783," BL, Add. MSS 12.431.

9. Coleman, *Railway Navvies*, 23.

10. Rule, *Fortification*, 145.

addition to rules of proportionality, he calculated productivity.[11] A man was expected to excavate a cubic yard in an hour in ordinary soil conditions: "throwing the earth 12 feet horizontally, or 6 feet vertically." Seven men equaled a horse. Peter Way describes the blasting, grubbing, mucking, hacking, bending, thrusting, straightening, hauling.[12]

Unlike West Africa, where the hoe was the principal implement of cultivation, Ireland was a spade culture; the spade was essential to large-scale drainage projects and lazybed cultivation alike. It combined many of the functions of the mattock, axe, crowbar, mallet, shovel, and hoe. When Despard left Ireland in the 1760s, he left a country that had just embarked on the most intensive land cultivation of its history. In consequence, the specialization and differentiation of the spade were at their highest. The English planters introduced the two-sided spade; there was a spade type particular to Despard's region, the Slieve Bloom loy;, and already stewards were discussing the rules of proportionality with respect to other implements (shovels).

Despard was part of a military proletariat. He supervised the slaves of Hercules Ross in artillery construction. He worked in an extreme variety of site conditions, ranging from marsh to mountain, where he faced, with everybody else, the dangers of slippage, irregularities, weight of boulders, surprising dangers of compacted earth, the flooding in trenches, the hazards of falling objects, failed pilings, and weak shoring.[13]

To mature as a military commander he had to learn, according to Clausewitz, acumen, firmness, lucidity, intellect, and intuition.[14] Lucidity posed particular problems in commanding irregular troops in the Caribbean. To be understood by the polyglot crew, Despard had to become familiar with pidgin or Creole. The importance of coherence increased in direct proportion as cooperation became more intricate, extensive, and expensive. Thus, from the midsixties to the mideighties, when he lived mainly in Jamaica, Despard became Creole.[15] Who taught him?

"The distinguishing feature of the slave was not his race," wrote C. L. R. James, "but the concentrated impact of his work on the extensive cultivation of the soil." That is one contribution, and it is one that the engineer Despard, as an earthmoving man, knew. James notes a second significant contribution:

11. Lendy, *Treatise on Fortification*, 147.
12. Way, *Common Labour*, 47.
13. Budleigh, *Trench Excavation and Support*, 62.
14. Clausewitz, *On War*, 178.
15. Braithwaite, *Development of Creole Society*, passim.

"The important point of the slave's contribution to civilization is that he recognized and did battle with the slavery system every day. "[16] Despard landed in Jamaica in the aftermath of Tacky's Revolt (1760), and its inauguration of terror. Four hundred slaves lost their lives in battle or by mutilations, gibbetings, and slow burning. In June 1768, more rebel slaves were hanged. In 1776, slaves revolted in the western parishes of Jamaica. British legislation against obeah, or the spiritual practices of the slaves that were believed to lead to invulnerability, was created. So fearful was the ruling class that the privy council discussed its power in 1788–89.[17]

Europeans, Africans, and Indians came from different biological environments: they carried different pathogens and possessed different immunological strengths. Africans developed tolerance for most European diseases, while Europeans remained susceptible to African pathogens. Owing to the cruel selection process of West African slave traders, those who came to the West Indies were "incredibly well suited to survive the nutritional and epidemiological rigors awaiting them from capture, through the middle passage to the plantations of the New World."[18] For Europeans, it was a dangerous biological environment.

The health of the English officers depended on the nursing they received from Jamaican women. The period of the internationally esteemed tradition of Jamaican (and Belizean) nursing begins in this period. J. B. Moreton, the small planter of Clarendon parish, believed that in the case of fever it was essential, "when a person is confined to his bed, [that] some careful discrete black woman, should be appointed to attend him all day and night." "A soldier should be nursed," asserted Benjamin Moseley, the senior physician to the British military in Jamaica. "All drudgery and labour should be performed by negroes, and others, inured to the climate."[19] They were lifesavers. After Nelson fell sick on the San Juan expedition, and was all but given up for dead, it was Cuba Cornwallis who nursed him to back to health.[20] Catherine may have nursed and nurtured Despard, helping to reproduce his health in a hostile pathogenic environment.

Moreton advised the recently arrived English officer or gentleman to quickly find a Creole or African American woman: "if you please and

16. James, "Atlantic Slave Trade," 256–77.
17. NA, CO 138/28.
18. Kiple, *Caribbean Slave*, 5.
19. Moseley, *Treatise on Tropical Diseases*, 184.
20. Hibbert, *Nelson: A Personal Biography*, 27, 28.

humour her properly, she will make and mend all your clothes, attend you when sick, and when she can afford it will assist you with any thing in her power." The celebrated Mary Seacole, the nurse of the British Army in the Crimea and the masseuse to the Prince of Wales, was the daughter of an African boardinghouse keeper in Kingston, who "was, like very many of the Creole women, an admirable doctress."[21] The West Indian boardinghouse indeed was something of a hospital as well as a restaurant and dance hall. With much affection, R. R. Madden, the historian of the United Irishmen, who had considerable West Indian experience, described two of them in Barbados before observing, "The free women of colour are generally represented as a class of persons possessed of considerable personal charms, of a frank and generous yet a loving nature, which betrays them too often into connections which custom sanctions, but religion does not sanctify. It is inferred from such connexions that they are a class of women depraved and dissolute, as the females are who are similarly situated in Europe. Nothing can be more unjust, or, I believe, unfounded."[22]

The Caribbean woman of color at the end of the eighteenth century was subject to stereotypes—the sable queen, the passive workhorse, the domineering matriarch, the lascivious Hottentot, the evil sorceress.[23] Catherine Despard fit none of these. Like all Caribbean slave women, she helped the process of creolization. Certainly she would have known of women rebels: "That the head Negro Women about Lucea, even those kept by white men, were concerned [in the 1776 rebellion]."[24] It was not inconsistent to be kept by white men *and* to be a rebel. Poisoning was her most feared form of resistance. Monk Lewis attended court when Minetta was tried for attempting to poison her master. He was appalled by her "hardened conduct." She heard the death sentence pronounced "without the least emotion and was laughing as she was escorted away." Cubah, "the queen of Kingston," and one of the true leaders of Tacky's Revolt was hanged. Thisbe led a rebellion in Trinidad in 1794. Nanny Grigg was famous for her role in the rebellion in Barbados in 1816. If Kate were a Kingston woman, she may also have accepted the free and easy approach here expressed in a Jamaica ballad, which concludes on an unexpected note of antinomianism. It is to be sung to the air of *What Care I for Mam or Dad.*

21. Seacole, *Wonderful Adventures*, 2–5, 60.
22. *Twelvemonth's Residence*, 117.
23. Bush, *Slave Women.*
24. Hall, *In Miserable Slavery*, 122, 129, 133, 142, 165, 235, 243, 158, 193, 219.

Me know no law, me know no sin,
Me is just what ebba them make me;
This is the way dem bring me in;
So God nor devil take me!

While we have no direct evidence of Despard's relationship with Catherine in Jamaica, there are suggestive parallels. Cuba Cornwallis who looked after Nelson is one. She had been a slave to Lord Cornwallis, the British general who commanded forces against the Americans and who surrendered at Yorktown in October 1781. She ran a boardinghouse in Kingston. We have already mentioned Edward Fitzgerald and Tony Small.

In 1801, Bryan Edwards made clear that Jamaica was a sexual playground for white men.[25] The "fancy girl" aroused desire, which was essential to the commodity market in human beings. These were regimes of unremitting cruelty in the forms of rape, torture, and death. Another parallel is provided by the extensive and salacious diary of Thomas Thistlewood (1721–86), the owner of Egypt Plantation in Westmoreland parish, Jamaica. He ruled by flogging and rape. He had a relationship of thirty-three years with one of his victims, Phibbah, who acquired property in land, livestock, and slaves. A third parallel might be found in Joanna, the slave companion of Captain John Gabriel Stedman (1744–97), who was a Scottish officer in the Dutch occupying army in Surinam. His published *Narrative* (1796) contains a frankly erotic picture of her—a bare breast, the back of her hand on her backside, anklets above her bare feet, necklace, and a broad brimmed hat in hand. Joanna nursed him when sick: "by her unwearied care and attention, I had the good fortune to regain my health." He described the "Surinam marriage":

> ... Gentlemen all without Exception have a female Slave /mostly a creole/ in their keeping who preserves their linens clean and decent, dresses their Victuals with Skill, carefully attends them /they being most excellent nurses/ during the frequent illnesses to which Europeans are exposed in this Country, prevents them from keeping late hours, knits for them, sews for them, &c.— while these Girls who are some times Indians, sometime Mulattos and often negroes, naturally pride themselves in living with an European whom they serve with as much tenderness, and to whom they are Generally as faithful as if he were their lawful Husband.[26]

25. *History Civil and Commercial.*
26. Stedman, *Narrative*, 20.

He brutally waged war against maroons. They had a son, John. He deserted mother and child when he returned to Holland in 1777. He freed his son, who joined the Royal Navy. These people possessed botanical knowledge, a knowledge derived from, and dependent on, the commons.

We may accept these parallels in some ways: a powerful sexual attraction; a complex negotiation concerning slavery, freedom, and property; "unwearied" attentions of nursing; and a host of other unmentioned duties (cooking? laundry? cleaning?). These parallels are inexact in two crucial ways. First, Kate accompanied Ned back to England. Second, she too was a revolutionary. Their relationship is the basis of his reproduction as a person and their reproduction in the birth of a son.

Catherine's mother, Sarah Gordon, was a free woman of color of St. Andrew's parish (Kingston), Jamaica, whose will of May 1799 and probated in August gave four slaves (three adults named Jack, Maria, and Louisa, and one child named December) to "my dear daughter Catherine Gordon Despard now in London."[27] In addition to the possible wealth which this may have provided in sustaining Kate in an independent manner proper for her journalism, Parliamentary lobbying, and prison advocacy, it is clear that she came from a complex Creole society in contrast to the hardening of racial society in England where the binary of black or white prevailed.

27. Will of Sarah Gordon, 19 May, 1799, LOS 66, fol. 6, Registrar General, Twickenham Park, Jamaica, as cited in Erin Trahey, "Free Women and the Making of Colonial Jamaican Economy and Society, 1760-1834" (PhD thesis., History Department, University of Cambridge, 2018).

FIFTEEN

Nicaragua and the Miskito Commons

"Q. *How long has your Lordship known Colonel Despard?*

A. It is twenty-three years since I saw him. I became acquainted with him in the year 1779, at Jamaica. He was, at that time, lieutenant in what were called the Liverpool Blues. For his abilities as an Engineer, I knew he was expected to be appointed.

Q. *I am sorry to be obliged to interrupt your Lordship; but we cannot hear, what I dare say your Lordship would give with great effect, the history of this gentleman's military life; but you will state what has been his general character.*

A. We went on the Spanish Main together; we slept many nights together in our clothes upon the ground; we measured the height of the enemy's wall together. In all that period of time no man could have shewn more zealous attachment to his Sovereign and his Country, than Colonel Despard did."

Ellenborough cut off Horatio Nelson before he could continue with his testimonial to Despard, so he did not get a chance to speak his whole mind to the court.[1] Why was he interrupted? Most likely because at the time Nelson was already the nation's hero from his victory over Napoleon on the Nile. Nelson had returned with the laurels of the Egyptian campaign; the plunder was being distributed throughout London at the same time the trial took place. The nation's hero could not have spoken more favorably, or with more credibility, of the nation's villain. Certainly, his testimony influenced the jury in its verdict recommending mercy.

1. *Trial of Edward Marcus Despard*, 176.

We easily detect a note of pleasure, perhaps joy, in Nelson's recollections. The very sharing to which Nelson attests became a more generalized experience during the disastrous San Juan expedition of 1780, in which Despard participated. The means of doing this was to be an expedition up the San Juan River to Lake Nicaragua investing on the way the castle of San Juan regarded as "the inland Gibraltar of Spanish America." Success would "produce a new order of things." Disaster, not success, was the result. An historian of the expedition provided the following summary: "Of nearly two thousand men sent up the river between February and November only about a hundred survived. In addition more than a thousand sailors died in the ships that had anchored off the mouth of the river."[2]

Despard distinguished himself for his prowess, his initiative, his vision, his stamina, his organization, and his leadership. Some of this was recognized and described, notably by Nelson at a later date but also at the time by the commanding officers of the expedition. Polson wrote, "There was scarcely a Gun fired but was pointed by [Nelson] or Lieut. Despard chief engineer who has exerted himself on every occasion." His exertions were rewarded by promotion and eventually the superintendency of British Honduras, or Belize.

The plan posed problems of logistics and communication that stretched the capacity of available resources to the limit. First, troops, ships, and provisions had to be mobilized in Jamaica. Second, they had to be transported across a thousand miles of sea. Third, a base of operations, or a headquarters, had to be established on an unknown coast. Fourth, men and provisions had to disembark and reassemble on river craft in order to ascend the sixty miles, overcoming rapids, shoals, shifting sandbars, and blind tributaries. Fifth, these forces had to lay siege on the castle, built in 1655. Sixth, having taken command of all strong points along the river, they had to build vessels and outfit a fleet for operations in Lake Nicaragua. These goals had be achieved in a debilitating milieu of heat, incessant rains, unfamiliar fauna and flora, and fever.

Irregular troops formed a conglomeration of the motley proletariat. They were made up of Jamaican, African-American, Irish, Moskito, or Central American Indians, whose task, as became increasingly apparent as time wore on, was to do the labor of building and transporting that such an expedition required. Migratory labor from several continents, unfamiliar with one another's food, mores, and languages, was brought together to construct the infrastructure of a military operation intended to produce "a new order of

2. Pocock, *Horatio Nelson*, 49. See also Pocock, *Young Nelson*.

things." This was the human milieu in which Despard acted out his deeds of war.

The lieutenant governor, Archibald Campbell, took the farewell salute as the irregulars were ready to embark from Kingston. He wrote, "In a ragged line, half-clothed and half-drunk, they seemed to possess the true complexion of buccaneers and it would be illiberal to suppose their principles were not in harmony with their faces."[3] The names of their formations—Royal Jamaica Volunteers, the Loyal Irish, the Jamaica Legion, the Black Regiment, and the Royal Batteaux Corps—the ornate military nomenclature for people who were otherwise without dignity and which, by August, deceived no one, as General Kemble wrote Governor Dalling, "Whites receive no addition of Constitution from being called Batteaux Men, &c., and fall sick as fast as others."[4]

Stephen Kemble (1740–1822), colonel to the 60th Regiment of Foot, sailed to Jamaica, where he took command of the San Juan expedition. He had been deputy adjutant general of British forces in North America. He resigned from American command in June 1778, after the evacuation of Philadelphia, when numerous women and children joined the evacuation. Could Catherine have been one of them? The expedition falls into two phases: the first was from February to the end of April, a dry season, and resulted in the defeat of the garrison at the castle up the St. John's river. The second phase fell during the rainy season and was characterized by mismanagement, chaos, disease, huge mortality, miscommunication, and withdrawal in December 1780. The first was a westward movement upriver, and the second was eastward downstream. In the first, we see Despard as a bold and daring soldier, in the second as embittered, and wasted but alive.

Nelson found an anchorage. The transports were disembarked. A camp of sorts was established in Greytown, or St. John's Harbor. Pitpans and panangs were obtained for river travel. A series of parties left the coast for the interior, Despard and Nelson in the lead canoe. Leaping out to engage the enemy, Nelson got his boots stuck in the mud. In extracting his feet, he lost time, and Despard got to the enemy outpost first. Despard distinguished himself over and over again—he was the first, he did the reconnoitering, he suggested

3. Moreton, *Manners and Customs*, 61. A. W. Haarmann takes the governor at his word and considers the men volunteers ("Notes").

4. Kemble, Documents and Correspondence, 26 August 1780.

a plan of attack, he led the first party and took fire. Nelson fell behind him. It was not long before they arrive at the castle. Despard again reconnoitered: he made the drawings. With Nelson, he sited the batteries for the artillery. Bombardment against the steep walls of the castle San Juan, El Castillo de la Immaculada Concepción, commenced on 11 April. The rains fell. Polson ordered the engineers to dig their way beneath the walls and bring them down with a mine, but after exhausting work they came upon solid rock. Despard was responsible for organizing parties of sappers to begin the attempt to mine the ramparts. Thanks to him the siege was successful and the garrison surrendered.

The sailors, soldiers, artificers, boat men, slaves, and laborers had to be constantly replaced as the original complement succumbed to disease. The soldiers were unable to crawl. At Greytown, there were times when no one was well enough to bury the dead. Dancer, the only physician on the expedition, refused to attend the hospital.[5] The motley proletariat began to desert, to mutiny, to get drunk, and to rebel.

Such an economy depended on scarcity, and this, to a degree, had to be created, because "the woods abound[ed] in game, such as warrus, or wild Hogs, guanas, Ducks, Pigeons, Currasoa Birds, Quams, both as big as Turkeys." Soldiers were disallowed barter, and could not exchange clothing for provisions. Soldiers and camp followers were forbidden to hunt in the woods without permission from their commanding officers. With scarcity came theft. This is the dynamic of capitalism, which creates scarcity by destroying the commons that are then criminalized by laws and punishments against the discommoned. It is a reality directly opposite to the tragedy of the commons proposed by James Wilson when the United States was imposed: "fierce and ungovernable competition for possession and enjoyment of things insufficient to satisfy all."[6]

One of the roots of Despard's egalitarianism came from his experiences in Nicaragua and on the Mosquito Shore. The Miskito Indians called their English allies the grey-eyed people. Nelson and Despard occupied a boat in a partnership similar to the turtling partnership of the Miskito turtlers, the captain or sternman working with the striker, or harpooner. The Miskito

5. Germain MSS, 7 Sept, 8 June, 5 August, William L. Clements Library, University of Michigan, Ann Arbor.
6. Wilson, *Works,* 195.

brought their knowledge of swidden agriculture (plantains, cassava, bananas), fishing, gathering (wild fruit, eggs, shellfish), turtling (green turtle, hawksbill), and hunting (white-lipped peccary, and white-tailed deer), essential to food provision in the tropical ecosystem. They held riverine and beach land collectively; they distributed food by generalized reciprocity or the rule of the "two haves," namely, "if have, have to give." Women maintained the luck of the gift, the sending, the receiving, and the remembering.[7]

Olaudah Equiano, with most commentators, remarked on the Miskito commons, "These Indians live under an almost perfect equality, and there are no rich or poor among them. They do not strive to accumulate, and the great unwearied exertion, found among our civilized societies, is unknown among them."[8] George Pinkard, wrote a few years later of the Miskito Indians that they "have no interest in the accumulation of property, and therefore do not labour to obtain wealth. They live under the most perfect equality, and hence are not impelled to industry by that spirit of emulation which, in society, leads to great and unwearied exertion. Content with their simple means, they evince no desire to emulate the habits or the occupations of the colonists; but on the contrary, seem to regard their toils and customs with a sense of pity or contempt."[9]

During all of May and half of June, Hercules Ross, the Kingston provisioner, awaited the arrival of the Cork fleet with its supplies of salted pork and beef. Until then, he advised the provisioner in Greytown to feed turtles to the troops. In July, he pressed the turtle fishermen of Port Royal to service in Nicaragua. Clearly, the army in San Juan did not know how to supply itself. By the beginning of June, "the melancholy effects of famine" were beginning to be discerned at the Castle. In June, Pierce of the Jamaica Volunteers was pleading for the sick that "a little Oatmeal would be of infinite Service." The ships in the harbor had no food or water. At the castle, Leith reported, "We have no flour, oatmeal, rice, sugar, coffee, tobacco, or medicines—and whoever goes into the hospital comes out only to his grave." This political economy depends on keeping the soldiers ignorant of the methods of providing for themselves.[10] Again from Nelson's testimony:

7. Nietschmann, *Between Lane and Water*, 183–84.
8. Conzemius, *Ethnographical Survey*, 40.
9. Pinkard, *Notes*, 519.
10. Stephen Kemble Papers, vol. 1, 9 April–26 August 1780, William L. Clements Library.

Q. *Were there any means made use of, to furnish the Sick with any Vegetables, or were there any to be had?*

A. Yes, I sent a Boat as frequently as possible in search of plantains & fruits, which, on being brought to the Castle were divided by the Officers amongst the Soldiery.[11]

Rum was more important, a douceur, a palliative, a medicinal. It was also the cause of disasters. The rains were so heavy it was impossible to make a fire. The troops were on short allowance. Provisions were in arrears by two days. The pitpans were too small to carry rum puncheons: "The few people on board the Lord Germain have been without Rum these Ten Days." In August, Charles Dixon reported to Kemple from the castle that the men had gone twenty days without rum, "but not a murmur heard." The grey-eyed people depended most essentially on the Caribbean people for food and transportation: provisions and pitpans. Peter Hulme points out that etymologically the English words *barbeque* and *canoe* are both Caribbean words, and that children still chant "Yo ho and a bottle of rum."[12]

The soldiers were without shoes coats or blankets. "Great neglect in the Officers Commanding Parties, relative to the Care of Stores of all Sorts. The Battery at the Point much retarded on Account of the Want of Carpenters' and Engineers' Tools." The question of engineer's tools was at the heart of this political economy. "If we are able to employ two Carpenters at a time we think ourselves lucky, and I speak now of the whole, those belonging to the Expedition as well as those in the different Corps; the artificers of every other Occupation are in the same State, I need say no more to convince you of our incapacity to build Vessels, Erect Barracks or Redoubts. The records ring with calls for skilled men—someone who "understands burning of Charcoal." "A Man from each Corps who understands splitting and Cutting of Wood to be sent down to the Castle to be set at Work immediately." In July "A Return of the Masons in each Corps to be sent immediately . . . these People to be employed in repairing the Roofs of the different Apartments in the Fort." The most frequent call was for boatmen.[13] "When the working parties quit Working an Officer to see all the Tools collected and put under the Charge of Sentries, and every possible care taken that they are not broke or

11. Germain MSS, "Narrative of Sir Alexander Leith, Lieut. Col. 88th Regiment," 49, William L. Clements Library.

12. Hulme, *Colonial Encounters*, 210–11.

13. "Narrative of Sir Alexander Leith," vol. 21, 67.

damaged." "All the Spades, Shovels, Pick axes, Falling axes, and other intrenching Tools in possession of Officer or Soldier, to be sent immdiately to the Carptenter's Shop." Tools were to be kept at center of encampment. Pilferage was endemic. In May, Despard wrote, "All Soldiers Employed as Artificers, and who really understand their business, will from hence forward be allowed 5 Bitts per day for each day they Work; the Engineer to keep a list of them and settle their Accounts every Saturday Evening, that there may not be any complaints hereafter."[14]

A principle of divide and rule seems to have been asserted from the beginning, at least in theory: "No Regular Troops are to be employ'd in labour but when the Necessity is very pressing." By July the appeal is frankly racist, as shown by this general order: "it is by the superiority of their discipline we are to reap the greatest advantages. Impressed with this Idea, he flatters himself each Soldier will strive to distinguish himself, and show how superior disciplined and well-bred Troops are to a motley Crew of Indians and Mulattoes." The appeal is not altogether successful; the "Loyal Irish" in particular were given to inefficiencies and desertion.[15] Concerning the Englishmen of Rattan, Black River, and the Mosquito Shore, the British superintendent, Robert Hodgson, wrote to Germain, " I cannot but think this is a timely riddance. . . . The chief use expected from these people was from their knowledge of the country. . . . Many of them were known to be adverse to the interests of the Crown."[16]

A turning point of the entire expedition was reached in early May when the Miskito Indians decided to collect their boats and go home.[17] The Indians "have been for some past very uneasy to get home; and several of them ran away with their Crafts in the night—as they have the highest ideas of freedom, they would not let their Crafts be put under our guard," Polson wrote in April. They were essential as pilots. In June, "five of the Indian Prisoners, two of whom were Pilots (and whom I intended to Employ) upon the Lake, made their Escape through the shameful neglect of the Guard and Want of Discipline of the Corps." While Captain Lamb spoke Spanish, Polson noted there was "want of a Person to speak the Rama Language"[18]

14. "Narrative of Sir Alexander Leith," vol. 21, 52, 65–80.

15. "Narrative of Sir Alexander Leith, vol. 21.

16. Shelburne MSS, West India, misc. papers, vol. 78, fol. 151, William L. Clements Library.

17. Dozier, *Nicaragua's Mosquito Shore*, 20.

18. Stephen Kemble Papers, vol. 1, 17 June 1780, William L. Clements Library; *Kemble's Journal,* in *Collections of the New York Historical Society*, vol. 17 (New York, 1884), 28. See also Pocock, *Young Nelson*.

"After the Indians deserted, the Black River Negroes deserted, and took the most suitable boats, leaving the rest to face "the melancholy effects of famine." Negroes continued to desert through May and June. By September, the negroes of the corps were basically imprisoned in the fort. The ablest hunted as chasseurs to get the food. They were the most skilled as boatmen. "Black River Negroes are more expert in getting up the Craft than the Indians—the Bay Negroes the most expert of all—they may be had at Rattan." The Negroes did the heavy lifting and digging, constructing sheds, unloading boats, moving cannon. Cooperation fell apart. "The Mining business is extremely laborious; Negroes only are adequate to the task & many of them are indispensibly requisite to carry it into execution." Captain Clark was advised from Jamaica to treat the mulattoes kindly "being free People to use them Gently" "for fear that we should not be able to Raise more." The Bay Negroes were conscious of their value—"the Inhabitants expect their Merit will intitle them to this distinction that their Wants will be attended to and their Usage such as will make them fond of the Service." Strikes as well as desertions were reported.[19]

Communication among the motley crew was fast and uncontrollable. The Negroes from Rattan who were collected for shipment to the San Juan were "all disaffected and averse to the service. This I find is occasioned by certain Negroes sent from this to St. Johns who having deserted and returned back & have so strongly prejudiced the other slaves here by reports of the bad treatment they met with that I find it impossible to engage them to go without Compulsion."[20] In March, the officers were ordered to "take every Step that the Soldiery have little connection with them [Indians] in Order to avoid the possibility of Disgust on their Side."[21] In September, officers were distressed to learn that the Miskito Indians were warning the white lower class against service in San Juan.

The structure of command began to collapse. "Captain Polson's ill health and apparent decay of Intellect render him of little use." Nelson took to his bed with fever and hardly survived the long journey back to Jamaica; the Miskito Indian chiefs, the leaders of the Black River militia, quarreled or deserted; and in June the Loyal Irish were united with the Jamaica Volunteers to form a single corps under Colonel Dalrymple. The stress and the sickness

19. Germain MSS, vol. 21, 169, William L. Clements Library.
20. Kemble, Documents and Correspondence, 5 September 1780.
21. Kemble, Documents and Correspondence, 21 March 1780.

affected all officers. Sir Alexander Leith labored under delirium "and evident signs of madness to be discovered every moment." Captain Tod flipped out and attempted to seize the gunship *Germain*.[22]

In August, Alexander Leith, commander of the batteau men, complained from the castle to Stephen Kemble at Greytown about "the total inactivity that has pervaded every officer on this command." Dalyrmple in particular was "encumbered with a quantity of fat turkies, and some broods of fine young chickens." "This Gentlemen, during the extreme severities he has undergone in the course of this bloodless campaign, never stirred without his claret and hen roost." He "entertained me every evening with three or four Spanish whores rolling on his bed, with whom he practiced all the conduct of a Covent Garden brothel."[23]

The end of the story belongs to Despard. In December, the garrison at St. John's was evacuated, but Despard remained there for several months. He was instructed to blow up the fort, but, he wrote,

> that with the few hands, & small number of Tools at present in the Castle the business cannot be done in less than Ten weeks, and the calculation supposes the work of twenty men a day for the time above.... Tools we are totally in want of, I shall therefore be much obliged to you to send me Ten large Iron Mauls, twenty Pickaxes and twenty Iron Crows, as you have no doubt received a supply of those articles from Jamaica long ere this time.... The Intrenching Tools are arrived agreeable to the list. We have got from five and twenty to thirty Negroes at work together with some white men.[24]

"Never was there so complete a ruin," Kemble wrote. Dr. Benjamin Moseley wrote of the expedition that "the failure of that undertaking has been buried, with many of its kindred, in the silent tomb of government."[25] Despard was a survivor of a death expedition.

The sailors, soldiers, artificers, boatmen, and laborers had to be continually replaced as the original complement succumbed. The good Dr. Irving, Olaudah Equiano's friend, master, and partner, was supposed to have led a corps of Indians to reinforce the expedition, but he had seen some of the sick return and observed "several men wandered about in a phrenzy, and died

22. Germain MSS, vol. 21, John Dalling, *Narrative of the Late Expedition to St. Juan's Harbour and the Lake Nicaragua*, 22 August 1780, William L. Clements Library.

23. Germain MSS, vol. 21, Dalling, 22 August 1780, 38.

24. Stephen Kemble Papers, vol. 2, 16 December 1780, William L. Clements Library.

25. Moseley, *Treatise on Tropical Diseases*.

raving mad." The English forces, Moseley summarized, were "exterminated by the Bloody Flux."[26] He noted the symptoms: black tongue, livid spots, faltering speech, trembling, convulsive sighing, muttering, coma and death. "To shew equal humanity towards all, a partial neglect towards individuals was indispensable." He grew sick himself and refused to enter the hospital.[27] He prescribed opiates which he treated as a police measure, they being "the best means of allaying irritability."

"The troops, deserted by those Indians who had not already perished, languished in the extremist misery, and gradually mouldered away, until there was not sufficient strength alive to attend the sick, nor to bury the dead."[28] Implied is a relationship between the desertion of the Indians and the death of the soldiers. Thomas Dancer, unlike Moseley, attended the expedition. He wrote that they could not have moved up the river without the "spirited exertions and perseverance" of the Indians. They hunted and fished "which contributed not a little to the support of our men's health."[29]

People of the commons met people of empire. Ernesto Cardenal wrote about a similar expedition along the San Juan River:

> And their names were forgotten,
> in barracks with boards taken out to make their coffins
> and the drunken sergeant, pigs, crap;
> or in those hospitals consisting of mango, coconut and almond groves
> where they suffered from delirium with howler monkeys and
>   magpies all around
> getting chills from the wind off the Lake,[30]

Twenty-three years later, when Ellenborough cut Nelson's testimony short, he also prevented any mention of this awful killing: he kept the subject locked in "the silent tomb of government." Despard's personal triumphs and the Crown's military failure were alike dangerous subjects in 1803. There were many veterans of the West Indies in London, as well as relatives and loved ones of those who had died there. In shutting off Nelson's testimony, Ellenborough attempted to induce some class-based amnesia.

26. Moseley, *Treatise on Tropical Diseases*.
27. Germain MSS, 7 Sept, 8 June, 5 August; Dancer, *Brief History*.
28. Moseley, *Treatise on Tropical Diseases*, 133.
29. Dancer, *Brief History*, 12.
30. Cardenal, *With Walker in Nicaragua*.

Despard survived owing to the relationships he formed among the motley crews on the San Juan river and along the Mosquito shore. His personal triumph, even that zeal observed by Nelson, was made possible by the healthy cooperation and access to the commons of the Moskito Indians and by the black boatmen, miners, sappers, and builders with whom he lived and worked for nearly eighteen months. He would have learned about and respected multiethnic labor skills, communication in various languages, and the properties of nourishing fauna and flora, not to mention similarities between Irish and Mesoamerican commoning. Catherine may have been his prime mediator.

SIXTEEN

Honduras and the Maya Commons

IN SEPTEMBER 1787, JAMES BARTLETT wrote Despard in the aftermath of a devastating hurricane offering to "contribute to your ease or the comfort of your family in these distressing times." This may be the earliest evidence, at least in the written record, of Despard's relationship with Catherine. If so, their love story originated in conditions of tempest, both meteorological and historical. A hundred persons perished, five hundred habitations were blown down, and survivors ran about in "fear and consternation."[1] Meanwhile, in Philadelphia a historic convention met to write the constitution of the United States.

Since the disastrous San Juan expedition of 1780–81 Despard had been active up and down the coast of Honduras, as well as between Jamaica and Central America. He was superintendent of British Honduras (now Belize) from 1786 to 1790. His biographer says that he came close to establishing principles of racial equality, respect for international law, and democratic representation.[2] To this I want to add the principle of the commons, which was strengthened by his interaction with indigenous practices.

Commentators of the eighteenth and twentieth centuries agree that the Miskito Indians were and are a people of three continents: American, African, and European. The confluence of these cultures began in the sixteenth century and was nourished by the buccaneers and escaped slaves of the seventeenth. Shipwreck and mutiny were the historical midwives of the population. After the murderous defeat of Tacky's Revolt in Jamaica in 1760, five hundred

1. Robert English, Samuel Harrison, and Abraham Bull to Supt. Despard, 20 August 1798, NA, CO 123:5, f. 18. Millás, *Hurricanes of the Caribbean*, 278–79.
2. Jay, *Unfortunate Colonel Despard*, 167.

prisoners were transported to the Bay of Honduras, where according to the slave chronicler Edward Long, they "may some time or other prove very troublesome to the logwood cutters."[3] By the eighteenth century, the Miskito Indians had become an advanced maritime people with major settlements at Blewfields, Pearl Key Lagoon, Boca del Toro, Corn Island, St. Andres, and Old Providence, whence the men returned from hunting and gathering expeditions and where the women cultivated plantains, cassava, rice, yams, breadfruit, eddos, Indian corn and the edible arum root, with oranges, sapodillas, guavas, mammees, papaws, star-apple, pineapples, sour-sops, custard apple, sugar-cane and mangoes. Although they maintained diplomatic, political, and trading relations with the English, particularly in Jamaica, their own history, as well as their coastline of coral, cayes, and lagoon, preserved internal autonomy.

Malachy Postlethwayt, the encyclopediast of English mercantilism, drew on his extensive contacts in the logwood trade for what is essentially an oral history of the Miskito Coast. He defended the English logwood cutters with fulsome justifications of their conquest against the Indians and their competition against the Spanish. Burnaby's Code (1765) stipulated, "When a person finds a spot of Logwood unoccupied, and builds his hut, that spot shall be deemed his property; and no person shall presume to cut a tree, or grub a stump, within less than one thousand paces or yards of his hut." Postlethwayt was unabashed about the great profits to be made. Men worth "even up to £10 to £30,000 sterling" were living in Belize Town in the 1750s. He expounded on the autonomous traditions of the coast, observing of the Miskito that "they have no kind of vice among them, nor any occasion for magistrates," evidence counter to the privatizing theory of James Wilson. "They have a king chose among themselves, and his consort has the title queen, and they are governed by certain rules of their own making."[4]

Olaudah Equiano passed a year with the Miskito Indians. In fact, he sailed to Jamaica from London with four Miskito chiefs, including the son of the Miskito king with whom he studied Foxe's *Book of Martyrs*. ("How comes it that all the white men on board who can read and write, and observe the sun, and know all things, yet swear, lie, and get drunk, only excepting yourself?" asked the young prince.) Nor would they work, though they helped build his house south of Cape Gracias á Dios, "which they did exactly like the

3. Long, *History of Jamaica*, 2:461–62.
4. Postlethwayt, *Universal Dictionary of Trade*.

Africans, by the joint labor of men, women, and children." They celebrated by a *dryckbot,* or drinking about, "without the least discord in any person in the company, although it was made up of different nations and complexions," he writes.[5]

As a boy, Napier Bell was befriended by an ancient Mandingo woman, a Muslim from the headwaters of the Niger, who taught him the lore of the place. "Soon as the evening shades prevail the drum takes up its wondrous tale, and together with the fiddle inspires the mad capers of the jig, the cara-bini, the punta, or the country dance; while the horse's jaw-bone, the teeth rattled with a stick, and two other sticks beating time on a bench, with the drum and the wild snatches of song by the women, provide the stimulus for the weird and mystic African dances." Napier Bell grew up among the Miskito. English was his second language, and he understood the amplitude of the cockles; the plenty of the seas; the simplicity of plantain cultivation; and that the flowers, the birds, and the cricky jeen provided the information of an almanac. "We call these people savages, but it is impossible to deny that they lead a happier life than nine-tenths of all civilized men. There is among them a remarkable absence of crime; they are cheerful and merry, sympathetic and kind to each other."[6]

Today, Yucatan, Chiapas, Belize, Honduras, and Guatemala are the names of the political entities that enclose the various Mayan people. The Mayan people are heterogeneous with several languages and many communities from little hamlets to city-states. Their "system of communal landholding has remained practically intact through both the Aztec and Spanish conquests."[7] Two hundred years ago knowledge of this commons might have been transmitted from the mountainous highlands to the coastal lowlands. I gained knowledge of this possibility when I attended church one Sunday morning on a mountain promontory of the Emiliano Zapata *ejido* in Chiapas, Mexico. On the floor in front of the altar I found a six-foot circle of pine needles surrounded by candles. Within this fragrant, green space was a large, spiral conch shell. It was testimony to the ancient trade of the Mayan communities (stressed by J. Eric Thompson) and also seemed to symbolize rebellion and, like the Hebrew *yobel* or jubilee horn, land redistribution.[8] If a conch could make its way up river through wetlands and over mountains to

5. Equiano, *Interesting Narrative,* chapter 11.
6. Bell, *Tangweera,* 262.
7. Lewis, *Tepoztlán Village in Mexico,* 27.
8. J. Thompson, *Maya History and Religion.*

the *selva* Lacandón of Chiapas, there is no reason why collective and communal practices could not make themselves known from the highlands to the coast.

Despard's opponents, the Baymen, dominated the settlement and were responsible for getting rid of him. Named for the Bay of Honduras, they were in essence planters, who profited by resource extraction. Their interests were in cutting down mahogany trees in the interior, floating them down the rivers, and exporting them from Belize Town to the European furniture markets. The Baymen called Despard an "unlettered barbarian."[9] He relocated the shoremen—Indians, freed Afro-American former slaves, Miskitos. He cooperated with the Spanish governor of Yucatan. He distributed city lands according to lottery, a randomizing principle analogous to one he had learned in Ireland that was inconsistent with hierarchies of gender, race, or wealth. In words pregnant with meaning of another kind of human being, the Baymen referred to his "wild and Levelling principle of universal equality." The phrase combines three traditions of the commons, namely the indigenous ("wild"), the English ("Levelling"), and that of the enlightenment ("universal").[10]

The Baymen also opposed the Indian settlements. The logwood extraction threatened the Mayan maritime trade, with the result that the Mayan people were forced into the forests. By 1779, it was reported to the Colonial Office that "the Indians who live near the English are so inconsiderable that it is unnecessary to take any notice of them."[11] This would change as extraction moved from the wetlands of the coast (where logwood grew) to the high ground of the interior (where mahogany grew). But the Mayans had a strong history of resistance.[12] In 1788, an "attack of wild Indians" occurred on the New River, and attacks continued into the nineteenth century (1802, 1817).

The Mayan people domesticated corn seven to ten thousand years ago, and the *milpa* of corn, squash, and beans made an ideal nutritional practice. Mayan settlement practices have been subjected to historical forces of war, invasion, and conquest. "The *milpa* system" was a new phrase of the 1920s. Joel Wainwright explains that the *Maya Atlas* (1997), itself the authorial product of ethnic sovereignty, while saying "Mayas live in a communal land system"

9. J. Thompson, *Maya History and Religion*, 158.
10. NA, CO 123.
11. Bolland, *Formation*, 192.
12. Grant D. Jones's *Maya Resistance to Spanish Rule* is largely about Tipu, Belize. Robert W. Patch's *Maya Revolt and Revolution in the Eighteenth Century* concerns Yucatan in the 1760s.

actually means to say that the Mayans would *prefer* such a system.[13] Armed with the machete since the sixteenth century, and with abundant forests at their disposal, Mayan communities and their *milpas* were wandering with slash-and-burn, or swidden, agriculture. Women tended the *milpas*.

British Honduras (Belize) was on the southeastern frontier of colonial Yucatan. The Mayans had been driven south by the Spanish, and entire towns harbored millenarian leaders, fugitives, refugees, rebels, and runaways. After the conquest of the Itza confederacy in 1697, "the jungle was the world's most effective prison." *Milpas,* villages, and temples were reduced, and with frontier interaction, there was rapid movement of ideas, individuals, goods, and activities, "often hidden from the watchful eyes of those who seek to monitor it."[14] "These places . . . were supremely alive, swarming with ideas both written and spoken, with pragmatic programs for rebellion and with the organizational skills to recruit followings and mount effective resistance." Many could read and write in "This complex underground world of the Mayas." "Villagers bitterly resented hacienda efforts to curb their customary practices of chopping wood, burning charcoal, tapping maguey, picking prickly pear, gathering wild lettuce, or grazing their few animals on lands hitherto utilized by estate owners." Conflicts over such rights turned earnest in 1803, when villagers threw down fences, invaded disputed lands, and began planting.[15]

Liza Grandia shows the dynamic character of Mayan, or Q'eqchi', settlements and migration in her study of Petén, the region of Guatemala that separates the jungles of Chiapas from the swamps of Belize. Five hundred years of experience of displacement meant that enclosure had as much to do with the control of labor as with the seizure of land. Shared village lands and community social organization were threatened by privatization. Dispersed *milpas* made possible integration of hunting and fishing practices, as well as herbal or medicinal gathering on the long, apparently leisurely, walks to and from the various planted areas.[16]

After he returned to London in 1790, Despard responded to the attacks of the Baymen on his government by writing a several-hundred-page account describing his superintendence of British Honduras.[17] It provides one of the

13. Wainwright, *Decolonizing Development*.

14. Jones, *Maya Resistance*, 21, 274.

15. Hamnett, *Roots of Insurgency*, 90.

16. Grandia, *Enclosed*.

17. Daniel Hill, Deposition, 4 July 1788, NA, CO 123:11; E.M. Despard, Appendix to the Narrative of Publick Transactions in the Bay of Honduras 1784–1790, NA, CO 123:11.

main sources of our knowledge. In addition to this, we rely on the letters that he and others in Honduras wrote to the Colonial Office between 1784 and 1790.[18] Together these provide materials for telling the administrative story from Despard's triumphal beginning in this imperial post to his withdrawal from it in the face of opposition from the merchants, slave dealers, and big land grabbers.

Two of the most powerful generators of eighteenth-century commoning met in Honduras, one from the interior, the other from the sea. Honduras in the east was protected by a coral frontier—in fact the second largest coral reef in the world: "The area's natural isolation, its geographical position outside the central shipping lanes, and the hazardous coral reef running offshore made an excellent buccaneer haven."[19]

The gnarled, crooked logwood grows in swamps and karstic depressions around freshwater lagoons. It is compact, valuable, and free of deterioration; hence, it was a means of exchange. The Maya taught the Spanish about logwood. Logwood produced an impermanent red if treated with acid; it supplied a mordant that rendered any color permanent.[20] "Logwood is the fundamental fixing Dye to almost every other Colour, and therefore absolutely essential to our Woolen Manufactures."[21] Camps went further upriver with settlement. Logwood floated downriver in cradles made of cabbage palm. The merchant seamen responded to the lack of institutionalized authority by becoming egalitarian and cooperative.[22] Eight thousand seamen were involved in the logwood and mahogany trades.[23]

"Shortly after 1770 a transition began to occur with the exploitation of logwood giving way to that of mahogany."[24] Mahogany trees could be seven to seventeen feet in girth and seventy to one hundred feet in height.[25] Labor on a mahogany gang called for good health, strength, and skill. There were no whip drivers, running away was relatively simple, supervision was lacking, and there was a five-day work week and a four-hour day. Mahogany was what European nobility sat on and what they put their clocks in. It filled the palaces

18. Honduras Bay Letter Books, 1787–1790, NA, CO 123:5–9.
19. Ashcraft, *Colonialism and Underdevelopment*.
20. Fairlie, "Dyestuffs," 488–510.
21. Burdon, *Archives of British Honduras*, 1:56–57.
22. Finamore, "Documentary Evidence."
23. Burdon, *Archives of British Honduras*, 1:135.
24. Craig, "Logwood as a Factor."
25. Bolland, *Formation*.

and cathedrals of the English Whigs. Chippendale was a great carver and a greater entrepreneur. His publication of *The Gentleman and Cabinet Maker's Director* (1754), with its four hundred designs and 160 folio copperplates was a turning point in his career and an important development of standardization in the transition from handicraft production to manufacture.[26]

By 1787, about fifteen men by collusive copartnerships between master and servant owned about twelve-fifteenths of all mahogany works.[27] By 1779, slaves outnumbered nonslaves by six to one. The settlement at the barcadares (the heaps of chips on which huts are built) had evolved into "convention Town." In 1787, Despard instructed David Lamb to draw a map. Huts and cabins were on the north of the river, while provision grounds were on the south. Barcadares were sources of dispute with respect to provision grounds, salvage rights on wrecks, and land ownership that eventually led to Despard's removal.

Despard arrived in Honduras amid these changes, which by no means seemed inevitable to him. The first dispute was about the settlement of the Miskito shore people. In May 1787, 1,740 people from the Miskito shore arrived. Despard was loyal to the Miskito people, to the Indians, to the people of colour, and to families and women, whom he defended against the baymen, or planters, merchants, and slavers. The disputes were over the fundamental laws.[28] Disputes were also about the metal box bringing the laws from haulover and the minutes to meetings. The Baymen complained that their slaves were encouraged to desert. Women who used to raise plantains, yams, corn, "and other vegetables fit for culinary purposes . . . must now forsake their casual and natural avocations and . . . hire themselves for hard labour in the woods to those who have it more in their power to pay their services in bread and clothing." In February 1788, Despard signed a deed of manumission for a slave belonging to him in consideration of good services done on the Miskito shore.[29]

It was a heterogeneous population controlled by segregation and the gallows. In May 1784, eighty convicts aboard the ship Mercury arrived in July to cut wood. For a month they were prohibited from disembarking, though Despard favored landing of the convicts. "Never permit a marine on any pretence whatever to pass thro' the barracade or to have any communication or conversation with the convicts between decks and as much as possible

26. Layton, *Thomas Chippendale.*
27. Ashcraft, *Colonialism and Underdevelopment,* 30.
28. NA, CO 123/11, Despard, Appendix, 17.
29. NA, CO 123:6, vol. 2, f. 130.

prevent the sailors from having anything to say to them."[30] In December 1786, a Negro man charged with murdering a white man was to be hanged and put in chains. "I have also directions to represent, that the present case of a cruel and wanton murder would be ill deserving of lenity; and that an example is wanting among the Negroes, who have of late acted as if they thought it improbable for the Country to punish them." Despard evidently did not agree.

Despard instructed Mr. David Lamb (an assistant engineer in the 1780 expedition) to lay out the lots. "One Joshua Jones having drawn the Lott No. 69, I was informed that Mr Aaron Young, one of the Magistrates, would not allow him to take possession of it." Jones was prevented from entering the courthouse. He and other Negroes "were so grossly abused by persons in the Character of Magistrates as even to have common walking sticks forcibly taken out of their hands and thrown into the river." A bayman named O'Brien said to Lamb "that he despised the authority of Col. Despard or mine either, and he would give the lotts to whom he pleased; he did not understand that a person of his extensive property should be placed on a footing with fellows of the lowest class and have no more land allowed him than . . . a fellow as Able Tayler (this is a man of Collour)." Later Despard reported that "the Negroes mentioned in the paper are in a state little short of rebellion, and the person Mr. O'Brien who lays claim to them will not relinquish his pretentions."[31]

Despard was later charged with leading the people of color in rescuing Joshua Jones, who had been seized by the Baymen. On Despard's order, Jones took down the cookhouse of Aaron Young: "The Superintendent then putting his hand upon the prisoner's Arm or Shoulder, said, in the King's name I discharge or release this man—Mr Bartlett on the other side said in the name of the people I detain him." The committee of magistrates of baymen threatened "to take Arms in defence of our Lives and properties against an armed banditti of people of all colours." They believed there was not a single person in "Despard's train who can possess or obtain a credit for One shilling in London."

In August 1787, the People of Colour appealed, "We your Petitioners the Inhabitants of the Musquito Shore humbly sheweth that the many circumstances that immediately occur to us gives the most assured reason to expect that it will be really impossible for us to procure a livelihood in this Country,

30. NA, CO, 19 April 1788, 123:6, 265.
31. Jay, *Unfortunate Colonel Despard,* chapter 4.

as we are not allowed the privileges of British subjects, and as Coloured persons treated with the utmost disrespect." Further,

> There is one particular hardship sustained by people of colour from the partiality of one of the rules laid down by those, who have taken upon themselves the legislative authority in this country, whereby they are totally excluded from possessing any mahogany or logwood works in this Settlement, unless they be what they call *naturalized,* by the unanimous Consent of the whole Magistrates; by which law not less than eighty people under that description who have come from the Mosquito Shore are entirely excluded from any means of gaining a Subsistence, unless they will become the Servants of these Legislators, which really seems to be the principle intention of this partial rule.[32]

Slaves rebelled in 1765 and 1768. In 1773, a rebellion lasting five months was suppressed only with the help of a naval force from Jamaica. They traveled a hundred miles in the bush to reach the Spanish.[33] The slaves "make plantations" or have gardens in which they grow rows of plantains with pineapples and melons in between. Caribbeans, Mayas, free coloreds, as well as slaves, grew gardens, despite the provisions of great power treaties. In 1830, it was observed that "their affection for their countrymen is very conspicuous; a black man will share his last plantain with another native of his own land, and seldom distinguishes or addresses him by any other appellation than countrymen." No legal fruit and vegetable market existed in Belize Town until 1803.[34]

In May 1789, Despard sent his secretary, Bannantine, with a canoe and five men up the river Siburn to inspect the plantain gardens. He found widespread destruction of provision grounds. Despard's deputy, James Hutchinson, was sent fifteen miles up Belize River "to a village called Convention Town ... where houses ... erect[ed] for the poorer sort" carried beef, pork, flower, hoes, axes, grindstones, linen, brown sugar, and medicines. Creole women such as Kate had botanical knowledge unknown to officers of the Crown such as Despard, but we do not know whether she accompanied those tending these plantations.

The pharmacopeia of Belize has given the world cortisone, the contraceptive pill, and vincristine (to relieve childhood leukemia). Guided by the bush

32. NA, CO, 24 August 1787, 123:5.
33. Burdon, *Archives of British Honduras,* 147.
34. Matin, *History,* 412.

doctors, healing women, *curanderos* of the commons, and in consultation with other ethnobotanists, Dr. Rosita Arvigo of the Ix Chel Tropical Research Foundation in San Ignacio, at the border between Belize and Guatemala, wrote a field guide to the traditional plants having medicinal and other useful properties belonging to the local forests.[35] The leaves of the trumpet tree could relieve rheumatism, mahogany bark might remedy skin cancer, skunk root helped intestinal ulcers, cockspur helped against snake-bites, red gumbolimbo soothed a burn, steamed leaves of the pheasant's tail tree relieved sore muscles, the duck flower could cure fever and flu, tinctures of jackass bitters killed parasites, the fiddlewood tree might eliminate foot fungus, the bark of the simaruba tree relieved dysentery and diarrhea, and the give-and-take tree might staunch wounds.

Plants were essential to reproductive health: the boiled bark of the hog plum tree eased pregnancy, midwives relied on Bay Cedar, the leaves of the allspice tree relieved menstrual cramps, and the bull hoof vine was a form of birth control. Maria Sibylla Merian recorded in 1705 how African slaves, as well as Indians of Surinam, a Dutch colony, "who are not treated well by their Dutch masters use the seeds [of this plant] to abort their children, so that their children will not become slaves like they are. The black slaves from Guinea and Angola have demanded to be well treated, threatening to refuse to have children." The "peacock flower" with its brilliant red and yellow grows plentifully in the Caribbean and is still brewed as an abortifacient by herb women and bush doctors. The red bird of paradise, or Barbados pride, is still known as an emmenagogue (i.e., it induces menses). In 1799, a "mula-tress" Creole taught many cures to Michel Descourtilz, who collected infor-mation on abortifacients and aphrodisiacs. In 1801, Moreau de Saint-Méry sold material for abortion in a Philadelphia shop, where he moved after leav-ing Haiti. The women were determined to "confound their masters' efforts to have them reduced to breedable beasts of burden."[36] These plants were part of the global commons until 1992.

Zapatista good government was based on three tiers—the *ejido,* the municipality, and the *caracol,* or snail. The snail's slow locomotion leaves a slippery trail. However, this is not the case with the marine gastropod mol-lusk of the Caribbean known as the Queen conch (*Strombus giga* or *Lobatus giga*). It was the presence of this mollusk shell among the Christmas

35. Arvigo, *Panti Maya Medicine.*
36. Schiebinger, *Plants and Empire.*

decorations of the Zapatistas that inspired me to study the commons that Despard found in Honduras. In an important 1922 article in the *Journal of Experimental Zoology,* called "The Leaping of the Stromb," G. H. Parker observed that from the soft, fleshy parts external to the shell of *Strombus giga* could extrude a rigid protrusion called the sickle-shaped operculum, which was used as a fixed point or fulcrum permitting the queen conch to leap over itself without leaving a continuous track for its predators to follow. The motion resembles pole vaulting.[37] History too moves occasionally by leaps.

37. G. H. Parker, "The Leaping of the Stromb," *Journal of Experimental Zoology* 32, no. 2 (1922).

F

HAITI

SEVENTEEN

Haiti and Thelwall

ALL THE ATLANTIC MOUNTAINS, to paraphrase Blake, had begun to shake with the Tupac Amarú revolt in the Andes of 1780. At the *cerro ricco* in Potosí, the source of the world's silver and the world's money, the murderous *mita* system of labor prevailed.[1] The 1780 revolt has been likened to "a great Civil War," whose drama, mobilization, and consequences rank with those of the Haitian revolution of 1791–1803. In this era, new mountains of geopolitics seemed to emerge out of nowhere—the expanding United States and the French Republic and Empire—to join old ones, such as the newly named United Kingdom. These imperial entities depended on islands of the Atlantic, whose volcaniclike eruptions threatened colonial capitalism. Labor was most intensely exploited, enslaved, and immiserated in Haiti and Ireland. Labor was imported into the former and exported from the latter.

The wealth of San Domingue originated in the suffering labor of hundreds of thousands of people forced into slavery from Africa. Their resistance exploded in the historic fury that took place on the night of 22 August 1791, at the Bois de Caïman. An all-out war began that culminated twelve years later—at the time of the Despard conspiracy—in the abolition of slavery and the independence of Haiti. It is a great and horrifying story of human freedom that reverberated throughout the Atlantic mountains, shaking every peak and valley.[2]

The people of San Domingue—the slaves—produced sugar on plantations in organized gangs. They worked in "factories in the field" in the telling

---

1. Nash, *We Eat the Mines*, xxxiii. See also Taussig, *Devil and Commodity Fetishism*; and Stern, "Age of Andean Insurrection."
2. J. Scott, *Common Wind*.

phrase. Their enormous production was expressed as money or as weight or as volume in exports to Europe, where the cuisine changed as a result—hunger suppressants for those thin for want of bread and fancy confections for those fat from their superfluities. The revolt of the slaves threatened this wealth—not the cuisine necessarily but the rate of surplus value and the pattern of investments. In short the most profitable and dynamic exploitation began to shift from sugar to cotton.

This tendency was further encouraged by the allies of the slaves in Europe, who in 1787 formed the abolitionist movement. It began to dawn on the planters, shippers, merchants, and bankers that another source of labor, besides Africa, was needed if they were to maintain the plantation labor supply. That source was staring them in the face: it was the women on the plantation who conceived, birthed, nursed, and nurtured a new, creole generation of labor. These were the pressures that formed the historical context of class, race, and gender during the 1790s. Reproduction of labor shifted from Africa to America. New trails of blood marked the geography of the internal slave trade.

In Haiti, Moreau described a "kind of republic" in the estuary of the Artibonite River, where property was not inherited but was returned to the community. The slaves defended customary rights to common provision grounds of potatoes and manioc. Polverel, one of the French commissioners, issued a proclamation in August 1793, saying that the plantations belonged "in common" to the "universality" of the "warriors" and eligible "cultivators."[3] Napoleon sent Leclerc and Rochambeau to recapture Haiti, "to exterminate," as Marcus Rainsford reported, "the whole race of color."[4] Their expedition sailed in December 1801. The Europeans suffered lack of food, lack of shelter, and devastating disease again, and worse, they listened to their enemies singing the song of liberty, "La Marseillaise," calling citizens to arms against tyranny, although now they were the tyrants and the blacks the soldiers of liberty. The men and women of Haiti fought for their own lives and land in a familiar landscape and in an ecology that their labors had nurtured or cultivated. Rainsford made it clear that these advantages enabled them to find repose and food—they knew the location of spring waters and ate well on the many varieties of yam and banana. The English West Indian interest, fearful of losing its possessions, contemplated making common cause against the elevation of a revolutionary hydra.

3. Dubois, *Avengers*, 20, 48, 162, 230.
4. Dubois, *Avengers,* 413.

In late 1801, the British government signed the preliminaries of the treaty that in March 1802 resulted in the Treaty of Amiens, which brought a period of peace between Britain and France. It enabled the Leclerc expedition necessitated by Toussaint's constitution of 1802, which was a de facto declaration of independence. Napoleon resolved to "make them go back to nothingness." Leclerc was Napoleon's brother-in-law. Sixty-seven ships carrying twenty-two thousand soldiers and twenty thousand sailors set sail across the Atlantic without fear of attack by the British navy. "Rid us of these gilded negroes and we will have nothing more to wish for," Napoleon wrote Leclerc in July 1802. Henry Addington, the prime minister, declared that the interests of the two governments were exactly the same—"to destroy Jacobinism, especially that of the blacks." Napoleon wished to restore slavery. James Stephen wrote Addington in 1802 predicting rebellion, "when the negroes shall discover, that not to the fasces of the Consul only, but to the whip of the driver, their submission is demanded."[5] Only late in the year did Bonaparte publicly announce his intention to restore slavery, which happened in Martinique in May. Le Cap was burned in February 1802. The French troops were without shoes or hats.[6] They listened to the blacks sing "Ça Ira," an iconic song of the French Revolution. Leclerc hanged sixty in Le Cap on one day and dumped a thousand in the sea on another. Rochambeau was "an expert in atrocity." Hundreds of man-hunting dogs were brought in. Race war began, and the Haitian flag was created by stripping white from the French tricolor. In June 1802, L'Ouverture was arrested: "you have cut down in Saint-Domingue only the trunk of the tree of the liberty of the blacks; it will grow back from the roots, because they are deep and numerous."[7]

By 1803, Jean-Jacques Dessalines had taken command of "the Army of the Incas," which had achieved victory by November. The significance of the name was twofold: it signified the total renunciation of France in particular and solidarity with resisting European colonialism in general. In the interests of eliminating color prejudice, all citizens were to be known as "black." In 1792, the powerful and politically dangerous English reformer John Thelwall composed a historical opera called *The Incas,* about which his modern editors commented, "It is as though the Amerindian uprising of 1780–91 in the Andes had succeeded."[8] Looking back to the past, to Thelwall's opera *The Incas,* and projecting forward, to Dessaline's "Army of the Incas," we observe

5. Stephen, *Crisis,* 45–46.
6. Dubois, *Avengers,* 268.
7. Dubois, *Avengers,* 278.
8. In Thelwall, *Incle and Yarico,* 85.

FIGURE 10. "A Real San Culotte!" Hand-colored etching by Richard Newton, December 1792. Courtesy of the Trustees of the British Museum.

that the former was unperformed but plagiarized, while in the latter, Rochambeau is driven out of the country and independence is secured.

"Every plantation is a factory that requires the union of cultivators and workers; it is the tranquil refuge of an active and loyal family, whose father is necessarily the owner of the soil or his representative." So said Toussaint's constitution of July 1801. The factory housed machines; the plantation was the place of slavery. The opposite was just as true: the sugar mill was an expensive machine, the factories were attached to dormitories of child workers. The zenith of technology coincided with the nadir of slavery, a unity of heaven above and hell below.

In France, the Montgolfier released the first hot air balloon in 1783. Soon the channel was crossed, then the Irish Sea. For the next two decades, ballooning helped to transform the imagination, the application of fire, technological innovation (a cloud in a paper bag), and the acquisition of a totally new view of the earth, one in which hills and buildings were flattened and the fragmentation of enclosure, road, and nature, or the separation of town and country, could be seen as a whole.[9] The hot air balloon inspired the first Ordnance Survey maps.

On the basalt piedmont of Acul and the Plaine du Nord of Haiti, three wealthy sugar plantations of more than eight hundred slaves—the Gallifet plantations—were managed by Odelucq. Anxious to show that the creoles were no less advanced, a balloon thirty feet tall and eighteen feet in diameter was released in April 1784 and ascended eighteen hundred feet. Odelucq helped to sponsor the flight, the first in the Americas, and provided one of the Gallifet plantations as its proving ground. What did the slaves think of this remarkable apparition/vision, this defiance of gravity, this impossibility? On the Gallifet plantation, Moreau, a contemporary scholar, observed that the "black spectators did not allow themselves to cry out over the insatiable passion of man to submit nature to his power."[10] Let Aimé Césaire describe such spectators:

> Eia for those who have never invented anything
> For those who never explored anything
> For those who never conquered anything
> But yield, captivated, to the essence of things
> Ignorant of surfaces but captivated by the motion of all things
> Indifferent to conquering, but playing the game of the world.[11]

9. Holmes, *Age of Wonder*.
10. Moreau de St. Méry, quoted in McClelland, *Colonialism and Science*, 170.
11. *Collected Poetry*, 69.

The passion that could not be satisfied was for avarice and accumulation. Odelucq had asked, "How can we make a lot of sugar when we work only sixteen hours [a day]?" Answering his own question, he proclaimed the only way "was by consuming men and animals." Seven years later in August 1791, slaves met who believed that the news from Paris included a decree that prohibited the use of the whip and provided slaves with three rather than two free days a week. The Gallifet plantation was the first attacked in the rising of the slaves that began the Haitian Revolution. Odelucq was among its first victims.[12] The game of the world was now to be played with new essence and new motion.

The earliest record we have of the legendary night of 22 August 1791 comes from a physician, writing in exile in 1793: "*ils célébrèrent une espece de fête ou de sacrifice, un milieu d'un terrain boisé et non cultivé de l'habitation Choiseul, appelé le Caïman, ou les nègres se réunirent en très grand nombre.*"[13] Boukman. who had been a literate slave in Jamaica (hence "Book Man"), led a religious ceremony for the conspirators the night before in the Bois Caïman, halfway between Le Cap and Gallifet, in a gathering place in the woods for slaves returning from market. It is unclear whether this place was a swamp in the plains surrounded by woods or a logwood forest on the Red Mountain, the Morne Rouge.[14] We can be sure only that it was not property owned by planters for the exploitation of slaves. It was a commons that provided the common ground for the flash point of a continental explosion.

Thunder and lightning accompanied by drums and animal sacrifice surrounded the taking of an oath of liberation. Then Boukman offered a prayer to "the god who created the sun which gives us light, who rouses the waves and rules the storm, though hidden in clouds, he watches us. He sees all that the white man does. The god of the white man inspires him with crime, but our god calls upon us to do good works . . . listen to the voice of liberty which speaks in the hearts of us all."[15] Fire and the commons were the ingredients for this flash point of the first successful slave revolution in history. The mysteries of the *houngans* and *mambos* were such that what European political science deemed impossible was turned into a new epoch of human history. The invocation of the sun and the voice of liberty anticipated the religious anthropology of Constantine Volney. On 4 April 1792, the French National

12. Dubois, *Avengers,* 92ff.
13. Dalmar, *Histoire de la révolution,* 117.
14. Geggus, *Haitian Revolutionary Studies,* 81ff.
15. James, *Black Jacobins,* 87.

Assembly declared, "The *hommes de couleur* and the *negres libres* must enjoy along with the white *colon,* equality of political rights." "In the heart of the slave societies of the Americas, legal distinctions on the basis of race were outlawed.... The slave insurgents of Saint-Domingue had expanded the political horizon in a paradoxical way, making it necessary to grant racial equality in order to save slavery."[16]

In the early months of 1798, the British position began to collapse—sixty thousand troops had died, had deserted, or had been discharged as unfit for service. No major offensives had been mounted. Casualties in the lesser Antilles were twice those in St Domingue.[17] In July–August, an agreement was struck for a complete British withdrawal. The election of 1799 and Jefferson's victory were ominous harbingers for St Domingue because Jefferson was a slave holder, was pro-French, and detested Toussaint.

In 1802, the Haitian war grew as yellow fever began to take its toll; Leclerc himself fell sick in October and died on 2 November. His last letter to Napoleon says, "You will have to exterminate all the blacks in the mountains, women as well as men, except for children under twelve. Wipe out half the population of the lowlands and do not leave in the colony a single black who has worn an epaulette." Also that year, Despard's conspiracy gathered steam, culminating in the arrests of November. Leclerc's force was made up of sixteen thousand men. Bonaparte, who wished to create a new French Empire in the Americas, had sent Leclerc to command his attempt to reestablish the French Empire in America; it was the final European bid to hold onto the colony. On 6 June 1802, Toussaint was arrested and deported to France, where he died in an icy cell in the French Alps only a few weeks after Despard suffered hanging and beheading in London. William Wordsworth's sonnet to Toussaint was published in the *Morning Post,* on 3 February 1803:

> Though fallen thyself, never to rise again,
> Live and take comfort. Thou has left behind
> Powers that will work for thee; air, earth, skies;
> There's not a breath of the common wind
> That will forget thee; thou has great allies;
> Thy friends are exultations, agonies,
> And Love, and man's unconquerable mind.

16. Dubois, *Avengers,* 130–31.
17. Blackburn, *Overthrow of Colonial Slavery.*

The common wind but not the commons. Wordsworth's common is abstract. The unconquerable mind only reminds us that the earth has actually been conquered. The proclamations of the two independence movements, Robert Emmet's The Provisional Government to the People of Ireland and Dessalines, Christophe, and Clervaux's The Declaration of the Independence of the Blacks of St. Domingo (29 November 1803), both contained explicit provisions protecting the property of some kinds of property holders and confiscating that of others.

After proclaiming independence and the restoration "to our primitive dignity," the declaration of Dessalines, Christophe, and Clervaux reassures exiled landholders that their return is welcome provided that they renounce former errors, abjure exorbitant pretensions, and acknowledge the lawfulness of the revolution. Those intoxicated with pride, enslaved to pretension, and blinded by the belief that they are "the essence of human nature" had best stay away.

In his Proclamation of Labor and in his Constitution of 1801, Toussaint sought to enforce the plantation system with wage labor instead of slavery. A decree of October 1800 put agriculture under military discipline.[18] The constitution banned voodoo; Alexander Hamilton advised installing a military government. Toussaint's nephew Moïse was executed for advocating land reform and the *lakou*. The *lakou* was an egalitarian, dignified community approach to working the soil for purposes of subsistence, not export, that advocated "living as much as possible beyond the gaze of the state."[19] The working masses themselves soon developed it as a kind of counterplantation: "*Moins pas esclave, moin pas travaye*" (I'm not a slave, I don't have to work).

Quitting the confines of the town, Rainsford ventured into the country, where "every individual employed a portion of his time in labor, and received an allotted part of the produce for his reward, while all took the field, from a sense of duty to themselves. A perfect combination appeared in their conduct, and every action came directly from the heart." And then in an apparent diversion from agricultural to military action, he continues, "More than sixty thousand men frequently exercise together on the plain of the Cape, in excellent discipline, whose united determination against an invading enemy, would be victory or death." Little coercion was necessary, the people were united. So here is a version of the commons—cooperative labor on a mass scale that is also in its form a military exercise. "Labor was so much abridged,

18. Kaisary, "Hercules."
19. Dubois, *Haiti*, 104–8.

that no want of leisure was felt; it would be a great gratification to the feeling heart, to see the peasant in other countries with a regulated toil similar to that of the laborer in St. Domingo."[20]

Rainsford wrote of "the system of equality" he found at the hotel, and further wrote that "the productive system of the earth seemed to be founded on original principles." The references to system and to principles are marks of the philosophes, the thinkers of the Enlightenment. These practices of commons were neither utopian nor feudal; they were part of a "modern" project of abolition and emancipation. Practices of cooperation such as the *lakou* and the *kombite* were essential to the Haitian commons. The Irish playwright Samuel Beckett translated an essay by a witness to such practices on Gonaive, among the Congo societies, which is reminiscent of the Homeric period and is called "black socialism."[21]

The traditions of radical craftsmen and of Romantic poets failed to find a junction point to mount a revolutionary challenge, according to E. P. Thompson. The Haitian revolt and the expansion of racial slavery help to explain that failure and a famous, oft-repeated anecdote gives us the point where that junction failed. John Thelwall was the radical English Jacobin, while Samuel Coleridge and William Wordsworth were the young romantic poets:

"Citizen John, this is a fine place to talk treason in!" mocked Samuel Coleridge to John Thelwall, as they strolled with William Wordsworth among the pretty dells or "coombes" of the Quantock Hills in the west of England.

"Nay, Citizen Samuel," Thelwall retorted, "it is rather a place to make a man forget that there is any necessity of treason."

That is how Samuel Coleridge recorded the exchange in 1835, more than thirty years after it took place in July 1797. William Wordsworth remembered it in a milder way. John Thelwall recorded his version earlier still, only three or four years after it occurred.[22] The anecdote marks the beginning of Wordsworth's and Coleridge's apostasy from the principles of the French Revolution. Of the three poets, only Thelwall remained steadfast. This was

20. Dubois, *Haiti*, 227–28.
21. Boulenger, "King of Gonaives," 291–92.
22. Coleridge, *Specimens*, 105. Wordsworth and Wordsworth, *Letters*, 3:640. Wordsworth thought Coleridge said that it was a place to soften one's remembrances of the strife and turmoil of the world, and that Thelwall said only "Nay . . . to make one forget the world altogether."

1797, the year the first generation of Romantic poets formed its like-minded, supportive community in an environment of gossip, informants, and spies. They began to refer to themselves as "romantic."

Wordsworth rented Alfoxden on the eastern side of the Quantocks. On 13 July, William and Dorothy moved in. The house is not far from the Holford village commons. The road to the house passes a stream down a steep bank and a sequestered waterfall, which became a symbol to the poets and the place to talk treason in, or *not* to talk treason in. Thelwall arrived at Alfoxden as a guest of Wordsworth and Coleridge on 17 July, after his lectures had been broken up, his life threatened, and his papers seized. There had recently been naval mutinies in the ports, and invasion was threatened off Fishguard in nearby Wales. In August, the Home Office sent an agent to spy on the poets now harboring Thelwall. The three went for a "delightful ramble among the plantations, and along a wild romantic dell." Later Thelwall wrote of finding the group a basis for the revival of "a golden age."[23]

Thelwall's version of the anecdote about treason is contained in his 1801 novel *The Daughter of Adoption: A Tale of Modern Times*. It isn't even set in England but in revolutionary San Domingue.[24] Concerned not with the *possibility* of treason but with the actuality of revolution, it is about the only successful slave revolt in human history: the second republic of the new world to throw off the empire of the old. Thelwall had published *The Rights of Nature against the Usurpation of Establishments* in 1796. In its first paragraph, he rouses readers to get up from the couch of lethargy by referring to the tens of thousands that have already been sacrificed to "the Moloch of West Indian avarice who immolates the flower of British youth for the perpetuity of the African slave trade." He obviously knew these events were of an entirely different magnitude and consequence than Romantic personal friendship. Even so, Thelwall's project in the novel is to reconcile the romantic ideal of sensitive friendship with the revolutionary solidarity of necessary comradeship.

The protagonist is Henry Montfort, the son of a sugar planter and slaver in both Jamaica and San Domingue. Henry is thrown out of Eton at harvest time in 1785, after stealing chickens from a neighboring cottager. He learns

23. Holmes, *Coleridge: Early Visions*.

24. Johnston notes that Thelwall too has a version, but he says only that it "follows Coleridge's." But it doesn't. Johnston, *Hidden Wordsworth*, 647. I use the edition of *The Daughter of Adoption* that was published in Dublin in 1801.

that the cottager was made economically desperate "when the commons was closed." The cottager comments bitterly, "*If the poor rob the rich, here is a great cry about justice; but nobody says any thing about justice when the rich rob the poor*" (italics in the original). One thing leads to another (shame, honor, debt, credit) and the ardent young Henry boards ship for the West Indies, where his father has put him under the care of a French planter from Santo Domingo. On board, he meets Edmund, who becomes his servant, an "enthusiast," who was expelled from seminary for his strong opinions. Although Edmund has led a vagrant life, he is English, "*a free-born Briton.*" Edmund has passed pamphlets in Paris on behalf of the Sociétés des Amis des Noirs and listened to Ogé speak, before the latter leads an October 1790 revolt that precedes the great revolt of the following year. Edmunds reminds them that thirty years ago, Tacky the Koromantyn chief led the slaves of Jamaica against the man-stealers. "The story is notorious through the two hemispheres."[25]

Thelwall did not actually go to Haiti, but he knew something about its topography, its history, and the history of antislavery. As a medical student, Thelwall hung out with creoles around Guy's and St. Thomas's hospitals in London: "Among the professional youth with whom he now associated were several West Indians."[26] He sets much of the novel in the north of Haiti between Port au Paix and Cape Haitian (formerly Cape Français) in Port Margot and the Bay of Acul. "As a Briton," says the fictional sailor in *The Daughter of Adoption*, "I like other folks to be as free as myself, and, love my eyes, if I can see what right we have to make slaves of these here people, tho' they be of a different colour than ourselves."[27]

"All was excitement—all was ensnaring voluptuousness—all fascination." Henry wakes up after his first night in Port au Prince (watching the celebrated dances, the *Gragement* and the *Chicca*) to the cries of the whipped and the blandishments of the prostitute. "Is this human nature?" he asks of the planters. Henry asks of himself, "But what is there of fair and beautiful in this magnificent structure of the universe that commercial rapacity will not deform? Where is the elysian scene that vice and misery will not pervade, when oppression bears sway in the land? When impious man, trampling the sacred rights of nature in the dust, erects the arbitrary distinctions of races

25. *Daughter of Adoption,* 145, 147.
26. Thelwall's introduction to *Poems, Chiefly Written,* xxi.
27. *Daughter of Adoption,* 242.

and of colors?" Seraphina is "a literary Creole," a feminist. As a dark Creole, and in her commitment to equality, she is a parallel for Catherine Despard.[28]

Harry strays from the plantation to "the brink of a deep luxuriantly wooden glen, from the bottom of which the dashing murmur of the stream arose in reverberating echoes." Thelwall is remembering the episode in the Quantocks. "What a scene, and what an hour, sir," replies Edmunds, with the most undisturbed composure, "to make one forget that treason was ever necessary in the world!" Henry responds with the facts of history, by pointing to a cavern the entrance to a mine where "the barbarous Spaniards consumed the whole aboriginal population of this ill-fated island." He then invites Edmund to join him in a sympathetic fantasy. "Could you and I become Indians . . . I suspect that our minds would be occupied by other ideas than those of the picturesque and the romantic—that these rocks, these pendant forests . . . might only embolden us by a sense of security to question the authority of our oppressors, and to demonstrate that against the ravages of foreign usurpation, at least, it is at all times lawful both to conspire and to act."[29]

Harry meets Parkinson, a white-haired Englishman, who has lived in seclusion in Haiti for six years, playing the flute.[30] The fictional Parkinson looks after a sick Negro. He explains that the stupendous cataract, which inspired their romantic imagination, was produced by his art of engineering to drain a marsh. He breached the rock with gunpowder and drained the marsh. Parkinson admits it was for "the vulgar purposes of utility . . . I determined to unite the useful and the delightful—the picturesque with agricultural improvement." It is left to Edmund to point out another consequence: it is "the negroes who cultivate that waste." He realizes that "in my zeal for agricultural improvement, I did not consider that circumstance till it was too late." Thelwall unites themes of the time: the genocidal past, romantic illusion, militaristic technology, and an invisible commons.[31]

In 1801, Thelwall also published a volume of poetry, which describes his departure from the encounter with the Romantics Wordsworth and Coleridge. "On Leaving the Bottoms of Gloucestershire" thanks the hospitality of cottagers, who live where not yet

28. *Daughter of Adoption*, 153, 165.
29. *Daughter of Adoption*, 169, 179.
30. He shares a name with a well-known English physician and democrat, James Parkinson.
31. *Daughter of Adoption*, 187–89.

Towers from each peaceful dell the unwieldy pride
Of Factory over-grown; where Opulence,
Dispeopling the neat cottage, crowds his walls
(Made pestilent by congregated lungs,
And lewd association) with a race
Of infant slaves, brok'n timely to the yoke
Of unremitting Drudgery[32]

Thelwall summarizes child labor, polluted air, and dispossession. In these years, 1800–02, a fierce struggle transpired in the west country of England against the technological innovations that were undermining traditional handicraft production of textiles and imposing on the workers the enclosed factory as the location of work.[33] Widespread episodes of machine-breaking resulted, and underground textile unions were formed. It was here, as we described in chapter 4, that Thomas Helliker was hanged in order to terrify the worker's solidarity.

The warmth and generosity of the common people contrasted with a people

... wrapp'd up in Self,
In sordid avarice, luxurious pomp,
And profligate intemperance

as he wrote a fortnight earlier in "Lines Written at Bridgewater in Somersetshire."[34] In that poem he dreams of friendship with Coleridge,

... and it would be sweet
With kindly interchange of mutual aid,
To delve our little garden plots, the while
Sweet converse flow'd, suspending oft the arm
And half-driven spade, while, eager, one propounds,
And listens one, weighing each pregnant word,
And pondering fit reply, that may untwist
The knotty point—perchance, of import high—
Of Moral Truth, of Causes Infinite,
Creating Power.

Enclosure destroys the commons and its human work rhythms. In *The Peripatetic* (1793) Thelwall wrote, "If a Gentleman ... purchases a small

32. *Poems, Chiefly Written.*
33. Ponting, *Woollen Industry.*
34. Thelwall, *Poems, Chiefly Written.*

estate . . . almost the first step he takes towards accomplishing his projected improvements, is to level the surrounding cottagers to the ground, and drive the wretched inhabitants from the spot, dear to them, perhaps, from the remembrance of their own infantile sports, or from the comfort it has afforded to their little families."[35] He warns that the dispossessed might lay the axe to the root and exclaimed, referring to the works of the gentry, "why cumbereth it the ground?"[36]

The transition from sugar to cotton production in the Americas was hastened by the Haitian war of independence and emancipation, and by the related election of the cotton planter (Thomas Jefferson) to the presidency of the expanding nation. This transition on one side of the Atlantic was parallel to the transition from wool to cotton in textile production on the other side. The supply of wool to the factory could not keep pace with the introduction of new machinery or indeed construction of new textile mills. The production of wool was limited by the resistance to enclosure, which reduced grazing lands available for sheep. In contrast, cotton "may be produced *ad infinitum*."[37]

35. *Peripatetic,* 138.

36. Thelwall sold the novel to a London publisher and with the proceeds purchased a lease on a small farm in Wales, where he fell into disputes with neighbors, partly from his failure to understand the unwritten customs concerning water and grazing: "There are several in this very neighbourhood who carry on every species of petty depredation." In a fit of sarcasm worthy of a Garrett Hardin nightmare, he wrote, "It is lawful and right to keep twenty times as much stock (particularly sheep) as you have land to maintain; to consider all the farms in the neighbourhood as a common; to graze everything your neighbor has upon his ground, ripe and unripe, except his wheat; and abuse him if he murmurs or complains. It is lawful and right to turn your horses, when idle, loose upon the roads, to shift for themselves, tear down your neighbour's hedges, and destroy his hay or grain. It is lawful and right to keep pigs which you never feed, and turn them loose with out yoke or ring, so that no hedge or fence may be able go resist them." E. Thompson, "Hunting the Jacobin Fox," in *Romantics,* 180.

37. *Observations on Woollen Machinery,* 9–12.

EIGHTEEN

Ireland and Volney

IN THE POLITICAL ECONOMY OF THE ATLANTIC, two islands stand out as mountains of capitalist accumulation. Demographically, one, Ireland (soon to lose its political identity in the United Kingdom), exported labor, while the other, San Domingue (soon to become Haiti), imported labor. Geologically, these islands had different formations—one being part of the Eurasian continental shelf (a continental island) and the other originating from volcanic upheavals at the bottom of the Atlantic (an oceanic island). Technically, one was formed by orogenesis and the other by epeirogenesis. Politically, one lost independence in the formation of the United Kingdom (1800), while the other gained it as the Republic of Haiti (1803). Economically, one provided a major source of labor, spinning and weaving, for mechanized cotton, while the other was all about sugar.

Writing from Paris in November 1802, Thomas Emmet sent his brother, Robert, a copy of the new edition of C. F. Volney's *Ruins* (1791), translated by Thomas Jefferson, the third president of the United States, and Joel Barlow, the former American ambassador to Tripoli, North Africa. Their translation of Volney has stood the test of time. Thomas Jefferson had distanced himself from the noted deist during a break in his campaign for president, but after his inauguration as the third president of the United States in March 1801, he resumed his correspondence with Volney. In March he sent him his translation of the first nineteen chapters of *Ruins,* including the revolutionary invocation, "Hail solitary ruins, holy sepulchers and silent walls! ... confounding the dust of the king with that of the meanest slave, [you] had announced to man the sacred dogma of Equality." Electoral victory gave Jefferson some latitude from the attacks by Federalists, and he could without fear of religious smear resume both his correspondence with the deported

Volney and send him by a third party a package containing his translation of *Ruins*. He only asked for anonymity. Joel Barlow finished the translation in Paris.[1] Social Jacobinism, or equality of property, was no longer a battle cry of the revolutionary people. The times had changed. Volney was a servant of Napoleon, Jefferson the enemy of Toussaint.[2]

Robert Emmet received the book the same month that Despard, with forty others, was arrested at the Oakley Arms. A continuation of the liberation struggle for Irish independence was to have had a London component led by Despard, in addition to those led by Emmet in Dublin and Russell in Belfast. Counterrevolution was not to them inevitable. When Robert received *The Ruins,* hot off the press, he feared for its safety and thus secreted it up the chimney with fifty musket balls, a number of bayonets, pike handles, and the equipment of a rocket lab in his St. Patrick Street arms depot (Dublin), along with other instruments of insurrection.[3]

Volney was one of those aristocratic Frenchmen whose enlightened outlook contributed to the breakdown of the old regime and whose thinking soared with the revolutionary waves that began to break in 1789.[4] Although he was in his later years an apostate to these ideals and actually an ideologue for Napoleon, his earlier outlook produced a remarkable anthropological critique of human religions. When Despard spoke of his visiting several places of worship a day, he expressed the spirit of Volney. And it was this critique that provided him with an account of the origin of *class* in human history—that one class, the poor, works for the other class, the rich. His critique had the effect of extending the range of human agency within human history, and it is this, evidently, that inspired the apostle of emancipation in Ireland Robert Emmet.

The Ruins; Or, Meditation on the Revolutions of Empires, to give the full English title, was a basic text of European materialism and free thought. In Volney's account, religion was "nothing more than a political engine to conduct the credulous vulgar."[5] Divinity was a universal trope for domination.

1. Jefferson, 440–41.
2. Dubois, *Avengers,* 187–88, 239–40, 244. Dubois writes, "Louverture had turned himself into a dictator, and the colony he ruled over into a society based on social hierarchy, forced labor, and violent repression" (250).
3. Geoghegan, *Robert Emmet,* 136, 147–48.
4. Chinard, *Volney et l'Amerique.*
5. The edition used here is a reprint of the Peter Eckler edition of 1890, which follows the translation published in Paris in 1802. Earlier translations lacked "many original beauties" of the French, according to the translator's November 1802 preface.

Volney imagined the common classes of people, the "untaught men of all countries and of every nation, without prophets, without doctors, and without doctrine," assembling in a circle questioning the religious leaders."[6] The subaltern began to speak; the inarticulate found a voice. To the rulers of society this was dangerous. Popular sovereignty was all very well as theory, but when actual people took it into their heads to put it into practice, then it was time for the rulers to close ranks.

There was already debate in Ireland based on earlier translations. The Reverend John Barrett in 1800 wrote that *Ruins* "menaces destruction to every thing that has justly commanded the respect and veneration of Man." Volney's theory of the zodiac provided the basis of "modern infidelity."[7] The author of *Ancient Irish Prophecies,* also writing in 1800, sarcastically scorned Volney, "One great philosopher (Mr Volney) has discovered that there was no such man as Jesus Christ." "The Hindoos worship Crisna and Crislien is the sun; therefore the worship of Christ is only the worship of the sun; it is astronomical worship." They are ancient prophecies.[8] *Ruins* was considered dangerous enough that a Castle informant reported its purchase by a Liverpool merchant.[9]

In 1799, Captain Marcus Rainsford was shipwrecked off Cape François en route from Jamaica to Martinique, and so it came about that he spent some considerable but unexpected time in the midst of the Haitian revolutionary achievement. He recorded his experiences with the view that "the rise of the Haytian empire is an event which may powerfully affect the condition of the human race."[10] He was a Freemason and an enlightened man with twenty-four years of experience in the British army, a fact that he prudently concealed by posing as an American.

Rainsford immediately breathed in the heady bloom of revolution. The spirit of equality was everywhere, and hierarchy was leveled. About making his way to the Hotel de la République, Rainsford wrote, "On entering the house . . . he immediately perceived that the usual subordinations of society were entirely disregarded, and that he was to witness, for the first time, a real system of equality." He continued, "Here were officers and privates, the colonel and the drummer, at the same table indiscriminately; and the writer had

6. Volney, *Ruins,* 162.
7. Barrett, *Enquiry,* 197.
8. *Ancient Irish Prophecies,* 6, 8, 15, 33, 38.
9. Rebellion Papers, 620/12/145, National Archives of Ireland.
10. Rainsford, *Historical Account.*

been scarcely seated at a repast in the first room to which he was conducted, when a fat negro, to initiate him in the general system, helped himself frequently from his dish, and took occasion to season his character by large draughts of the wine, accompanied with the address of 'Mon Americain.'"[11] The sons of revolution, American and Haitian, ate from a common dish.

The experience of the shared meal was Atlantic in scale and revolutionary in scope. Joseph Brant, the Iroquois leader, spoke of the "dish with one spoon," and later Lewis Henry Morgan, the ally of the Iroquois, built his theory of "primitive communism" from the experience of Montezuma's dinner. The "dinner in question," he wrote, "was the usual single daily meal of a communal household, prepared in a common cookhouse from common stores, and divided, Indian fashion, from the kettle."[12]

The meal may be the basis of human solidarity or a mirror of social hierarchy. By the seventeenth century, at least among European nobility, eating from a common dish was finished; everyone had a spoon and fork and their own plate.[13] Such became the bourgeois savoir vivre by the eighteenth century. These notions of *civilité* and *politesse* slowly became a means of differentiating *humanité*. The common dish could no longer be taken for granted. This change in table manners accompanied differentiation in the menu as well. The bill of fare for rich and poor was as different as could be.

After his billiard game with Toussaint and his meal at the communal table, Rainsford was introduced to the cottage of a black laborer. Its furnishings "even to the smallest utensil" were made by the ingenuity by this artificer. "The wife of this laborer ... was nearly as ingenious as himself, and equally intelligent." "On a neat shelf, appropriated peculiarly to their use, lay a mass book, and a mutilated volume of Volney's *Travels,* some part of which he understood more than his visitor."[14] The Irish revolutionary and the Haitian "black laborer" kept Volney's books in special places: Emmet in a chimney with the weapons of popular insurrection, the Haitian on a special shelf with a holy book. Clearly, Captain Rainsford and the black laborer had had a discussion about Volney's book. What might it have involved?

Emmet received Volney's *Ruins* (1791), while the black laborer possessed Volney's *Travels* (1788). *Ruins* is a revolutionary meditation written during the most optimistic phase of the French Revolution, while *Travels* is a 1787

11. Rainsford, *Historical Account*, 216.
12. "Montezuma's Dinner."
13. Elias, *Civilizing Process*, 92.
14. Rainsford, *Historical Account*, 223–25.

travelogue of a trip that he took to Egypt and Syria in 1783–85. It mixes politics, chronicle, natural history, climate, costume, manners, and so on. Yet, clearly the latter book is the basis for the former.[15]

This was a time of intense construction of the doctrine of white supremacy, some of which was based on concepts of literacy, so it is unusual to find a European officer admitting that his understanding of a European text was inferior to that of a black laborer. We do know, though, that for later generations of the black freedom struggle, Volney's *Ruins* was deeply admired for placing the origin of human civilization in Africa, a fact that remained largely concealed, as Martin Bernal has shown, in the Euro-American world. The cultures of Africa, far from being the ignorant and despised cultures of the lowest of peoples, for several thousand years of human history were the most advanced. This was not a theme in harmony with the growth of racial slave power, nor was it a theme in concord with determinist theories of the stages of history.

Another theme in Volney was essential to both the Haitian and the Irish struggles for independence and emancipation. Volney advocated the abolition of class society and its inherent oppression. His concept of revolution was as deep as the object of his analysis was old. Certainly its success required a change in the "mode of production" and its relations. This is not to say that Volney was a communist in the Marxist sense—and he certainly was not a commoner who depended on customary access to subsistence. The historical anthropology of religion was his forte. Volney's account of the origin and progress of human oppression was based on the few who are rich exploiting the many who are not. Religion maintained the difference. He provided a series of stages in the evolution of religions. While Volney's account is assuredly a class analysis of property, and while it is described with direct, biting humor, and even an ecstatic, rhapsodic idealism, he was not an agitator among the sans culottes in the mold of Babeuf or Spence.

"We ask you whether it be gospel charity which has made you exterminate whole nations in America, to annihilate the empires of Mexico and Peru; which makes you continue to dispeople Africa and sell its inhabitants like cattle, notwithstanding your abolition of slavery; which makes you ravage India and usurp its dominions?"[16] By 1802, those inhabitants of Africa who had been dispeopled to America were no longer cattle but were showing "the

15. Volney, *Travels through Egypt*.
16. Volney, *Travels through Egypt*, 167.

very age and body of the time its form and pressure." This quotation from *Hamlet* appeared on the masthead of the progressive German newspaper, *Minerva,* which also translated Rainsford and carried news about Haiti. The Haitian struggle was far from primitive; it inspired the most powerful philosophy of Europe. Susan Buck-Morss shows convincingly that G. W. F. Hegel's dialectics, later published as *The Phenomenology of Mind,* were developed from contemplating the Haitian revolution.[17] Dialectical reasoning, including the unity of opposites, enabled the historian to understand the struggle between technology and poverty.

In 1781, Volney, age twenty-four, inherited a small sum, which enabled him to travel. He sailed for Cairo in 1782 and spent three years in North Africa and the Near East, traveling and studying Arabic before returning to France. At first he was tempted to visit revolutionary America "and the savages," but he chose instead to go to Egypt and Syria, opting for antiquity over revolution. "'Those are the countries,' said I, 'in which the greater part of the opinions that govern us at this day have had their origin. In them, those religious ideas took their rise, which have operated so powerfully on our private and public manners, on our laws, and our social state.'"[18]

He was impressed by the extreme poverty and the small class of people enjoying wealth. He concluded his two volumes with "'If formerly,' said I, 'the states of Asia enjoyed this splendor, who can assure us that those of Europe will not one day experience the same reverse?' This thought appeared to me distressing, yet perhaps it may be useful. . . . Their example may be a lesson to us." This was written on the eve of the Tennis Court Oath (affirming populist sovereignty) and the storming of the Bastille (enforcing it).[19]

Among pastoral people—the Bedouins, the Kurds, the Turkomen—he found absolute hospitality, writing "His generosity is so sincere that he does not look upon it as a merit. To observe the manner in which the Arabs conduct themselves towards each other, one would imagine that they possessed all their goods in common. Nevertheless, they are no strangers to property, but it has none of that selfishness which the increase of imaginary wants of luxury has given it among polished nations. . . . They are fortunate, at least, that this necessity [of circumstance] should have established among them a state of things, which has appeared to the wisest legislators as the perfection

17. *Hegel, Haiti.*
18. Preface to *Travels through Egypt,* iv.
19. *Travels through Egypt,* 2:499.

of human policy: I mean, a kind of equality in the partition of property, and the variety of conditions."

Change came about from foreign invasion and conquest, not from internal class struggles. The danger he faced as a foreigner arose because "the superstitious natives believe [Europeans] to be sorcerers come to discover by magic, treasures which the Genii have concealed under the ruins."[20] He was amazed by the pigeons of Aleppo, which carried messages to Alexandria in just a few days. He listened to the songs of porters and sailors and poetic declamations, which might last two or three hours. The most celebrated dancers were in Cairo: "in the eastern world dancing is not an imitation of war, as among the Greeks, nor a combination of graceful attitudes and movements, as with us; but a licentious imitation of the utmost wantonness of love." The dance was taken to Spain by the Arabs, where it "still subsists there under the title of the *Fandango.*" They reminded him of the popular dances of the Paris winehouses. When the peasant Druze shared his last morsel with the hungry traveler, he said, "God is liberal and great, and all men are brethren."[21]

To Volney the workers were dupes of the priests. In Irish popular culture, this was challenged by the prophecies of the saints, St. Bridget, St. Columbe, Columcill. "Benevolence and good neighborhood will disappear"; "there will be neither abundance nor generosity, but want and penury"; "the powerful will oppress the poor with false law and perverted judgments"; "lying will overflow the country"; "all will be addicted to pilfering"; "the churls will be driven over the main." "Dismal, dark, melancholy, mournful, woeful days will come in the latter times. . . . Hard hearted avarice, penury, and impiety will prevail." "The stars will become red." Volney gives no credit to such inspiration and insight from below.

In Ireland, we witness popular mobilization for the cooperative production of subsistence, in a powerful political practice known as "hasty diggings." *The Northern Star,* the Belfast newspaper of the United Irish, reported that when William Orr of county Antrim was imprisoned, between five and six hundred of his neighbors assembled "and cut down his entire harvest before one o'clock on that day—and what is passing strange, and will, no doubt alarm *some* people, would accept of no compensation." The cooperative assemblies might reslate a roof or cut and carry in the summer hay. Three

20. Edward Said in *Orientalism* cautions us against a naïve reading of Volney, who assisted Napoleon's invasion of Egypt in 1798.

21. *Travels through Egypt,* 2:48.

thousand people assembled "and in the space of fourteen minutes and a half they carefully dug and covered up two acres and a half of potatoes—same time sowing and trenching the field with wheat. Whilst one party was thus employed, another, to the amount of several hundreds, built a barn, timbered and thatched it!" Generally, though, it was potatoes that were dug in these large, sober, assemblies of solidarity. Fifteen hundred people dug Samuel Neilson's potatoes "*in seven minutes.*" A thousand dug the potatoes of a jailed shoemaker; two hundred people dug "upwards of 400 bushels of potatoes" in two hours and fourteen minutes. These generous acts of cooperative labor were performed not just for political prisoners—"the Potatoes of three poor men, who are confined to bed with fevers, etc. were raised this week by large bodies of people assembled to pay this tribute to humanity"—though we distinguish "hasty diggings" from the many forms of *meitheal,* or cooperative labor, mutual aid, and seasonal reciprocities integral to rural Ireland.[22] The potato diggers sang this song:

> The time now is when frost severe
> Potatoe stalks nips low;
> Therefore, my lads, with hearty cheer,
>
> A digging let us go
> A digging let us go,
> A digging let us go,
> To show our love for those brave men
> Who to jail for Truth did go.
>
> Let Strife and Disagreement cease,
> And Union take their place;
> Let Truth and Virtue still increase,
> And bless those happy days –
>
> When a digging we do go, etc.

Against these displays of solidarity, the authorities, led by Lord Carhampton, proclaimed martial law in the counties of Tyrone, Derry, Antrim, Down, and Armagh. The dragoons and Orangemen were let loose to attack men and women in the fields, beating them up, forcing them to swear oaths of loyalty, and, for those who refused, confining them in offshore

22. O'Dowd, *Meitheal.*

tenders.[23] Robert's brother, Thomas Addis Emmet, wrote *Letters from the Mountains,* which appeared in Dublin in November 1797. "The country is under the reign of terror," he wrote, and heaped scorn on the government: "Under the auspices of a military government, the digging of potatoes has become high treason, the reaping of corn a felony of death."[24] The criminalization of the *meitheal.*

The Bishop of Dromore wrote the Lord Downshire, "I am told it has been discover'd that these assemblies of Men for what is called *Hasty Diggings,* are made by United Irishmen under the pretence, but with the further view of collecting in Bodies in order to know their own strength, & after the Digging is over they meet at night for the purpose of mustering, & even Drilling and Training." The digging was a blind, the bishop said. As proof of their disaffection the bishop noted that they marched "from one field to other two & two with all the regularity of drilled soldiers."[25]

Thomas Emmet believed that the creation of the Yeomanry was part of a dangerous experiment, namely, "to establish a smothered war, originating in a system of coercion, between the opulent and the poor of this country," to maintain good order and protect property while regular troops were used only to repel invaders. The government did nothing against death squads and village burnings. "The greatest part of Ireland groans under military execution. *Rapine, conflagration,* and *butchery,* rage without compassion or control."[26]

Volney was perhaps not so dangerous after all. He was a threat to organized religion but not to private property. He did not appeal to the actualities of the commons among the indigenous, the enslaved, the peasantry, or the artisans. On the contrary, as we shall find, these disgusted him as crime, as savagery, or as backwardness. Thomas Addis Emmet wrote, "I will add certain philosophical and speculative minds; that filled with abstract notions of freedom and smit with the charms of theoretical perfection in government, aim at a general participation of the Rights of Man, on the broad principles of the French Revolution."[27] Revolutionaries could not merely speculate or

---

23. A selection of reports of hasty diggings as reported in the *Northern Star* (September–November 1796) has been assembled by Brendan Clifford in *Prison Adverts and Potatoe Diggings.*

24. Emmet, *Memoir,* 2:416.

25. *Northern Star,* 5 November 1796, item 33, in Clifford, *Prison Averts.*

26. Emmet, *Memoir.*

27. *Letters from the Mountains,* letter 5, 412.

philosophize or submit to the charms of theory. United Irishmen to change society had to meet it on its own terms. And what were those? The oppression of a foreign power, the bigotry and prejudice of religion, the prohibition of cultural autonomy, and the exploitation by landlords over the peasantry produced social terms of a cultural and class nature.

In his sixth letter, Thomas Addis Emmet turned to "the lower classes of the people; the artisans and peasants" and "even the rude, the thoughtless and illiterate." The war has overwhelmed the land with wretchedness—"the perpetuated abuse, the prescriptive grievance; and the code written in blood, dictated by the exterminating spirit of an avenging demon." They grieved the loss of land 1) because of "the custom of casting lands and selling them at the highest penny, without any regard to the antient possessors"; 2) because tithes that were rigorously exacted discouraged improvements, and 3) because of the presence of middlemen and land jobbers serving absentees. "Goaded by misery, and irritated by contempt, they have proceeded to tumultuary risings and local outrage; from time to time, under the various denominations of white-boys, right-boys, oak-boys, hearts-of-steel, and defenders. The high price of lands—the low price of labour—the exaction of tithe-farmers, stood foremost in their catalogue of grievances."[28]

Especially strong voices of abolition emerged from the Celtic fringe. Morgan John Rhees, the Welsh bard, was a fervent abolitionist. Belfast refused to enter the slave trade, though it was integral to the Atlantic commerce. At the celebrated Belfast Academy at the end of the eighteenth century "were to be seen young lads of colour, sent, by their fathers, for education, both from the East and the West Indies, intermingled with the sons of the proudest gentry and nobility of the land."[29] "News and verse about slavery frequently appeared in *The Northern Star*." For instance, William Cowper's poem "The Negroes Complaint" appeared in the first issue, published on 2 January 1792. Thomas Russell's version of the poem, "The African's Complaint on Board a Slave Ship," removed the dialect. Denis Driscoll wrote in 1794 against slavery on behalf of the "persecuted sons of Africa." In 1802, he said "where slavery is practised, there real happiness cannot be." "SLAVERY IS ODIOUS WHEREVER IT IS PRACTISED."[30]

28. *Letters from the Mountains,* letter 6, 414.
29. Grimshaw, *Incidents Recalled,* 17.
30. Thuente, *Harp Re-strung,* 90, 92.

The Reverend James Coigly was imprisoned in Maidstone Gaol in May and June 1798. His *Address to the People of Ireland* concludes on a note of militant antislavery: "Behold the scourge of war, and all its evils, shall not be removed from their doors, until the shackles of bondmen and slaves are broken, and the oppressed delivered from their afflictions." To the Orangemen he asked, "Why have you rejected the glorious title of United Irishmen, to accept that of West-Indian Bloodhounds?," which refers to the notorious decision of the British military authorities in Jamaica to send to Cuba trained bloodhounds to track down the freedom fighters within inhospitable terrain of the Jamaican Cockpit country during the Trelawny Town maroon war of 1796. His identification of the Irish struggle with the Jamaican could not be more explicit.[31] According to Stewart Castlereagh, "A vast number of United Irishmen, transported from this Kingdom, have been landed there [Jamaica] and incautiously drafted into the regiments. . . . As soon as they got arms into their hands they deserted, and fled to the mountains, where they have been joined by large bodies of the natives and such of the French as were in the island. There have already been some engagements between this part and the King's troops; several have been killed and wounded on both sides."[32]

"The condition of the human race" was deeply affected by the Haitian revolutionary achievement, as Captain Rainsford said. Even in this excursus, we can distinguish four meanings of commons: 1) the common dish at the meal, 2) the action of collective labor on behalf of the politically disabled, 3) the equality that abolishes the gap between rich and poor, and 4) the emergency exigency of cooperation in war.

31. Keogh, *Patriot Priest*, 68–69.
32. Castlereagh, *Memoirs and Correspondence*, 2:417.

NINETEEN

A Spot in Time

THE CONSCIOUSNESS OF RACE AND CLASS DEVELOPED in relation to the mass and movement of human labor. We were struck by a coincidence in the elite and in the plebeian politics of England on 2 April 1792. The slave trade was almost abolished and the working class was almost made, and these happened almost on the same day. As Wordsworth might say, it was "a spot in time."

The House of Commons met on 2 April 1792 as a committee to debate a resolution proposed by Wilberforce "that it is the opinion of this committee that the trade carried on by British subjects, for the purpose of obtaining slaves on the coast of Africa, ought to be abolished."[1] Henry Dundas, the home secretary and a Scotsman, amended the resolution by inserting the word "gradually." Pitt's is the voice of perfidious Albion. *Gradually* became a term of defeat. It was the term used against the civil rights movement in the USA.[2]

The prime minister of England rose well after midnight to speak in favor of the original, unamended motion. He was fatigued. "That the greatest stigma on our national character which ever yet existed, is about to be removed! And, Sir, (which is still more important,) that mankind, I trust, in general, are now likely to be delivered from the greatest practical evil that ever has afflicted the human race—from the severest and most extensive calamity recorded in the history of the world!" He spoke a long time for immediate abolition of the slave trade. He wished to atone for the crime of the slave trade by practicing the new ideology of "improvement" in Africa.

1. Quoted in Linebaugh and Rediker, *Many-Headed Hydra*, 340.
2. John Lewis at the August 1963 March on Washington spoke of social revolution: "To those who have said, be patient and wait, we must say that we cannot be patient, we do not want to be free gradually." Forman, *Making of Black Revolutionaries*, 337.

Unto "the present dark, uncultivated, and uncivilized state of that continent," he wished to cast the light of civilization. In July 1968, Sir Robert Birley addressed Parliament, on the subject of *The Discovery of Africa: Some Lessons for Today,* in which he commented on Pitt's speech on the night of 2–3 April 1792. Pitt's speech "marked a turning-point in history; it raised in the most insistent way some questions that still face us today." That question was decolonization.[3]

On 2 April 1792, the London Corresponding Society issued its first address to the public. Edward Thompson, in *The Making of the English Working Class* (1963), sees it as the beginning of the working class in England: "In the 1790s something like an 'English Revolution' took place, of profound importance in shaping the consciousness of the post-war working class."[4] That shaping began when the artisans of London made contact with the workers of Sheffield, a contact made possible by Olaudah Equiano, Cugoano's associate, a leading abolitionist, and author. "In the decades after 1795 there was a profound alienation between classes in Britain, and working people were thrust into a state of apartheid whose effects . . . can be felt to this day." Apartheid was based on the doctrine of white supremacy, which had important origins in the 1790s.[5]

William Wordsworth described his arrival in London at the time in his autobiographical poem *The Prelude.* He encountered an expropriated woman uttering blasphemy.

> Saw woman as she is to open shame
> Abandoned, and the pride of public vice.
> Full surely from the bottom of my heart
> I shuddered, but the pain was almost lost,
> Absorbed and buried in the immensity
> Of the effect: a barrier seemed at once
> Thrown in, that from humanity divorced
> The human form, splitting the race of man
> In twain, yet leaving the same outward shape. (bk. 7, 418–20)

Prostitution, or the buying and selling of a woman, leads the poet to an insight, the splitting of the race of man. The phrase is echoed in Despard's

3. Hearnden, *Red Robert,* 51. He retired as head of Eton and went to South Africa in 1962, the year Mandela was jailed.
4. E. Thompson, *Making,* 177.
5. E. Thompson, *Making,* 177.

gallows speech. It hearkens to James White's three-fifth's clause of the US Constitution. He fractionates the body for politics. The English physician Charles White, in April 1794, fractionated the body for "science" when he began to measure the feet, limbs, breasts, and craniums of men at Liverpool's Lunatic Asylum and of women at Manchester's Lying-in Hospital.[6] Among white people, he measured a butler, gardener, footman, coachman, apothecary, and hairdresser—the servant class. Among black people, he examined a glazier from Ghana (Gold Coast), a cattleman from Jamaica, a dragoon from the West Indies Regiment, and a cattleman from Long Island. The human being was reified, or made into a thing, which Edmund Burke called human labor, the *instrumentum vocale,* in contrast to "the *semivocale* in the ancient classification, that is, the working stock of cattle, and the *instrumentum mutum,* such as carts, ploughs, spades, and so forth."[7] This is how humans were *split.* Ned and Kate were *not* split, and it was that unity that partly explained their danger to the Atlantic ruling class.

Wordsworth continues,

> We ... thought of each bright spot
> That could be found in all recorded time
> Of truth preserved and error passed away
> Of single spirits that catch the flame from Heaven,
> And how the multitude of men will feed
> And fan each other ... (bk. 9, 372–78)
> ... And finally, beheld
> A living confirmation of the whole
> Before us in a people risen up
> Fresh as the morning star. Elate we looked
> Upon their virtues, saw in rudest men
> Self-sacrifice the firmest, generous love
> And continence of mind, and sense of right
> Uppermost in the midst of fiercest strife. (bk. 9, 372–78, 389–96)

In the phrase, "a people risen up," we immediately conjure up the great revolutions of the era, such as the night of the Bois de Caïman on 22 August 1791, when the slaves of Santo Domingo inaugurated the struggle culminating in Haitian independence, or the assault on the Bastille in Paris on 14 July 1789, or the beginnings of working-class reform in England, or the risings that will culminate in Ireland in 1798. Wordsworth refers to historical moments of

6. C. White, *Account.*
7. Burke, *Thoughts and Details.*

honorable deeds, virtue made visible, still celebrated as holidays throughout the world.

Some lines later he elaborates the "spot of time," now not as history, but as biography.

> There are in our existence spots of time
> Which with distinct pre-eminence retain
> A vivifying virtue, (bk. 11, 257–72)

And he provides an example from his childhood. A spot of time is also a spot on earth, on a commons, on a terrifying place of the commons. Separated from his guide, he became lost at a terrible place, where a murderer had been hanged in a gibbet of iron chains:

> Forthwith I left the spot
> And reascending the bare common saw
> A naked pool that lay beneath the hills,
> The beacon on the summit, and more near,
> A girl with a pitcher on her head
> And seemed with difficult steps to force her way
> Against the blowing wind. (bk. 11, 301–7)

The spot of time is also a spot on earth, a particular place on the commons. Time and space are conflated. These are the two images of great power: the hanging of a murderer and a girl with a pitcher on her head, who, when brought into relationship with each other are images of immense tension. The moment of terror and sustenance was sublime, and its recollection provided Wordsworth's spirit with power for the rest of his life.

The April 1792 historical spot in time was also sublime insofar as it compressed a contradiction. The contradiction was expressed in the technology of the new death machine, the guillotine, which combined "reason" with death. The first victim, a highway robber, suffered under the guillotine in April 1792. The contradiction was expressed on 2 April 1792, when Washington signed the congressional bill establishing the US Mint, whose coins were prescribed to display a device: "Upon one side . . . there shall be an impression emblematic of liberty."[8] On 4 April 1792, the National Assembly declared, "the *hommes de couleur* and the *negres libres* must enjoy along with the white *colon,* equality of political rights." "In the heart of the slave societies

8. Stack, *United States Type Coins,* 2.

of the Americas, legal distinctions on the basis of race were outlawed. . . . The slave insurgents of Saint-Domingue had expanded the political horizon in a paradoxical way, making it necessary to grant racial equality in order to save slavery."[9]

In addition to involving terror, Wordsworth's childhood spot of time includes the nourishing image of the girl with a pitcher of water on her head. Jacques Roumain, in the national novel of Haiti *Masters of the Dew* (1947), describes the *negresse:* "When she came out of the stream, cool bracelets ripple from her legs. She places the gourds in a wicker basket that she placed on her head." "Formerly the water had flowed freely there in the sun, its rippling and its light mingling like the soft laughter of cutting knives . . . In those days when they had all lived in harmony, united as the fingers of the hand, they had assembled all the neighborhood in collective *coumbites* for the harvest or the clearing."[10] In Goethe's *The Sorrows of Young Werther* (1774), the novel that swept the revolutionary bourgeoisie of late eighteenth-century Germany, there is a young servant girl at a spring, who could not lift the water jar to her head. "'Let's not stand on ceremony,' I said. She adjusted the pad on her head, I helped her with her pitcher, she thanked me, and up she went!" This transgression of age, class, and gender boundaries provided an allegory of the revolutionary epoch, both egalitarian and biblical. "'Sir,' the Samaritan woman said, 'you have no bucket and this well is deep. How can you give me living water?' (John 4:11). Jesus offers spiritual sustenance, and the Samaritan woman offers water. The resources are common, and the ideology is egalitarian.

9. Dubois, *Avengers*, 130–31.
10. Roumain, *Masters of the Dew*.

TWENTY

Their Son

JANE DESPARD DESCRIBED CATHERINE DESPARD THIS WAY: "She was one of a train of black servants he brought over with him and maintained at a hotel in London, for, like his father, he thought his pocket had no bottom." Jane treated her as a servant, though they were married. Elizabeth Despard wrote about her this way: "The Negro woman who first lived with him as his housekeeper never could have inflamed a mind like his, and it is likely that it was her fidelity to him in every situation and to the last that engaged his confidence and his affections."[1] The nieces give us clues to Ned and Kate's material circumstances. The phrase "a pocket with no bottom" might issue from selfish exaggeration, or describe a man willing to risk debt for his family's sake. "A mind inflamed" is not the only hint at the passion shared by Ned and Kate; Nelson would say that she was "violently in love" with Ned. That one niece describes Kate as "Negro" and the other niece describes her as "black" may or may not be significant during a time when in white supremacist usage of the time "black" included lascars, or South Asians.

In the spring of 1790, Ned and Kate crossed the Atlantic for England, for him a return and for her a new destination. They avoided the West Indian hurricane season and the winter gales of European waters. They waded the surf to enter a longboat, which rowed them out to deeper waters, where a sailing ship anchored. In Jamaica, they re-embarked on a transatlantic vessel. Accompanying them was their son, John Edward, a child at the time. James Bannantine, his secretary, joined the entourage, and, if we credit family memory, "a train of black servants" accompanied them.

1. J. Despard, "Memoranda," 54; E. Despard, "Recollections," 22.

We can only imagine what the voyage was like. Did Ned sleep in bed or hammock? Was he tended for fever? After Despard's death, some who knew him claimed that he suffered from a disease (malaria?) contracted in tropical America. Was Kate's care work shared by others—perhaps a servant? Did he obtain information about the French Revolution from others sailing on the vessel? What books did they read? They had large, interesting crews. The warm waters of the Gulf Stream carried them northward, parallel to the mainland coast, before swerving east, south of Iceland, to Ireland and Britain.

Besides crossing the ocean, they were crossing invisible lines of longitude and latitude. These were fictive and recently manmade. He as an Anglo-Irishman and she as an African American were also crossing the color line. Unlike the coordinates that took their bearing from the stars, the color line referred to skin tones at a time when the theory of color still played a role in alchemy and its search for gold and the transformation of the soul. In a year when tens of thousands traversed the Middle Passage, in conditions of extreme cruelty, to be sold as property to planters, the color line was drawn deep in response to the resistance and frequent revolts of Africans on board ship and ashore. It became integral to the search for gold and to the destruction of the soul. Although alchemy was giving way to chemistry, color was still a marker signifying wealth and domination.

As Wordsworth described it,

> ... a barrier seemed at once
> Thrown in, that from humanity divorced
> The human form, splitting the race of man
> In twain. (*Prelude,* bk. 7, lines 424–27)

What was "humanity"? "We hold these truths to be self-evident, that all men are created equal, that they are endowed by their Creator with certain unalienable Rights, that among these are Life, Liberty and the pursuit of Happiness." Such truths indeed set in motion events in France that would topple the ancien régime and nearly do the same in Ireland. That was inspirational in 1776 but by 1787, the author of these lines had changed his tune. He wrote, "Whether originally a distinct race, or made distinct by time and circumstances [black people] are inferior to the whites in the endowments both of body and mind." Jefferson described black people as disagreeable in odor, inferior in beauty, wanting forethought, dull in imagination, and existing in sensation rather than reflection. These differences expressed a politics. These "real distinctions which nature has made" will produce convulsions, Jefferson wrote, that will end "in the extermination of one or the other race." The auction block, the coffle, and the whip put paid to life, liberty, and the pursuit of happiness. They were directly contrary to the inalienable rights. Black people were alienable in all three respects: *lives* were bought and sold on the auction block; *liberty* was enchained on wrists, ankles and necks; and the *pursuit of happiness* had the whip at the back and blood hounds at the heel.[2]

Ideologically, one of the color line's most fervent expressions was found in the only book that Thomas Jefferson ever published, *Notes on the State of Virginia*. Jefferson's *Notes* joined Edward Long's *History of Jamaica* (1774) as vicious screeds of white supremacy, which did not prevent them from becoming seeds of "scientific racism." For Jefferson you had to be either white or black—mixing was forbidden. The racial bifurcation of people supported enslavement, anticipated his antagonism against Saint Domingue, and prepared him for the vast expansion of slave territory, even while in his person he copulated with/raped Sally Hemings.

Yet witnesses attest to the mixed-race characteristics of his plantation people. He himself sired children on the body of Sally Hemings, who was herself a mixed-race slave. She sailed to Paris in 1787 to join Jefferson's household, and stayed until December 1789, a few months before Ned and Kate voyaged in the opposite direction. She was present at the time and in the city of revolutionary popular sovereignty: the Tennis Court Oath, the storming of the Bastille, the abolition of feudal dues, the march of the women on Versailles. Sally Hemings bore between five and seven children.[3] One of them at least was probably fathered by Jefferson, according to James Callender writing in September 1802.

Little more is known about Sally Hemings than is known about Kate Despard. Sally Hemings was born in 1773 and became one of Jefferson's two hundred slaves on his plantation in Monticello. Her relationship to Jefferson was scandalous not so much because it was a master-slave relation with its inherent violence, including rape, but because it flew in the face of Jefferson's belief that blacks and whites should not mix, despite its widespread practice

2. Thomas Jefferson, *Notes on the State of Virginia*, query 14.
3. Lewis and Onuf, *Sally Hemings*.

throughout the American South and the British Caribbean.[4] According to Jefferson, "No man will labour for himself who can make another labour for him." There is the basis of the color line! It distinguishes those who labor from those who don't. "The whole commerce between master and slave is a perpetual exercise of the most boisterous passions, the most unremitting despotism on the one part, and degrading submission on the other," Jefferson wrote.[5] The observation applies with minor modification to the commerce between master and servant. Forelock-tugging deference to "the quality" was early taught at the end of the rod. Social cringing was maintained by the lash in the army and navy and by the gallows for the rest held *in terrorem*.

These were years of Atlantic-wide political re-alignment and economic re-structuring.[6] The potential link between the white working class of England and the black slaves of the Caribbean, mediated by Irish workers, threatened power, not just in its (historically) temporary forms—monarchy, republic, federal, "united"—but with respect to the economic mode of production at its base. The London riots in June 1780 displayed this danger in an insurrectionary form when Benjamin Bowsey and John Glover, both former African American slaves, led the break in of Newgate prison in London. In 1783, another African American former slave, Olaudah Equiano, brought to the attention of the leading English abolitionist, Granville Sharpe, the horrifying news that in November 1781, Luke Collingwood, the captain of the slave ship *Zong*, owned by a Liverpool banker, had deliberately thrown 133 slaves overboard to drown in the ocean in order to collect the insurance. The court awarded the owners thirty pounds for each murdered person. These two events—the *Zong* massacre and the delivery of Newgate—determined the terms of the struggle for the next decade: mass racial murder, on the one hand, or multiracial liberation, on the other. The former crime was never far from the mind of the abolitionist struggle, and the latter was nearly always present among the fears of the propertied.

While English riches derived from slave labor, England itself was not directly a slave society, yet here too the color line was being drawn. Kate had

---

4. James Callender himself had advocated for the independence of Scotland in his book *The Political Progress of Britain* (1792). He described Britain as a war-making machine and "a conspiracy of the rich against the poor." With the help of the London Corresponding Society and the Dublin United Irishmen, he escaped Scotland for Philadelphia and later was imprisoned under the Alien and Sedition Acts (1798). Durey, *"With the Hammer."*

5. Jefferson, *Notes on the State of Virginia*, query 14.

6. Sinha, *Slave's Cause*, 122.

to deal with it on arrival in England in the spring of 1790. We can learn about it from Ottobah Cugoano, born in Ghana and a former slave in Grenada, who in 1787 London published *Thoughts and Sentiments on the Evil and Wicked Traffic of the Slavery and Commerce of the Human Species*. "But why should total abolition, and an universal emancipation of slaves, and the enfranchisement of all the Black People employed in the culture of the Colonies, taking place as it ought to do, and without any hesitation, or delay for a moment?"[7] Cugoano was the first African in England to call for the immediate abolition of the slave trade. He linked racial slavery to its roots in imperialist ambition and capitalist accumulation. The African may boast greater liberty than the English, he wrote, because in Africa the commons with its inherent mutuality is primary, "for the poorest amongst us are never in distress for want."[8] His was the strongest and longest denunciation of racial slavery ever written, as well as the first abolitionist book published by an African. The different colors and complexions are no more unbecoming, Ottobah Cugoano wrote, "than the different shades of the rainbow are unseemly to the whole." Ned and Kate were the avatars of the rainbow coalition. Cugoano wrote without a trace of servility, and with utter command of biblical texts. In the vocative voice of Jude or Amos, and addressing his readers as "beloved," Cugoano appealed directly to people such as Despard: "But wherefore, O beloved, should your watchmen sit still, when they hear tell that the enemy is invading all the out-posts and camp of the British empire, where many of your dwellings are? Are they all fallen asleep, and lying down to slumber in assimilation of the workers of iniquity? Should not those who are awake, arise, and give alarm, that others may arise and awake also?"[9]

Catherine arrived in the aftermath of the Gordon Riots. The working-class composition in London was composed, broadly speaking, of servants, craftsmen, sailors, and slaves. They showed themselves 1) as the "mob," or relatedly as the criminal underworld; 2) as loose and disorderly persons; 3) as "freeborn Englishmen"; 4) as members of a confusing welter of Christian sects and storefront churches; and 5) as the population that made up the common life of the town—a bustling market, widespread public houses, and intense street traffic.

7. Sinha, *Slave's Cause*, 91.
8. Sinha, 103.
9. Cugoano, *Thoughts and Sentiments*, 41, 94.

The term *mob* described two things: on the one hand, the frequent public assembly of those who were ready to take direct action to redress grievances. This mob could be manipulated or bought by politicians. On the other hand, as with the Gordon Riots, the gathering could ignite into insurrectionary conflagration. The term itself is a shortened version of *mobility*, which takes us to a second reality of the working class in London. Its working conditions were not stationary. This was obviously true of porters, sailors, carters, and coach drivers, as well as, increasingly, craftworkers, whose skills were devalued.

The love between Ned and Kate—eros—resulted in a son. Eros, however, did not cavort Cupidlike in pure delight. Eros was dragged down by *meum et tuum,* that is, property, whose legal and matrimonial expression—to have and to hold—was identical to the marriage vows. The range of possible liaisons was changing. In September 1791, a butcher's daughter named Olympe de Gouges issued a declaration of the rights of women in Paris. On behalf of the sex that is superior in beauty and courage, she abandoned the patronymic and property basis of marriage. In her "social contract between man and woman," she asserted that all children have the right to bear the names of their fathers and that their wealth becomes "communal property."

The "making" of a child and the "making" of that class of people forced to labor for others are related by the concept of reproduction. In this era of enclosures, the population explosion, which was an abstract demographic fact, increased the numbers available for labor. A common place of eighteenth-century statecraft and mercantilist policy held that the foundation of the state rested on a multitude of inhabitants for agriculture, manufactures, and war. Who else would till the field, turn the wheel, or wield the sword? Obstetricians were taught that poor women, stereotyped as "hardy Scots," "wild Irish," "doxies," or "women of the town," were especially suitable for this work, unlike dainty upper-class bodies.[10] They were true proletarians

Numbers do not tell the whole story, because the issue is not "population" but available labor power. Enclosure released labor power; prison disciplined it. Prisons were as necessary as "breeding" or immigration or the slave trade. Furthermore, the working class was divided within itself. New divisions of race and nation were added to older divisions—religion, country versus city, gender, and age. Workers were of woman born. Her labors of pregnancy, parturition, nursing, infant care, socialization, and acculturation—or what

10. J. Lawless, "Images of 'Poor' Women."

in animal husbandry is called "breeding"—were essential prerequisites to the making of the class of workers. This was *ektrophe* rather than *eros*.

William Bollan's *Britannia Libera* (1772) argues against mixed marriage, "to prevent Britannia's pure and noble blood from being polluted by the multiplicity of those conjunctions which produce such a motley disagreeable race."[11] In summer 1802, William Cobbett, England's most voluminous journalist, published lurid expressions of racial supremacy. A mutiny among the black soldiers of a West Indian regiment on the Caribbean island of Dominica provoked him to say that negroes should not be "put upon a level with white men, even as musicians and drummers." He found it "truly shocking to see the number of English women married to Negroes," calling it "Negromania." He wanted to find "some means to put a stop to the increase of Blacks in this country, at any rate, where they have made no little progress in changing the color of the inhabitants."[12] It is important to remember how this train of thought began, because its origin colors the conclusion. Racist bigotry began as a response to the mob or working-class rebellion. In January 1808, C. S. Sonnini published a critique of physical racism titled "On the Varieties in the Human Species." "The augmentation of population in some parts, the spirit of inquietude and agitation, the madness of conquests, the violence of invasion, and force of voluntary migrations, have all concurred to intermingle the races; room has been given in the great family of human nature for ancient alliances which have challenged the physiognomy of nations, and confounded their features."[13]

The 1787 struggle to establish a regime of institutionalized white supremacy in Honduras took place in a broader context of racist ideology. This was the year Thomas Clarkson was nearly assassinated in Liverpool by slavers, who wanted to stop his investigation into the nautical organization of the slave trade. He published *A Summary View of the Slave Trade* that year, when he also visited two reformers of Manchester, Thomas Cooper and Thomas Walker, who were beginning to link slave emancipation and the working-class movement in England. "The idea of abolishing the slave trade," said an aristocrat with a long historical memory, "is connected with the levelling system and the rights of man."[14] Also in 1787, the Society for the Abolition of the Slave Trade was formed in London, and in the following year, William

11. *Britannia Libera*, 47.
12. *Cobbett's Political Register*, 12 June 1802.
13. *The Irish Magazine and Monthly Asylum for Neglected Biography*, January 1808.
14. Fryer, *Staying Power*, 210–11.

Dolben's bill regulating overcrowding on slave ships was passed. A boycott of sugar and mass petitioning of Parliament soon became novel means of popular agitation. Ned and Kate arrived in London at the same time that Vincent Ogé, having returned to Haiti after arguing before the Paris revolutionary national assembly for the abolition of slavery in Haiti, visited Thomas Clarkson in London. Ned and Kate made brave decisions—to have a child and to return with it to Europe. Both acts violated the emerging color lines and tell us that their relationship was no ordinary one between an English imperialist and a colonial mistress, dumped before the former returned to the metropolis. To violate the color line in this way was also to challenge the class relationship.

By 1787, the planters of the American South, as were those in Honduras, were intent on constructing a racist government of white power. That summer, planters and merchants in America met in a constitutional convention to form that government. Their extraordinary solution was, first, to square the circle by counting each slave as three-fifths of a human being and, second, to permit slavery in the southwest while prohibiting it in the northwest (Ohio, Illinois, Michigan, Indiana, and Wisconsin). These provisions accounting for slavery without mentioning it were part of a constitution intended to protect all kinds of property and prevent any formation of commons. For as Jefferson wrote, "In a warm climate, no man will labour for himself who can make another labour for him." For him, racism was linked to class.

This was the historical context of Despard's struggle in Belize. Racism and slavery were at stake in a transatlantic struggle. The supply of labor was threatened by the prospect of the abolition of the transatlantic slave trade. With the growth of that threat, slave owners tended toward an "internal slave trade," or the reproduction of slaves on and among the plantations. This too met fundamental resistance having profound consequences for slaves and for women (whether slave or free) everywhere. Rape was inherent in the social relations of slavery, with the lascivious creole woman becoming a stereotype to the master class. In partial defense, women preserved and treasured a knowledge of birth control.

For the English feminist Mary Wollstonecraft, 1787 was also important. That year, she left England to become a servant to an aristocratic family in Ireland, joining one of the most numerous categories of workers in English society. As a servant in Ireland, she was part of an oppressed society that in the geopolitical world was a reservoir, or warehouse, of labor—seasonal, annual, or forever. As a woman of eighteenth-century England, her patriotic destiny was pregnancy and childbirth. Cugoano called such people as the ascendant English in Ireland "colonians." In the context of state population policy, which was to encourage births in every way, Mary Wollstonecraft sought a destiny that was not dependent on "biology." That year, she completed her novel *Maria—a Fiction,* whose closing words tell us that Maria was "hastening to that world where there is neither marrying, nor giving in marriage." From Ireland as a live-in servant, she called for what amounted to the abolition of the habendum clause. She wrote her sister, "I am . . . going to be the first of a new genus—I tremble at the attempt."[15] Etymologically associated with birth, and also associated with the new science of biology, the classification she chose—genus—was a powerful one below that of family and above that of species. Specifically, she decided to work as a writer for the publisher Joseph Johnson, an economic exchange that might make her independent. No wonder she trembled.

Policies or views toward sexuality culminated at one extreme in the cruelties of absolute power and at another extreme in the utilitarian duty to renew the nation's labor powers. There is a continuum between sexual pleasure obtained by painful degradation on the one hand and patriotic duty served by fecundity for economic growth on the other. The one was expressed by the Marquis de Sade and the other by Thomas Malthus, both in 1802. London contained fifty thousand prostitutes, fully one tenth of its population. William Wilberforce obtained a Royal Proclamation against Vice and Immorality and promoted the Vice Society and overall prudery. This was the atmosphere of gender relations and racial life, at least as encouraged by the rulers of society, that faced Ned, Kate, and their son on arriving in England. "The Eternal Female groaned!" William Blake sang in his Song of Liberty.

In September 1787, after a hurricane, one of the Baymen in Honduras wrote Despard offering to help "contribute to your ease and comfort of your family in these distressing times."[16] When Despard petitioned Parliament in February 1799 requesting examination before the House concerning the conditions of his imprisonment, he said "that the affairs of his family are

15. Wollstonecraft, *Collected Letters,* 164.
16. E.M. Despard, Appendix to the Narrative of Publick Transactions in the Bay of Honduras, 1784–1790, NA, CO 123/11.

entirely ruined by his long confinement."[17] Ned referred to Kate's son as his son. In particular, he stated to them "that within this month his son who had come a great distance to see him, was refused admittance."[18]

In their family histories, Despard's nieces question the paternity of Kate's son, which is in line with the mercenary motives on display in their writings. Jane asserted that, while Despard *did* permit the boy to take his name, when his son claimed support, his uncles denied him, saying "he had not even an illegitimate claim."[19] Property relations were supreme. Elizabeth Despard wrote, "Her son was born long before they met and was the child of an officer, an ensign (an Irishman) in the 18th. I regret much having forgotten his name which Uncle Andrew told me, and as he was in the same Regiment with his brother, he could hardly have been mistaken."[20] Jane says that he was sent to Paris in 1802 at the Peace of Amiens but he did not support Bonaparte and so returned to live "in the neighborhood of Cambridge," so she heard. He ran away with a lady of fortune from a boarding school, "a flashy creole," a conventional plot of abduction, especially towards Irishmen. The London *Times* reported that the funeral of his father was delayed to 1 March so that the son, "of respectable character and has been in Paris about three months, with his wife" could be present. The *Times* described him as an Ensign in Ireland who had been left "a comfortable maintenance by his grandfather."[21]

John Edward Despard is named as a captain in the Royal East London Regiment of Militia, which was disembodied in February 1816. He led a company of soldiers and was billeted in stationary quarters with an allowance of eleven pounds, fourteen shillings a month. In 1820, he was listed as a quartermaster.[22] He was a figure worthy of Stendhal or Dickens, and a man of two cities—Paris and London. As a captain of militia in London's East End, his life was amid the ragged people living in the slums of the docklands, again like his father.

Cugoano served in the household of the painter Richard Cosway, and in that artistic setting William Blake came into contact with this African

17. *Parliamentary History*, vol. 34.
18. Henry Burdett Papers, MS English History, c. 296, folio pages 9–11, Bodleian Library, University of Oxford.
19. J. Despard, "Memoranda."
20. E. Despard, "Recollections," 23.
21. *Times*, 28 February 1803.
22. NA, WO 13/1369.

FIGURE 11. *Joanna,* the wife in Surinam of Captain John Steadman, 1770s. Illustration by John Gabriel Stedman in his *Narrative of a Five Years Expedition against the Revolted Negroes of Surinam* (London).

prophet of abolition. He was not the only person Blake may have relied on for knowledge of the racial slavery of America. Blake made the engravings for Captain Steadman's watercolors, which depict his years of fighting the slave revolt in Surinam. The engravings became part of a book published by Joseph Johnson. His familiarity with the unexpurgated journal gave him full details of his relationship with Joanna, a slave. Captain Steadman and Joanna had a son. Where their story differs from Despard's is that Steadman obeyed the racist practice among the slave owners and refused to bring Joanna with him when he returned to Europe. Their son grew up to live neither in America nor England but in the Royal Navy, where he died.

William Blake's visionary and prophetic power arose from an urban optics that compressed sexual desire, antinomian thinking, and historical remnants with an Atlantic scope. In 1793, William Blake published two long poems about America, which poetically express the lurking ruling-class fear of an alliance between the African American slave and the white working class in England. At the same time, and for all time, they show that such an alliance made possible a manifold of liberation. On the one hand, "Let the slave grinding at the mill run out into the field." On the other hand, "Let the inchained soul shut up in darkness and in sighing . . . rise and look out." As prisoner and slave burst their bonds and bars, the wife and children are freed from the oppressor's scourge. In the prophetic poem *America,* Blake describes the image of God dwelling in Africa, while the higher power, Urizen ("your reason"), who perverts thinking into calculation, is described as pale and "all over white." "Pale religious letchery" represses the revolutionary spirit, which therefore becomes antinomian: the "stony law I stamp to dust, and scatter religion abroad."[23] Cugoano adhered to the revolutionary theological doctrine called "the everlasting gospel," which had inspired the seventeenth-century Levellers and Diggers, as well as William Blake.

Blake's poem *Visions of the Daughters of Albion* tells the story of a rape and the resulting paternity dispute. It is also an allegory of transatlantic oppression.[24] Oothoon, a female slave, is raped and impregnated by Bromion, a thunderous slave master. As one of "the swarthy children of the sun" she is possessively stamped with his signet. Bromion commands Theotormon, a subaltern of some kind, either a slave or a worker in England, to marry her and protect her child. He refuses. The rest of the poem consists of arguments between Theotormon and her, as the choral-like daughters of Albion (the Roman name for England) weep to the side. Blake moves quickly to an inspired attack on the dominant ideology that is composed of equal parts religious repression and empiricist abstraction. Theotormon prefers to remain in pious sorrow adhering to a single law based on enclosure:

23. Blake, *Poetry and Prose,* 203.
24. Erdman, *Blake: Prophet against Empire,* chapter 10.

> They told me I had five senses to inclose me up,
> And they inclos'd my infinite brain into a narrow circle
> And sunk my heart into the Abyss, a red round globe hot burning
> Till all from life I was obliterated and erased.[25]

The limited knowledge of the five senses leads to narrow-minded thinking without even the proprioceptive and vestibular knowledge arising from the motions and balance of life.

Oothoon poetically depicts the existing economic and religious orders as contrary to the solar system and to creatures of the world. Both the spirit of possession and the mercantilist spirit oppose generosity and mutualism. The principle of infinite love is her alternative to enclosure. Her erotic energy evolves into a divinelike love of all creation as she enunciates the pleasure principle in her pleas to him. The moment of erotic desire can succeed against the "shadow wailing on the margin of non-entity." Both "slaves beneath the sun and children bought with money," that is, slave labor in America and child labor in England, suffer from the failure of Theotormon to accept Oothoon.[26] That failure is the failure to link directly the energies of the slave revolt begun in San Domingue, where the swarthy children of the sun rise against Bromion, their oppressor, with the beginnings of the political organization of the working-class in England.

Blake did not write an allegory of Ned and Kate. He created a dynamic myth from the binaries of slavery and freedom, black and white, male and female. Just as we distrust the nieces when they dispute the paternity of Ned and Kate's son, we must doubt Elizabeth Despard's veracity when she opines that Kate could never have "inflamed" a mind like Ned's. They fled a continent where a huge slave resistance had taken place during the American War of Independence and where another one was about to occur.

The nature of their love is of that between a man and a woman, or eros; it is between two people from different British colonies. Their story is one of cooperation between equals, or philia, and between them and their kind, which at the end embraced the human race, or *agape*. Eros, philia, and *agape* propel the commons; they form the basis of community. With the expropriation of the commons, all three forms of love became alienated: *eros* as prostitution and pornography; *philia* as exploitation, not cooperation; and *agape* as

---

25. In *Poetry and Prose,* 196.
26. *Poetry and Prose,* 195.

associated with empire. In keeping with this Greek classification of love as eros, philia, and agape, we make a quartet by adding *ektrophe,* signifying calculated, mercenary breeding and the political science of reproduction. Population policy and property management became its foundations. *Ektrophe* stands in for the Malthusian purpose and manner of calculations of life and death. It includes prostitution and marriage. Beside the abortion law of 1803 is de Sade's publication in the same year of his applications of the principles of the Code Noir to sexual relations. That and Malthus provide the contrast to what Ned and Kate were up to.

G

ENGLAND

TWENTY-ONE

"A System of Man-Eaters"

WE DESCRIBED IN "ATLANTIC MOUNTAINS" three colonial geographies of Despard and the commons, namely, Ireland, America, and Haiti. In this and the next three chapters, we return to England, where Ned and Kate embarked on a revolutionary project with its woeful termination. England was ruled by landlords of both an aristocratic kind, with military pride, and a bourgeois kind intent on profit and rent. Enclosure of land and the abolition of commons became part and parcel of the conquest of other countries. Thus empire and privatization went hand in hand. Ned and Kate returned to a decade of counterrevolution against the principles of *liberté, égalité,* and *fraternité.* The present chapter describes the systematic worldwide violence led by William Pitt, prime minister of England. The next approaches the commons from the standpoint of an animal, the goose. "The Den of Thieves" examines a single act of enclosure in Enfield that transpired at the time of Despard's plot. "Commons or True Commons" concludes with a direct examination of what "the commons" meant to the reformer and common people during the 1790s and, to employ a geological metaphor, how the sedimentary rock of English resistance now confronted explosive igneous rock from the Atlantic mountains.

Inspired by the American Revolution, calloused by the brutal repression of the Gordon Riots, starved by the high prices of bread, experienced in crowds of redress, increasingly enclosed by field and factory, quickened with hopes by news of popular mobilization in Paris, the common people of London during the first half of the 1790s assembled in the open fields of the north, west, and south of London. Copenhagen Fields, St. George's Fields, Marylebone Fields, Tothill Fields—these were the commons of popular mobilization, where people learned from one another, protested, petitioned, and demonstrated such popular power that a humble engraver (Blake) might actually envision the slave grinding at the mill running away or the chained soul shut in darkness bursting his bonds. Government's answer to popular mobilization was mobilization for war. In Blake's terms, Bromion intervened to prevent the woman and the man, the slave and the artisan, from creating a commons.

John Emblin, a watchmaker by trade, was among those arrested with Despard at the Oakley Arms on 16 November 1802. He called the government *"the Man Eaters,"* an expression that in the printed text of the trial was emphasized by italics, and which was brought up again in the sentencing address by Lord Ellenborough, in which he accused them of seeking to extinguish and annihilate the legitimate government by calling it *"a system of man eaters."*[1] What did he mean by a system? What did he mean by a system of man-eaters? Emblin meant war. The "system" was an acquisitive, bellicose state, whose raison d'être was the development and provision of the power to kill its enemies. At its core was the army and navy. Two quotations, one by the Tory Henry Dundas and the other by city money men, summarize its imperial, global ambition.

Henry Dundas (1742–1811), a Scotsman, a Tory, a scourge of radicals, and an ally of the slave trade, left the Home Office to become secretary of war in 1794. He wrote, "By our commerce and our fleet, we have been enabled to perform those prodigies of exertion which have placed us in the proud state of pre-eminence we now hold."[2] In 1803, the merchants, bankers, and traders of the city of London declared their loyalty to the Crown in these terms, "We fight for that Constitution and System of Society which is at once the noblest Monument and the firmest Bulwark of Civilization! We fight to preserve the *whole Earth* from the barbarous Yoke of military Despotism!"[3] The merchant fleet and the Royal Navy grew by a factor of eight once war began. After Louis XVI was guillotined in January 1793, war was declared against France and the principles of its revolution, *liberté, égalité,* and *fraternité.* Dundas personally profited at the Admiralty (1802) and was impeached for corruption.

The regime was led by globalizers, and blood and fire followed them—"red round globe hot burning." The theaters of war were worldwide. For English

1. *Trial of Edward Marcus Despard,* 123, 265.
2. Cobbett, *Parliamentary History,* vol. 35, columns 1072–73.
3. Klingberg and Hustvedt, *Warning Drum,* 127.

arms, they were Flanders, the Caribbean, the Ohio Valley, India, and then the Mediterranean, Egypt, and South Africa. In 1794, the campaigns in Flanders commanded by the king's son, the duke of York, were disastrous. Flanders was a point on the coast of continental Europe, from which an invasion of England could be launched. It was considered essential to the balance of power, a key principle of English diplomacy. The soldiers in Flanders were untrained, undisciplined, dirty, diseased, and unshod. English armies retreated from "a bleak winter and a hostile land." War was capitalism's delivery system, soldiers being one of its commodities.

Perhaps John Emblin, watchmaker, had listened to Thelwall speaking on 26 October 1795, at one of the huge meetings in Copenhagen Fields. "It is not the crimp, it is not the baker, a miller or a malster, no nor even a few disperate and avaricious monopolizers—those are not the authors of your sufferings. . . . It is the system that you must reform."[4] William Godwin named the system as follows: "Property is that which occupies the most vigilant attention in the civilized states of Europe. It is a system, in whatever manner established, by which one man enters into the faculty of disposing of the produce of another man's industry."[5]

Clausewitz, the classic military theorist, studied this war systematically. Populousness had acquired a military significance. The 1801 census helped define the manpower reserves. Armies were larger in his time, and the troops were no longer feudal levies but mercenaries. Armies could not live off the land, at least not at home. It was better to fight on enemy soil, and armies had to keep moving. Provisioning by requisition was a necessary evil, and was possible only with limited numbers of troops. Otherwise government had to organize supply. "Nourished often by only a meager crust of bread, soldiers tottered about like shadows." A horse's rations weighed ten times that of a man—poorly clad, thirty or forty pounds on his back, plodding along for days in every kind of weather, endangering his health and life without a crust to nourish him.[6]

War was a huge consumer of manpower (this is why people called government "a system of man-eaters"), and government began to plan policy with this knowledge in mind. In 1800, the first national census was taken; in 1798, Malthus began to publish his studies of birth and deaths. Soldiering was a

4. Wells, *Wretched Faces*.
5. Godwin, *Enquiry concerning Political Justice*, 710–11.
6. Clausewitz, *On War*, 331, 339.

sentence regarded as severe as hanging. While Adam Smith described it as "the noblest of all arts," it was no longer skilled work. Its central requirement was obedience. "Regularity, order, and prompt obedience to command are qualities which, in modern armies, are of more importance towards determining the fate of battles than the dexterity and skill of the soldiers in the use of their arms," he wrote.[7]

The population policy of the European mercantilist state was to produce soldiers. The century of incessant war between England and France and between England and its colonies was the work of soldiering, a craft with its own distinctive tools, language, and organization. And it was the work of sailors. The navy depended on compulsory labor; at least half of its men were impressed. After 1795, the Quota Acts put the manning of the navy into the hands of magistrates.[8] The soldier was a wage laborer, as was the sailor. In this context, William Cobbett's *Soldier's Friend* (1792) is significant in demanding simply the wage of sixpence a day. The soldiers were trained to destruction, to kill. "Tush, man, mortal man, mortal man," said Falstaff, quietly adding, "I had most of them out of prison" (Henry IV, pt. 1, act 4, scene 2). Recruitment was by conscription, impressment, or crimping.

The state mobilized the population; the entire economy was affected. Cornwallis in August 1796 originated the mass mobilization of the armed nation. In 1798, 116,000 volunteered; in 1801, the volunteer establishment increased to 146,000; by the end of 1803, the number of volunteers had more than doubled to 380,000. The Defense Act of 1803 defined "military age" to be between seventeen and fifty-five. Total mobilization in 1801 neared half a million. Military forces included, besides the army, the militia, the volunteers, the yeomanry, and the fencibles (with the same etymological derivation as fence). These were attempts to mobilize the civilian property holders.

Opposition to the war was widespread. William Frend, a mathematics instructor at Jesus College, Cambridge, and a Unitarian, was tried and fired by the university for writing and publishing an antiwar pamphlet.[9] He published it in the week after the execution of Louis XVI and a week before England's declaration of war against France:

> Three days after the debate on the king's message, I was walking from my friend's house to the neighbouring town to inspect the printing of these few

7. *Wealth of Nations,* 2:187.
8. C. Lloyd, *British Seaman,* 181.
9. Frend, *Peace and Union.*

sheets, and in my way joined company with two men of the village, who, being employed by the woolstaplers let out spinning to the poor, had lately received orders to lower the value of labour. We were talking on this subject, when the exclamations of a group of poor women going to market overhearing our conversation made an impression on my mind, which all the eloquence of the houses of lords and commons cannot efface. We are to be sconced three-pence in the shilling, let others work, for me I'll not. We are to be sconced a fourth part of our labor. What is all this for?[10]

Thomas Paine suggested an answer in *Rights of Man*. War, he wrote, "is the art of conquering at home." Thomas Beddoes the physician agreed, noting that the purpose of the hostilities is "the unconditional submission of the republicans."[11] William Godwin, likewise noted, "It is clear then that war, in all its aggravations, is the growth of unequal property."[12] Charles Pigott wrote a *Political Dictionary* with a long entry under "War":

War, Oh soldiers, soldiers! Lay not the flattering unction to your souls, that you are heroes! You are nothing but murderers; butchers. When you began to be soldiers, you ceased to be men! . . . Still I am bewildered how to account for this universal and brutal rage for massacre, which seems to have stagnated and palsied every human sentiment, and stopped at once all the noble work-ings of nature which once glowed in your bosoms! I have only one cause more that could possibly induce you to such a dreadful effect, and that cause is, want. . . . It is then to you, O iniquitous Governments! That mankind is indebted for this awful calamity! You starve your people, and then the loud calls of Nature force them into a compliance and concurrence with you in plunder and murder! You take away their earnings and destroy their com-merce, and then inlist them under your bloody banners![13]

The theme of warfare's class nature is brought up again by a pamphleteer, himself a former army officer, who expressed his views in a printed letter to a friend. The soldier is dragged to the West Indies or "the bloody plains of Flanders, whither they have been dragged by cruel force to the deliberate destruction of men, against whom they have never conceived the least emo-tion to resentment, and whom they are doomed to hew in pieces, or be killed themselves—without one impulse of private animosity; merely at the *instiga-tion* of their superiors!!!" In response to the argument that they have to

10. Frend, *Peace and Union*.
11. Frend, *What Shall the Rich*.
12. Godwin, *Enquiry concerning Political Justice*, 734.
13. Pigott, *Political Dictionary*.

recruit to defend the country, he attacks the premise: "if wicked wars were not so often wickedly undertaken for the selfish purposes of wicked Governors, that we should not then have occasion for so many man-killers under the delusive name of Soldiers." Soldiers are decoyed into war "for the ease of their betters who never dream of fighting their own battles."[14]

The author had served in Jamaica, where he learned of a soldier in the 79th Regiment who deserted to relieve his wife and children by returning to his loom or plowshare. He was caught and shot. He too compared the recruitment to the slave trade. Hundreds of soldiers disembarked in conditions as noisome as those endured by the slaves from the Guinea coast. Soldiers were marched to London in handcuffs, imprisoned in the Savoy, and then marched to Chatham barracks, the king's crimping house. The mortality was great in the West Indies. Soldiers pinched their bellies to scrape a few pounds together to buy themselves coffins, for once health had quitted the soldier, government would incur no further expense on his behalf. "Carrion men, groaning for burial" (*Julius Caesar,* act 3, scene 1, 290).

The eagerness of the people to join the army must be qualified by the evidence that many were willing to mutilate themselves in order to avoid it. The poet John Clare reported from Northamptonshire, "Men had crooked fingers because their parents had disabled the finger of every male child in wartime to keep them from being drawn for the Militia or sent for soldiers for any petty theft they might commit."[15] It was practiced often enough for a slang term to be created: "to fake your pin" was to cut your leg as if accidentally "in hopes to obtain a discharge from the army or navy." John Horne Tooke tells the story of a loyal wife, who concealed a mallet and chisel when she went to visit her husband, imprisoned as a vagabond until he could be put on board one of the king's ships. He slid his hand underneath the iron door of his cell while she chopped off a finger and thumb, rendering him unfit for his Majesty's service.[16]

Pigott concludes with Shakespeare: "Cry 'Havoc!' and let slip the dogs of war," says Mark Anthony, seeking to avenge the death of Caesar (act 3, scene 1, 1502).[17] "*Havoc!* was the signal to an army for the seizure of spoil," according to the OED, the opposite of commoning. John Oswald wrote of the king,

14. *Reflections on the Pernicious Custom.*
15. *Prose of John Clare,* 37.
16. Tooke, *Diversions of Purley,* 320.
17. Pigott, *Political Dictionary.* His brother, Robert, wrote a disquisition, published in France, against hats and in favor of caps, when headdress was highly politicized.

"He unfurls the bloody banner of strife, lets loose the hounds of havoc, and whirling furious in his hand the firebrand of war, involves in ruin and desolation half the inhabitants of the globe."[18] Red round globe hot burning.

The physician and London Corresponding Society (LCS) member Dr. William Hodgson was tried for declaring the British king to be no better than a hog butcher in giving up his Hanoverian troops to be led to the slaughter for thirty pounds. Tried in December 1793, he was sentenced to two years in Newgate. In Newgate, he was forced into solitary confinement for refusing to pay the jailer his extortionate fees.[19] In 1801, Gilbert Wakefield died as a result of imprisonment in King's Bench. He opposed the war, and wrote that ministers of government "have reduced thousands and tens of thousands to wretchedness and beggary; they have occasioned a devastation of the human species infinitely tremendous beyond the most merciless tyrants of ancient or modern times; the death of a fellow creature is no more to them than the fall of an autumnal leaf in the pathless desert; land and sea is covered with the carcasses of their slain. The real motives for the war were given as being "beyond all controversy, the suppression of a reforming spirit in the societies at home," behind "the pretended ones to the preservation of property from republicans and levelers."[20] Wakefield identified the most awful dynamic of modernity, the one tying together domestic enclosures and imperial expansion by means of the enhancing military capacity of the state. Despard lived this dynamic, came to refuse it, and fell victim to it.

The mob protested conscription by shouting "No War, no Pitt, cheap Bread!" and by pelting the prime minister's house with stones. In May 1794, the government acted decisively, with the proclamation against seditious publication and arrests of members of the LCS. The LCS was formed in January 1792—"a spot in time"—by Thomas Hardy with the help of Olaudah Equiano. It favored written correspondence with like-minded people elsewhere; cheap publications; and mass meetings to abolish slavery, reform Parliament, and reduce the price of bread. Clubs like it spread like wildfire in the English provinces, in Scotland, and in Ireland. Traditionally, it is considered the beginning of the modern English working class. Government feared its links with Ireland. Troops had to be used to cover the judges comings and goings at the Courts. The Attorney General was surrounded by a mob. The

18. Erdman, *Commerce des Lumières*, 98.
19. T. Lloyd, "Impositions and Abuses," 72.
20. Wakefield, *Reply to the Bishop*, 12.

harvests were bad in 1795, prices mounted. People rioted for food under the moral economy.

The government began the barracks-building program to insulate the soldiery from civilians; it was an enclosure too. In Britain in 1794, there was sufficient barrack accommodation for 18,000 men; by 1806, the number had risen to 125,000. Forty-eight barracks each capable of holding more than 1,000 were available by that time. Arms depots were scattered in warehouses all over the kingdom in 1803. By 1803 the artillery volunteers consisted only of men called out to man the great guns of harbor batteries. One such man, a sailor, was part of Despard's conspiracy.

Radicalism and popular unrest followed different courses. The second half of 1795 saw the biggest explosion of political and economic protest. It looked to Pitt at one point like revolution. Thelwall's public lectures and the LCS's mass meetings were the new features. The growing unpopularity of war was combined with the rising cost of food. People rioted ferociously against the crimps. Despard was a soldier from a family of conquerors. His brothers were distinguished officers of the Crown. Like Napoleon he was an engineer, skilled in mathematics. He owed his promotion to these skills. "Careers open to talent" was a slogan of the era. Certainly Despard's talent opened his career. But he changed. Despard encountered *Rights of Man* in King's Bench Prison and read therein that "all monarchical governments are military. War is their trade, plunder and revenue their objects."[21] Paine looked forward to the day when "the oppressed soldier will become a freeman; and the tortured sailor no longer dragged along the streets like a felon."[22]

War was an incentive to innovation, a dizzying encouragement to commerce, a powerful intensification of production, and a huge opportunity for profiteering. The mobilization of vast armies and navies shook up old institutions and prepared for new ones. The war was instrumental to the ruling class, regardless of country. This was obvious to many at the time. The recruitment of soldiers and sailors rid the cities of dangerous populations, London and Paris alike, and it weakened rural social structures. War was not only the "health of the state," it was an exciting tonic to the economy.[23]

The idea of the "nation" became a popular creed. The army was one half English, one sixth Scottish, and one third Irish. War was not only about

21. Paine, *Rights of Man*, 99.
22. *Rights of Man*, 290.
23. Cookson, *British Armed Nation*.

plunder; in an era of mass mobilization it was about killing. Thus, it was not an accident that Major General Henry Shrapnel's invention—the antipersonnel weapon that bears his name—was adopted in 1803 and first used in Surinam the following year. Capable of transforming the iron ball into an artillery shell that exploded bullets *after* it left the cannon's muzzle, this was a weapon not for breaking down castle walls or breaching city gates; it was a weapon to disable a person, a weapon to maim. Pure butchery.

The militia joined food rioters in Portsmouth, Chichester, and Plymouth. "Crimps were like pimps, except that they dealt in recruits not prostitutes."[24] Their slogans included, "No war, no soldiers," "Liberty and no crimps," "Liberty, Fraternity and Peace with France,"' or 'Damn the King, Damn Pitt, We Will Have Bread at 6d. a Loaf." Foot guards, horse guards, and militia suppressed the attack on Pitt's house in summer 1794. "I can point out the houses and the names of persons by whom men have been bought and sold; where you might have gone and chosen men as you would hogs or horses, according to their size, their make, their ages, and their appearance; some, for eight, ten twelve, guineas; and now I am told that the price is rais'd to more than Twenty Guineas for fine young men."[25] One recruit was enlisted by the beat of the drum for every five procured by crimps.

Three days of rioting in August 1794 destroyed the crimping houses of Holborn, Clerkenwell, and Shoreditch. Crimps had to go before a justice of the peace within four days to certify their recruitment was "voluntary." The crimping houses were "places of rendezvous for the recruiting officers and the magistrates."[26] They also provided a secure place of detention for men impressed to the navy. The crimp dealt in these men, trading them to the army or merchant marine and getting money from the bounty on their enlistment or from an advance on wages. The houses were "scenes of enormities committed in this atrocious and inhuman traffic for fresh supplies of blood, the liberties of our country are invaded! The seamen is forcibly torn from his family! The peasant kidnapped from the plough! And the starving labourer is compelled to sell his life and his liberty for bread."[27] In August 1794, a young man named George Howe was found dead with his hands tied outside a crimping house in Charing Cross. On the night of 20

24. Gilmour, *Riot, Risings and Revolution,* 408.
25. *Reflections on the Pernicious Custom,* 14.
26. Goodwin, *Friends of Liberty,* 359.
27. *An Address to the Nation from the London Corresponding Society* (1793), repr. in Claeys, *Political Writings,* 4:63.

August, three houses were pulled down. A detachment of guards from the Tower, a hundred armed and accoutered men of the artillery company, constables, and the Light Horse Volunteers, were mobilized to suppress "the present Attempts to renew the Riots of 1780," as the Lord Mayor wrote the Home Secretary.[28]

Patrick Colquhoun reported, "I have strong grounds to believe that the riots are the result of a deliberate system originating with the corresponding societies for the purpose of overthrowing the government." But the leadership was in prison awaiting trial.

> Beware Britons of the hordes of crimps and kidnappers that infest the metropolis and its environs, who rot and imprison its peaceful inhabitants. . . .
> Would such atrocious acts have been suffered in the days of Alfred?[29]

Of the twenty-three committed to trial, four were condemned to be executed. Two crimping housekeepers were brought before the justice and released.

In January 1795, eighteen men were released when a crimping house in Southwark was attacked. The door was chalked, "the empty Bastille." A thousand assembled in the spring in Westminster against crimping. On 29 June, the LCS called a meeting in St. George's Fields, Southwark, and demanded an immediate end "to the ravages of a cruel and destructive war." On 7 July, crimping houses were attacked in Newington, and another in Soho. The Horse Guards were called out to disperse crowds in Seven Dials demanding bread. Going over Westminster Bridge into Southwark, they beset two crimping houses with a bonfire in the street, and were dispersed by a troop of cavalry. A mob assembled in Charing Cross and marched down Whitehall, breaking Pitt's windows in Downing Street.

Edward Marcus Despard was in the thick of it. In May 1796, his brother, John, wrote Andrew, another brother, "I have had no account of Marcus since last July, when the Newspapers mentioned his being taken up and carried before a Magistrate for being amongst the Mob that was breaking Mr. Pitt's Windows. I should not be surprised to hear of his having gone to France, as his political sentiments seem to agree perfectly with those of that Country,"—that is *liberté, égalité,* and *fraternité*.[30] If he had gone to revolu-

---

28. NA, HO 42/33.
29. Stevenson, *Popular Disturbances in England,* 166–76.
30. Letter to Andrew Despard from J. Despard, 28 May 1796, Despard Collection.

tionary France as a military man, he would have worked with John Oswald, a Scottish artisan and vegetarian, who lived poor as a sansculotte in 1790 Paris, and whose sons fed on what they gathered in "neighboring gardens and forests." He advised the revolutionary army to exhibit their fury by song and dance at the moment of action. John Oswald called for universal arming of the population in France as the only way of disarming the few who ruled the many. This he argued in a manifesto he put on the city walls near the Bastille.[31] The prime minister, William Pitt, lived at Number 10 Downing Street from 1783 to 1801. Minor alterations were made to the building in 1796, but no significant expense appears to have been incurred the year that his windows were broken.[32] Pitt played down the incident in a letter to his mother: "A mob is magnified by report; but that which visited my window with a single pebble was really so young and so little versed in its business, that it hardly merited the notice of a newspaper."[33]

Henry Martin Saunders dramatized the conflict in a broad one-act play called *The Crimps, or the Death of Poor Howe*. It served as excellent agitprop. "Poor Howe" is a simpleminded recruit driven to suicide. Scene 1 takes us to a house of ill fame, where Captain Cut-throat orders Sergeant Blood to raise more men for the war in Flanders. Captain Gab explains that "ragged, and tired, and hungry" laborers were "up" to them, meaning they considered the recruiting pitch and the bounty as humbug. Sal Slash'em said,

> Not long agon, I could have got a score
> Of *cliver* lads, to serve his majesty,
> In no time, as it were; but now, in no time
> I can't get none; if I but begs them to
> Step in a bit, they only damnes my eyes,
> And calls me gallows b—ch.[34]

Mother Hannau robs those who refuse to enlist and then kills them. Bet Brimstone says she likes "to catch 'em when they're *tosticated*." Captain Gab seeks "to curb their Jacobine spirits." They go out to their stands first offering toasts to "Pitt, Windham, Dundas and Irish Edmund too" and damns the

31. Oswald, *De La Marche Universelle*, placard (1792).
32. Crook and Port, *History*, 562. Large-scale renovations of Windsor Castle, in the amount of tens of thousands of pounds, commenced after 1797.
33. Stanhope, *Life of Pitt*, 2:324.
34. *Crimps*, 3.

swinish multitude. They drink to the suspension of habeas corpus, to imprison-ment of all who complain, to church and king, to taxes and tithes, and to spies, informers, and Mr. Reeves. They sing "God Save the King." Scene 2 brings Mrs. Howe, the mother, and Maria, the sister, on stage to warn the young Howe of kidnappers on the streets. He answers them reassuringly, "London is a place of liberty," and then declares "None but Levellers, reformers, or Jacobins" would oppose the good, great men before departing. Maria sings "Rule Britannia" to calm herself down when it becomes clear that Howe is not returning. In scene 3, Hannau and Cut-throat confer about a sailor who was dragged to a crimping house and then had his teeth knocked out. Howe is dragged in from the streets and threatened with slavery—"He shall to Africa to learn submission." Then he's stripped and confined to the garret. In scene 4, Howe, bleeding from a beating, moans, "I shall be transported unheard, unknown, to Africa or India, or on the purple plains of ravaged Flanders." "There is no justice here but for the rich and powerful; and all else, I find are deemed a swinish multitude." He then heaves himself out the window and dies.

Antiwar propaganda was creative. Thomas Spence struck coinage of political sophistication. A halfpenny piece with two civilians approaching a soldier with outstretched hand bears the slogan, "We also Are the People." Another with three soldiers standing at attention with bayonets fixed on shouldered muskets declares, "Who Know Their Rights and Knowing Dare Maintain." The obverse side of the coin depicts a war-ravaged village with the ominous reminder, "One Only Master Grasps the Whole Domain." Another coin shows a man from a press gang bludgeoning a resisting victim. These are coins of class struggle!

The LCS planned another mass meeting, this one in Copenhagen Fields, Islington, for 26 October 1795. It was called in light of "the rapid approxima-tion of national destruction thro' the continuation of the present detestable war." It opened at midday to one hundred thousand people. John Binns, the Irish plumber, was in the chair. The organizers were aware of the global impor-tance: we meet "in the open face of day, and call the heavens and earth to wit-ness the purity of our proceedings. Amidst the dreadful storm and hurricanes which at present assail the political hemisphere of our country."[35] The authori-ties were alarmed; the Home Office informed the commander of the volunteer corps that it "exactly resembling that which fifteen years before had nearly led to the destruction of the metropolis."[36] The Gordon Riots of 1780 had been a

35. London Corresponding Society, *Selections from the Papers,* 315.
36. Lord Mayor to the Duke of Portland, 22 August 1794, NA, HO 42/33.

serious threat. Among the resolutions passed by the meeting was one declaring "that the inflexible obstinacy of Ministers, in continuing the present cruel, unjust, and disgraceful war—a war which has stained the earth and seas with so much human blood—calls aloud for the execration of every friend of humanity."[37]

Three days later, crowds assembled for the opening of Parliament—"No Pitt," "No war," "Give us bread" were the slogans. A stone was thrown and struck the king's carriage. The king switched coaches—the state coach was nearly destroyed and the king nearly dragged out of the private coach carrying him. Four people were charged with throwing stones, but only the journeyman printer Kyd Wake was found guilty. The two bills were passed, one against seditious meetings and the other making seditious written or spoken words treasonable. Spence struck a new coin: on one side was a bust of Thelwall, while on the other was "A Free-Born Englishman" with his legs shackled, his hands tied behind his back, and a padlock shutting his mouth!

The last of the mass meetings of the LCS was called for Marylebone Fields (now Regent's Park) on 7 December 1795. On 17 December, Pitt, while riding back from Parliament through St. James Park, was attacked and pelted with mud. Pitt's house was again attacked in June 1796, and he was hissed at in December 1797 as he went to St Paul's for a thanksgiving service after the victory at Camperdown. At the same time, Thomas Hardy's, a founder of the LCS, house was attacked by a loyalist mob and defended by about a hundred men, "many of them Irish, armed with good shillelahs."

"A Familiar Letter from John Bull to his Countrymen" admitted that prices were high and taxes heavy "and many of us are at a loss to subsist ourselves and Families." This was partly owing to the greed of monopolizers and regraters. Invasion, however, would have been worse because it would have brought "a confiscation of all Property."[38] A broadside addressed to the "Men of England" and signed by an "Englishwoman" began by acknowledging that the men were discontented. "Heaven from the beginning intended you should have kings and superiors—Equality never was intended—it never can be on this earth—Heaven and reason forbid it—and Bonaparte himself has shown you how little he intended to establish it."[39]

---

37. London Corresponding Society, *Selections from the Papers,* 314.
38. *Dialogue between a Labourer.*
39. *Invasion! A Familiar Letter.*

TWENTY-TWO

The Goose and the Commons, c. 1802

THE LAW LOCKS UP THE MAN or woman who steals the goose from off the common, but lets the greater villain loose who steals the common from the goose.

The Quatrain Expresses the quintessence of the enclosure time: the loss of commons and the criminalization of the man or woman. The great English communist of the previous century Gerrard Winstanley had said as much: "The law is the fox, poor men are the geese; he pulls off their feathers and feeds upon them."[1] These four lines refer to two institutions—the enclosed field and the prison—and propose a relationship between them: the police process of criminalization. Ned and Kate Despard had to deal with them. Their prison experiences are related in the next section of this book. This chapter begins an account of the English loss of commons by studying the particulars of this poem, while the next chapter concerns one out of hundreds of enclosure acts. Together they offer some similarities to and some differences from Despard's Irish experience, already described in "Habendum" and "Hotchpot."

"Parliamentary enclosure only got underway in earnest in Middlesex around 1800," say the historians of the cartography of enclosure, Middlesex being the county containing of much of London.[2] John Middleton, an advocate of enclosure and its Middlesex historian, writes that,

> the Commons were of real injury to the Public, by holding out a lure to the poor man; by affording him materials wherewith to build his cottage, and ground to erect it upon; together with firing, and the run of his poultry and pigs for nothing. This is, of course, temptation sufficient to induce a great number of poor persons to settle upon the borders of such Commons. But

1. Winstanley, *Fire in the Bush*, in *Works of Gerrard Winstanley*, 468.
2. Kain, Chapman, and Oliver, *Enclosure Maps of England*, 29, 45, 94.

the mischief does not end here; for having gained these trifling advantages, through the neglect or connivance of the Lord of the Manor, it unfortunately gives their minds an improper bias, and inculcates a desire to live, from that time forward, without labour, or at least with as little as possible.

before concluding, "The Commons of this Country are well known to be the constant resort of footpads and highwaymen."[3]

Let us examine the goose quatrain literally. Between 1789 and 1803, in fifteen cases at the Old Bailey, sixteen men and one woman were tried for offenses that included stealing a goose or geese. Juries found four not guilty. Of the guilty, six were sentenced to transportation for seven years, three were sentenced to public whippings, two were fined a shilling and imprisoned in Newgate for a month, one was sentenced to a whipping and six months in the House of Correction, and one man was sentenced to death. That was John Moore, a thirty-four-year-old, who on the night of 28 September 1800 had broken into Thomas Hopwood's public house in Spitalfields The White Horse to steal a large copper pot, some cloths "hanging on a cloaths-horse to dry," and a goose valued at seven shillings. He was to hang not so much for the goose as the B and E.

The date was significant. Of the fifteen cases, all but two of the offences occurred in the autumn or winter months, six in September alone.

The Month of London Goose Thefts, 1789 to 1803

Jan	Feb	Mar	April	May	June	July	Aug	Sept	Oct	Nov	Dec
2	–	–	–	–	–	2	–	6	3	1	1

The cross-examination of William Archer, a Whitechapel tailor, explains the significance of the September date. William Thomas had taken a pair of geese on 30 September 1799, and Archer had found his goose in the boneyard behind his washhouse.

Q. *When was it that you lost this goose?*

A. The 29th or 30th of September.

Q. *Just about Michaelmas you know?*

A. Yes.

3. Middleton, *View*, 83, 85.

Q. *All the persons about London, if they can, will have a goose upon Michaelmas-day?*

A. Yes.

Geese were in their prime, having fattened on the postharvest stubble. Michaelmas was one of the four quarter days of the English calendar named for the archangel Michael, who led the "army of God" against Satan (Rev., 12:7–9). The 29 September Michaelmas was the quarter day when rents were due. The Michaelmas goose was part and parcel of traditional relations between landlord and tenant. In manorial tenancy agreements from at least the fifteenth century, a goose was stipulated as part of the rent. A goose on Michaelmas proverbially provided prosperity: "Eat a goose on Michaelmas day, Want not for money all the year." A royalist legend emerged in the seventeenth century that Queen Elizabeth I learned of the victory over the Spanish Armada while dining on a goose at Michaelmas. Thereafter, loyal subjects were thus expected to do the same. In Ireland the day was known as the Feast of the Goose (*Fomhar na nGeanna*).

The very fragrance of the feast day seems to waft out of the court testimony, goose fat sizzling in the pan with onions and sage an irresistible temptation. In the William Thomas case (30 October 1799), John Griffiths, a Lambeth officer, found the fire under the tin kettle and two pair of giblets cooking. Jacob Stone was apprehended in his room with Mary Tapp "cutting sage and onion." Dorothy Hartley suggests that such goose recipes with this traditional stuffing arose simply from seasonal synchronizing—the first apple windfalls, fattened rabbits, and scallions all became available around Michaelmas.[4]

It's a point underscored in William Cobbett's *Cottage Economy*. According to Cobbett, geese "can be kept to advantage only where there are green commons, and there they are easily kept, live to a very great age, and are amongst the hardiest animals in the world." They lay a hundred eggs a year. Opinionated in all things, Cobbett preferred his geese in late October not September. "It is a very great error to suppose that what is called a Michaelmas goose is the thing."[5] He claimed he could buy one off the common for half a crown, fatten it on cabbage and lettuce, and end up with a tasty meal that could not be had in London for less than seven shillings.

4. *Food in England,* 194. In *The Every Day Book,* William Hone describes collecting crab apples on Michaelmas (2:464); he also describes the custom of "griggling" apples, when boys were permitted to glean in the orchards (2:1270).

5. *Cottage Economy,* para. 167.

Goose fairs at Michaelmas were an annual event. Daniel Defoe painted a vivid picture of the geese waddling from Norfolk and Suffolk to London in droves numbering one or two thousand each. They began the drive in August, so the geese could feed on the stubble after the harvest as they went along, completing the work of the other gleaners. The drive continued into October, when the roads become too deep with mud for their webbed feet and short legs to march in.[6] (The soldier's goosestep derives from the view that the goose can stand on one leg.)

The location of the thefts varied—some were at market, others at shop or stall. Two offenses took place at the main poultry market, Leadenhall. Mary Powis was picking a goose that Andrew Banks took on Michaelmas Day. Removing the feathers seems to have been work of men, the removal of downy feathers ("stubbing") the work of women. On 29 September 1789, Andrew Banks was caught taking "a flat of geese off the stall" (a "flat" being both a shallow basket and a unit of measure) by a journeyman poulterer, a salesman, and the market watchman. He defended himself by saying that "they were fat geese," nothing you could run away with.

Richard Smith, convicted of stealing a goose from a Leadenhall poulterer in January 1800, could say only that he was "very much in liquor." The thefts took place in shops. Andrew Finch was a worker who "turned a wheel" at a glass cutters, and in mid-September 1790, he took a goose, along with "96 shoe-shapes" from a neighboring cobbler almost as an afterthought. On November 1802, James Higgs stole a goose from a stall on Whitechapel High Street. Richard Knight was a laborer too. He worked at the oil mills pressing seeds and fruits to extract the oils. With his coworkers, he worked on Sundays, and on the 19 October 1800, he showed them four bags that he had found. He was charged with stealing them from a Tottenham coach house that he passed on his way to work, and then throwing the dead goose into a ditch to claim after work. A servant bringing the cows in from the field saw him do it.

In July 1800, James Robins and Patrick Moreing stole seven geese from a butcher's premises in Mile End. Robins defended himself as follows: "I was going to see the new docks, and going through the field, a man asked me if I would have a goose, and he went down into the saw-pit, and chucked me up two." The "new docks" were one of the sights of the time. On 3 December 1796, Eleanor Connor, who kept a stand in Petticoat Lane along with her partner, Mary Prinnan, fell victim to the quick Aaron Levi, a ten-year-old

6. Defoe, *Tour*, 1:59–60.

orphan boy, who grabbed a goose by the neck from her stall and sprinted away. A local bully halted his progress, but Aaron was able to pass the goose off to "another chap" before submitting himself to a beating. Elizabeth Pratt, who sold fish and fruit on the corner, tried to soften the punishment. The goose was retrieved covered with mud, and Aaron Levi was pronounced guilty.

By their nature, criminal records are inclined to express the inherent aggression of mine and thine. In October 1800, at The Adam and Eve public house, Mr. Castle called for a pint of beer and saw a goose lying on the table. "I took the goose up and said, 'if any body here has more right to this goose than I have let them own it.'" Anderson said he bought it from a wagoner at the Kingsland turnpike for four shillings. Castle claimed to have bought it as part of a pair from the Leeds wagoner in Hoxton for thirteen shillings and six pence. "The prisoner said it is my property, Mr. Castle said it was his." Anderson, the prisoner, was sixty-six-years-old.[7]

A Twickenham farmer found a goose hidden in straw three yards from a barn. He lay in watch from seven to midnight. "It was a moon-light night, I heard a rustling in the straw." The future prisoner came. After the prisoner dropped the goose and ran, the farmer drew his gun and fired, wounding the prisoner, William Hall, in his leg. The people knew Hall, who had four children. Hall defended himself as follows: "On Saturday evening I got too much liquor, my wife came to fetch me home, and I would not go, we had some words and she said, she would lock me out; I said, I did not mind if she did; I went to lie down in the straw." That was in October 1803.[8]

Juries valued geese in varying monetary amounts from one shilling and six pence to eight shillings; the average seems to have been about two shillings. These valuations were essential to the indictments determining the severity of the punishment. But the value of the geese to the people taking them cannot be expressed simply by money. We need to take a moment to remember some of our fine feathered friend's other contributions. Geese supplied many benefits—feathers, eggs, down, quills, and medicines. Their ample fat was rubbed on the chest against wheeziness or "the brown kitties."[9] Goose grease had many uses: creams to prevent skin from chapping and to soften leather shoes, harnesses, and leather tackle were made from it. It was also

7. *Proceedings of the Peace,* October 1800.
8. *Proceedings of the Peace,* October 1883.
9. Mrs. Field of Holloway, London, told me in the winter of 1970 that pressing a sheet of brown paper soaked in goose fat against the chest was a sure palliative to the "brown kitties" (bronchitis).

used to create ointments, poultices, and lineaments of embrocation. On behalf of the London literary scene, Lord Byron paid geese this tribute:

> Oh, nature's noblest gift, my grey goose quill
> Slave of my thoughts, obedient to my will,
> Torn from the parent bird to form a pen,
> That mighty instrument of little men.

"The law locks up the man or *woman*." The loss of commons hit women particularly hard. Although a charity for "lying-in women" had been established in 1797, in Enfield, to pay home visits to women in labor, parturition was a mortal danger to mother and child alike. For a poor woman, an unwanted pregnancy could mean disaster and shame.[10] In her expansive study of the sensational burning of Bridget Cleary, Angela Bourke sums up Irish experience: "Poultry keeping, like talkativeness, was a sign that a woman was not under a man's control."[11] Geese were categorized as poultry, along with ducks, chickens and turkeys, and the keeping of them was one of the tasks of the wife of the farmer, cottager, or squatter. Good management of the livestock could add substantially to income, true, though let us not lose sight of other ways of valuing these creatures.[12] In February 1792, Sarah Pearce took an unstubbed goose from a poultry shop in Shadwell High Street. She was caught and asked to say pardon. "She said, there is your property," but when it came to begging pardon, she declared, "I shall not do any thing of the kind." Her refusal hints at a conception of justice that had not been discussed in the court at Old Bailey. What was meant by "property"? How was it connected to "rights"?

Country people thus grew up with this knowledge and the understanding of the usefulness of these creatures. Much of it was vernacular knowledge that was lost with enclosure, commercial agriculture, and proletarianization of farm families.[13] One of the Brothers Grimm's fairy tales published in 1815, "The Goose Girl," is a story of role reversal between a haughty, duplicitous princess and an honest, common goosegirl. Riches and avarice are pitted against innocence and virtue; it is the palace versus the common.[14]

---

10. Robinson, *History and Antiquities*, 2:130.

11. *Burning of Bridget Cleary*, 50.

12. See Ivy Pinchbeck's *Women Workers and the Industrial Revolution, 1750–1850*.

13. Not entirely lost, as the state acquired it. In 1966, the US Department of the Interior issued *Birds in Our Lives*, a report from its Division of Fish and Wildlife, which pointed out for the uninformed that "geese like grass."

14. A statue in Göttingen, the *Gänseliesel*, honors the common girl and her goose.

Children might grow up tending geese by performing a simple array of tasks. Not only did the children look after the geese but the geese, playing their role in animal husbandry's daily caretaking complexities, in many ways formed the kind of human beings that the children would become. The youngster simply by stretching out his arms and waving them, winglike, could nudge the flock along from one place to another, from the farmyard to the common, for example. These creatures flock together and travel vast distances; they flock for protection, for company, no one knows why. The children might have learned solidarity from them. The children were knowledgeable; ignorance befell them in the workhouse, the factory, the city. None of this suited that concept of "discipline," which might make a man "fit to kill or be killed." Middleton, the Middlesex advocate of enclosures, observed the children not through rose-tinted glasses but through a dirtier lens: "The poor children who are brought up on the borders of commons and copses, are accustomed to little labour, but to much idleness and pilfering."

With the enclosure of the fenlands in Lincolnshire, the price of feathers rose about 40 percent. Adam Smith commented on the disappearance of goose down, associated with enclosure and the decline of small proprietors.[15]

For centuries, Mother Goose told rhymes and stories to children. Part of European oral tradition, the stories were not printed and published in English until the eighteenth century.[16] Mother Goose was among several "mothers" of English common lore—Mother Hubbard, Mother Bunch, Mother Shipton (Tudor prophetess), Mother Carey (among sailors)—figures who arose in the Early Modern era as figures of comfort and power. Their disappearance coincided with the destruction of the commons. Or if they did not totally disappear, they became figures of amusement for polite, literary culture or attained a lasting position in the lore of the weakest part of the population, the children. Children preserved vestiges of older popular beliefs that could not survive in the world of mercantile rationality and capitalist enclosures, in a process analogous to the transformation of the productive subsistence commons into the nineteenth-century folkish village green.[17] Did such childhood memories provide a fund of latent knowledge?

15. *Wealth of Nations* (1937), 227–28, quoted in Neeson, *Commoners,* 68.

16. Charles Perrault published *Histoires ou Contes du Temps Passé* in 1695, which was translated into English in 1729 as *Histories or Tales of Past Times, Told by Mother Goose.* John Newbury in 1768 published *Melodies.* See also Tsurumi, "Development of Mother Goose," 28–35.

17. Ariès, *Centuries of Childhood,* 62–99.

Thomas Carnan edited *Mother Goose's Melody* in 1780. The rhymes—"Solomon Grundy," "Pat-a-Cake," "Georgy Porgy," "Little Bo Peep," "Jack Be Nimble"—are more than melodies; they are rhymes for games, for sport, and for play. The stories—"Sleeping Beauty," "Jack and the Beanstalk," "Cinderella," "Little Red Riding Hood"—are evidence of plebeian life, the frank recognition of death, cheating the dangers of the market, the hazards of the road, sexual symbolism. They make it easier to understand Blake's *Songs of Innocence* (1789) and the profound alterations in social reproduction, especially as they affect children.

By 1806, Mother Goose seems to have left the open air of children's street games for the sheltered enclosure of the stage, becoming the subject of Christmas pantomime and cast as a witch. When *Harlequin and Mother Goose* was performed at the Theatre Royal in Drury Lane, she had acquired supernatural powers and defended the young against the avarice of an ugly squire:

> Old Mother Goose when
> She wanted to wander
> Would ride through the air
> On a very fine gander.

Beginning in the sixteenth century, witches in England were given the sobriquet "mother"—Mother Eve, Mother Waterhouse, Mother Dutten, Mother Devell, Mother Stile, Mother Seder, Mother Staunton, Mother Nokes, Mother Bennett, Mother Tredsall, and so on. These were elderly, poor, proletarian women, who possessed not only folk knowledge but the general knowledge of life and death, illness and health, which was essential to poor village communities. Her historian writes, "The witch, good or bad, usually had nothing but a herbal remedy or two, several commonplace spells, and an effective tongue for cursing or blessing. Therein lay her danger, because she could not be separated from her power except by death."[18]

I have described only one traditional English custom, the Michaelmas goose, and its criminalization. Taking the whole country, over the last several centuries into consideration, however, there were hundreds, probably thousands, of such customs—estovers, pannage, piscary, turbary, gleaning, to name a few of the major classes of customary right. These have been analyzed in a skilled scholarly literature of social history and memorialized in

18. Rosen, *Witchcraft in England*, ix, 73, 77, 87–89, 97–98, 118, 135.

generations of lore of various cultural kinds—children's story, local praxis, or "heritage." The contrast with the "barbarous usages," as the conservative Irish neighbor of Despard called them, or what the Irish novelist Maria Edgeworth might called "minute facts," lies in the relation to a different linguistic and religious matrix determined by conqueror and conquered or colonizer and colonized. These customs will be fought for in the nineteenth and twentieth centuries in a transformed context of either Irish nationalism or what James Connolly called "Celtic communism." In the 1790s, however, these differences had not become implacable; they were still in the gristle. In fact, as will be recalled from the chapter on the Irish Whiteboy insurgence, the famous poetic quatrain that led us to the custom of the Michaelmas goose, the quatrain with its Foucaultlike insight into enclosure, seems to have arisen first in Ireland.

TWENTY-THREE

"The Den of Thieves"

"OH HOW THE BUYERS AND SELLERS ARE GUARDED, fenced with walls, and defended with Laws!" William Covel cried in 1659, during the struggle to prevent the enclosure of the commons in Enfield, northeast of London. This was during the "interregnum" of the monarchy, when Parliament alone made laws. Covel plays with words: the spelling of wall and law are (almost) an anadrome, and fence is an aphetic of defense. So, what appears to be politically opposite—one physical and the other not, one connoting violence and the other justice—are etymologically and orthographically identical. Code expresses content and, in this case, imitates it as well.

At Despard's trial in February 1803, Thomas Blades, a soldier, testified for the government about another soldier, Thomas Francis, and the meetings they had had during the previous September. In addition to soldiers like Blades and Francis, the conspirators included some craftsmen (a watchmaker, a shoemaker, a tailor), some sailors, and several Irishmen, who met at the Black Raven down Tooley Street. At this particular meeting at the Bleeding Heart in Hatton Garden, when the timing of attack was under discussion, Francis *"thought it would be better to make the attack as soon as possible, at least before the Den of Thieves met'* which was the term he made use of for Parliament."[1] Some historians have agreed. "Enclosure (when all the sophistications are allowed for) was a plain enough case of class robbery," writes Thompson.[2] It is the goose again.

Parliament, indeed, consisted of landlords, and in 1802 alone they passed ninety-six enclosure acts. These privatized common lands and removed

1. *Trial of Edward Marcus,* 93.
2. E. Thompson, *Making,* 218.

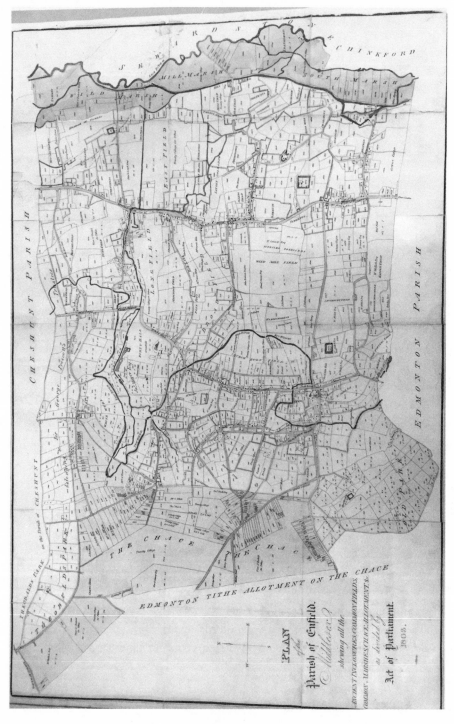

FIGURE 12. Enfield Enclosure Map, 1803. London Metropolitan Library.

customary rights of access. In 1793, Pitt agreed to help fund a Board of Agriculture, the brainchild of the Scotsman Sir John Sinclair. Arthur Young was its first secretary and a vigorous traveler, researcher, and promoter of enclosure, at least until c. 1801, when its miserable consequences began to affect him.

Not only were the Despard conspirators themselves victims of enclosures or its effects, but one of the their goals was to right this wrong. The land was fenced off and hedged, permanently altering the landscape. It was a major intervention in the economy and its social relations, augmenting rent rolls, dispossessing commoners, and criminalizing customs. With the plantation, the ship, the factory, and the prison, the enclosed arable field defined the epoch, the epoch of enclosures.

Certainly, enclosure of land in England refers to a major process of world economic significance that lasted several centuries. Unlike the expropriations of imperial conquest, it was a piecemeal process that took place one parish at a time. The first years of nineteenth century were exceptional, inasmuch as enclosure became a central, generalized policy. We can show this by law and statistics. In terms of law, in the summer of 1801, Parliament finally passed the General Enclosure Act (41 George III, c. 109). For the first time, the following provisions applied to all enclosure acts. The act requires that an enclosure commissioner ascertain and fix all boundaries, "reducing" oral accounts to writing. Also in writing, he must receive a "schedule of particulars" naming everyone with a claim to the commons and quantifying each common right. The commissioner is then required to extinguish all rights of common. In terms of statistics, the number of enclosure acts roughly doubled from 1789 to the mid-1790s. By 1801, the number had almost doubled again. These were their land grabs.

Decisive to this transformation was a visit by John Oswald to Parliament, when a bill of enclosure was brought before the House of Commons. Not having made "political inquiries" of his own, he accepted the pro-bill propaganda, which maintained it would "improve" agriculture and divide land among the poor. Instead, he "found that the poor and indigent were to be driven from the commons and that the land which before was common to all was now to become the exclusive property of the rich." He concluded, "The honorable House of Commons vanished from my sight; and I saw in its stead a den of thieves, plotting in their midnight conspiracies the murder of the innocent, and the ruin of the fatherless and the widow!"[3] He was also present at the passage of another bill, one "For the Better Protection of Nurseries" against "pilfering

3. As quoted in Erdman, *Commerce des Lumières*, 96.

rogues," who made free with what formerly had been common. The penalty for "the horrid crime of cutting cabbage" was changed from transportation to hanging by the neck. Most of the vegetables hawked in carts about the streets of London were purloined. This was before the green grocery, as with most all retail, was enclosed in shops leaving the streets strictly for transport. Until then, the streets had resounded with the "cries of London": "Six a penny Cucumbers," "Rue a farthing a bunch," "Two pence large Potatoes," and so on.

The garden grounds around the city were monopolized by the class of people who made the law. Those who fell victim to the noose became heroes or martyrs. They became, as Oswald put it, "the unfortunate champions of the indefeasible rights of man." They become the admired subjects of song and ballad.[4] Here's one from 1803.

> It's of a famous highway-man a story I will tell;
> His name was Willie Brennan, and in Ireland he did dwell;
> And on the Kilworth mountains he commenced his wild career,
> Where many a wealthy gentleman before him shook with fear.
> Brennan on the Moor, Brennan on the Moor,
> A brave undaunted robber was bold Brennan on the Moor.

Ballads of social bandits were prevalent in border country as (besides Ireland) between England and Scotland. where the musician, horse thief, and escape artist, Jamie Allen thrived until he was hanged in 1803.[5]

Parliament with its House of Lords and its House of Commons was the "public sphere" of the den of thieves. We might see market, stall, or street as part of a plebeian public sphere or as an out-of-door urban common, because this is where most of the goose thefts took place. Actually, there is one that did happen on the agrarian common. The case was this. On 15 July 1800, Thomas Purvitt, a soldier, took a goose (value 2 shillings) belonging to Daniel Rogers from the common in Enfield. Daniel Rogers lived on Forty Hill, and the goose was commoned on Forty Green. Rogers had recently bought it and marked its wing with a pair of scissors. He noticed the goose was missing and saw the prisoner with a bloody bag covered with a jacket. He fetched the constable (a butcher), and together they went to the prisoner's lodging, where they found the marked goose. Purvitt defended himself by saying he was quartered with five other soldiers and that "this was a bag belonging to the regiment that I always fetched our meat in; how the goose came there I do

---

4. *Review of the Constitution of Great Britain,* in Gregory Claeys, ed., *Political Writings,* 3:423–24.

5. Pickard, *Ballad of Jamie Allen.*

not know." The jury found him not guilty. Why, we can only conjecture. Knowing Michaelmas was coming up (the trial was on 17 September), the jury perhaps took pity on the soldiers. Perhaps quartered soldiers in time of war could help themselves to "meat" where they found it. Perhaps jurors knew something about commoning that has been lost to us. This was neither the first time soldiers had robbed commonable beasts in Enfield nor the first time that its commons had been the site of significant conflict.

The commons lost a goose, and in the following year the geese lost the commons. An act of Parliament for the enclosure of nearly the entire parish of Enfield, eight thousand acres, was passed in 1801, taking effect in 1803.[6] At a stroke, the marsh commons by the river Lea and the arable commons on higher ground were extinguished. Enfield Chase, traditionally the denizen of poachers and squatters, had been enclosed in 1777. Edmonton, the parish to the south, had been enclosed by parliamentary act in 1801. It was a Crown manor, and its tenants, being tenacious of their customs and low rents, held off enclosure for three centuries, until 1801.[7]

Judging by the evidence of the *Proceedings* at the Old Bailey, Enfield in the 1790s was an agricultural and pastoral parish intersected by major transportation routes of road and river. The river Lea carried coal and grain to London. In July 1795, three bushels of coal valued at four shillings were taken from a warehouse by the river and used as partial payment for a pot of beer and bread and cheese. A considerable number of people were specialized workers, skilled in metal working and allied trades.[8] Most cases were theft, and the thefts were mostly of country products; for example, two heifers (twelve pounds), two beehives and twenty pounds of honey, nine ewe sheep, nineteen wether sheep, and so on.

Whose England was it? To whom did the land belong? The expropriation of land, "the colossal spoliation" had begun in the sixteenth century with the birth of the modern state. By the eighteenth century, the law itself had become the instrument of the theft of land. Parliament as the House of Lords and the House of Commons stole the common lands from the common people. Milk, cheese, meat, vegetables, bread, and fuel depended on the common lands, customary access to common pool resources, and open field agriculture with its narrow strips. Communal property provided neither modern comforts nor equality for all. To understand *custom*, we have to enter into local, productive

6. Baker and Pugh, *History of the County*; 41 George III, c. 143.

7. Avery, *Irregular Common Fields*.

8. For knowledge of Enfield, I have relied on Baker and Pugh's *A History of the County of Middlesex*, 232–41.

relations, where we find a particular lexicon. Its purpose is not to hide or seal off a community; it is the language of community communication.

Arthur Young engaged in debate about agrarian policy in 1802. Lord Kenyon, as Doug Hay explained, was replaced by Edward Law (later Lord Ellenborough) as chief justice of the King's Bench in 1802, and he put an end to the widespread paternalist view that the "moral economy" was recognized in common law, if not by parliamentary statute.[9] Arthur Young toured Norfolk in 1803 and published the results in 1804. His longest chapter is on enclosures. He visited seventy-nine enclosed parishes, talked to the enclosure commissioners and the landowners, tabulated births and deaths—did everything, it seems, except engage in serious intercourse with the commoners themselves, though he did include a section on the "poor" for each place. Here's what he came up with regarding customary access before enclosure (the date in parentheses after each place is the date of its enclosure): At Ashill (1785), the poor took in stock and called it their own. At Banham (1789), the poor had herbage and turf fen. The poor of Bintry (1795) had 46 commonable rights. At Brancaster (1755), each dwelling house could keep two cows and cut furze. At Burnham Norton, common-right cottagers could keep twenty-four cows, but how they supported them is an enigma. The people of Cranworth (1796) kept geese on the commons, of which they are deprived. In Little Dunham (1794), coals were provided, so the poor did not have to cut whins (a prickly shrub, furze, or gorse). At Ellingham (1798), 64 common rights existed. Poachers harbored in the commons of Felthorpe (1779). Hetherset (1798) was permitted fifty or sixty allotments. In Heveningham (1799), "the commons was the source of all sorts of immorality, poaching, smuggling, &c., &c." A stinted common remained at Heacham (1780). At Ludham (1801), the poor commoners were left destitute. When Smeeth and the Fen (1797) were drained, 528 common rights were lost. At Northwold (1796), the commons was allotted to the great proprietors, and all the commoners were able to do was mow it. At Sayham and Ovington (1800), the poor received coals as a substitute for their lost fuel rights. The commoners of Shouldham (1794) "used to keep cows, mares, geese, ducks, but now nothing." At Shottisham St. Mary (1781), commoners could keep a colt, an ass, and three geese; the children of the workhouse were let out to farmers. At Snettisham (1762), the poor had no right to cut flag (any reed or rush). The object of the enclosure of Stiffkey and Morston was "to extinguish rights of shackage" (after harvest, to release pigs into the stubble or shack).[10]

9. Hay, "State and the Market."
10. Young, *General View.*

What were these common rights? The inhabitants claimed that for more than three hundred years, they enjoyed commons "for all manner of commonable beasts without number, and common of estovers, and divers other great priviledges and advantages in Enfield Chace, which of late have been endeavoured to be taken from them." According to a 1650 survey, which was still applied in 1777, at the time of the enclosure of Enfield Chase, common rights were defined as "herbage, mastage for swine, green boughs to garnish horses, thorns for fences, and crabs and acorns gathered under trees."[11] Estovers meant wood, particular wood that in 1685 had been specified as "browse, strammet, or sprey" for the inhabitants of Enfield to carry away "for their necessity without controulment." Forest officials might have "the old dotrells, swooners, and dead trees." Furthermore the "inhabitants of Enfield might take clay, sand, and gravel in Enfield Chase, or any of the King's common places, without doing any annoyance, for the repairs of their houses." They might also "cut, mow, and take furze, heath, and fearne for their necessary uses."

"Whelmes" are wooden drainpipes or water courses that have been fashioned by sawing a tree trunk in half vertically and then turning its concavity downward on top of the other half. "Sprey" consists of the slender twigs of a tree used for fuel. Hazel or birch spray was used in thatching. "Strammell," or strummel, is straw; in cant, it means hair. "Strammet" does not appear in the OED. "Dotrells" are dotterel, or doddered, trees, that is, trees without a head, like pollards. It might refer also to an old oak. "Swooners" refers to someone who has sunk into a state of rest, has fainted, or is a deep sleeper, a figurative meaning for a fallen tree.

Dorothy Hartley reminds us that "a countryman's family, even under the most slavish conditions, often had as good food as their own industry could provide for themselves. The wool on his back, the leather shoes on his feet, the pork in his larder, the corn in his bin, were a man's own growing. . . . He lived in good clean air, had clean water, and was able to make a fire and build a house." With enclosures "the people are driven off the land; they are cut off from their natural food supply, and are compelled for the first time to buy food." Money, she says, became a necessity of life.[12]

On 2 July 1801, "an Act [41 George III, c. 143] for dividing and inclosing the open and common fields, common marshes, and lammas grounds, chace allotment, and other commonable and waste lands, within the parish of

11. Robinson, *History and Antiquities*, 1:198, 208–9.
12. *Food in England*, 578.

Enfield, in the county of Middlesex" was passed by Parliament.[13] Because it was a private act of Parliament, its thirty-nine printed pages are not included in *Statutes at Large*. These pages set out the procedures of expropriation and allotment. They, with the map and the numbered assignments made in the following years, provide a list of the "villains" in the case—namely, the new private owners, or "possessioners," to use the sixteenth-century term.

The commissioners of enclosure directed the course of husbandry "with respect to the laying down, plowing, sowing, fallowing, and tilling thereof as for the stocking and feeding the Fallows and Stubbles . . . they shall . . . suspend or totally extinguish all or any Parts of the Rights of Common." Horses, cattle, sheep, lamb, or swine, "go, depasture, or feed on any of the Lands or Grounds so exonerated from Common Rights" the new proprietor or occupier may impound them. The "Plan of the Parish of Enfield, Middlesex, shewing all the Ancient Inclosures, Common Fields, Common, Marshes, Chase, Allotment, &c. as divided by Act of Parliament 1803" is reprinted in Robinson.[14] The Lammas lands along the river Lea are shaded in blue, parish roads are delineated by orange, the chase is tinted in yellow, former common fields are demarked with dark blue lines, and the boundaries of the new properties are inked and identified by number. The overall effect was pretty, if you didn't know it was a map of thieves divvying up the loot just the same, not a buried treasure map.

Robinson lists by name and numbered allotment more than six hundred new possessioners. He describes the area of each allotment by acres, rods, and perch and orders the mode of fencing, as well as its location in relation to roads or adjacent properties. In that same year (1802), Thomas N. Parker published his *Essay on the Construction of . . . Gates,* which was praised by the *Anti-Jacobin Review* for helping to keep common Jacobin cows from entering privatized fields and trampling the privatized corn! The London Metropolitan Archives contains a few deeds of the sale of common rights in Enfield during 1803–4.[15] These delineated parcels of freehold were granted to compensate for lost common field, marsh, meadow, and so on. Robinson, writing before 1823, could easily name the common fields by memory or by consulting the recollections of others. We can infer from their appearance in print that the names still lived on the tongue and within the understanding of the common people, even after common access to their referents had passed. This persistence of landscape memory over enclosure we learn from the poetry of John Clare.

13. ACC/1437/5, London Metropolitan Archive.
14. *History and Antiquities*, 1:180ff.
15. ACC/1057/088–091, ACC/1437/1–12, London Metropolitan Archive.

The tissue of custom, its infrastructural networks, and its local understandings were far from timeless. These printed descriptions have their place in time, and the time was that of the bourgeois revolution, when common property began to be transformed into private property, and private property into capital. Enfield was the scene of riots in June 1649, and again ten years later with the enclosure of Enfield Chase. A Digger colony was located in Enfield.[16] Soldiers had enforced the enclosure of Enfield to begin with, working on behalf of their paymasters. In 1659, *A Relation of the Cruelties and Barbarous Murthers Committed by Some Foot-Souldiers and Others, upon the Inhabitants of Enfield, Edmonton, &c.* was printed and published.[17] Commissioners and military officers took away the goods of commoners and beat and wounded them. Traditional proprietors and commoners claimed two thirds of soil and wood. The purchasers were great officers of the army, including Colonel Joyce, the man who had arrested King Charles. They bought up poor soldiers' debentures at one to two shillings in the pound. Two hundred families were forced to take alms. Some hired troops, plying them with wine, beer, and money and paying them an extra six pence a day. The soldiers "knocked them down, and cut and slashed with their swords divers of them and their servants and other poor laboring men coming from their labour at night." A justice threatened to send some of them "to Barbadoes to dig for tobacco." Some of the judges, themselves purchasers, were ready "to take off the courage of the proprietors and commoners from their claymes to their common."

The soldiers shot and killed several of the commoners' sheep "and carried some of them to their quarters, and there dressed them, and eat them, and also did shoot and kill divers cows and horses of the said commoners to a good value with their muskets charged with stones and bullets." Calling them rogues and cowards, the commander challenged the commoners to fight, threatening to burn their houses down. The commoners "had with them cudgels, mattocks, axes, and two forks, and no other weapons." "And about the number of 10 red-coats, and the rest gray-coats, on the Lord's day, the 10th July" marched upon Enfield discharging their muskets "towards some of the inhabitants walking upon the common, who heard bullets fly closer by them." The next day, 11 July, twenty-five soldiers were urged to kill three or four of the commoners, so "the rest would be quiet from their claymes." This was class war.

16. Hill, *World Turned Upside Down*, 101, 279.
17. Reprinted in Robinson, *History and Antiquities*, 1:180.

Arguing that some commons was better than none, Timothy Nourse reasoned that commoners were "most useful in Time of War, for the same reason of being bred hardy, and when reform'd by Discipline will make good rough, cross-grain'd Soldiers enough, fit to kill or be kill'd."[18] We can see commons as remnants from a defeat, the defeat of the Levellers and Diggers of the English Revolution, when the notion of the commons burst parochial bounds and the activity of commoning could be imagined as encompassing all. This was clear from William Covel's *Declaration* of 1659.

Covel moved to Enfield, where he spoke and wrote on behalf of its squatters and commoners "without respect of persons."[19] He published a brilliant tract combining prayer, prophecy, plan, and program, in the kind of revolutionary language typical of Bunyan or Winstanley. Holding a pantheist conception of the deity, he wished to see divine creation restored by preventing buying and selling and limiting money (state idols possessing the images of kings). "What slaves men are made to fetch Gold out of other Nations?"

His class consciousness was vivid. He inveighed against the possessors, their fat and scornful eyes, their taunting speech—"What lyings! What cheatings! What blood! What murders! What divisions! What tumults! What pride! What covetousness!" "Oh how the buyers and sellers are guarded, fenced with walls, and defended with Laws!" He said that the wicked of the world rule by three principles:1) strength united is stronger, 2) "divide and spoil," and 3) "make poor enough, and you will rule well enough." In particular, he denounced lawyers, clergymen, corporations, and great tradesmen. Gold and silver were their signs of glory "but to others [they were] a sign of death." In contrast, mariners, those who follow the plow, and those who practice handicrafts were useful, for on their labors all others depended.

He anticipated objection: "You say I am a *Leveller,* and would destroy Propriety. I answer, I am not." Only four laws were required: 1) that tithe lands, delinquent estates, lands of court chancery and university be used to pay public debts; 2) that gavelkind tenure be reestablished or, in other words, that land be divided equally among all children of the deceased; 3) "settling all Waste-lands, and Commons on the poor for ever"; and 4) that the rich maintain the impotent and aged poor and that every parish have a hospital. And that was it! That was all the legislation required for the commonwealth.

He advocated religious toleration, a commonwealth not of theory but of actuality, equality of privilege, the removal of churches (they "bewitch the

18. *Campania Foelix.*
19. Patrick, "William Covell," 45–57.

hearts of the youth"), wastelands for the poor, and abolition of church tithes. He was appalled that the lords were so cruel that they did not permit the poor even "to gather a bagge of chips." He anticipated small communities of a hundred houses and forty families on one or two thousand acres, where the "gifts of nature" were not bought and sold and where the resources used by handicrafts were "a common stock." As it was, the poor were compelled to steal, "all men are weary and at their wits-ends, unless it be a few, whose hearts are as hard as a nether mill-stone."

He listed thirty "callings" (crafts or trades)—shepherd, gardener, smith, carpenter, turner, dyer, weaver, shearman, tailor, currier, shoemaker, hatter, oatmeal maker, basket maker, sieve maker, collar maker, rope maker, fell-monger, barber, physician or chemist, schoolmaster, cooper, wheelwright, plowman, bricklayer, earthen pot maker, glazier, herdsman, and slaughter-man (butcher). He favored a mix of marine, handicraft, and farming work. "The disjointing of them spoils all: experience makes it true all over England: the uniting the plow, and handy-crafts, and mariners, and arts recovers it all again: It was never done in the world yet." The whole end, he said, was "that people may enjoy the labours of each other."

On the margin of town and country, Enfield was already notorious for two noted criminals—the social bandit Dick Turpin, and the kidnapped servant maid Elizabeth Canning. During this period, several highway robberies of coach or carriage passengers took place, with the perpetrators often sentenced to death—for example, the man who robbed a carriage on the road between Edmonton Common and Enfield Common on 28 May 1800 and Henry Lazarus, who was tried for stealing two pairs of leather breeches from the Enfield stagecoach on 1 December 1802. On 30 November 1803, an Enfield laborer was tried for stealing seven hundred crab quicksets (for hedging) from John Irons. "I follow ditching and planting," he explained. Timothy Nourse observed that "banks of Earth they are most us'd near Cities, where 'tis impossible almost to raise a Quick-Hedge, by reason of the great Numbers of Poor who inhabit the Out-skirts, who upon all Occasions, and especially in cold Weather, will make Plunder of whatsoever is combustible."[20] In another case from April 1789, a father and son were tried for stealing a plough pin, plough spindle, and other bits of ironmongery belonging to a farmer on Enfield Chase, who found them missing when he came to plough on Monday morning. The prisoners had worked for a neighboring farmer. They were starving. In defense they said, "We had no

20. Nourse, *Campania Foelix*, 59. Felix here doesn't mean "happy" but rather "fertile," as in blessed with productive soil and rainfall.

bread for two days, and we found them under a hedge." The result of enclosure was the extinction of the open field system of farming.

Fifty years earlier, most of Enfield was farmed in open fields, whose strips, called "journeys," were divided from each other by "bulks." This was the open-field system of farming, a community task in common. Hay, wheat, turnips, and corn were the principal crops. In 1803, 2,891 acres were enclosed and 3,540 were unenclosed (apart from the chase). Commoners could graze livestock on the Lammas lands adjoining the river Lea. These were lands commoned after the wheat harvest ("loaf mass") on 1 August.

On 30 October 1799, a working millwright was sentenced to two years in the House of Correction for stealing some of his master's tools ("cast steel mill bills" and an iron winch) on the day that the Enfield races began. The races, starting in 1788, drew a disreputable crowd.[21] Enfield had a raunchy history of profane amusements, dice, cards, and bowls. Twenty thousand people gathered in 1801 for a boxing match. These bloody spectacles were turning the commons surrounding London into muddy sites. Boxing flourished as a sport during the wars, when poor men become soldiers and made spectacles of themselves fighting each other senseless. In Enfield in 1789, William Ward, a notorious prizefighter, beat his challenger, a blacksmith, to death.[22] In addition to this boisterous, rough-and-ready crowd, the plebeian population of Enfield had established several box clubs, or friendly societies, such as the United Society, the Amicable Union, and the Society of Good Fellowship. These provided a base of artisanal solidarity and social security while avoiding the prohibitions of the Combination Acts. The working class on London's outskirts was composed of both metalworkers and rural craftsmen, who were generally controlled by "a moment of coercion" or "a moment of consent," as two cases from January 1798 illustrate.

A crew of building tradesmen, including a sawyer, a wheelwright, a blacksmith, and a carpenter, gathered at The Swan at Tottenham High Cross on Saturday, 16 December. "It was pay night." A tremendous scuffle broke over pay, and the ownership of some building materials from an adjacent washhouse. A little incident in the overall scheme of things, it might be thought, but the moment was fraught with epochal meaning—money payment was replacing customary taking. Constables were called, and a file of soldiers was sent for from Enfield. Two of the belligerents were handcuffed, caged, and

21. *Victoria County History.*
22. Robinson, *History and Antiquities,* 2:155.

carted to Newgate, where several rescue attempts failed. This was the moment of force, and it was reflected in two meanings of the verb "to pay." The payment of wages for work done was one meaning, and the other came up in testimony—"one man paid me about the head and the constable too with a stick," and when a knife was drawn "I began to pay him about the head."[23]

Agricultural workers were hired annually at Enfield's "statute" or "statute fair," the winter gathering at which farmers hired servants. Sir William Dolben rented "a certain enclosed ground," where on "a thickish morning, and only a glimmer of light" three men cut down a horse chestnut tree of "fifty or sixty years growth." Thomas Eady, who worked with pickaxe and shovel among farm laborers, was apprehended. The carter carried the four pieces of wood to Finsbury Square in London, where they were sold to the turners or cabinetmakers. Although Thomas Eady was found guilty, he was fined only one shilling and discharged, having been given "an excellent character" by the prosecutor, Sir William Dolben! In this way, gentry paternalism might produce "the moment of consent."

William Dolben (1727–1814) represented Oxford University in the House of Commons. Between 1789 and 1793, he introduced bills to enclose common and open fields in Oxfordshire, including the parishes of Dunstew, Stoke Lyne, Little Barford, Milcomb, Little Tew, Lewknor, and Sibford Ferris, as well as two in Northamptonshire (where he was born)—one at Wollaston and the other at Laxton, the parish famous for having the longest lasting open-field agriculture in England, right into the 1940s.[24] The historian of Northamptonshire's commoners, Jeanette Neeson, informs us that, while Dolben favored enclosures, he was a paternalist critic of their excesses. For example, in Parliament, he opposed the enclosure of the Northamptonshire parish of Burton Latimer in 1803, unless greater acknowledgment of the poor's right to the wold was included, a fortieth part of each enclosure was planted for timber, and charity lands were fenced free of charge.[25]

Handicrafts came to Enfield because of the arms industry, encouraged by the presence of the Royal Gunpowder Works up the river Lea and by the ease of transportation to London and the Thames downstream. The Bren gun, the

23. *Proceedings of the Peace,* January 1798.

24. *Journal of the House of Lords,* vols. 33, 38, 39.

25. The *Dictionary of National Biography* stresses his alliance with Wilberforce in working toward abolition of the slave trade, including the 1788 act named after him requiring that the number of slaves be limited according to the tonnage of the ship. But it says not a word about enclosure. See also, Neeson, *Commoners,* 209–10.

Enfield rifle, and the Royal Small Arms Factory were not established until 1815, but had already been proposed in 1803. The hungry and the dispossessed enlisted as soldiers or were made to "volunteer" in lieu of prison.[26] Enfield produced guns. The famous Lee-Enfield bolt action rifle (1895); the Bren gun, or light machine gun (1935); and the Sten gun, or submachine gun (1941) were the firearms of choice for twentieth-century British armies. Enfield's association with handguns began in 1800, when the Whitechapel gunsmith Ezekiel Baker designed and made what was to become the standard-issue, muzzle-loading, flintlock rifle bearing his name. The Baker rifle went into mass production in 1805, but its patterns were produced in 1800, in Enfield, where it was tested. Thousands were made for the rifle corps of the Napoleonic wars. Enfield's Royal Small Arms factory had been established by 1816.

While proximity to the Royal Gunpowder Works and to the waterways of the river Lea partly explain the location of Enfield's Small Arms factory, the military site managers also saw the benefit of a dispossessed and enclosed local populace. Integrated factory production could take place without the delays and obstacles inherent in component manufacturing, which characterized production in Birmingham and was thought to be responsible for an inferior product. The Baker rifle, more reliable and with greater range could kill a target at two-to-three hundred yards.

In 1802, a militia force was mobilized in England. Those who could, paid substitutes to serve in their place. Enfield had eleven such substitutes quartered in public houses, and Purvitt, our goose thief, may have been one of them. In Enfield's revolutionary past, commoners and soldiers had fought each other in a parochial microcosm of class struggle, the former with vision and the latter with greed.

26. Pam, *History of Enfield*, vol. 1, *Before 1837*, 323–24. I am grateful to Christine Noone of the Enfield Local Studies Library and Archives for this reference.

TWENTY-FOUR

Commons or True Commons

THE BAYMEN OF HONDURAS CHARGED Despard with being wild, a Leveler, and a universalist. The charges gathered force in the 1790s and culminated in 1803. Leveling has a historical meaning; it has socialist connotations of economic equality; it has restorative properties of reparations (jubilee); and it has political implications, a political party. As for "wild" the reference is to savages, if not barbarians. It refers to the time before cultivation, and thus to the forest, the uplands, or wetlands, like marshes and the fens—places of independent people, such as the indigenous people whom he worked with in Central America. This chapter begins to explore the political ramifications of these "wild" places in the years after Ned and Kate Despard arrived in London.

Adam Ferguson (1723–1816), the Scottish philosopher and friend of David Hume and Adam Smith, promoted the idea of progress in human history. He was the sociologist of stadialism, or the stages theory of history (savagery, barbarism, feudalism, commerce), which he analyzed in *An Essay on the History of Civil Society* (1767). The book had a big impact on the liberal ruling class, especially among European political thinkers, American constitution makers, Scottish political economists, and English moral philosophers. Despite setbacks, according to Ferguson, human history progressed providentially toward perfection. The commons was a thing of savagery or barbarism, hence of the past. Ferguson wrote, "Some having thought, that the unequal distribution of wealth is unjust, required a new division of property, as the foundation of freedom. New settlements, like that of the people of Israel, and singular establishments, like those of Sparta and Crete, have furnished examples of its actual execution; but in most other states, even the democratical spirit could attain no more than to prolong the struggle for

Agrarian laws; to procure, on occasion, the expunging of debts; and to keep the people in mind, under all the distinctions of fortune, that they still had a claim to equality."[1]

The Agrarian Law was derived from antiquity. Lycurgus in Sparta seized all landed property and divided it among citizens equally. The Roman agrarian law limited the size of holdings and restricted private exploitation of public lands. Acceptance of the idea behind the Agrarian Law was widespread in the eighteenth century. Mably in 1776 called for an agrarian law in his book *De la legislation*. In February 1791, Sylvain Maréchal, who later collaborated with Gracchus Babeuf, published an essay "Concerning the Poor and the Rich." He claimed that "the French Revolution is a veritable agrarian law put into execution by the people."[2] By the first months of 1791, the cosmopolitan Cercle Social (Society of the Friends of the Truth, a proponent of Rousseau's ideas) called for it. In January 1791, James Rutledge, an Englishman, who was in Cordeliers Club (Society of the Friends of the Rights of Man and the Citizen, whose motto was *liberté, égalité, fraternité*), started the new journal *Le Creuset* with a discussion of the agrarian law. Restif de la Bretonne called for equalization of land. The starting point of the counterrevolution or, at least, the separation of the propertied from the maximum demand of the unpropertied took place in March 1793, when the French National Convention decreed the death penalty for "anyone who shall propose the agrarian law."

In England, William Godwin espoused a republican position, in this classic Enlightenment discourse of human progress: "The rich are in all countries ... directly or indirectly the legislators of the state; and of consequence are perpetually reducing oppression to a system, and depriving the poor of that little commonage of nature which might otherwise still have remained to them." "It follows upon the principles of equal and impartial justice, that the good things of the world are a common stock, upon which one man has as valid a title as another to draw for what he wants."[3] Godwin was a reformer and a thinker. He was not a conservative like Edmund Burke, whose *Reflections on the Revolution in France* (1790) started a massive debate on the principles of the French Revolution, particularly the right of resistance. After, Burke referred to the people as "the swinish multitude," and advocates for the

1. *Essay,* pt. 3, sec. 6, 156.
2. Rose, "'Red Scare.'"
3. *Enquiry concerning Political Justice,* 92, 703.

people began referring to themselves humorously as pigs. This included Thomas Spence, who using the current term for food (*meat*) started a newspaper called *Pig's Meat; Or, Lessons for the Swinish Multitude*, which sold for one penny. This contrasted with William Godwin's book, which cost several guineas, a price well outside the range of a common person's budget. The elite theoretician (Godwin) and common plebeian (Spence) were both important, but Spence spoke to the people. In his newspaper, he quoted the seventeenth-century politician and political philosopher James Harrington's *Oceana* to explain, "This kind of Law fixing the balance in lands is called *Agrarian,* and was introduced by God himself, who divided the land of *Canaan* to his people by lots, and is of such virtue, that wherever it is held, that government is not altered except by consent."[4]

Edmund Burke wrote, "When the Anabaptists of Munster, in the sixteenth century, had filled Germany with confusion by their system of levelling and their wild opinions concerning property, to what country in Europe did not the progress of their fury furnish just cause of alarm?" Even in *Rights of Man,* published a year after Burke's *Reflections on the Revolution in France* (November 1790), Thomas Paine found it necessary to deny that "rights of man" was "a leveling system."[5] *Leveling* was a term used to bait opponents. Not all reformers were ready to embrace all its many implications, which included universal franchise, regicide, equality, confiscation of the superfluities of the rich, restoration of commons, and knocking down opponents!

In 1647, in Saint Mary's Church in Putney, the soldiers debated their officers about the franchise and property. The soldiers, led by Levelers, threatened mutiny within Cromwell's revolutionary army unless they were listened to, and so they were. Speaking for the soldiers, Rainborough famously said, "For truly I think that the poorest he that is in England hath a life to live as the greatest he"; less than two years later, in August 1649, Gerrard Winstanley wrote, "that the poorest man hath as true a title and just right to the Land, as the richest man, and that undeniably the earth ought to be a common treasury of livelihood for all, without respecting persons."[6]

There is no evidence that Winstanley participated at Putney, yet the audible resonance suggests he was listening. Had some of the speeches reached his ears? Or was his egalitarian utterance a Leveler commonplace? Equality

4. *Pig's Meat,* 3:197.
5. *Rights of Man,* pt. 2, 194.
6. *A Watch-Word to the City of London and the Armie* (1649), in Winstanley, *Works,* 321.

arises only from the negation of the difference between social classes: poorest he, greatest he; poorest man, richest man. There's a difference: one hath a life to live, the other hath a right to land. This difference, this debate, appeared again in the 1790s. The right to live was an empty promise unless it was accompanied by access to subsistence commons. Let's listen a little more closely. Rainborough continued," And therefore truly, sir, I think it's clear, that every man that is to live under a government ought first by his own consent to put himself under that government; and I do think that the poorest man in England is not at all bound in a strict sense to that government that he hath not had a voice to put himself under." In political theory this is called contract theory. This variation asserts the right of resistance.

By contrast, Winstanley's statement is followed by "it is a great trespass before the Lord God Almighty, for one to hinder another of his liberty to dig the earth, that he might feed and cloath himself with the fruits of his labor therefrom freely, without owning any Landlord, or paying any rent to any person of his own kind."[7] Asserting divine authority to invert the meaning of trespass, Winstanley propounds a communist theory of land. Rainborough is all about government and the nation, whereas Winstanley is all about land and subsistence. Rainborough was a Leveler, while Winstanley called himself a "True Leveller." Rainborough is deferential ("truly, sir"), while Winstanley is declarative ("freedom is the man that will turn the world upside downe").

The English Revolution did not settle this debate by chopping the king's head off. It was a class issue. Diggers in Buckinghamshire addressed the rich as follows: "Mark this you great Curmudgings [misers], you hang a man for stealing for his wants, when you yourselves have stole from your fellow brethren all Lands, Creatures, &c." *The True Levellers* said, "The Powers of the World made the Earth stink everywhere.... The earth stinks with their Hypocrisie, Covetousness, Envie, sottish Ignorance and pride."[8] Gerrard Winstanley said that "the true levelling is the community of mankind joined with the community of the earth." The distinction between leveling and true leveling in the mid-seventeenth century parallels the distinction between the commons and the true commons of the late eighteenth. The former stresses equality before the law, the latter material equality. One appears to be limited to the sphere of politics ("civil rights"), the other is based in economic reality (economic rights). We shall see, despite shifting opinions during the turmoil

7. *Watch-Word,* 321.
8. *The True Levellers Standard Advanced* (1649), in Winstanley, *Works,* 263.

of war and revolution, that the distinction differentiates the thought of Thomas Paine from Thomas Spence's. The difference also corresponds to class differences.

The transmission of these discussions from the mid-seventeenth century to the 1790s found several vectors. One was Irish. In a previous chapter, we described how Irish redresser movements claimed the title. Captain Rock's father was a Whiteboy or "Leveler" ("their interference with public matters being as yet confined to leveling enclosures of commons").[9] In Despard's home county, county Queens, Eyre Coote wrote to his wife that his estates were "in a ticklish way," warning her that it was impossible to say how matters would turn out. He added, however, "I think the levelers are more dangerous by far than the Catholics."[10]

Another vector was maritime transmission. After the restoration of the monarchy and the end of Cromwell's revolution, the Levelers' ideas were preserved among pirates, who found a stable ecological refuge on the Miskito Coast and British Honduras. The struggle against slavery was the third and major vector. Tacky's revolt in Jamaica (1760) had a huge impact, as did the great uprising of Tupac Amaru in 1780. Another vector of transmission was the dissenting church on both sides of the Atlantic. In a biblical culture, the words of the prophet Isaiah would be well-known: "Let every mountain and hill be brought low, uneven ground be made smooth, and steep places become level" (40:3–5). It was in one of these cultures that Thomas Spence, the most consistent among the common communists of the 1790s, grew up.

Thomas Spence (1750–1814) witnessed the battle over the enclosure of the Town Moor in Newcastle. In 1775, at the Newcastle Philosophical Society, Spence first enunciated his plan that the land should revert to parish ownership: "The country of any people, in a native state, is properly their common, in which each of them has an equal property, with free liberty to sustain himself and family with the animals, fruits and other products thereof. Thus such a people reap jointly the whole advantages of their country or neighborhood, without having their right in so doing called in question by any, not even by the most selfish and corrupt."[11] The *Newcastle Chronicle* (25 November 1775) was "informed that he [Spence] ... became a member, apparently for the purpose of obtruding upon the world the erroneous and

---

9. Moore, *Memoirs of Captain Rock,* 82.
10. Eyre Coote to Sarah Coote, 16 February 1793, Cootes Papers, 32/7.
11. *Rights of Man.*

dangerous levelling principles with which the lecture is replete." Besides lecturing philosophers, he chalked on walls and pavements such pithy theorems as, "Fat Bairns, Full Bellies," "You Rogues, No Landlords," "War or Land."[12]

Reflecting on jubilee passages in Leviticus Thomas Spence concluded that "God Almighty himself is a very notorious leveller." Thomas Spence called for "a levelling Constitution" in the twelfth letter dated 18 October 1800. Spence quoted *Paradise Lost* (bk. 12) in his first letter *"Man over man, he made not Lord."* It was not long before it became a slogan in the abolitionist movement in the Caribbean and on the American mainland. Spence favored divorce, public granaries, scalping the landed proprietors, returning the land to the people (as easily done as mutiny in the fleet!), abolishing the press gangs, swimming pools in every parish, and health care for all. "I should have the Hospitals open for the admission of the sick of every description, every Day of the week, without previous application."[13]

Spence combined the practicalities of the commons' customary rights with the ideals of universal equality. He drew on several ideas and traditions, the Garden of Eden, jubilee, the golden age, utopian, Christian, Jewish, American Indian, millenarian, dissenting. All of these ideas were experienced in a context of a commons of the sea (his mother was from the Orkney Islands) and of the land (the Newcastle Town Moor, not yet enclosed).[14] Shaking the dust from his feet, Spence moved to London in 1792, or perhaps earlier, where he became the publisher of the London Corresponding Society (LCS). He distributed its printed matter from a street stall at Holborn and Chancery Lane. He was arrested twice in 1792 for selling Thomas Paine's *Rights of Man,* and a third time in 1794. As noted above, he began issuing his weekly one-penny paper *Pig's Meat.* He was abused, attacked, and evicted.

Spence sold salop from his stall in High Holborn. The working man's coffee, salop supposedly had Viagra-like powers. It was derived from several varieties of orchids—the bee orchid, the great orchid, the meadow orchid, and the early spotted orchid—which could be gathered in London's vicinity. as we learn from the botanist William Curtis, whose *Flora Londinensis* appeared in two volumes, one in 1777 and the other in 1798. "Should it ever

12. His lecture was published as *Property in Land Every One's Right.* In 1793, he published it as *The Rights of Man* with interesting modifications—he removed its anti-Catholicism, substituted "congress" for "Parliament," and omitted capital punishment.

13. *Pig's Meat,* 3:231.

14. Cazzola, "'All Shall Be Happy.'"

be found practicable, as well as profitable of making *Salop,* this species appears as likely to answer as any of them. The extraordinary invigorating powers of the roots of these plants [which consisted of two roundish testicular appearing bulbs] have been handed down to us with ceremony by many great names amongst antiquity."[15]

In London, he countermarked the coin of the realm by minting his own coins.[16] On one side of a penny entitled "Before the Revolution" is the image of a chained, skeletal prisoner in a stone dungeon gnawing on a bone, while on its obverse side, entitled "After the Revolution," is a man happily feasting at table while three figures gaily dance beneath a leafy tree. His tokens depict heroes and martyrs—Thomas More, Horne Tooke, John Thelwall, Thomas Paine, Lord George Gordon, Charles James Fox, and Mendoza the boxing champion. Others had striking images—a bonfire of title deeds, a guillotine, a gallows, a state prisoner, a bridewell boy, a truehearted sailor, an Indian, a Westminster scholar. The pennies and halfpennies display radical mottoes ringed around the coins' edges, laurel-like: "If rents I once consent to pay My Liberty is past away," "Man over Man He Made Not Lord," "We Were Born Free and Will Never Die Slave," "Let Tyrants Tremble at the Crow of Liberty," "Spence's Glorious Plan Is Parochial Partnership in Land," "Am I Not a Man and a Brother?" and "Who Know Their Rights and Knowing Dare Maintain." Spence knew that the parish was the unit of government and the unit of production: "Our debates are in every parish how we shall work such a mine, make such a river navigable, drain such a fen, or improve such a waste. These things we are all immediately interested in, and have each a vote in executing; and thus we are not mere spectators in the world, but as all men ought to be, actors, and that only for our own benefit."[17]

All of these ideas were experienced in a context of the commons of the sea and of the land. The dispute over the Newcastle Town Moor delayed the enclosure of the urban commons. Fishing communities, though traditionally poor, were also among the most solid of human communities. The evolution of Spence's notion of the commons into a precursor of communism was complex, open to varieties human experience, knowledgeable of the practices of several crafts. When he spoke he did not sound like a book. He took on the landed interest in England, France, and America. Suppose "that men have

15. *Flora Londinensis,* 2:299.
16. R. Thompson, "Dies of Thomas Spence," 2126–67.
17. Spence, "A Further Account of Spensonia," in *Pig's Meat,* 2:214.

the same right to property of land as they have to liberty, and the light and heat of the sun."[18]

Spence's *The Rights of Infants* (1797) further develops his thought and recommendations. He advocates women's suffrage: "We have found our husbands, to their indelible shame, woefully negligent and deficient about their own rights, as well as those of their wives and infants, we women mean to take up the business ourselves." He had two wives but had separated from them by the time he joined the LCS. Recognizing women's association to commoning in agriculture—keeping a pig, caring for chickens, tilling a vegetable garden, and working in the open field—helps us understand that his advocacy of rights for women was supported by such knowledge. He would have known of Mary Houghton, who lost her case for gleaning to Cornwallis in 1788, or the case of Elizabeth Salmon, who was hanged in 1802 over a dispute about gleaning. When we call Spence a working-class thinker, what we mean is he thought about the workers and knew about work. He listed twenty of Paine's quotes in one column and twenty of his own in opposition in a second column to draw the sharpest contrast between their agrarian policies, though each began with the premise that the earth was common to all. In his pamphlet *Agrarian Justice* (1797), Paine claimed that agricultural "improvement" permitted landlords greater reward. "But," Spence asked, "may we not ask who improved the land?" This question was followed by a simple declaration: "the earth has been cultivated either by slaves, compelled, like beasts, to labour, or by the indigent objects whom they first exclude from a share in the soil, that want may compel them to sell their labour for daily bread." The whole product of the common belonged to the people.

In *The End of Oppression* (1795), Spence "suffers no private Property in Land, but gives it all to the Parishes." "Landed Property always was originally acquired either by conquest or encroachment on the common Property of Mankind." On insurrection, he writes "let us suppose a few thousands of hearty determined Fellows well armed and appointed with Officers, and having a Committee of honest, firm, and intelligent Men to act as a provisionary Government and to direct their Actions to the proper Object." This Committee published "a Manifesto or proclamation, directing the People in every Parish to take, on receipt thereof, immediate possession of the whole Landed Property," imprisoning those landlords who refused and burning "all

18. *Pig's Meat,* 3:230.

Writings and Documents relating to their Estates." On the possibility of the landlords persisting to resist, he says "Let the People be firm and desperate, destroying them Root and Branch, and strengthening their Hands by the rich Confiscations."[19]

His emphasis on land is not a limitation of his communism, as if "the land question" applied merely to one sector of the population, and that one whose proportion to the whole was diminishing. On the contrary, he believed that everything and everyone depended on land. There is an extraordinary passage uniting the prose of the naturalist with the polemic of the communist in 1797's *The Rights of Infants*:

> Is not this earth our common also, as well as it is the common of brutes? May we not eat herbs, berries, or nuts as well as other creatures? Have we not a right to hunt and prowl for prey with she-wolves? And have we not a right to fish with she-otters? Or may we not dig coals or cut wood for fuel? Nay, does nature provide as luxuriant and abundant feast for all her numerous tribes of animals except us? As if sorrow were our portion alone, and as if we and our helpless babes came into this world only to weep over each other?

An old folktale, popular through simple chapbooks and a favorite of Thomas Spence, tells of Thomas Hickathrift, the lazy son of a laborer but very big and strong. When a forester offers his mother a tree, Tom is able to take a very big one. A giant appears, angrily exclaiming, "Does thou not see how many heads hang upon yonder tree that have offended my law?" to which Tom rudely replies, "a turd in your teeth." This makes the giant even angrier, so they fight. When Tom wins, he takes not only the big tree but all the giant's ground, "which he gave to the poor for their common, the rest he made pasture of and divided the most part into tillage, to maintain him and his mother."[20]

In March 1801, the first Spencean meeting, one of "*Real Friends to Truth, Justice,* and HUMAN HAPPINESS," resolved "to meet frequently, though in ever smaller numbers, in their respective neighborhoods, after a Free and Easy manner, without encumbering themselves with Rules."[21] A month later "F.G." informed the Home Office that a book "which explains the way of dividing the Land and Property after a Revolution is gained" was part of

19. *Pig's Meat.*
20. Smith, *Politics of Language,* 102.
21. Quoted in Chase, *People's Farm,* 61.

conversation at a free and easy.[22] The Oakley Arms, where the mass arrest of November took place, was one such "free and easy."

Spence was for all creatures—animals, as well as humans—regardless of gender, race, or age. In 1800, the governor of Jamaica, Lord Balcarres, wrote that the Kingston population was made up of "turbulent people of all nations engaged in illicit trade; a most abandoned class of Negroes, up to every scene of mischief, and a general levelling spirit throughout."[23] Bussa's Rebellion in Barbados (1816) was inspired by a vision of liberty built on the ruins of the "privileged class," "whether promulgated under the authority of Spencean or African philanthropists." A year later, the *Royal Gazette* in Jamaica criticized "the dangerous and leveling doctrines" of Spence, deemed "not the less dangerous because its supporters belong to the lower classes of the community." In 1803, Spence himself promised to send his constitution "to St. Domingo: To the Republic of the Incas."[24]

In the Yorkshire Dales in 1792, "with the bell ringing, and the clamour of the mill, all the vale is disturb'd; treason and levelling systems are the discourse; and rebellion may be near at hand." Mr. J.A. Busfield was a leading cotton spinner and magistrate in the West Riding of Yorkshire, who wrote the home secretary, the duke of Portland, in 1795 "that turbulent and levelling Principle, my Lord, which was so recently display'd in the horrid outrage upon his Majesty's Person, is by no means confined to the Metropolis."[25] In Despard's home county Queens, Eyre Coote privately wrote Sarah Coote on 16 February 1793 that "in my mind estates are in a ticklish way. Many counties are this day ruled by a mob—Louth, Meath, Armagh, and Monaghan. How matters will turn out is impossible to say, & I think the levelers are more dangerous by far than the Catholics."[26]

The Association for the Protection of Liberty and Property from Republicans and Levellers was founded on 20 November 1792 at the Crown and Anchor Inn by John Reeves (1752–1829), whose previous work included counsel to the Royal Mint, superintendent of aliens, and paymaster to the Metropolitan Police. John Reeves testified against Despard at the parliamentary inquiry into the conditions of the Cold Bath Fields Prison: "The mixture

22. NA, HO 42/61/484.
23. Julius Scott, *Common Wind,* 33.
24. Cazzola, "'All Shall Be Happy.'"
25. E.E. Dodd, "Alarm at Elland," *Bradford Antiquary,* n.s., 42 (1964).
26. Estate and Legal papers, Ireland 1798–1827, 32/7, Cootes Papers.

of Whigs and democrats advocate universal suffrage and annual Parliaments though they know that "the destruction of Monarchy must inevitably follow; and a leveling Republic may then be substituted according to the imaginations and will of this rabble."[27]

A broadsheet titled "The Perverse Definition Imposed on the Word Equality" (c. 1792) contrasts the equality of rights with the equality of wealth "The rule is not '*Let all mankind be perpetually equal*.'—God and nature have forbidden it. But '*Let all mankind start fair in the race of life*.' The *inequality* derived from labour and successful enterprise, the result of superior industry and good fortune, is *an inequality essential to the very existence of Society*." "Let us hear no more of LEVELLERS and LEVELLING SYSTEMS; nor let an odium be thrown on GREAT UNCHANGEABLE TRUTHS from the equivocal meaning of a word."[28]

Dr. Vincent's *Short Hints upon Levelling* was published by the Association for the Protection of Liberty and Property against Republicans and Levellers after the founding of the association in November 1792. Twenty thousand copies were sold at one penny each. William Vincent (1739–1815) was the dean of Westminster and chaplain to the king. As headmaster of the Westminster School, he was known for "his love for the rod." "All history and all experience prove, that wherever Society exists there must exist a class of poor. Those who deny the necessary existence of such a class, who assert that the gifts of Nature and the bounties of providence are common to all, intend no good to the poor themselves, but mean to excite discontent and tumult, and use the poor as an instrument in an attack meditated upon the rich." Poverty "is a good when compared with the miseries of savage life" and New Zealanders and American Indians prove this, "their hand is against every man, and every man's hand against them."[29]

Hannah More (1745–1833), the bluestocking philanthropist and evangelical moralist, published a brilliant short pamphlet called *Village Politics: Addressed to All the Mechanics, Journeymen, and Day Labourers in Great Britain* (1793). Prompted by the bishop of London, and designed, according to More, "for the most vulgar class, this hugely successful work was characterized as "Burke for Beginners." In it she imagined a dialogue between Tom Hod, a mason, and Jack Anvil, a blacksmith.

27. Reeves, *Thoughts on English Government*, 74.
28. Claeys, *Political Writings*, 3:403–4.
29. Vincent, *Short Hints*.

TOM. I want Liberty and Equality.

JACK. Thou art a Leveller and a republican.

TOM. I'm a friend of the people.

TOM. What are gaols for? Down with the gaols, I say; all men should be free.

JACK. A few rogues in prison keep the rest in order.

TOM. I'm for a Constitution and Organization and Equalization.

JACK. If everyone is digging potatoes on their half acre no one is available to make clothes or repair a broken spade.

Effective among children and the near literate, this pamphlet was the opening salvo of a barrage of simpleminded pieties called cheap repository tracts that was launched at the end of the decade. For Hannah More those advocating the equalization of the commons became an "Other" in her *Black Giles, the Poacher* (1801), who with his wife "Tawney Rachel" associated the perpetrators of violent robberies with black people.[30]

Against this onslaught the LCS took a defensive stance. On 29 November 1792, the chairman M. Margarot and secretary T. Hardy published a small pamphlet titled *Address of the London Corresponding Society,* in which they call the accusations made by the aristocratic association that the clubs and societies were designed to invade property, "a willful, an impudent, and a malicious Falsehood." "We know and are sensible that the Wages of every Man are his Right; that *Difference of Strength, of Talents, and of Industry, do and ought to afford proportional Distinctions of Property, which,* when acquired and confirmed by the Laws, is *sacred and inviolable.*"[31]

On 10 January 1793, a motion for printing an explanation of the word equality was defeated by the LCS. Days later it recommended publishing instead "resolutions to refute the charge of being Levelors [*sic*]." In July, the LCS addressed the nation, "Those who would restore the House of Commons to a state of independence have been labeled levellers." In 1795, it issued the handbill "An Explicit Declaration of the Principles and Views of the L.C.S." In their ideas of equality, "they have never included (nor, till the associations of alarmists broached the frantic notion, could they ever have conceived that so wild and detestable a sentiment could have entered the brain of man) . . . the equalization of property."[32] The LCS suffered from its inability to clarify

30. More, *Village Politics.*
31. London Corresponding Society, *Selections from the Papers.*
32. London Corresponding Society, *Selections from the Papers.*

the commons: did it mean equitable land distribution or access to subsistence?

The doubts and confusions were widespread among the respectable radicals, if not among plebeians and proletarians. Here for example is the physician, Thomas Beddoes: "we have LEVELLERS at home, who would equally divide our lands and houses, goods and chattels, assign to each man his lot." The thought is prompted by the negro revolt. "No individual, I believe, of sound mind, has hinted a wish for this species of equalization. It is true, that a few benevolent enthusiasts, seeing that almost all crimes may be referred to extreme poverty, to the desire or abuse of wealth, have imagined that in some distant age men would become Christian in more than profession, 'love their neighbour as themselves,' and agree that the ground might be tilled for the common benefit."[33]

In Elizabeth Inchbald's powerful and radical novel *Nature and Art,* begun in 1794 and published in 1796, the matter is quickly laid to rest in a short dialogue:

"And what are the rich for?"
"To be served by the poor."
"But suppose the poor would not serve them?"
"Then they must starve."

In other words, "In respect to placing all persons on a level, it is utterly impossible—God has ordained it otherwise." It is a revolutionary catechism employed to great effect in chapter 15 of Volney's *The Ruins of Empire,* published in English in 1793, the year before Inchbald started *Nature and Art.* The chapter was frequently published as a leaflet.

PEOPLE. "And what labor to you perform in our society?"
PRIVILEGED CLASS. "None; we are not made to work."
PEOPLE. "How, then, have you acquired these riches?"
PRIVILEGED CLASS. "By taking the pains to govern you."

Inchbald's novel puts the class analysis in the mouth of Hannah Primrose, an agricultural worker, who walks to London with her infant to find a scanty subsistence, first as a kitchen pot washer and then as a sexual prostitute. At that point, "She began to suspect that dishonesty was only held a sin to secure

33. *Where Would Be the Harm of a Speedy Peace* (London, 1795), 8.

the property of the rich; and that to take from those who did not want by the art of stealing was less guilty than to take from those who did want by the power of law."[34]

Also published in 1796 was *Man as He Is Not; or, Hermsprong,* written by the paper mill owner Robert Bage (1728–1801). Hermsprong is an egalitarian, who prefers going on foot to riding a horse or sitting in a carriage. He says, "I was born a savage." His father and mother go to Michillimakinac from England, and he speaks the language of an Indian tribe from infancy and finds the Indians his equal, but superior in friendship, hospitality, and integrity. In 1792, at age six, he leaves America. "Savages like me have no idea of the happiness of incessant labour." "You have built cities, no doubt, and filled them full of improvement, if magnificence be improvement; and of poverty also, if poverty be improvement." Wealth does not bring happiness. Of the word equality, Hermsprong says, "The poor word, my lord, has been so used and abused, has been made to mean so many things it did not mean, that I do not choose to have any thing to do with it." He warns, "People of family, now there are so many levellers about, ought to be more careful than ever." During a food riot among Cornish miners, he tells the rioters, "My friends, we cannot all be rich; there is no possible equality of property which can last a day. If you were capable of desiring it, which I hope you are not, you must wade through such scenes of guilt and horror to obtain it as you would tremble to think of."[35]

The practices and the theories of commons were Atlantic—that is, Scottish, Irish, and Native American. While John Oswald was a Scotsman and Despard an Irishman, they were both soldiers who became revolutionaries. Both met violent deaths: Despard on the scaffold and Oswald on the field of battle. Emissaries of the commons, they helped to expand its meanings from particular localities, enriching its universalist claims by grounding them in experience. Oswald, born in Edinburgh (1760) and apprenticed to a jeweler, embarked on a thirteen-month journey to India. Stopping north of Madagascar on the isle of Joanna, he met an Abyssinian oracle, who informed him that "Englishman and Joannaman were all one brother."[36]

In 1793 France, John Oswald published *The Government of the People; or, A Sketch of a Constitution for the Universal Common-Wealth.* He advocated

34. *Nature and Art*; Volney, *Ruins,* 64.
35. *Man as He Is Not,* 179, 319.
36. Erdman, *Commerce des Lumières,* 22.

direct democracy based on neighborhood assemblies, where people might debate such questions as "Whether the land should be cultivated in common, or divided equally between the individuals of the nation?" To him the commons was worldly, not at all parochial, in scope. He commoned with his sons on the outskirts of Paris by foraging in the woods for food. It became part of revolutionary discourse; he made it part of the "rights of man." We see this evolution of the rights of man to include the commons in the project of the United Irish; in Wolfe Tone's "men of no property," in Robert Emmet's proclamation in the summer of 1803, and in William Drennan's intended defense in June 1794 against a charge of sedition. It was Drennan who suggested allying with England, France, Scotland, and America to form a republican brotherhood, which would become the United Irishmen. He composed its oath of allegiance: "I shall do whatever lies in my power to forward a brotherhood of affection, an identity of interests, a communion of rights, and an union of power among Irishmen of all religious persuasions." Three years later he faced a sedition charge.

Drennan called for "the common rights of humanity," which were threatened by the claims of property "to dominion and ascendancy" and which converted "persons into things, and men into cattle. To Drennan, the tenant in the hovel and the wretch lying in the street are products of an estranged humanity created by one great corporation of the propertied. He wrote,

> It appears to me that the fluctuation which attends property is, of itself, a proof, how absurd it is to base the rights of man on a bottom so instable; and still more so to draw circles around places, as if to encompass or confine a quality so fugitive, and to seat the genius of the constitution on the still revolving wheel of blind and capricious fortune.... By attaching the oldest inheritance of the whole people to certain round spots of earth, gives a locality to liberty, inconsistent with its nature: turns legislators into land-measurers, and land-measurers into legislators; extending lines of demarcation, on the one side of which privilege is heaped up, and on the other, common right trodden down.[37]

That Native Americans held "all things in common" was a commonplace.[38] Irish people in particular allied with Native Americans during the Indian Wars of the 1790s. Lord Edward Fitzgerald, the assassinated commander of the liberation army of the United Irish, befriended Tom Paine in

37. Deane, *Field Day Anthology*, 3:323.
38. Winterbotham, *Historical, Geographical, Commercial,* 1:102–5.

Paris, where in 1792, he substituted his aristocratic title for the revolutionary designation Citizen Edward. His lifelong servant and partner, Tony Small, a former slave from South Carolina, accompanied him on a long journey from the Atlantic along the waterways of the North American Great Lakes and down the Mississippi River. Their journey included induction into the commoning ways of the Seneca, of the Iroquois Confederacy, who conferred on Edward the name Eghnidal at a ceremony in 1788.[39]

Denis Driscol, once editor of the *Cork Gazette* formerly a Catholic priest, and once imprisoned for advocating an agrarian law became a deist in America. He had been tried in Ireland for equating private property with robbery and imprisoned for advocating the agrarian law. A month before Despard was executed, he wrote, "The earth is the common inheritance of all men. Every man has a right to a proportionate share of the country he lies in. He who possesses a greater share of the land he lives in, than another is a monopolist and a usurper of the rights of his fellow citizens." Further, "The whole moral system, as far as it respects property, must be revised."[40]

James Reynolds, county Tyrone, traced the roots of social evil not to hereditary privilege or to private property in land but to private property itself and to the class structure that was its social formulation.[41] In an address to the people of Ireland, he wrote, "Property is merely the collection of labour: it possesses the very same qualities before, as after, it is collected into a heap." It's the cause of despotism. In 1794, Reynolds moved to the United States, where he attacked George Washington, declaring in March 1797 that the victory of his successor ought to bring about "a jubilee in the United States"[42]

Charles Pigott, satirical author of the *Political Dictionary* (1795), wrote that the biblical Adam was "a true Sans Culottes and the first revolutionist" and defined *weal* as follows: "*Weal*. The common weal, the public weal, the general weal, so much regarded in Saxon antiquity, is now out of date, and sneered at by our legislators; in so much, that if a man talks of the public weal, he is a visionary; and if he by action, strives to promote the general weal, he is a rebel, and a leveller." Relatedly, the hero of William Godwin's novel *Caleb Williams* (1794) escapes from wrongful imprisonment, exclaiming "Ah, this

39. Tillyard, *Citizen Lord*. See also my comparison of the careers of Fitzgerald and Despard in "'A Dish with One Spoon.'"

40. *American Patriot,* 25 January 1803.

41. Twomey, *Jacobins and Jeffersonians*, 214.

42. Durey, *Transatlantic Radicals*.

is indeed to be a man!" He finds refuge with a gang of thieves in the forest: "Our profession is the profession of justice," says one. "One man steals in one way, and another in another." The captain of the thieves insists that Caleb take "a share at the time that each man received his dividend from the common stock."[43]

The debate between the commons and the true commons was not restricted to advanced thinkers in polite drawing rooms or to the closely surveilled public houses of London. It was also found among the enclosed workers of the textile industries in the north of England, where the discussion was closely attached to illegalities and insurrection: Writing to Earl Fitzwilliam, William Cookson observed that "a System of Combination has for some time been forming which is now so compleat, that the Clothworkers or Shearmen act & move by one general plan, throughout the Kingdom. The Nocturnal Meetings are not Immediately Connected with the System to which I allude. Very few of the Clothworkers are supos'd to attend those Meetings—they are Compos'd of Labouring poor of all descriptions—... The abolition of Taxes, of pensions, *the natural rights of mankind to the produce of the Soil,* [my emphasis] form the leading Points with the abettors of the Nocturnal meetings."[44]

In December 1800, Cookson wrote to Fitzwilliam warning that in Stavely "there are a few Sicklesmiths . . . who call themselves White Boys," who with private signals, nocturnal insults, overturn haystacks and mutilate sheep on enclosed land. "Several meetings have been lately held in the neighbourhood, at 10 o'clock in the Evening—an orator in a mask harangues the people— reads letters from distant societies by the light of a candle & immediately burns them." In May 1802, he related events in Huddersfield, where authorities stopped a riot by taking away the football. In June 1802, he described midnight meetings in Barnsley, where the "lower ranks . . . speak consistently & steadily of a time approaching when a sudden and midnight insurrection shall lead them to assert & regain their native rights." In July 1802, the mayor of Leeds reported that "several meetings have been held in fields & on open Commons - at which 3 to 400 Men have been present—Chiefly of the Labouring Poor."[45] The commons was thus a point of resistance, a place from whence an offensive, such as Despard's, might take place.

43. Pigott, *Political Dictionary*; Godwin, *Caleb Williams.*
44. William Cookson to Earl Fitzwilliam, 16 August 1802, Leeds, F.45/79, Wentworth Woodhouse Collection.
45. F.45/42–114.

PART THREE

———

LOVE AND STRUGGLE

FIGURES 13 AND 14. "We Also Are the People" and
"Who Know Their Rights and Knowing Dare Maintain."
Two trade tokens struck by Thomas Spence.

H

THE "BUSINESS"

TWENTY-FIVE

"The Business"

WE ARE NEVER GOING TO KNOW the facts of Despard's conspiracy for certain, but it is a fact that on the evening of Tuesday, 16 November 1802, Despard was arrested with forty others at the Oakley Arms public house in Oakley Street, Lambeth. Despard's role in the conspiracy can be teased out from the reports of spies preserved in the national archives of England, France, and Ireland—what was said at Dublin dinner parties, what paid informants saw or heard, a report on a sermon at a remote moorland chapel, what a fellow traveler said in the coach, who in prison would snitch.[1] This produces history by rumor and whispers but leaves out both social forces and ideas. Moreover, since evidence of the conspiracy is inconclusive, we are compelled to broaden the context. From this we find connections from London to the midlands to the north of England. We also find continuities to 1798 (and even the seventeenth century, as in Enfield), as well as continuities going forward to Robert Emmet's revolt of 1803. Despard aligned himself with an Irish militant *republican* party, though he is generally not extolled in Irish *nationalist* history, mainly because his theater of action was England. The Irish republicans were closely associated with the Scottish Convention movement and with the democratic societies in England, such as the London Corresponding Society, the United English, or the United Britons, all of which propounded popular sovereignty inspired by the American and French revolutions. Government had suppressed them by the time Despard was imprisoned as a suspect in 1798.

We can approach the conspiracy through its public houses. In the course of Despard's trial, eighteen different public houses were mentioned:[2] the Oakley

---

1. Madden, *United Irishmen*, 2:293.
2. Howell, *Complete Collection*.

London Corresponding Society, alarm'd, Vide. Guilty Conscience

FIGURE 15. *London Corresponding Society, Alarm'd*. Etching by James Gillray, 20 April 1798. The simian look of the democrats of the London Corresponding Society anticipates the bestialization of the Atlantic proletariat in hostile graphic arts. Irish people and then African people were portrayed to look like monkeys, thereby contributing to the formation of racist stereotypes in the nineteenth century.

Arms, the Ham and Windmill, the Black Horse, the Bleeding Heart, the Flying Horse, the Tyger, the Coach and Horses, the Brown Bear, the Running Horse, the Spread Eagle, the Hoop and Ram, the Bell, the Two Bells, the Black Raven, the King's Head, the Coach and Horses, the Queen's Arms, and the Angel. Five were in Saint Giles-in-the-Fields, a virtual autonomous zone of the proletariat; three were south of the river; six were East End river parishes; and one or two were around Moorfields. The public house was the principal urban institution of plebeian social life. There a night's sleep could be obtained or long term lodging for single people, couples, and families. There a meal might be taken. Certainly, drink, beer especially, was consumed. Wages were paid there and work gangs were organized there. Songs were sung and stories told. Credit might be obtained, with services rendered on the tick. Plots might be hatched, treasons whispered, curses uttered, visions expressed, or books discussed. Conviviality reigned supreme. There were thousands in London alone. They helped constitute the common life of the common people.

Consequently, they were licensed, which is to say they were watched or policed. A few years earlier, the police magistrate Patrick Colquhoun conducted a study of the six thousand London alehouses. He believed a substantial proportion of the London poor lived in them with their families. Because "in modern times they are become the general receptacle of the vicious, the idle, and the profligate," licensing them was the important work of police. Colquhoun proposed numerous regulations combining censorship, union prohibition, and wage regulation, including the following,:

> No licensed publican shall permit, on any pretence whatsoever, any debating or political club, for the purpose of seditious or traitorous designs against the government or constitution of the country, to assemble in his house, nor suffer any books or papers to be read, or songs to be sung, of a seditious or immoral tendency, on pain of losing the license. . . .

> No publican shall permit journeymen, or working people of any description, to assemble in his house, for the purpose of unlawful combinations or confederacies, which may disturb or obstruct the general industry of the country, on any pretence whatsoever.

> No pay tables shall be permitted in any licensed alehouse, since journeymen and laborers are thereby often enticed improvidently to spend a large proportion of their weekly earnings, which ought to be set apart for the support of their families.[3]

3. Colquhoun *Treatise on Indigence*, 284–92.

Public houses could not be an effective base of organization. Despard was overhead to say, "a regular organization in London is dangerous to us, it is under the eye of the Government; but a regular organization in the country is necessary, and, I believe, general; and that the people were everywhere ripe and anxious for the moment of attack ... particularly in Leeds, Sheffield, in Birmingham." Graffiti appeared in Birmingham expressing the bloody minded mood: "May Pitt's ribs be converted to a gridiron and the King's heart roasted thereon."[4] Despard, with his characteristic green silk umbrella with its yellow-hook handle, was upstairs attending a meeting at the Oakley Arms. "The business," as they called it, of the evening was treason—to launch an insurrection on the following Tuesday.

John Emblin recalled what Colonel Despard said at the Queen's Arms in Vauxhall: "The day was fixed for the attack to be made when the King went to the House. The King will be stopped when he goes to the House, and the business will be settled."[5] Later he heard Thomas Broughton say, "My boy, we have the completest plan in the world, which will do the business without any trouble.... To load the great gun in the park with four balls or chain shot, and fire it at his Majesty as he returns from the house."[6] The "business" was evolving in both its goals and its methods. Thomas Blades recalled the conversation and seating arrangements at the Oakley Arms: "Those who came to settle the business" should have preference of the fire and those who come "to show their good will" should go to the far end of the room. When a number of people are "upon such business" wrangles arise, so it's best to reduce the number.[7]

Asked the object of the meetings, the conspirator Thomas Windsor, who turned state's evidence, replied, "to unite ourselves, to raise subscriptions to pay delegates, to go into the country, and to pay the expence of printing these affidavits, to overturn the system of Government, and to destroy the Royal Family."[8] Of a two-and-a-half hour meeting at the Flying Horse in Newington on 12 November, the Friday after Lord Mayor's Day, Thomas Windsor remembered that Broughton, Emblin, Samuel Smith, and Arthur Graham were present. He mentioned Leeds, Sheffield, Manchester, and Birmingham, among other cities. The "mail coaches were to be stopped, as a signal to the

4. NA, HO, 42/62/1645.
5. *Trial of Edward Marcus Despard*, 124.
6. *Trial*, 133.
7. *Trial*, 100.
8. *Trial*, 72.

people in the country, that they had revolted in town." William Francis, a guard at the Tower, was told by Despard that "there was nothing to be done, for he expected some money and news to come from France." This was the strategic argument that had divided the leadership of the United Irishmen.

The guns and the money, these were the instruments of power if not sovereignty. "Surely the Bank ought to be almost the first consideration, for if we have the Bank and the Tower, we have everything: that he could from the Tower, if necessary, burn the town and batter it to pieces."[9] Windsor said that they had been deceived by the number of arms in the Bank: "there are no more than six hundred, and they have taken the hammers off, to render them useless, as they must have been apprised of our intention." Despard discussed the plans that they take the arms belonging to the East India Company, gather the artillery pieces at the Artillery Ground, and dispatch mounted couriers to gather their own intelligence at a central location.

Some of the conspirators were given to study and possessed books. At the Bleeding Heart in Hatton Garden. Blades, Wood, Macnamara, and others met Despard who read a paper "concerning the plan of taking the Tower, the Bank, and the Horse Guards" and then asked them to kiss it.[10] John Bird read the card but would not kiss the book: "I put it to my head as if I kissed it [and then] chucked it to him, and it fell on the floor, and he took it up and put it in his pocket."[11] In August, John Francis invited John Bird, a shoemaker of Oakingham, New Windsor, whose master worked for the royal family, to join the society. The king will be dethroned, said Francis, who was present in Windsor with his regiment. There would be a new Parliament, he declared, and "every parish was to form themselves into a committee of fourteen, and then into seven, and one out of every seven was to come into the Parliament house."

This reflects the plan of Thomas Spence, who to quote his *End of Oppression* (1795) "suffers no private Property in Land, but gives it all to the Parishes." Thomas Spence came to London and, despite repeated arrests and ugly harassments, determinedly agitated and argued for this plan throughout the 1790s and through the first decade and a half of the nineteenth century. "Landed Property always was originally acquired either by conquest or

---

9. *Trial,* 134–35, 82–83. These rumors reached the ears of the Privy Council. See NA, PC 1/3117/48, 51.

10. *Trial,* 106.

11. *Trial,* 114.

encroachment on the common Property of Mankind." The "business" certainly included the return of land to the common.

Spence was tried in May 1801, but not by a jury of his peers, which at least in his opinion ought to have included propertyless laborers. He was sentenced to a year in prison for writing and publishing *The Restorer of Society to its Natural State.*[12] He read aloud the entire text at his defense, which enabled him to publish it as *The Important Trial of Thomas Spence,* thereby avoiding censorship. (Lord Ellenborough, later the judge at Despard's trial, was attorney general at the time under the name Edward Law. He filed the information against Spence for seditious libel.)

The End of Oppression (1795) outlined a revolutionary scenario: "Let us suppose a few thousands of hearty determined Fellows well armed and appointed with Officers, and having a Committee of honest, firm, and intelligent Men to act as a provisionary Government and to direct their Actions to the proper Object. If this Committee published a Manifesto or proclamation, directing the People in every Parish to take, on receipt thereof, immediate possession of the whole Landed Property," imprisoning those landlords who refused and burning "all Writings and Documents relating to their Estates," and if the landlords persisted in resistance, "let the People be firm and desperate, destroying them Root and Branch, and strengthening their Hands by the rich Confiscations."[13] In 1801, a radical of the United Englishmen recommended a book "which explains the way of dividing the Land and Property after a Revolution is gained."[14]

Francis offered a book to Bird, asking him to kiss it and safeguard it, because "he did not like to keep it at the barracks." What could this book have been if not one by Thomas Spence? Bird was asked to join his society. For what? *"To fight, to burst the chain of bondage and slavery."*[15] William Francis, who could not read, was told that the purpose was "to overthrow the present system of Government, and kill all the Royal Family; and *help me God* was at the bottom of it; it was a small card."[16]

The coconspirators referred to their own organization as "the society." Thomas Blades was invited by John Francis "to take an oath to join into their

12. Worrall, *Radical Culture,* 47–53.
13. Spence, *Pig's Meat.*
14. NA, HO 42/61/484, "F.J.," April 1801.
15. *Trial,* 115.
16. *Trial,* 104.

society."[17] He took the oath by reading from the card. Despard asked Windsor at the Coach and Horses, Whitechapel, whether he knew the two soldiers sitting at the top of the table. Despard said, "I believe they belong to us," meaning "belonging to the society the same as myself."[18] John Emblin objected to "the plan for overturning the present government. Broughton called them "the Man Eaters" (see chapter 21). Emblin was invited to attend the meetings of "this society." He said he couldn't because he had to attend to his family. So Broughton called at Emblin's house and spoke to his wife, pressing him to attend meetings of the society.

Mack, or John Macnamara, swore Thomas Tomlinson into "a free and easy society, to overthrow the Government, and have our nation the same as France."[19] Is this the United Britons, or the United English? What is "a free and easy society"? A year earlier, in March 1801, the first Spencean group met in London and adopted Spence's principles, resolving, as a broadside put it, to recommend to well wishers "to meet frequently, though in ever so small Numbers, in their respective Neighbourhoods, after a Free and Easy manner, without encumbering themselves with Rules, to converse on the Subject, provoke investigation, and answer such objections as may be stated, and to promote the circulation of Citizen Spence's Pamphlets."[20] To "have our nation the same as France" begs many questions, while at the same time it reasserts revolutionary change.

Thomas Blades remembered a meeting on Monday, 13 September 1802, at the Bleeding Heart, Hatton Garden. More than a dozen were present besides himself. Wratten had come from Southwark to learn when the attack would take place. Penderill answered one way, John Francis another, saying, "*He thought it would be better to make the attack as soon as possible, at least before the Den of Thieves met*,'" which was the term he made use of for Parliament." The Parliament of landlords passed ninety-six enclosure acts in 1802 alone. Each one was an outright confiscation of common lands or the common rights of commoners, and a major augmentation of the rent rolls, revenues, and produce of the enclosers, or discommoners.

John Stafford, the first witness for the Crown and chief clerk of the Police Office, provided "paper no. 1" as evidence. It read as follows:

17. *Trial,* 94–95.
18. *Trial,* 83.
19. *Trial,* 123, 120.
20. Quoted in Chase, *People's Farm,* 61.

The independence of Great Britain and Ireland. An equalization of Civil, Political, and Religious Rights; an ample Provision for the families of the Heroes who shall fall in the contest.

A liberal Reward for distinguished Merit.

These are the objects for which we contend; and to obtain these objects we swear to be united.

In the awful Presence of Almighty God, I, A.B. do voluntarily declare that I will endeavor to the utmost of my power to obtain the objects of this Union; namely, to recover those rights which the Supreme Being in his infinite bounty has given to all men; that neither hopes nor fears, rewards nor punishments shall ever induce me to give any Information, directly or indirectly, concerning the Business, of any member of this or any similar Society.

So help me God.[21]

In Thomas Blades's recollection of the oath, "the society was determined to get those rights which God had ordained for them."[22] He had been told, "A great number of independent gentlemen had united themselves together, to form and establish a free and independent constitution for the present constitution was much broken." Labeling paper no. 1 a "constitution" showed the purpose of the society or the business was clearly to repair what had been broken. *United* and *equalization* are the key terms, with the former invoking the United Irishmen and the latter indicating Spencean influence.

In opening the case against Despard, the attorney general said, "It seems to me to be clear that an annihilation of all distinctions and inequalities of rank, property, or political right whatever, is the fair, the reasonable, and the necessary interpretation of [these words]."[23] The purpose of the union being "to recover those rights which the Supreme Being in his infinite bounty has given to all men" certainly suggests not just rights, or notional equality but an actuality—namely, "infinite bounty."

The techniques of the planned insurrection remain murky, because evidence depends on dubious testimony, hidden government spies, and censored

---

21. *People's Farm,* 64.
22. *People's Farm,* 94.
23. *People's Farm,* 37.

or repressed witnesses. In the wake of defeat, of course, the plan seems impossible, or insane—foolhardy at best. A notion of "infinite bounty" combined with the goal of annihilating inequalities provided "the business" with its attraction to a working class prohibited from discussing fundamental goals or acting to obtain them.

TWENTY-SIX

The Kiss of Love and Equalization

THE KISS OF THE CARD was an act of commitment to ideas and a gesture of union with people. The kiss might signify a greeting or peace, marriage, or love. It might be a kiss of death, or indicate a betrayal or sexuality. For Despard and his coconspirators, it was a gesture of allegiance and loyalty. Some of these inherent incompatibilities arose in the trial. The contradiction between the kiss as part of a ritual of allegiance and the kiss as a gesture of sexual pleasure will undermine the solemnity of the proceedings. Following is Thomas Blades's examination and testimony:

Q. What did you do when you read the card?

A. I kissed the card.

Q. Who told you to kiss the card.

A. John Francis.

Q. Why did you kiss the card; was that the manner in which you were to be sworn?

A. It was.

Q. In consequence of kissing the card where did you go with it?

A. After we had settled our business on the parade, we went up to the Ham and Windmill.

LORD ELLENBOROUGH. Did this pass upon the parade?

A. Yes, I was sworn upon the parade.[1]

The Horse Guards Parade was the headquarters of the British army. It was a paved open space reserved for exhibitions of power. It was also a

1. *Trial of Edward Marcus Despard*, 25.

precious urban space in Whitehall that is surrounded today by the Admiralty and the Banqueting House in front of a Palladian palace built in 1750–58. There Charles I was beheaded. It became the site of significant reviews, parades, and ceremonies, such as the Trooping of the Colors, and the location of military trophies, such as a Turkish cannon taken from Egypt in 1801. In asking whether the kiss took place on the Parade, Ellenborough was drawing out the symbolism of the oath to show the depth of Despard's subversion of authority. William Francis refused to kiss the card. When Despard offered to swear him in some time around Bartholomew Fair Day, William Francis said never, having already "been sworn once to my King and Country."[2]

In times of war and developing class consciousness, the question of allegiance becomes fraught as we find in the story of the spy Thomas Hirst. Solidarity here was tied to the labor theory of value. Hirst was with the Twenty-Eighth Light Dragoons in Ireland, when it was disbanded at Clonmel, county Tipperary, in May 1802. He marched to Dublin, from whence he sailed to Liverpool. On board ship, he met a man called Johnston Blood, who was evidently an experienced agitator for revolutionary causes. Blood asked Thomas Hirst,

> "How do you do, Sir, you appear to me to have been in the army."
>
> I answered "I have, sir."
>
> ". . . and are you fond of the Army?
>
> "I like it pretty well."
>
> "That's because you have no common sense—why sir—why sir, are you blind, a promising youth like you and knows no better and been in Ireland too?"

Having obtained his attention, Blood told him his society was strong in Yorkshire, "a good part for humanity and the cause." What cause could that be, wondered Hirst. "A cause of Justice my dear fellow." Then Hirst fell seasick. "I then dropt discourse and fell very sick with the Sea, where he attended me very much."

In Liverpool, they met again and resumed their conversation. "I hope we will yet become Brothers," said Blood. He added, quoting the constitution card "In love and Equalization."

2. *Trial,* 108.

"I wonder very much at the people of England been so very blind."

"In what Sir?"

"To see themselves Imposed on by a Government."

I then said "are you a Man of Property, Sir?"

"No, Sir."

"You labour for your living?"

"Yes."

"Any Gentleman that employs you I dare say pays you your Wages?"

"Yes, Sir."

"And what have you to do with Government? Why taxes are too heavy: You have no taxes to pay if you have no property."

"Why, Sir, but my wages is not enough for my Labour."

"I suppose you want the whole to yourself alone?"

"No Sir, I do not, but the fruits of me [blank]."

"Is not your Wages the fruits of your Labour?"

"Not half, Sir, there is too many Noblemen for me to have the fruits of me labour."

After these conversations, Hirst swore the oath of the United Irishmen, received a printed ticket, and soon attended meetings with conductors from Portsmouth, London, and Ireland. "I then see Instruction of this cause of which I read, was to seize at the Breach, the Arms, and every King's store, to take the Gentlemen of each County and their property and Provisions, that Government would not starve out before overturned, each Man after was according to his family to have his equal part of Ground & choose their own Government every season—no Government to sit twice after their seizure, &c."[3]

The language is garbled, but we hear fragments from Thomas Spence. When not conveyed by word of mouth, these ideas were transmitted by "paper" and "cards." These ideas included the labor theory of value, the rotation of government, the confiscation of estates, the *taxation populaire* of provisioning, and the notion that equality was an active accomplishment rather than a static or stationary state.[4] In this respect, the ends and the means of revolution are united. Equality is *acted* as much as it is *enacted*; performed rather than proclaimed. The evidence, even at the trial, did not

3. Rebellion Papers, 1798, National Archive of Ireland.
4. F.45/78, 12 July 1802, Wentworth Woodhouse Collection, Sheffield Archives.

show that they were imagining the King's death, as the law of treason required. Rather they were talking about it in relation to the restoration of the constitution, the equalization of rights, and the provision of subsistence. Everyone was to get "his equal part of Ground."

When Thomas Blades was sworn in at the Parade in June 1802, he was able to remember the day because it was "the same evening the balloon went off from Lord's cricket ground."[5] Such crowds expressed a "collective gasp of hope and longing," writes Richard Holmes, who compares the balloon crowd to the revolutionary crowd as both uplifting and terrifying. Such evenings were "communal expressions of hope and wonder."[6] They inspired Luke Howard, the first professional meteorologist, who published *On the Modification of Clouds* (1803), seeing the earth in a new way, as a giant organism of mutual interaction of waters, land, and sky. Its effect was like that of the first NASA photo of planet earth.[7] His nomenclature of clouds (cirrus, cumulus, stratus, and nimbus) was designed "to apply the key of Analysis to the experience of others," which he expropriated from mariners and husbandmen, whose knowledge was expressed simply as a "mass of simple aphorisms." Goethe wrote a poem for Howard, and J. M. W. Turner found ways of representing atmosphere. The gaze of these visionaries was an ambitious, accumulating, classifying one akin to Humboldt's as he at the same time traversed the mountains and rivers of South America.

Thomas Broughton asked Thomas Windsor to join him at the Flying Horse, where Windsor used to buy his regular beer. At first he refused, saying "I could not neglect my business, that I had a wife and family to maintain." When Broughton replied that he neglected his, Windsor relented. At the meeting, he heard Despard expound on the business and conclude with a "remarkable expression." Despard said, "I have weighed the matter well, and my heart is callous."

LORD ELLENBOROUGH. What immediately preceded that?

A. I believe it was at the time when he said the people are every where ripe; he said, "the people are every where ripe, I have weighed the matter well and my heart is callous."

5. *Trial,* 95.
6. Holmes, *Age of Wonder,* 160–61.
7. Holmes, *Age of Wonder,* 160–61.

LORD ELLENBOROUGH. Had he, before that, mentioned that an attack was to be made on his Majesty, and his Majesty was to be put to death, before he said, his heart was callous?

A. He had mentioned that.[8]

Thomas Emblin also testified to Despard's "callous heart." After a laughable dispute concerning whether to shoot the horses of the king's carriage to make it stop, the question arose of what would happen if someone shot the horses. The person doing so would be cut to pieces by the horse riders. "Who would execute so dangerous a thing?" According to Emblin, Despard replied, "I would do it with my own hand." He then said, "I have weighed this matter well, and my heart is callous."[9]

It is Despard's heart that condemns him. How romantic! More romance is to follow, for another kind of kiss often figures in these proceedings. Three people describe it. First, Windsor.

Q. Did you see the servant girl that night?

A. The servant girl came into the room several times that night.

Q. Did any body give her any thing?

A. Mr. Emblin gave her two or three pence, and he said, "I will kiss you when I come again," or, "I'll have a kiss when I come again."

Second, Thomas Emblin. Speaking to the prosecutor, he said, "I hope you will not think of mentioning what was said jocosely; there is no harm attaches to it."[10] "The girl seemed awkward taking it, and I said, never mind, I will have a kiss the next time. It was spoke only jocosely."

These proceedings show that several witnesses were family men, whose responsibilities might have curtailed their presence at some meetings. Further, meetings took place not at the lodging house but at the public house, where men and women could freely mix and a kiss might be bought and sold, taken or given. These were elements of the urban commons.

The third person to describe the kiss was Mary Plowman, keeper of the Flying Horse. She remembered the man with the umbrella coming in a little before eight o'clock. The others gathered in the backroom and drew the curtain. Leaning over the bar, she heard one say that "he'd weighed every thing

8. *Trial of Edward Marcus Despard,* 80.
9. *Trial,* 128.
10. *Trial,* 130.

well within him, and God may know, his heart was callous." When it came to the reckoning, she said, "They came to the bar and had four glasses of gin and a glass of rum, which came to nine pence. I gave threepence change to a little man; he gave it to my maid, and turned and told her he would have a kiss for it next time he came. There was a tall swarthy man desired I might not give him wash; Windsor answered and said, what he had would be good here."[11] This is the third version of the incident that shows the close association between the callous heart and the wanton kiss. Thomas Malthus included prostitution, along with famine, plague, and war, as a "positive check" on population. In Dr. Johnson's *Dictionary,* one of the meanings of "common" is prostitution. Blake's "London" concludes with syphilis. The prostitute's curse blasts the newborn infant and "blights with plagues the Marriage hearse." Malthus was right: the control of reproduction was the center of Atlantic capitalism, in all its varieties and expansions of forced labor.

Mary Plowman introduces a racial theme by including the detail that "a tall swarthy man desired I might not give him wash." She was referring to one of Aesop's fables (himself an Ethiopian, according to tradition): "Washing the Blackamore White." Godwin retold the fable in *Fables Ancient and Modern.* In 1793, Godwin was the author of a theory of human benevolence and the commons that Thomas Malthus refuted in the 1798 and 1803 editions of his *Essay on the Principles of Population,* which formed part of the reaction against "love and equalization." Godwin persisted, writing under the pseudonym Edward Baldwin and changing the direction of his writing to reach young readers. To continue the political discussion, he chose traditional subjects. His *Bible Stories* appeared in 1802 and his *Fables Ancient and Modern* in 1805. His retelling of "Washing the Blackamoor White" avoids the message of the biological inferiority of African people found, for instance, in the 1776 comic opera *The Blackamoor Washed White* and promoted in Blumenbach's 1795 "scientific" hierarchy of races. Godwin's version stresses the manly beauty of the "blackamoor" Nango, who is employed as a footman by Miss Moggridge. Her ignorance and foolishness lead her to employ all her maids and three extra washerwomen, whom she sets to work scrubbing from nine in the morning until noon. The washerwomen, who are as easily familiar with black people as Mary Plowman, laugh with the neighbors behind Miss Moggridge's back, meanwhile collecting "Miss Moggridge's money for themselves and their families." The antiracist humanity of the washerwomen

11. *Trial,* 137, 138.

contrasts with aristocratic ignorance and greed (her uncle would not spare a farthing toward her education).

Back to Mary Plowman, keeper of the Flying Horse. The talk of kissing led to assumptions of common knowledge of this fable. Who was "the tall swarthy man," if not the Jamaican Robert Wedderburn, a biblically conversant man of color and Spencean radical. In 1802, the same year as Despard's trial, Wedderburn, age thirty-one, published *Truth Self Supported*. In it, he also references washing, using the application of water and Fuller's soap as a metaphor for conversion to Christian salvation.[12] He writes,

> And are we Wretches yet alive?
> And do we yet rebel?
> 'Tis boundless, 'tis amazing Love,
> That bears us up from Hell.[13]

We are back to love again, now as a means of survival and rebellion. This contrasts with the Malthusian conception, for which we need other terms besides *eros, philia,* and *agape* to express the mercenary purposes of breeding future labor power, which was becoming an urgent legal matter on an Atlantic scale. Perhaps another Greek word, *ektrophe,* meaning a mercenary, calculating reproduction, or breeding, will suffice. Wedderburn invokes a "love" to overcome the enclosed hells of factory, plantation, mine, ship, and field. The presence of a black man—a Jamaican and an African American —within the circles of the Despard conspiracy points to one dynamic revolutionary forces, that is, a person who was descended from those Africans who provided the labor producing the riches of the Atlantic world.

Labor was also available in places like Ireland or even England, if women would only bear children. Lord Ellenborough succeeded Lord Kenyon as lord chief justice in 1802. Born Edward Law in Cumberland to an upper-class family, he was bad tempered, hasty, severe, overbearing, and sarcastic. Early in life he was known as a womanizer and later in life as a voluptuary. He has been praised for his contributions to commercial law, especially concerning insurance and bills of exchange, and he himself acquired a fortune at the bar. In 1803, he ruled in *R. v. Fletcher* that the body of a felon convicted of murder could be dissected without sentence of dissection having been pronounced.

12. Wedderburn, *Horrors of Slavery*, 9, 15. See also chapter 9 of Linebaugh and Rediker, *Many-Headed Hydra*.
13. Wedderburn, *Truth Self Supported*.

The corpse was removed from legal notice, and its disposal lay entirely in the hands of the state. During the same year, as a member of Parliament in the House of Lords, he introduced Lord Ellenborough's Act, which was the first statutory prohibition of abortion. It made abortion punishable by death without benefit of clergy. In 1802, the Crown drew up an indictment against abortion. While the common law seems also to have prohibited abortion, there was sufficient confusion so as to permit popular, or customary, beliefs to survive. Ellenborough's Act defined abortion as the administering of abortifacients (in England, this would have been juniper berries and birthwort), by potion or instrument, *with the intent* of causing miscarriage; prosecution no longer had to prove stillbirth or death after a live birth. Most important, the law did not accept that life began only with the "quickening" of the fetus. Since only the pregnant woman could feel when that quickening moment begins, she had significant say, albeit a de facto say, in the legality of abortion. It was her role that the statute diminished, indeed criminalized by imposition of the death penalty. As we'll see, what was at stake was not life but young, useful life.

The disapprobation of prequickening abortion among surgeons, doctors, and apothecaries grew in the 1790s. Samuel Farr in *Elements of Medical Jurisprudence* (1788) defined life as commencing with conception, explaining that the embryo "might live and become of use to mankind." The same year as Ellenborough's Act, Dr. Thomas Percival in *Medical Ethics* argued that "the first spark of life" was, like infancy, childhood, or adulthood, a "successive stage of existence . . . appointed as the exclusive means of preserving the race, and multiplying the enjoyments of mankind."[14] Thus, consistent with this argument and with respect to abortion, the women and the midwives were excluded on penalty of death from determining the social utility, social preservation, and enjoyment of mankind. Inasmuch as the family, or the relation between parent and child, was the basis for the commons, Ellenborough's bill was another nail in its coffin.

Ellenborough disregarded the jury's recommendation that mercy be shown to Despard, and he snubbed Horatio Nelson's testimony on behalf of his former comrade. What do we find if we compare his few interruptions during the trial—Was Despard's heart callous? Was the card kissed on the Parade? Could Despard move closer in order to hear a soft-spoken witness?—

14. 43 George III, c.58 (1803); Keown, *Abortion, Doctors and Law*; *Dictionary of National Biography*; J. Campbell, *Lives*.

to his decision in *R. v. Fletcher* that same year and to the criminalization of abortion accomplished by his act of Parliament the month after Despard's gruesome sentence? Not the freedom of romance but the contrary, state control over the body—its sentiments and its motions, as well as its political actions and beliefs. Ellenborough was the lord of all he surveyed. His interruptions suggested more than the bad temper of an irascible personality. They demonstrated a tendency of the entire ruling class to sugar punitive severity with sentimentalism. Furthermore, what was at stake in ending some lives and preserving others was not love for the fetus but opposition to the commons.

TWENTY-SEVEN

Criminalization in the Labor Process

ECONOMICALLY, ADAM SMITH'S *Wealth of Nations* (1776) developed the idea of the division of labor. This combined two meanings. The first was geographic specialization connected by an infrastructure of transport, and the second was the separation of different tasks within the labor process of skilled handicrafts that had formerly been performed by one person. These changes took place under conditions of systematic and differential violence. The violence of war and conquest for settler colonization and for wealth extraction was essential to the globalization of sugar and cotton. This was accompanied by the violence inherent in the factory, where police and the prison, science and technology, compelled those who had been expropriated from land and subsistence to submit to painful and punitive discipline. Mechanization destroyed family, community, and commons, reversing the relationship between man and tool. The resulting devaluation hit slaves, children, and women.

The philosopher of the factory wrote, "When capital enlists science into her service, the refractory hand of labour will always be taught docility."[1] The enclosed isolated factory increased productivity by, among other things, removing the possibility of customary taking of the materials and wastes of production, or embezzlement. The 1802 debate about the factory and the shearing machine, made the link between the factory and the enclosed field clear: "A large new mill can be much sooner erected, than additional sheep reared to keep it in motion. Indeed, without some restriction to the slaughter of lambs, or general enclosure bill, we may pretty safely conclude that little or

1. Ure, *Philosophy of Manufactures*, 368.

no addition can be made to our growth of wool." In contrast, cotton "may be produced *ad infinitum*."[2]

The factory was an enclosure in two senses: first, as an architectural location of machine production, and second, as an expropriation of customary usages. As to the former, at this time factories located largely in the west or north of England, were places where human beings, such as ten-year-old Mary Richardson, whose apron was caught in the drive shaft in a cotton mill, were consumed. Robert Blincoe witnessed the terror: "He saw her whirled round and round with the shaft—he heard the bones of her arms, legs, thighs, &c., successively snap asunder, crushed, seemingly to atoms, as the machinery whirled her round, and drew tighter and tighter her body within the works, her blood was scattered over the frame and streamed upon the floor, her head appeared dashed to pieces."[3] As an expropriation of customary usages, the factory altered the way workers derived value. To understand this, let us return to the Oakley Arms.

Who attended that November meeting at the Oakley Arms? John Emblin, reports "They appeared most of them to be workingmen; some were soldiers, and in regimentals." Otherwise, "There were some dirty and some clean; they were of all descriptions." John Francis and John Bird were shoemakers; John Wood, Pollard, and Tyndall were carpenters; Connelly "passed for a breeches-maker"; Emblin and Cassel were watchmakers; and another was a bricklayer. Owing to the peace, there were more sailors than usual beached or at liberty in London. In his testimony about those at the Spread Eagle in Mill Lane, Thomas Windsor said the people were made up "principally of persons who have been discharged from the navy, or who have been in the great gun exercise."[4]

Workers, artisans, soldiers, and sailors attended the meeting. They were in the midst of a deep historical transition to the monetized wage relationship, which entailed an exclusive claim on compensation. During this transition, customary forms of appropriation were criminalized. In general, the criminalization of custom expropriated workers from forms of the urban commons and from their work itself. The subject has been scarcely recognized, much less analyzed or understood, yet it reflects what was becoming a profound division by criminalizing part of the working class and creating the criminal.

2. *Observations on Woollen Machinery*, 9–10.
3. *Memoir*, 19.
4. *Trial of Edward Marcus Despard*, 73.

The soldiers at the Oakley Arms looked up deferentially to Despard. Thomas Windsor, the first to testify, if not the first to betray Despard and the conspiracy, was a grenadier in the Third Battalion of Foot Guards. Others attending the meeting were identified with the army; Winterbottom was a soldier, as were Lynch, Herron, William Francis, and John Wood. John Emblin was a soldier too. As with soldiers everywhere, they were dealers of death, which they were conscious of as the great equalizer. As clandestine insurrectionists, they adopted an organizational model based on cells of ten members, each led by a captain, then a district of several cells led by a colonel.

War abroad came home as class war. What was the relationship between crime and the commons? We need historical sources for the commons at the time that Despard suffered. The Old Bailey tried major property crimes in London, sentencing the guilty to various punishments, such as hanging, prison, transportation, and whipping. We must read hostile sources with a "Satanic light" to find occasional glimmers of the commons shining through them. One such case was Thomas Blades, another who gave evidence against Despard. He was a soldier, and not an obedient one, having been flogged twice and brought before three or four courts martial. Despard's counsel attempted to discredit his character further by suggesting he was a thief. "I was never brought to any bar," answered Blades. You swear it? "I swear positively I was never brought before any justice." Has a theft been imputed to you? "Never to my knowledge." Have you never been charged to your face with theft? "That I am pretty sure of." Only pretty sure? "I am quite sure of it." Then,

Q. Do you know a person of the name of Tibbetts?

A. I do.

Q. Do you mean to swear you never were charged by Tibbetts, and to your face, with having stolen something from him?

A. I worked for him. I had some leather by me, and some of it was lost.

Q. Did he charge you with stealing any of it?

A. He did not charge me with stealing of it; he said I had made away with it.[5]

---

5. *Trial of Edward Marcus Despard*, 93–103.

Such distinctions are commonplace in the records of the Old Bailey. A profound fissure grew even wider in the composition of the laborers of London, the process of criminalizing custom. The division between the unrespectable and the respectable poor, as Francis Place saw it, between poverty and indigence, as Colquhoun put it, or between the deserving and the undeserving poor, required continual acts of separation.[6] It was never a simple bifurcation.

As to the Old Bailey, the evidence is seductive. You can hear the whimpering of the desperate or the defiance of the obdurate. You hear the plain statement of commonsense against harsh sentences. You get a sense of how intimidating the Old Bailey could be from the testimony of those who chose not to say much, if anything, or of those who submitted written statements. Sometimes you hear the jury being addressed distinctly, and its members, always propertied, sometimes hard of heart, were capable of making distinctions between theft and custom unknown to the Bench.

There was a slippery slope between community-sanctioned customs and criminality that was unknown to law but vital to the commonality. It would be vain to titrate a precise gradation of excuses along this slope. Equally it would fly against all we know to say that it did not exist. For Blades and the court, there was a big difference between "stealing" and "making away." At another moment in Despard's trial, the distinction came up incidentally. Loss appears in the archives upside down as crime. Ireland, Atlantic, Iroquois, Scotland, and the English enclosures provide direct evidence of this massive alteration in land possession. Yet the idea of the commons persisted. It found fugitive expression in the Gothic, in the dream, in the hidden, in the surreal, in the utopian, in the communist, or in the indicted felon at the Old Bailey. The Sessions House at the Old Bailey printed its *Proceedings,* and these annals of larceny provide us with a glimpse into a partial urban commons, and sometimes with direct evidence of the criminalization of custom, or lost liberties.

The Peace of Amiens was signed between England and France on 25 March 1802 and lasted over a year. War did not resume until 18 May 1803, so London consequently had more idle soldiers home from the wars than usual. At midnight, a month after peace was declared on 22 April 1802, two soldiers assaulted a man coming home from the circus in Saint George's Fields and took his hat, a pair of gloves, a half guinea, and a half crown, making it high-

6. Colquhoun, *Treatise on Indigence.*

way robbery. They were found guilty and sentenced to death.[7] A couple months later, on 29 June 1802, two soldiers stole a child's cloth dress and a cloth gaiter from a tailor's shop. One of them tried to hide them in his regimental long cap, but it fell out. They were tried, found guilty, and transported for seven years.[8] James Munyard on 21 June was listening to a balladeer, when Simon Linn picked his pocket of a gilded medal. Munyard had it "in consequence of being out the 1st August in the action of the Nile." Linn, age forty, was found guilty and sentenced to seven years' transportation.[9]

The poverty was pathetic. The fifty-nine-year-old nurse to the boys of the Saint Andrew's, Holborn, workhouse was charged with stealing six sheets, which she had taken and pawned ("I meant to get them out in a day or two"). Found guilty, she was sentenced to be whipped and confined six months in Newgate. The crimes were desperate. Sam Tapster on 14 May 1802 had nothing to eat. He offered to help unload a cartload of hay and load it up again with dung in exchange for some victuals. He stole a greatcoat and shovel belonging to the carter and was sentenced to twelve months in the House of Correction.[10]

People were without money. These included sailors like George Brown, who was sentenced to death for burglary. He said in his own defense, "I am a foreigner, and very much distressed; poverty brought me to it; I leave it to your Lordship, and mercy of the Court; I sailed with Lord Camelford round the world, and I have fought for this country though I belong to the City of Hanover." Or a seafaring man, who on 22 June 1802 was seen leaving his lodging at the Ship and Horseshoe, Nightingale Lane, "rather thicker in the body than the night before." A practitioner of the lodging-slum, he took a sheet, testifying "I had no money to pay for my lodging, or to support me, so I meant to pawn the sheet in order to pay him, and to take it out again." He was found guilty, imprisoned in Newgate, and whipped. William Thompson, a black, was transported for seven years after being found guilty of stealing six pairs of shoes. He had been at sea for two years "and could not get any money of the purser, but he let him have the shoes to make money of."[11]

Sailors flush with money on reaching shore made easy targets. Seventeen-year-old John Rutland took a hammock, blankets, and clothing from a

7. *Proceedings*, 2 June 1802.
8. *Proceedings*, 4 July 1802.
9. *Proceedings*, 15 September 1802.
10. *Proceedings*, 2 June 1802.
11. *Proceedings*, 15 September 1802; 4 July 1802; 12 January 1803.

mariner, who had hired him as a porter to carry them into Wapping. He was transported for seven years. As the foreman of the New River Company, who had finished paying his men on 15 May 1802 at the Three Jolly Butchers, returned to his lodging in Hoxton, Sarah Fox accosted him asking whether she might join him. He said no but in the transaction lost his watch, which was later found in the lining at the bottom of her petticoat.

One sailor fell asleep in a ditch by the roadside in the heat of a June day, when Morris Scully came along and stole his hat and two mackerel. He was discharged with a whipping. Sophia and John Johnson ("two blacks") stole two twenty-pound banknotes from the seaman Joseph Howard ("a black"), who had received them for wages at Woolwich after a West Indian voyage aboard a man-of-war. They had all known each other in Saint Thomas in the Caribbean. Sophia was "a common prostitute." Adam Stearstray, a white man, sailed in the West Indies with Anthony Martin, a black man. Ashore in London, they went drinking gin. In a room together, Martin took a Stearstray's watch and pawned it. He was sentenced to a whipping and one year in the 'Steel.[12]

Mary Cheeseman was transported for seven years for taking five pairs of shoes from her master, a shoemaker, who had attempted to seduce her: "No sooner was I taken than he went to my father in hopes of making property of me." Is there an opposition here between slavery and the commons? Were the shoes she took a meal ticket to an option other than patriarchal enslavement?[13]

If we understand the commons to be a means of subsistence, then we can look at all actions undertaken to use the means of production as a kind of commoning. Thus two warehouse laborers took bladders of misappropriated rum and concealed them in their leather aprons ("a common appendage to men in that line of business"). According to custom, rum sat in the warehouse trade before it was sold to become "perfectly fine." This was ascertained by use of the "dip," with an allowance of two gallons called the "flow."[14] An intoxicated soldier passing through the quays took some linen yarn to make a mop for his wife ("it is a very common thing for goods to lay upon the quays"). It was an apt description for the huge worldwide congelation of commodities that were funneled into England through the Thames.[15]

12. *Proceedings*, 2 June 1802; 15 September 1802.
13. *Proceedings*, 17 September 1794.
14. *Proceedings*, 2 December 1795.
15. *Proceedings*, 30 June 1796.

Ann Priestly, who was a tobacco stripper in a Whitechapel cellar, was sent to the House of Correction for three months for taking six and a half pounds of tobacco. The prosecutor admitted, "We are in the constant habit of allowing them every Saturday night a quantity of tobacco or snuff, which ever they like, in order to keep them from pilfering." This case is important for illustrating the relationship between prison and the wage. "The constant habit of allowing them" provides evidence of how an action could become a custom— not contractual but customary.[16] Edward Smith, who worked eight years for a tobacconist, took ten ounces of "shag tobacco." The tobacconist allowed his men an allowance "to prevent their stealing, every Saturday night, to each man a quarter of a pound."[17]

A carman, married to a washerwoman, got two years in the House or Correction for taking soap from his master, a Bethnal Green soap manufacturer. "My master used to make exceeding good weight, and when I have carried quantities of soap home, the over-weight I have brought home to my own house; but I never took a piece off my master's premises." We might see the domestic setting as a place of common. Indeed, this was a principal problem of the domestic system of putting-out, and the problem was resolved by means of enclosure and architectural separation of home and work.[18] Thomas Hayes was transported for seven years for taking a yard of printed calico from his employer, a calico glazier. "Do you allow your men any perquisites?" None was the answer. Don't you "when you glaze this calico cut off the fag end?" He cut two folds instead of one with his knife. Hayes's master demanded he let down his breeches, in which he had concealed the calico thrum.[19]

A shipwright, who took iron, called them "chips" and considered them one of his entitlements. 10 January 1798.[20] Philip Bramley, a cooper, hooped and unhooped casks of coffee. When he was rubbed down, "as is customary," six pounds of coffee fell out of his knee breeches. "Are there any perquisites belonging to the persons using the warehouses?" "Are not the droppings from the casks perquisites?"[21] James Rotter, who worked for a Ratcliffe brewery, was caught taking four gallons of twopenny. "Well then, hang me for a little

16. *Proceedings,* 14 September 1796.
17. *Proceedings,* 6 December 1797.
18. *Proceedings,* 6 December 1797.
19. *Proceedings,* 15 February 1797.
20. *Proceedings,* 10 January 1798.
21. *Proceedings,* 14 February 1798.

small beer," he said contemptuously. He was spared the gallows, and given six months in the House of Correction on 30 November 1796. Sarcasm would not be accepted with its implied charges of cruelty, mercilessness, and wrong. To attempt it was to turn the theatrical message of the courtroom upside down.

Of these kinds of misappropriations, those involving sugar were the most frequent and resulted in severe consequences. John Burn was sentenced to a year in prison for taking a pound a sugar. He had a special container sewed in the left leg of his trousers. As a "lumper," he was notorious. The questioning went from "plunder" to "stealing" to "taking."[22] Colquhoun wrote, "What was at first considered as the wages of turpitude, at length assumes the form, and is viewed in the light of a fair perquisite of office. . . . Custom and example sanction the greatest enormities which at length become fortified by immemorial and progressive usage."[23] Two Irishmen took eight pounds of sugar from a West Indiaman. They argued the sugar was "sweepings" off the floor, rather than "clean sugar." It was concealed in a bag under his "smock frock." "I found this sugar in the street. . . . I thought I had a right to it," said John Purdy.[24]

When John Emblin was brought to meet Colonel Despard, who was with Windsor and the others, the conversation turned to the wet docks. "Some complaint of the guards being employed at the Wet Docks?" asked the prosecutor. Emblin replied as follows: "Yes; but after some time I asked Colonel Despard whether there was any particular business at hand, and what he thought of it; he said, *'nothing particular; only it seems the wish of a great many people, that an effort should be made on Tuesday week next to recover some of those liberties which we have lost.'*" The transition from the subject of the wet docks to the subject of lost liberties was not as far fetched as it might seem. Here was the material connection between the West Indies and the United Kingdom. Here the sugar and the coffee, the stimulant and the hunger suppressant, both the labor of slaves, were transferred to the tables in the form of cups of tea and baked goods, the cuisine of Europe. That labor became surplus value to the bankers, merchants, and rulers of an empire. The plantation workers produced the calories for the factory workers. For these

22. *Proceedings,* 30 November 1796.
23. *Treatise on the Police,* 252.
24. *Proceedings,* 30 November 1796.

transferences to occur, the lumpers (as dockers were called) had to bear the weight.

The twenty-five-year-old Joseph Dixon stole twenty-eight pounds of sugar from a cart on 28 June 1802. Pursued to the cry of "Stop thief" in Moor Street, Seven Dials, he was taken but made "a stout resistance." He was sentenced to seven years transportation. Many possessed specialized tools, equipment, or clothing. William Williams stole a gallon of rum on 13 October. He was apprehended by a private in the First Regiment of Foot Guards, who was employed as a sentinel on the Wet Docks and had seen him bore a hole in a cask to let the liquor run into a can. Sugar was taken in blackstrap bags to prevent their being seen at night. These formed part of the clothing of delinquency.[25] Ellis and Amos were sentenced to transportation for seven years for stealing 139 pounds of coffee on 24 February 1803. They were in a wherry in the Hamburg tier, Saint Catherine's dock, coming under the bows of the ship *Henrietta,* when the Thames Police surveyor apprehended them and their "*jemmy bag.*" Amos, age twenty-two, had ten character witnesses, whereas Ellis, age twenty-one, wrote a defense. On 12 June 1802, William Williams, age nineteen, was found with nine pounds of coffee "in his breeches and in his trowsers, and different parts about him" at a wharf near Bear key.[26]

"I was very much in liquor. . . . I have a wife and three children," pleaded Robert Whittingham as he threw himself on the mercy of "the Court and Jury," which acquitted him of feloniously stealing eighty pounds of raw sugar from a warehouse. "I did not take it to make any property of it," said William Coles, indicted for stealing four quarts of oil, "but only for my own use— times are very hard and I have a family." Thomas Stewart, alias Caton, a porter for the East India Company, stole three pounds of sugar from a river lighter. "I have only been taking a little sugar for some beer." "I picked up the sugar as it scattered from a cart where the packages had broke." He was whipped and spent six months in Newgate.[27]

An East India Company warehouse laborer, indicted for stealing three ounces of tea, testified that "in walking among such a quantity of tea, some of it got into my shoes." Another company laborer informed the court, "It is considered no crime in the warehouse for a man to take up a bit." On 5 May

25. Colquhoun, *Treatise on the Police,* 62.
26. *Proceedings,* 2 June 1802; 27 October 1802; April 1803; 4 July 1802.
27. *Proceedings,* 15 September 1802; 27 October 1802.

1802, John Payne, a twenty-nine-year-old porter for the East India Company warehouse, was seen at eight o'clock in the morning taking ten pounds of sugar out of "a kind of butter-firkin, put it in a paper, and tie it up in a hand-kerchief, . . . put the head of the small cask on, and went away." He was found guilty and sentenced to seven years transportation.[28]

On 8 October 1802, sixty-year-old William Rawley stole three-and-a-half pounds of raw sugar. He was employed as a lumper and was apprehended during a routine body search ("rubbing down"). He was whipped and imprisoned for six months in the House of Correction. Also taken from a river lighter was three pounds of coffee stolen by John Watson from the scuttle. He explained that he "saw the coffee running out of the bag; I was picking it up, with intent to save it." He was whipped and spent two weeks in Newgate. On 4 July 1802, William Thomas, age twenty-five, saying he was starving, and would work for his victuals, asked a shipmaster for work as a lumper. He took forty-five pounds of sugar from the cook's caboose. The sugar came from an open hogshead in the hold, and he claimed it as his "sea-stock." He was sentenced to seven years' transportation.[29]

In London, the problem of customary direct appropriation stimulated the owners to preventive innovation, such as the enclosed wet docks. But it was a national problem. In November 1802, the mayor of Leeds wrote the lord lieutenant Earl Fitzwilliam about "the momentous shape which the spirit of combination of almost every class (but particularly amongst the shearmen) has now assumed: perquisites, privileges, time, mode of labour, rate, who shall be employed, &c., &c.—all are now dependent upon the fiats of our workmen, beyond all appeal."[30] He mentions "perquisites" first. This was the issue of waste products, an issue of recycling. It resisted that expropriation from the means of production, the precondition of capitalism. Criminalization of the workers' appropriation of the materials of production was essential to the separation, the alienation, and the expropriation of the worker. "Perquisites" were often called "custom" or "customs of the trade." Abstractly considered, they were usages and practices that retained a worker's possessive link to the means and materials of production. Perquisites were criminalized.[31] In this regard, they were similar to the customary rights

28. *Proceedings,* September 1803; April 1803; 2 June 1802. In my "London's London," I describe more tea or sugar thefts and their relation to sailoring from India by lascars.
29. *Proceedings,* 27 October 1802; 27 October 1802; 4 July 1802.
30. Aspinall, *Early Trade Union,* 41, 45–46.
31. Linebaugh, chapter 12 of *London Hanged.*

enjoyed by agrarian commoners as a source of subsistence and met comparable systematic, savage repression. Allowances. Droppings. Sweepings. From an economic standpoint, they were analogous to estovers, turbary, herbage, and pannage, that is, they were means of subsistence among the direct producers, urban or rural, manufactures or agriculture. Their names signified types of access to the means of production and subsistence.

In April 1794, a coal merchant prosecuted two coalheavers for stealing three bushels of coal. But was it not "customary to give small quantity of coals to men who load and unload?" Mr. Knowlys for the defense asked. "I don't know that," replied the prosecutor, "some time back they might when men worked on different terms to what they do now." Times had changed: "Years ago it was a customary thing to take the tobacco from the men & let them go," said a warehouseman in court in May 1800.

Between January 1789 and December 1803, 209 cases were tried at the Old Bailey, either for theft of coal or involving such people connected to the provision of coal to London, such as porters, heavers, merchants, shippers, charwomen, and cooks. Indeed urban space was marked by its ubiquity in the metropolis—coal yards, coal wharfs, coal holes, coal shops, and the like. The coal ("sea coal" it was called) came along the North Sea coast from Newcastle, and many of the "thefts" were from barges, lighters, or larger vessels, such as the Newcastle collier, on the river. It is no surprise that Thomas Spence came from Newcastle. This struggle was most advanced and most widespread in London, where the product of most intense interest was coal, as it provided the energy of the heat engine—the new thermodynamics. The contest over these inputs was the direct cause of the establishment of police. Let John Harriot, a founder of the police, explain:

> Previously to the establishment (of the police) [in 1798], these men had long been in the constant practice of each man taking his sack, containing two or three bushels of coals, whenever he went on shore from the ship he was unloading. Neither the captain nor the owner of the ship or cargo durst resist their taking what they claimed as a perquisite; and most of these men, having followed it as a custom of their predecessors, thought they had a fair title to such coals. . . . Custom was their invariable plea (and so it was with every other description of working men on the river, when detected in the act of bringing on shore with them forty pounds to two hundred weight of sugar, coffee, pepper, tea, and other articles), and in vain was it, that Mr. Colquhoun and myself laboured hard to convince them of their error.[32]

32. Harriot, *Struggles through Life*, 2:261.

The Old Bailey provides direct evidence. For example, Edward Hatred, tried in December 1792, testified, "I heaved out the coals, from a West-country-barge; and they gave me 1 s. and the sweepings out; I don't rightly know whose barge it was; I heaved five chaldrons out, Jones was heaving the head room out, and I was heaving at the stern room; accordingly I came ashore with my coals; and Mr. Rodbard stopped me, and I was taken before the Alderman." A witness "asked them where they got the coals, they said they were sweepings." He was whipped and spent six months in Newgate.[33]

The regulations adopted in 1790 by the West Indian merchants prohibited giving sweepings to the gangsmen.[34] In 1798, the Marine Police was founded to organize, control, patrol, and punish, as well as apprehend, the lumpers, gangsmen, and heavy horsemen. "The Lumping Rates have been ultimately settled on the lowest terms for which honest labour can be procured for daily wages." Their working day as set was from six in the morning to six at night, during which time they were prohibited from leaving the ship. On 2 February 2003, Thomas Spencer stole from a warehouse thirty-three pounds of sugar he found lying on the dock among the hogsheads. He was sentenced to Newgate for six months and a whipping.

Q. Was this sweepings?

A. No; it was taken out of the hogshead.[35]

In another case, John Overington, a laboring cooper, was caught with six pounds of coffee when he was searched at the warehouse on 5 April. Mr. Knapp examined the customhouse locker:

Q. Is there any thing called sweepings?

A. Yes.

Q. Is there a perquisite of the sweepings of coffee spilt on the floor?

A. No.[36]

There was a kind of urban commons of necessity, whose currency was product, not money. The pawnbroker mediated it; Patrick Colquhoun

33. *Proceedings,* 15 December 1792.
34. Colquhoun, *Treatise on the Commerce,* 104, 619, 625.
35. *Proceedings,* 16 February 1803.
36. *Proceedings,* April 1803.

described it. From the standpoint of merchant capital, the enclosure of the docks behind great walls of stone was decisive. From the standpoint of manufacturing capital, the economic transition at this time was also a form of enclosure, from a domestic system, in which various processes of manufacture were "put-out" to the homes of workers, to a system enclosed within the walls of the factory or manufactory. In both cases, the transition was accompanied by serious challenges to the control of the materials of production. This too was a form of commoning. Now we see the connection between the construction of London's wet docks and the loss of liberties that Despard sought to recover.

Elizabeth King worked five years for a tailor, who suspecting her of stealing searched her lodgings and found pawn tickets At the pawnbroker's, he found one of the children's dresses that he had lost. She defended herself in writing: "My Lord, I very much lament my inability and my extreme poverty to procure legal assistance, but I trust to the humanity of your Lordship to supply that defect; I humbly take the liberty of informing your Lordship, I have worked for the prosecutor upwards of five years, without any impeachment of character, and I most solemnly assure your Lordship the property pledged was my own, and was bought by me in remnants, and made up for sale at my leisure intervals." Six witnesses gave her a good character. "Cabbage" was the tailor's vernacular for remnants. She was found guilty and sentenced to be whipped and confined six months in Newgate.[37]

A week before Despard and the others hanged, Ann Brown was brought to trial and convicted on twenty-three counts of assault on eleven-year-old Ann Harris, who had been apprenticed to her as a pinhead maker. Harris was sold along with the ten-year-old Ann Grace and others from the parish of Saint Giles's-in-the-Fields. She was forced to labor from seven in the morning until ten at night, unless her tasks were not done, in which case she had to work an additional hour, for a sixteen-hour day. The children sometimes were forced to go thirty hours without food. A witness saw her caned—nine-to-fourteen strokes at a time. Once she was forced to sit on the hob of the fire grate with a log of wood tied to her foot and her hand stretched into the chimney to hold a brick for two hours. The relation between the tool of labor and the worker was utterly reversed: a leaden weight, "which was a part of a machine used in the business," was used to knock her head. The intensity of the work was described as follows:

37. *Proceedings*, 4 July 1802.

An hour-glass stood continually by her, and it was expected by their mistress, that she was to produce (manufactured) six ounces of pins in the space of an hour; in default thereof, she was treated in the following manner: Part of the pins were run into her arms, and in different parts of her body, till the blood flowed from the wounds.

Thus did the eleven-year-old Ann Harris expire, "bruised from head to foot."[38]

Pin-making, as readers of Adam Smith's *Wealth of Nations* (1776) learn in its first pages, was the classic instance of the division of labor. Smith chose a "trifling manufacture" because the whole number of workers was small and could be collected in the same workhouse under the view of the supervisor. Smith pointed out that the division of labor increased the dexterity of the worker, reduced time lost from passing from one task to another, and ultimately facilitated the invention and introduction of machines. We see in the case of Ann Harris that the conditions Adam Smith identified—the simplification of tasks so that any child could do them—enabled the separation of children from home. Direct supervision allowed the torture of labor, and the mechanization of tasks may inflict pain, and continuous labor. The alienation of labor—from home, from the tool, from the product, and finally from life—could hardly have been exceeded. The church wardens intervened, and the other children were taken to the workhouse for their own safety.

It was the beginning of the Age of Iron, and old iron shops were a node of the underground economy. On the one hand, stolen iron could be fenced, while on the other hand, iron was the material of the legitimate, aboveground economy, enabling mechanization (machines), enclosure (locks and bars), and war (rifles, cannon). Iron was the medium of Colonel Despard's work as an engineer. In 1800, Henry Maudslay, the founder of the machine tool industry, invented the slide rest, the screw-cutting lathe, applying principles of standardization and interchangeability to iron production. The nuts and bolts of industry were standardized at his workshop in Saint Giles's-in-the-Fields. The Combination Acts of 1799 and 1800 (which prohibited workers from coordinating to raise wages or reduce hours) were directed in the first place against London engineers, the metal workers of this Age of Iron.

The day after the raid at the Oakley Arms on 17 November 1802, John Small was acquitted of stealing thirty-six pounds of wrought iron, a component of a chain pump, belonging to the London Dock Company, where he

38. *Times*, 15 February 1803.

was employed as a laborer. He said he found it buried in the sand, and "he was going to take it home, he thought it was his by right." The jury acquitted him. Earlier in the year on 7 July 1802, James Williams was pinched coming down a ladder from the fourth floor of a warehouse in Limehouse hole with twenty pounds of iron nails belonging to a carpenter he used to work for at the New Docks. The nails were covered with chips. "Going along, he said, he had a wife and family, and hoped I would let him go." He got six months in the 'Steel. On 6 September 1802, a forty-seven-year-old porter employed for five years at an ironmonger pocketed loose nails while sweeping behind the counter. He also spent six months in the 'Steel.[39] As Despard was tried for treason in January 1803, William Mines, a black man, was acquitted of stealing saws, chisels, hammer, gimlet, and other tools and selling them to an old Lambeth iron shop kept by William Baker, another defendant.

Francis Place, looking back on his precarious youth in the 1780s from the secure advantage point of a successful shopkeeper in the 1820s, said "Pilfering and thieving especially were not then as now almost wholly confined to the very lowest of the people but were practices by tradesmen's sons, by youths, and young men who would now no more commit such acts than would the sons of a well bred gentleman." He had an ax to grind; to him "improvement" did not mean the enclosure of land but "right thinking and better habits." The Londoners of his youth were a "barbarous people" given to drinking, whoring, gaming, fishing, and fighting.[40] Indecency, ignorance, immorality, grossness, dirtiness, and depravity were widespread. His observations cannot be dismissed as completely without validity, but his moralizing hides the vast material changes that were taking place.

At six o'clock one evening, Samuel De Graves stole a tin box with four shillings in it from an Elizabeth Sikes, who was "going to see Punch and his wife" at Bartholomew Fair in 1802. He was transported for seven years. In a suggestive coincidence, the subject of Ben Jonson's magnificent sprawling play *Bartholomew Fair* (1614) involves common people indulging their wits, lusts, appetites, and songs in permitted, licensed carnival against Justice Overdo. Nightingale, the ballad singer, sings, "Youth, youth, thou hadst better been starv'd by thy Nurse / Than live to be hanged for cutting a purse" (act 3, scene 5).[41] The joke is that as Nightingale sings, his confederate is cutting a purse.

39. *Proceedings,* December 1802; 12 January 1803; 4 July 1802; 15 September 1802.
40. Place, *Autobiography of Francis Place,* 14, 57.
41. Jonson, *Bartholomew Fair,* act 3, scene v.

By early 1792 and the passage of the Stipendiary Magistrates Act, Justice Overdo could not longer be laughed at. In 1797, the puppeteers were prosecuted for making their puppets talk too freely and causing just such laughter, despite the Licensing Act. An attempt to close the fair in 1798 failed for fear of "a concentrated tumult." The Puritans attempted to put an end to the fair, but a group called "Lady Holland's Mob" kept it open. In 1802, the same year Elizabeth Sykes had her shillings stolen, a "Lady Holland's Mob" riotously proclaimed the fair open, greatly disturbing the sleep of neighboring householders The historian of Bartholomew Fair notes the triumph of mere violence in the representations in the early nineteenth century: "The more ambitious puppet shows were in their decline, and Punch in the full tide of his popularity rioted over their decay."[42]

Bartholomew Fair took place at Smithfield, northwest of the city walls near the Old Bailey and Newgate Prison. At the southeast side of the city, by the docks on Tower Hill, William Francis, a solder, was sworn into the society by Colonel Despard on the same day in 1802 that Elizabeth Sikes's pocket was picked.[43] These people did not risk their lives, or lose them, for a song. By 1802, a revolutionary threat to the social order was cooking. The contrast was between two eras. The first was the confident Tudor capitalism of the sixteenth century, with its sturdy rogues and 'prentice riots, easily managed by the gallows, and occasional carnival. And the second, nearly two hundred years later, was the era of enclosure, mechanization, and slavery, when a revolutionary common people manifested their potential to turn the world upside down permanently.

42. Morley, *Memoirs of Bartholomew Fair*, 456–57, 470, 478, 479.
43. *Proceedings,* 15 September 1802; *Trial of Edward Marcus Despard,* 104.

TWENTY-EIGHT

Irish Labor, English Coal

THE LONDON WORKING CLASS—the plebs and proles, the crowd or mob, the settled and nomadic—was undergoing huge changes in access to land and urban space. Its sporting, raucous, even antinomian, cultural life was being stifled by a confining, suffocating spirit. Its children were put to work. Its customary ways of life were being criminalized. War, hunger, and brutalization were its realities. This was the state of things Ned and Kate Despard had to work with, not perhaps "the stuff at hand plastic as they could wish."

Despard was released from prison in May 1801. Between then and February 1802, he visited Ireland. The countryside of his birth was not peaceful. In June, an informant wrote from Naas, a town only a few miles from Mountrath, on the Dublin-to-Cork road, that "the rebellion though put down is by no means suppressed. The blaze is only smothered."[1] In the summer after Despard's death and Emmet's revolt, a lone traveler in county Queens stopped at a farmhouse, where the farmwife told him that "every Man in the Parishes for severall Miles Round were anxiously waiting until the harvest was over, that Every Man had his Pike and Pike Handle."[2] County Queens continued to simmer into 1804. A correspondent wrote Jonah Barrington that a general rising was planned in case the French should land, though leadership was lacking. Yet "nothing could be done without salt." Also in spring 1804, a schoolmaster of Donaghmore, county Queens, wrote that the people of the neighborhood were "ready to rise." The signal

1. Rebellion Papers, carton 620/63/11, National Archives of Ireland.
2. 16 August 1803, carton 620/11/130 f. 39, National Archives of Ireland.

was to be "a wisp to be lighted on every hill" or "the setting fire (as if by accident) to a house."[3]

Much of the London working class was Irish, and its ranks had been recently replenished, with thousands fleeing Ireland to escape the terror employed to suppress the Irish Rebellion of '98. It was to them, among others, that Despard appealed. At Despard's trial, Thomas Windsor attended meetings at the Brown Bear and the Running Horse public houses in Saint Giles's-in-the-Fields, where about two dozen might attend weekly meetings. He said, "They principally appeared to me to be Irishmen of the lower class; laboring men." "Mack," or Macnamara, proposed they should frequently change public houses to avoid detection. At another public house, the Black Raven down Tooley Street, six or seven Irishmen met as part of the "society." Thomas Windsor (who eventually testified against Despard and the conspiracy) brought to the Oakley Arms two day laborers, James Mayhem and Marney, both United Irishmen. John Pike, a soldier in the guards, testified at the trial that an Irishman helped raise the toast at one meeting, with "may the wings of liberty never lose a feather."[4] Thomas Windsor, his wings clipped by government, betrayed Despard by turning state's evidence.

The working class in England was often Irish anyway. Irish sailors played an important part in the great mutiny of the English fleet in summer 1797. Irish proletarians found work on the canals and docks, as well as in the factories of imperial Britain. Irish spalpeen roamed in large gangs to bring in the harvest in England. On a political level, the Act of Union of 1800 extinguished Irish political independence, while on an economic level, the savage repression of the Rebellion of 1798 siphoned off Irish rebels from Ireland and exacerbated wage, religious, and ethnic divisions in England. The deaths of Despard and Emmet with the many others along with each of these leaders, closed off alternatives. In fact, Irish England was the precondition of the Despard revolt and explains why it was so quickly nipped in the bud. Those deaths served as a warning. In Ireland, martyrs were created but two generations were silenced, while in England Irishmen labored in the mills of the factory towns and Irishwomen wore out their bodies with the labor of reproduction.

Parts of the London Irish spoke Irish. The father of George Borrow (1803–81) was a soldier sent to capture a couple of deserters in an Irish part of

3. Carton 620/13/176, National Archives of Ireland.
4. *Trial of Edward Marcus Despard*, 71, 99.

London at this time. "The whole district had become alarmed, and hundreds came pouring down upon us—men, women, and children. Women, did I say!—they looked fiends, half naked, with their hair hanging down over their bosoms; they tore up the very pavement to hurl at us, sticks rang about our ears, stones, and Irish. I liked the Irish worst of all, it sounded so horrid, especially as I did not understand it. It's a bad language."[5]

Consider the word *slum*. James Hardy Vaux (1782–1841) was the first to use it in print in his 1812 *Memoirs*, where he defines it as a room or a racket.[6] It was used by flash people to refer generically to various kinds of depredation or fraud, such as the lodging-slum (referring to the practice of renting furnished lodging and then stripping it of valuables), the area-slum (the practice of robbing the lower apartments of private homes), or the back-slum (going in the back entrance of any premises). The two meanings, illegality and architecture, had been joined by the 1820s, when the *Oxford English Dictionary* defined it as the streets, alleys, and courts forming a thickly populated district, where the houses and conditions of life are squalid and wretched. Here criminality and commons were mixed. It was an Irish urban formation. The *OED* also says it has a cant origin. Daniel Cassidy includes it among English slang deriving from the Irish "*'s lom*," or an exposed, vulnerable place.[7] Following is a physician describing slum conditions in 1802: "Air and light are, in a great measure, excluded from their habitations, whilst damp and cold frequently predominate. Human effluvia and exhalations from putrefying vegetable and animal substances, within and about their sordid dwellings, are constantly accumulating; and the atmosphere of one polluted cell is but exchanged, for that of another."[8]

The ancient London division between the East and West Ends, between the London of the court and the London of the port (with money, law, and entertainment in between), began to take on new meanings. In 1803, F. A. Winsor, who had court connections, illuminated Pall Mall with coal gas. The historian of the industry wrote in 1821, "We all remember the dismal appearance of our most public streets previous to the year 1810; before that time, the light afforded by the street lamps hardly enabled the passenger to distinguish a watchman from a thief, or the pavement from the gutter." Before then the well to do walked at night with linkboys carrying torches.

5. Borrow, *Lavengro*, 61.
6. *Memoirs*.
7. Cassidy, *How the Irish Invented*, 265.
8. Stranger, *Remarks*.

Urban life was organized to display the commodity, that form of wealth separating desire from possession. The commodity could be seen but not had. The invention of illuminating coal gas (along with the shop window) made this possible. Gas lighting thus enabled the urban spectacle. The spectacle itself put the commodity on display; display, however, opposed security. This was the dilemma of the shopkeeper, who had to both show off and secure. A tricky kind of peekaboo became integral to the city as the economics of the sale and the political science of police were joined.

As an illuminant, coal was essential to "the society of the spectacle." Bonaparte granted a patent in 1803 for distilling illuminating gas from wood. Gas was first distilled from burning coal in 1739, in experiments repeated by Richard Watson, the future bishop of Landaff, in 1767. The gas industry was born during the momentous year of 1792.[9] William Murdoch (1754–1839), working for Boulton and Watt, illuminated his office in the Cornwall mines with coal gas in 1792. In 1798, he constructed in Birmingham an apparatus for making and storing gas for use in factories. The first public exhibition of gas lighting to celebrate the Peace of Amiens took place in March 1802, on the exterior of the Soho Works, where steam engines were produced. Murdoch's innovation added three hours to the working day in mills and considerably cheapened, for example, the night shift at the Phillips and Lee factory in Salford. Gas light costing six hundred pounds per annum replaced candles costing more than three times as much.

A new epoch in the history of the body began around 1802. The cough became one of the human signs of the Anthropocene—"a change of air," in both its senses, was the solution. The raid on the Oakley Arms occurred in November 1802, the London's unhealthiest month. Lung ailments "rage more in this one city, than in the whole earth besides," wrote John Evelyn, the royalist ecologist, whose *Fumifugium* (1661) was the first study of smog. A fifth to a quarter of all deaths in London were lung related, according to John Graunt.[10] Cases of rickets, induced by lack of sunlight, increased in number. "Tisick," or consumption, as tuberculosis was known before it was named in 1820s, was also associated with the "stinking fogs" of November. These fogs could last several days.[11] The combination of smoke and fog, along with the action of sulfuric acid, corroded the granite stones of London build-

9. Chandler and Lacey, *Rise.*
10. Evelyn, *Fumifugium*; Graunt, *Natural and Political Observations.*
11. Brimblecombe, *Big Smoke.*

ings. Furnishings were dirtied. Plants suffered. In London, one of every seven deaths at the beginning of the eighteenth century was attributable to fog; by the beginning of the nineteenth century, fog accounted for one in four. So when we learn of thirty or forty men crowded in the upstairs of the Oakley Arms, some smoking pipes, others warmed by the coal fire in the grate, we can hear their respiration—coughing, wheezing, sneezing, heaving, panting, catarrh, nose blowing, the cacophony of the lungs, the dyspnea of the Anthropocene. Despard would have needed a moment to catch his breath.

Interest in lung diseases characterized the great Bristol physician Thomas Beddoes, who concluded that "the prevention of pulmonary consumption, and its cure, may be numbered among the things most wanting in our system of life."[12] Later in the winter of 1802–3, Dr. Charles Badham made a study of patients at the Westminster Dispensary Hospital, from which he became the first to diagnosis bronchitis as distinct from pleurisy and pneumonia Badham observed particularly among the artisans of the metropolis and the soldiers he examined a general sense of weight, anxiety, and tension all over the chest. The bronchial tubes were attacked with inflammation, the lungs became inspissated, and patients suffered shortness of breath, leaving them in a condition of inanition that led to debility and death. Relief depended less on opium or various tinctures of saffron and ginger than "on a favorable state of atmosphere."[13]

Coal, if not quite the "monument of felicity to the organization of Nature," as Erasmus Darwin dubbed it, was certainly the means of warming human bodies and cooking food. The chief hazard in those endeavors was chimney fires, caused when hot smoke met cool surroundings, leaving deposits of soot and inflammable creosote. Children were sent up the chimneys to clean them. Most sweeps were under twelve, sometimes even a four-year old was squeezed up the narrow apertures. Their elbows and knees were bloodied, and they slept in soot blankets ("to sleep black"). Sometimes these "human brushes" became stuck as the flues twisted and turned behind the walls. Fires were lit to force them out. Thousands of chimney sweeper apprentices were employed, and scores of them died in the chimneys.

In 1775, Percival Pott, who studied the diseases of London chimney sweeps, found an association between exposure to soot and a high incidence

12. *Essay on the Causes.*
13. Badham, *Observations.* I am grateful to Gillian Boal of the Wellcome Medical Library for making this text available to me.

of scrotal cancer (later found to be a type of squamous cell carcinoma) in chimney sweeps. This was the first occupational link to cancer, and Pott became the first person to associate human malignancy with an environmental carcinogen (benzo(a)pyrene). When Jonas Hanway argued that they should not be forced up chimneys that were actually on fire, or when David Porter argued that they deserved to have one good meal a week, these were taken as marks of humanitarianism. These children were slaves, slaves who preserved the border between the comfort of warm interiors and the deadly disaster of conflagration.

A small-diameter chimney meant a fire with a better draught. The Chimney Sweepers' Act of 1788 mandated that the diameter of chimneys not be less than nine inches, and this remains the standard diameter. In 1800, the Society for the Protection and Instruction of Chimney Sweep Apprentices was created. In 1803, the Society for Superseding the Necessity of Climbing Boys was formed. That year, George Smart's sweeping machine became available, but it applied only to chimneys that were truly vertical.[14]

In 1789, William Blake tells the story of the chimney sweeper as a song of innocence. The boy is orphaned and sold. One night he dreams of the death of thousands of sweepers, whom an angel sets free to laugh on the green plain and wash in the river, leaving their bags behind, and this dream comforts him to do his duty! Three years later, Blake returned to the subject, now as a song of experience. In 1791, the chimney sweep's parents are alive physically but dead spiritually. They go to church.

> And because I am happy & dance & sing,
> They think they have done me no injury,
> And are gone to praise God & his Priest & King,
> Who make up a heaven of our misery.[15]

Part 2 of Blake's poem replaces direct contradiction with indirect irony and the subconscious solace of the dream, or the religious doctrine of an afterlife, with revolutionary challenge. This shift directly reflects the opening possibilities of the French Revolution. The twin pillars of the establishment, monarchy and monotheism, hold up a regime of parentless unhappiness, in which the creaturely warmth of church and king ("heaven") arises from the cold

---

14. Strange, *Climbing Boys*; Porter, *Considerations*.

15. "The Chimney Sweeper: When My Mother Died, I Was Very Young" and "The Chimney Sweeper: A Little Black Thing among the Snow," in *Complete Poetry*.

heart of exploitation ("our misery"). This is the poetry of antinomianism, in which the last become first, and the least become the best—agents of a new humanity. Coal brings an end to human happiness. In "London," Blake listens to "How the Chimney-sweepers cry / Every blackning Church appalls" (lines 9–10). Enclosure here is measured at nine inches; the commons is suggested by the river, the heath, the sun. It is linked to Methodism, whose historical mission was to eliminate all signs of antinomianism from the dispossessed working class.

The first steam-powered factory was nicknamed Beelzebub. To the historian Paul Mantoux, the mixture of depravity and suffering found in the factory "offered a perfect picture of hell."[16] He notes there was a Lancashire spinning mill known as "Hell's Gate." These were dens of human malignancy. The anthem of the northeast pitmen of Durham and Northumberland, "The Colliers Rant," was old when it was first published in 1793:

> As me an' me marra wes gannin te wark
> We met wi' the Devil, it wes in the dark;
> I up wi' me pick, it was in the neet,
> I knocked off his horns, likewise his club feet.

In the Albion Mills, built in London between 1785 and 1788, were fifty pairs of millstones powered by two steam engines to grind grain. In 1791, a fire burned it to the ground; arson was suspected. A contemporary print portrays a devil squatting on the building.[17] These were the "Satanic Mills" that Blake wrote about around 1802:

> And did the Countenance Divine
> Shine forth upon our clouded hills?
> And was Jerusalem builded here
> Among these dark Satanic Mills? ("Jerusalem," lines 5–8)

The hills indeed were cloudy and the mills dark. This was the work of coal dust. Life in London was indeed hellish.

On 16 October 1798, Gabriel Franks was shot to death at Dung Wharf adjacent to the Marine Police Office on the river Thames. At eight o'clock in the evening, a riot broke out against the police office. Stones were thrown against the windows, which were quickly shuttered. Huge paving stones were

16. Mantoux, *Industrial Revolution*, 416.
17. Maidment, *Reading Popular Prints*, 27–53.

then heaved, which shattered them. The police fired a pistol, and one of the rioters fell. "Bloody murder," was cried, and some called for the magistrates' heads. In response, James Eyres shot and killed Gabriel Franks.

Earlier that day, Charles Eyres, the brother of James, had been detained with small amounts of coal in his possession after work on a collier. Colquhoun and Harriot fined him forty shillings. They were in earnest in expropriating the coal heavers from their last possessive connection with the means and material of their labor. The war had come home: battle raged on the Thames. Many of the coal heavers were Irish, and the recent massacres in Ireland contributed to their vengefulness. The Thames Police was the brainchild of Patrick Colquhoun, the practical political economist, East End magistrate, and government agent, who was responsible for organizing, at a general level of merchant capital, the transfer of the world's wealth from marine transportation to land. Colquhoun had worked in Jamaica and Virginia; Harriot in India. The Thames Police Act was passed by Parliament at the urging of the West Indian interest in reducing the losses on its sugar cargoes incurred by the lumpers and coopers responsible for getting the heavy hogsheads to shore. They too took their "sweepings" and "waxers." The police both enforced the criminalization of these customs and assembled the gangs required to unload the ships when they arrived unpredictably at their moorings. Gabriel Franks worked for the police office as a foreman lumper, or one who organized gangs of dockers (or lumpers) to offload ships. At the close of day and at the end of work, with scant illumination aside from candles and oil lamps, the issue had become bloody murder.

I

PRISON

TWENTY-NINE

In Debt in Prison

DESPARD RETURNED TO ENGLAND FROM THE CARIBBEAN in the summer of 1790. In London, he was subject to a vexatious lawsuit brought by American merchants, whose ships had been seized in British Honduras. He owed nearly three thousand pounds. To add to his difficulties, the government was not going to reinstate him as superintendent, though he patiently waited for two years, according to James Bannantine, his biographer of 1799. In March 1791, he completed a *Narrative of the Public Transactions in the Bay of Honduras.* The effort was unavailing. Despard scurried up and down the corridors of power in a futile search for official clarity on why he had not been reinstated. These efforts were met by months on end of putting-off (Dickens referred to the Circumlocution Office), until the position of superintendent of British Honduras was abolished. Not only was Despard's reinstatement rejected in October 1791 but early in 1792 he was confined as a debtor to King's Bench Prison, where he remained for nearly three years, until the end of 1794. This was the first stage of a decade he spent in and out of prison.[1]

By 1800, there were eighteen prisons in London, including the Fleet, Tothill Fields, Cold Bath Fields, King's Bench, Bridewell, and Newgate. The latter, according to John Summerson, "was an extraordinary building. Far from being a mere dump for felons, a gigantic lock up, it was a splendid and costly architecture, a great Palace of Retribution."[2] Horsemonger Lane Gaol was designed by the man who built the warehouses at the West India Docks. Despard was not the only one hanged at Horsemonger Lane; between

---

1. Conner, *Colonel Despard,* 141–44; Jay, *Unfortunate Colonel Despard,* 201–16.
2. As quoted in Porter, *London,* 154.

1798 and 1803, thirty-six people suffered this fate at this Surrey County prison, fifteen in 1803.

Despard was revolutionized during the decade and played a part in these changes even from prison. A lifetime of grievances, suffered directly or witnessed indirectly, found expression, as it did for millions of people throughout the Atlantic mountains, in the explosions of the French Revolution. In prison, Despard read Thomas Paine's *Rights of Man*. Prisons themselves underwent a transformation, one that Despard lived. When Despard entered prison in early 1792, not only had the French Revolution progressed three years but its worldwide effects were taking place. Debate in England about its principles was vigorous and remains so. The year 1792 was a turning point. The French Revolution opened prisons, while the English counterrevolution built them. Forty-five prisons were erected in England in the last quarter of the eighteenth century.

Jules Michelet counted thirty prisons in Paris in the eighteenth century. The Bastille was the most hated. Its interior garden was enclosed against the prisoners, and the windows were walled up.[3] George Lefebvre tells us that the existence of the French peasantry depended on collective rights: access to common land for pasture, access to woodlands for fuel and building materials, and the right to glean after the harvest for bread.[4] The encroachment on these common customs led to the vast uprisings of the summer of 1789. The enclosure of the commons and the storming of the Bastille started the revolution. Thomas Paine called it "the high altar and castle of despotism"; John Thelwall spoke of its "bars, iron doors, and caves forlorn" in his first sonnet from prison. William Hazlitt, the English radical, likened the liberation of the Bastille to the jubilee.[5]

The Prison Ship, the first extended poem of the American War of Independence, was written in four cantos by the prisoner of war Philip Freneau and published in 1781, the same year 133 kidnapped Africans on the slave ship Zong were thrown overboard so the ship owners could collect the insurance on them! *The Prison Ship* tells the horrors of three hundred prisoners in one hulk (11,000 altogether died in them). No water, no bedding, no protection from sun or rain, one meal a day, and cruelty:

3. Michelet, *History.*
4. Lefebvre, *Coming,* 140–41.
5. Paine, *Rights of Man*; John Thelwall, "The Feelings of a Parent," in *Poems … Written in the Tower*; Hazlitt, "The Causes of The French Revolution," in *William Hazlitt: Selected Writings,* 489.

See how they pant to stain the world with gore,
And millions murdered, still would murder more,
The selfish race from all the world disjoin'd,
Eternal discord sow among mankind;
Aim to extend their empire o'er the ball,
As if the power that form'd us did condemn
All other nations to be slaves to them. . . .
To such a race the rights of men deny.

Liberation from prison and liberation of the people figured in the revolutionary discourse. This is the importance of the Bastille.

In the eighteenth century, prisons were neither standard nor uniform. They depended on the prisoners to organize rooms, food, drink, sport, and gambling in their own way. Authority was dispersed among petty tyrants, whose incomes depended on garnishing the prisoners (extorting a fee from new prisoners), rather than on a salary from parish, county, or government. By contrast, the nineteenth-century regime was the prison of the Enlightenment reformers John Howard and Jeremy Bentham, with its silent system, isolation, obsession with sanitation, and incessant labor. The transition from one to the other paralleled the transition to industrial work discipline required in the factory.

In *The State of Prisons* (1776), John Howard exposed the hunger, cold, damp, vermin, noise, irreligion, profanity, and corruption of prisons. He recommended eliminating fees, early rising, uniforms, soap and cold water, prayers, Bible reading, solitary nighttime cellular confinement, frequent inspection, constant daytime work, and classification by age and gender in order to prevent communication. The goal was repentance, or penance— hence, "the penitentiary." His solution helped to destroy the inmate order, or the prisoner's forms of self-governance, that had allowed a vibrant political culture to flourish. Jeremy Bentham's "panopticon" combined oversight and overhearing in an architectural arrangement to render inspection and achieve omniscience, omnipotence, and omnipresence. He planned two hundred and fifty of them.

The "first penitentiary in the world" was not in England but Philadelphia, where the Walnut Street Penitentiary was established in April 1790, across the street from Independence Hall. Its inmates lived in "unremitted solitude and laborious employment."[6] Its inspectors found that the prison was "no

6. Teeters, *Cradle of the Penitentiary,* 39.

longer a scene of debauchery, idleness and profanity" but a school of reformation and a place of public labour (beating hemp and picking oakum). On May Day, Tom Paine presented George Washington with the key to the Bastille (in Paris, Lafayette asked him to carry it to the new president) and a note saying "that the principles of America opened the Bastille is not to be doubted, and therefore the key comes to the right place." Principles are one thing, practice is another. On the evening of the first day of the new regime, fifteen prisoners successfully escaped. Thus, did freedom ring.

In Newgate gathered feminists, millenarians, vegetarians, antinomians, prophets, poets, philosophers, historians, healers, and doctors—"guests of His Majesty." Lord George Gordon was at the center of "London's notorious prison republic." He was the apparent cause of those 1780 riots that bear his name and that released hundreds of prisoners from Newgate. He "divided his substance with those who had no money . . . He clothed the naked, and fed the hungry," his secretary wrote, saying of the prisoners, "They were composed of all ranks . . . the Jew and the Gentile, the legislator and the laboring mechanic, the officer and the soldier, all shared alike; liberty and equality were enjoyed in their full extent, as far as Newgate would allow."[7]

The main three-story building of King's Bench was one hundred yards long, with sixteen staircases and 176 rooms. It was surrounded by a stout twenty-five-foot wall surmounted with prickly *cheveux de frise*. Its doors were locked at nine o'clock at night, when women and children were required to vacate the prison. Otherwise, prisoners could come and go, as long as they remained within the "rules" of the prison, meaning its well-defined neighborhood. Sixty-to-seventy prisoners lived within the rules. The boundaries of the rules were changed in 1790. According to Dickens, who used to visit his father in the Marshalsea debtor's prison, moneylenders, lawyers, and pawnbrokers conducted their business at that boundary "along the North Side of Dirty Lane and Melancholy Walk to Black Friars Road."[8]

At King's Bench, debtors held the keys to their own rooms. Those on the common side and those on the masters side both had their own organization. The latter, called "the college," held general assemblies and controlled the allotment of rooms. Some prisoners were "on the box," or dependent on charity. "Whistling shops" were rooms where liquor was sold. The utterly destitute

7. Dr. Robert Watson was Gordon's secretary and wrote his biography in 1795. Hay, "Laws of God."

8. Dickens is quoting from *Rules and Orders on the Plea Side of the Court of King's Bench . . ., Volume 1*, 1795.

could avail themselves of charity from a begging grate. Three of the water pumps were laid out, "communicating now at high tide and after heavy rains with the common sewers." The stairwells were filthy. The criers escorted people to their rooms and made announcements; scavengers swept the floors and emptied the chamber pots, selling the urine to local leather makers.

While King's Bench was the reputed prison for gamesters and debtors of high social status, a 1795 breakdown of the occupations of the eight hundred prisoners shows the reality was otherwise:

40 mercantilists	5 percent
50 manufacturers	7 percent
60 army and navy	8 percent
110 mechanics	14 percent
150 in trade	19 percent
160 agriculturalists	20 percent
200 laborers	25 percent

While the first three categories (20 percent) might have been men of rank or fortune, the remaining groups, making up nearly 80 percent of the prisoners, were poor tradesmen, workers, peasants, or artisans.[9] The anonymous author of *The Debtors and Creditor's Assistant* (1793), after noting that it cost on average twelve shillings a week to live in King's Bench, reckoned "the great bulk of the prisoners live extremely hard, and seldom know what it is to have a good dinner." Some have perished from "a total deprivation of the common necessaries of life." Despard did not suffer the worst of it, having means to purchase prison's wherewithal.[10]

In April 1792, a committee of the House of Commons heard testimony about King's Bench Prison. At that time, the prison held 570 debtors, 340 of whom were with their wives and children. Kate may have accompanied Ned. Most were "manufacturers, labourers, and seamen. Many prisoners were without bed or bedding. While the prison was designed to provide one room per prisoner, prisoners in fact doubled up with "chums." Some rooms contained as many as eight prisoners. The deputy marshal had "to chum the prisoners" "to rooms most suitable to their rank and situation." Otherwise,

9. Innes, "King's Bench Prison," 262.
10. *Debtor and Creditor's Assistant.*

the prisoners slept in the stairwells or on top of the tables in the tap room or didn't sleep at all.[11]

The Insolvency Acts, which had regularly provided relief to imprisoned debtors (hundreds were discharged with each act), were temporarily abandoned between 1781 and 1793. This was in reaction to the Gordon Riots of 1780, when the prisons were opened by direct action of the London crowds. Fleet Prison was destroyed, Newgate was burned down, and the big gates of King's Bench were opened.[12]

In 1771, James Stephen launched a major campaign against imprisonment for debt, lecturing against the iniquity of it. To protest it, he advocated fixing a day and time for a national jailbreak. Prisoners in King's Bench in fact organized a hundred strong for such an action. He helped remove the door to the lodge from its hinges. He heard at an assembly that "their complaint was being illegally confined or against Magna Charta and that they were determined not to suffer confinement in that prison for debt any longer."[13] A year later, a charitable society to relieve poor debtors began meeting at the Thatched Roof Tavern. By 1792, the Thatched Roof Society had discharged 381 debtors, with half again as many wives and twice as many children.[14]

"In point of *personal* consideration, little or no superiority appears amongst the prisoners in the King's Bench or Fleet; like the grave, they level all distinctions! The poorest and the worst, fancy themselves upon an equality with the richest and the best, and think a mere locality [King's Bench] or situation [debt], arising from a similarity of causes, a sufficient title for mixing with company they never could otherwise have aspired to."[15] Joanna Innes, the Oxford social historian and expert on King's Bench prison, is rightly skeptical. The prison was not a society of equals. Money ruled. Daily markets, a group kitchen, a coffee room, a taproom, and single rooms were available for those who could pay. Furnishings, meals, medical assistance, funeral arrangements, and exit into the "'rules" could be bought. So not *all*

11. House of Commons, R*eport from the Committee Appointed to Enquire into the Practices and Effects*, 39.

12. House of Commons, *Report from the Committee Appointed to Enquire into the Practices and Effects*.

13. Innes, "King's Bench Prison," 296.

14. House of Commons, R*eport from the Committee Appointed to Enquire into the Practices and Effects, a*ppendix 9.

15. Innes, "King's Bench Prison."

distinctions were leveled. The verb *to level*, expresses a political reality from English history that the French *égalité* brought to life again.

On 26 November 1792, while Despard was imprisoned, five persons, including a minister, were charged "with conspiracy to demolish the walls of the King's Bench Prison and for that purpose introducing a large quantity of gunpowder near them."[16] Captain John Cummings, Richard Burgh, Thomas Macan, James Davis, and John Bourne were convicted in February 1793. The same day, "one or two Levelling Societies formed in the borough intended to proceed to Kennington Common, on Sunday at noon, for the purpose of planting a tree there and call it the Tree of Liberty." The minister of war sent a detachment of dragoons to prevent the planting of the tree.

In November 1792, P. W. Duffin and Thomas Lloyd were brought to trial for posting an inflammatory handbill on the door of Fleet Prison, the other major debtor's prison. With some cockney wit and revolutionary fervor it advertised,

> *A House to Lett*
>
> Peaceable possession will be given by the present tenants
> On or before the first day of January 1793, being the
> Commencement of the first year of liberty in Great Britain.
> The Republic of France having rooted out despotism, their
> Glorious example and eventful success against tyranny,
> Render such bastiles [*sic*] no longer necessary in Europe.

The lord chief justice himself, Lord Kenyon, sent them to Newgate. Duffin addressed the court, saying "he had heard much of the boasted constitution of the country and the glorious liberties enjoyed by its subjects, that he had for twenty-one days been kept in confinement." Kenyon did not give Lloyd a chance to speak.[17]

Patrick Duffin was an Irishman from Dublin and Thomas Lloyd an American from Philadelphia. Unpaid debts threw them into Fleet Prison; the warden's decision punished them further by chumming them in the "strong room," a place devoid of bed or bedding, water jug or urinal. One might reasonably expect that Duffin was influenced by the formation of the

16. *Annual Register* 34, November 26, 1792.
17. *Annual Register* 34, 29 November 1792.

United Irishmen, and Lloyd was affected by the debates in Philadelphia that led to the Bill of Rights. Yet their testimony at the trial was almost entirely confined to arguments designed to appeal to a jury of Englishmen. Duffin was sentenced to two years in prison.

Coming to London from Philadelphia, seriously in debt, Thomas Lloyd had been affected by the first financial panic in US history, a bubble that collapsed in March 1792. The new United States was a commercial and money republic from the beginning. Its first debtors' prisons came with political independence, and with them opposition. In 1798, forty prisoners escaped the New York jail; in 1800, twenty-five issues of the newspaper the *Forlorn Hope* were published from within its debtors' prison. The debtors met as "a shadow republic," electing officers, assigning rooms, organizing cleanliness, and settling disputes, all according to a "book of Constitution."[18]

Duffin operated a gaming house in the Strand. Earlier he had been sentenced to two years prison in the New Compter. The Dublin United Irishmen was founded in November 1791. Mainly a polemical and educational organization, it had in this early period far greater influence than its numbers suggest. Though it was dominated by mercantile and professional people, its fortnightly meetings were open to all. It maintained an active correspondence with similar organizations in Scotland and England. A year later, during Patrick Duffin's trial in London, the United Irishmen proposed a political program of universal manhood franchise.[19]

Duffin and Lloyd were tried in December 1792 at the Guildhall in the City of London as "wicked, seditious, and ill-disposed persons, greatly disaffected to the king, government and constitution." A hostile witness from the prison testified that they belonged to a "club" in the prison. Duffin had protested his imprisonment in a letter to the secretary of state. Writing in the strong cell of Fleet Prison, "this mansion of the oppressed," he protested against the denial of "locomotion" (this was how Blackstone defined liberty) as a violation of Magna Carta and against the refusal "to furnish any convenience or necessary to preserve life or health, in a dismal vaulted cell, flagged with stone." Lloyd, a lawyer, gave a long speech in self-defense, calling the poster or handbill a mere "*jeu d'esprit*" or "pasquinade. He argued that because he was a citizen of the United States, half of the jury that convicted him should have been composed of other "aliens." Referencing the Magna

18. Mann, *Republic of Debtors,* 148.
19. Curtin, *United Irishmen,* 24–25.

Carta and the commons, he protested that imprisonment for debt "is a crime against the natural, imprescriptible, and unalienable rights of man; and, in Great Britain, a crime also against what is called the great charter of English liberty." Debt without fraud cannot in itself be a crime, he argued. He pointed to the charitable societies, the insolvency acts, and the "popular commotions" liberating debtors from prison as evidence of the widespread opposition to imprisonment for debt. He imagined that once constitutional rights were restored, "the usurped jurisdiction of the court of King's Bench [will] tumble to the ground—the liberty and happiness of thousands will be restored, but the golden stream which so long has flowed through that channel, will flow no more." As if to explain "the golden flow," Lloyd then provided a history of finance capitalism since the Restoration.[20]

The excessive facility of credit caused the prices of the necessaries of life to rise "by which the day-labourer is deprived of two out of his three daily meals." The disposition "to engross the goods of life, to the exclusion of our neighbor" had become "an incurable disease." Cupidity, avarice, and selfishness were the growing evils hidden in the forms of money. "Fictitious contrivances," "legal fictions," "*hocus pocus*," "incomprehensible jargon," and "legerdemain" were some of the circumlocutions of money. Imprisonment for debt oppressed, he declared, the "swinish multitude." Tens of thousands were deprived of liberty. "All the horrors of the Bastile [*sic*] are incidental to a man's situation who is confined for debt." He appealed to the spirit of Alfred, the only monarch in English history popularly called "the Great," who ordered the execution of judges for illegalities. How shall these evils be rectified? By application to Parliament? By appeal to lawyers? What about appealing to "a more numerous and as well-informed a body of men"? At that point, Lord Kenyon interrupted his speech to warn Lloyd that "he was advancing to the edge of a precipice." This was the precipice of direct, popular action, such as that expressed in the handbill that brought them to trial; over the edge was the republic, a world without prison, and "liberty in Great Britain." Lloyd went on, noting that the poor trader rotted in jail while the "lordling is strutting about the purlieus of St. James's, like the jay in the fable, in the borrowed, or rather let me say, the stolen plumage of others." He pities the plumage but forgets the dying bird, Paine had admonished Burke. The reference was not lost on Lord Kenyon, who rebuked Lloyd and ordered him to sit down.[21]

20. Howell, *Complete Collection*, vol. 22, 317–48.
21. Howell, *Complete Collection*, vol. 22, 317–48.

In February 1793, in front of the Royal Exchange, Lloyd was placed in the stocks, a traditional wooden apparatus of punishment, in which the victim stood while his wrists and neck were immobilized between two boards, making him an easy target for the missiles and execrations of the public. The restraints were loosely attached at first, but at the sheriff's command, they were shut tightly; in the presence of a huge concourse of people, two hundred constables kept order.[22]

In 1794, Thomas Lloyd wrote and D.I. Eaton published his *Impositions and Abuses in the Management of the Jail of Newgate* (1794) against John Kirby, who was head jailer from 1792 to 1804.[23] The windows were unglazed— "there is not a drop of water to wash off the excrement and filth"—women were not permitted to attend the sermon for the condemned, tubs of urine were kept standing in the yard, and commodities were sold at exorbitant prices. Soap, butter, cheese, sugar, tea, tobacco, and coal cost three times what they would at an ordinary chandler's shop. Lloyd compared Kirby to Rhadamanthus, the judge of hell.

The diary of Thomas Lloyd has recently come to light. It is an important source for understanding the political convergence among Newgate prisoners during the 1790s. It details Lloyd's business dealings with America (bank loans, textile commerce, innovations in spinning) and his receipt of food (fresh vegetables, meat pies, currant pie, apple pie) It alludes often to the persecution of other democrats and provides a chronicle of his illnesses. It mentions his petitions to the home secretary and the chief justice and his observation of the Fourth of July. He notes the names of those who borrowed Paine's *Rights of Man* and *Age of Reason*. He joins the arguments about Robespierre and the meaning of the Thermidorean reaction, when Robespierre was denounced and then beheaded. In February 1795 "a number of prisoners made attempt to escape but could not effect it." He received money from the Society for the Relief of Prisoners Suffering for Their Political Opinions.

By the time Edward Despard entered King's Bench, the opposition to imprisonment for debt was drawing on both English constitutional history (habeas corpus and Magna Carta) and on the French Revolution. While the actuality of the storming of the Bastille supports the view that the liberation of prisoners was a minor accomplishment, the event had greater meaning in

22. *Annual Register,* 7 February 1793.
23. *Impositions and Abuses.*

England. There the "Bastille" quickly became both the symbol of oppression and of liberation. The English "bastilles" were prisons, not armories; they contained debtors, thieves, vagabonds, and the poor; they were the lock-ups for the working class. Any prison or crimping house would be called a "bastille," and by the 1830s, even the workhouses set up by the New Poor Law were referred to by this name.

In Philadelphia, "a Lady" compared the new Walnut Street Penitentiary to the commons: "It is a sort of little commonwealth (if I may be allowed the expression) which I shall entitle the commonwealth of nature—an excellent school to teach the utility of the government, which most attends to its operations, to the uniformity, beauty, and simplicity of her precepts." Others would not have allowed the expression! Thomas Lloyd stated unequivocally that "The public good is an estate in common, of the free possession and enjoyment of which no law can deprive the humblest individual." In the United States, a Bankruptcy Law of 1800 benefited some. To quote a journalist, "Those who get their living. . . by the various arts which draw the productions of labour into their hands without working themselves" contrast with the "labourers . . . who produce by their industry something to the common stock of the community."[24]

When he was a young man, Henry Hunt (1773–1835), or "Orator" Hunt, the national speaker for parliamentary reform, who was supposed to speak at Peterloo in 1819, insulted an aristocratic neighbor and was confined to King's Bench for six weeks at the end of 1800. "Circumstances brought me into strange company, and here I saw men of all persuasion in religion, and of all parties in politics."[25] Hunt's progress from zealous patriot and devoted subject to the king to democrat and reformer began in prison, where he learned "of rational liberty, of freedom as the natural rights of man, and as the law of God and nature." He met Henry Clifford (1768–1813), an attorney, a legal writer, a Catholic, and Despard's employee, who was imprisoned at the time in the Tower. Clifford knew Despard as "a mild gentleman-like man." So one day that winter, Clifford and Hunt walked from King's Bench (Hunt was sentenced to the custody of the marshal of King's Bench, not to the prison) to London Bridge, where they took a boat to the Tower stairs. Despard received Hunt with "great courtesy and politeness" and warmly inveighed against his imprisonment. Two beefeaters, or "Yeomen Extraordinary of the

24. Benjamin Franklin Brahe writing in the *Aurora*, 26 March 1798.
25. *Memoirs of Henry Hunt*, 471.

Guard," were in the room the whole time, not leaving even when Clifford visited with Catherine in order to make out Despard's will. If Despard wished to walk on the terrace,

> A guard of soldiers was called, and the procession was as follows:—One of the beef-eaters walked first, with his sword drawn; then followed two soldiers, carrying arms, with their bayonets fixed; then came Colonel Despard, with Mr. Clifford and myself, one on each side of him. Immediately behind us marched two more soldiers, carrying arms, with fixed bayonets; and another beef-eater, with a drawn sword, brought up the rear. In this manner we walked the parade or terrace for about half an hour, taking care to speak loud, so that the whole of our conversation was heard by the beef-eaters.

Hunt was outraged. Clifford explained that Despard refused to "crouch and truckle to his persecutors," and had fallen victim to "that monster" William Pitt, prime minister. Government hired spies to swear away the lives of its opponents! "Gracious God!" exclaimed Hunt. Hunt never forgot those words, and two years later at Despard's trial, they came true. The facts of Despard's case "created in my breast a deep-rooted never-ceasing antipathy to tyranny."[26]

26. *Memoirs of Henry Hunt*, 500.

THIRTY

In Prison without a Spoon:
The Commons of the Meal

MR. JACKSON, WHO HAD KNOWN Despard for twenty years as a humane, benevolent, honorable gentlemen, testified to the Parliamentary Committee on Cold Bath Fields Prison on 21 March 1799. "Mr Nicholson shewed me into the Cell; I viewed it with Horror and Astonishment; the room appeared to be about Five or Six feet wide, and Seven Feet in Length; there was neither Chair or Table, but as a Substitute for a Table was the Colonel's Portmanteau, on which was a Bowl or Bason of Water." He had a few planks for a bed. The floor was stone, and "the rain or snow might easily beat under and over the Door."[1] In his poem "The Cell," Thelwall wrote of suffering similar conditions earlier in Newgate: "The damp foul floor, the ragged wall, / And shattered window, grated high."[2] In his memoir, James Hardy Vaux described his experience on entering Cold Bath Fields as a prisoner in 1800:

> This was the first prison I had ever entered, every thing around me had an air of unspeakable horror. After being viewed and reviewed by the surly Cerberuses of this earthly hell, I was conducted up some stairs to a long gallery, or passage, six feet wide, having on either side a number of dismal cells, each about six feet by nine, formed entirely of stone, but having a small grated window near the roof, at the further end, which admitted a gloomy light, and overlooked a yard, in which other prisoners were confined; there was also a similar grate over the door; but, owing to their height, both these apertures were very difficult of access.

1. House of Commons, *Report from the Committee Appointed to Enquire into the State of His Majesty's Prison.*
2. *Poems Written.*

Unlike Despard, he had bed and blanket and three meals a day (though he paid "through the nose").[3]

Jackson found Despard in the kitchen, where dinner was being prepared. The meat was served in wooden bowls. "I asked Colonel Despard if he was to be of that Mess? He replied in the Affirmative, that he shared in common with the other Prisoners that when he was served was in a Bowl or Platter, without Knife, Fork, or Spoon, that his Allowance was One Pint of Porter per Day for his Drink." Jackson refused to eat the food that he had been offered as a visitor. One o'clock dinner, then, Despard "shared in common with the other Prisoners." After four, when he was locked up, it was different, no commons. Then, he was "without a Candle, or without being permitted to have any Book at any Time of the Day to amuse him; that he had neither Knife, Fork, or Spoon."[4] This was solitary confinement. He was not permitted to go into the garden. The idea was degradation by means of deprivation.

Prisoners called spoons "feeders" and teaspoons were called "slop feeders." Daily rations were called "crackers," and food in general was called "bum charter." Despard had been dispossessed of the simplest instrument of commoning; in the eighteenth century, a person was expected to possess a spoon. The meal was becoming individualized, and the instruments of its consumption had become a source of profit. The prisoner had to *buy* his eating utensils. For example, Andrew Bryson was a United Irishman, who was caught and sentenced to transportation to the West Indies in 1798. Before he embarked, he was imprisoned in Waterford without fire or food or straw for bedding, and in sight of the gallows. An experienced sympathizer informed him that "a tin and spoon are things you will find the want of immediately, and the friend offered to sell him the implements for 1s. instead of the purser's 4s. aboard the ship."[5] On the one hand, as with Despard, the proletariat was criminalized, while on the other, as with Bryson, the prisoner was proletarianized. At least Despard's condition was one he shared with others.

Of course, spoons, especially silver spoons, were valuable and could easily be sold to a pawnbroker. "To be born with a silver spoon in your mouth," was a marker of class superiority at this time.[6] Teaspoons, tablespoons, pap spoons,

3. *Memoirs*, 74.

4. House of Commons, *Report from the Committee Appointed to Enquire into the State of His Majesty's Prison.*

5. Bryson, *Andrew Bryson's Ordeal.*

6. According to the *Oxford English Dictionary,* the expression was first used in 1801, in America.

gravy spoons, pepper spoons, marrow spoons, dessert spoons, salt spoons, and Cadley spoons are all named in bills of indictment against suspected thieves in the Old Bailey. Refinement and larceny seem to grow together, though their connection is by no means a simple one. I have counted these indictments and found that between one and two dozen prosecutions for such thefts occurred annually between 1789 and 1812. The accused were generally household servants, and when they were found guilty, their punishments ranged from transportation (seven or fourteen years), whipping, hard labor in the House of Correction (two years), or imprisonment in Newgate (months).

Bannister Truelock was a silversmith, as were his companions. He met the veteran James Hadfield at White Conduit Fields, where they witnessed the flogging of two soldiers. "It was a shame there should be any soldiers," Truelock said, "that Jesus Christ was coming; and we should have neither King nor soldiers." His landlady recalled him saying that on Christmas Eve, kingship would be abolished and the necessities of life would be much reduced in price. He supported the rights of man and was a reader of seditious books. Truelock was imprisoned in Cold Bath Fields. On 15 May 1800, Hadfield shot at George III at the Drury Lane theater but missed. The attempt led to the Criminal Lunatics Act, which made it possible for Hadfield to be confined for life.[7]

Taking silver spoons was not anyone's customary right, but Thomas Pryer, who lived first as an errand boy and then as an apprentice for three years to a silversmith in Hatton Garden, was transported for seven years for taking silver *turnings*.[8] At the end of 1798, when Despard was in Cold Bath Fields Prison, John Bott, or Pott, was tried for stealing six silver dessert spoons valued at thirty-six shillings, a silver ladle, and three silver tablespoons also valued at thirty-six shillings. Pott had not been paid his wages of twenty-one pounds, one shilling, and one pence. His employer had three or four years earlier sent him to work as a butler to Richard Watson, the bishop of Llandaff, who gave Pott "an exceeding good character."[9] In 1792, the bishop of Llandaff had preached a famous sermon on the subject that God made the rich and the poor. Tom Paine replied that "no, God didn't, God made man and woman." William Blake and William Wordsworth also opposed Llandaff's crude ideology but not publically. Pott was sentenced to death.

7. Moran, "Origin of Insanity."
8. *Proceedings of the Peace,* 23 October 1797.
9. *Proceedings,* 5 December 1798.

Gilbert Wakefield of Hackney was imprisoned for writing a *Reply to the Bishop of Llandaff* (1798), who had praised "the wisdom of God in having made both Rich and Poor." The experience killed him. He had written, "I believe from my soul that within these three miles of this house, where I am writing these pages there is a much greater number of starving, miserable human beings, the hopeless victims of penury and distress, than on any equal portion of ground through the habitable globe." He was referring to Shoreditch and Spitalfields. The ministers "have reduced thousands and tens of thousands to wretchedness and beggary; they have occasioned a devastation of the human species infinitely tremendous beyond the most merciless tyrants of ancient or modern times; the death of a fellow creature is no more to them than the fall of an autumnal leaf in the pathless desert; land and sea is covered with the carcasses of their slain."[10] This was the spirit of the times when Despard was once again imprisoned. Authorities were suspicious and niggardly. For example, for the starving people of Dublin, during the "great" famine of 1846–47, the French chef of the London Reform Club designed a factorylike soup kitchen, to which a hundred bowls with a hundred spoons were attached to a single, long table by a hundred chains![11]

"La Carmagnole" was the song of the French Revolution when the sansculottes assaulted the royal palace of the Tuileries on 10 August 1792—the event that led to the downfall of the monarchy. The first verse asked, "What do republicans want" and answered "Liberty for the human race," in particular pickaxes to break out of the dungeons. "Torch to the castles and peace to the cottages" was its incendiary message. If only the people would apply common sense and cease cutting one another's throats and unite as one, then "*Ils viendraient tous manger / A la même gamelle*" (they would all come eat from the same plate).

It would be a mistake to regard such expressions as purely metaphorical. The commons begins with the meal and its preparation. Joseph Brant, the Iroquois leader and British ally during the American War of Independence, remained an enemy of the United States. He organized for a confederacy in one land, calling for "a dish with one spoon." In 1789, he struggled to maintain unity among the Seneca, Mohawk, Cayugas, Onondagas, Oswegos, and Oneidas. "A dish with one spoon" extended the political confederation of the Iroquois to the new peoples of the Ohio and the Old Northwest—the

10. *Reply to the Bishop,* 12.
11. Woodham-Smith, *Great Hunger,* 179.

Miami, Shawnee, Delaware, Wyandot, Sac, Chippewa, and Potawatomy. His confederacy, on a boundless hunting ground, was a classless society without private property. In 1803, Brant wrote a letter comparing Indians with the English:

> We have no law but that written on the heart of every rational creature by the immediate finger of the great Spirit of the universe himself. We have no prisons—we have no pompous parade of courts—we have no robbery under the color of law—daring wickedness here is never suffered to triumph over helpless innocence.... Our sachems, and our warriors, eat their own bread, and not the bread of wickedness.... The palaces and prisons among you form a most dreadful contrast. Go to the former places, and you will see, perhaps, a most deformed piece of earth swelled with pride.... Go to one of your prisons—here description utterly fails! Liberty to a rational creature, as much exceeds property, as the light of the sun does that of the most twinkling star, but you put them on a level, to the everlasting disgrace of civilization.[12]

The American anthropologist Lewis Henry Morgan (1818–81) described the law of hospitality in his book *Montezuma's Dinner*. Of the people of the longhouse, none was refused. Morgan quotes John Stephens among the Maya and their "practice of communism in food."[13] Karl Marx noted "at twilight each day a dinner in common served to the entire body in attendance"; with the commons came gratitude. Noting that the meal began with grace, Marx wrote, "It was a prolonged exclamation by a single person on a high shrill note, falling down in cadences into stillness."[14]

What is civilization? Norbert Elias defined it as emphasizing mediations of the body with things like the spoon. The custom of taking liquid with a spoon was the anonymous work of centuries that began at aristocratic courts and, like other behaviors or etiquette, spread first to other courts and then to other parts of the population. By 1790, the fork was no longer used to eat soup and had been replaced by the spoon. This was an accomplishment of the ancien régime, a legacy of the European aristocracy. Elias showed that these changes corresponded to psychological changes in the emotions and drives. To Elias, they provided a "second nature" to the civilized person and were indicators of shame and disgust.[15]

12. Stone, *Life of Joseph Brant*, 2:481.
13. *Montezuma's Dinner*, 75–77.
14. Marx, *Ethnological Notebooks*, 172–73.
15. *Civilizing Process*, 92.

The technology of consumption, even the shapes and functions of our eating utensils, remain decidedly *dix-huitième*. In the Middle Ages, "eating from the same dish or plate as others was taken for granted" as long as one did not fall into it like a pig. The ritual of living together was in flux. By the seventeenth century, "everyone eats with spoon and fork" "Here, step by step, the now accepted way of taking soup is being established: everyone has his own plate and his own spoon, and the soup is distributed with a specialized implement."[16]

The spoon could be a marker of class or civilization. Mother Goose says it's a mark of bounty:

> A swarm of bees in May
> Is worth a load of hay;
> A swarm of bees in June
> Is worth a silver spoon;
> A swarm of bees in July
> Is not worth a fly.

Denying Despard a spoon was part of his punishment and his dehumanization. The spoon was part of a standard of shame; hygiene had nothing to do with it. The shame was associated with individualized consumption. We can begin to see how the word *common* came to have two meanings—coarse conduct, or vulgarity, and a community of sharing—depending on the social rank of the person using it. It could express hierarchical scorn or a lofty ideal of welfare. The word contained a central contradiction of bourgeois society and placed its resolution in the working class. These two contradictory meanings—vulgarity and sharing—helped guide the transition from the commons of the meal to the commons of play. *Vulgarity* was an upper-class pejorative term only for the common people (Latin: *vulgus*), whose games, as we shall see, even when enclosed, provided space for commons.

16. Elias, *Civilizing Process,* 106–7.

THIRTY-ONE

Rackets in King's Bench Prison: The Commons of Play

THE TRANSITION IN THE PRISON corresponded to a transition in sport; sport and games were also enclosed, as Blake summarized it in "The Echoing Green," "And sport no more seen, / On the darkening Green" (lines 29–30). The social historians Barbara and John Hammond titled their chapter on enclosures "The Loss of Playgrounds." Sport became a spectacle, enclosed and authorized, and this corresponded with the double meaning of *common* as signifying both common fields of play and the vulgarity of its participants.

Space in King's Bench was not entirely enclosed, as there was an open yard used for rackets, skittles, and marketing. The old prison regime had room for sport, and the prison provided a level playing field inasmuch as skill and practice were rewarded rather than money or birth. At King's Bench, the field was called the "Parade." Thomas Rowlandson's 1809 illustration of the Parade on a beautiful sunny day depicts men at a table, a dozen small groups of men and women strolling and talking, several ground-floor stalls open to customers, flower pots on the windows of the upper stories, and men in shirt-sleeves playing rackets.[1] The overall impression is of a hundred people or so engaged in bustling social intercourse. This was the debtors' commons.

A contemporary wrote that "the lower sort" in King's Bench played skittles or bowls. Skittles has nine pins. As was gin, it was brought to London by the Dutch in the 1690s. The extreme lateral pins on the left and right were called, respectively, "the landlord" and "the copper." "The favorite game, however, and that which in a manner characterizes both the King's Bench and the Fleet prison is *rackets*."[2] It was played with a ball and racket against

1. Pyne, *Microcosm of London.*
2. *Debtor and Creditor's Assistant*, 46.

a wall (or two, if played at a corner). The game derived from tennis and was a progenitor of squash. If the ball were lobbed over the wall, the master of the ground might supply a new one at two- or threepence.[3]

This was an era of puritanical attack on games and sport by evangelicals, utilitarians, and politicians. Traditional sport required an open space, often a commons, whether it was the street in the city or the field in the country. Sport was occasion for intense sociality, even theater, and in a revolutionary time could itself become politicized. For example, in 1802, a tennis game in the prison yard of Kilmainham Gaol, Dublin, provided the occasion for clandestine communication between Robert Emmet and Anne Devlin. J. M. Neeson describes how football games in Northamptonshire during the 1760s were played in such a way as to destroy enclosures. Indeed, a huge football game in Lincolnshire was a major event in the struggle in the fenlands against enclosures at the time of the English Civil War.

The separation of recreation from work was an accomplishment of this time similar to the separation of production from reproduction. It had been a long time coming; homo ludens was not so easily crippled by a few generations of evangelical fulmination. The historian of sport counterposes it to industrial-work discipline, which games and sports undermined.[4] Patrick Colquhoun investigated the six thousand public houses of London in 1795–96, advising that minute attention be paid to their licensing, including the rule that the morals of laboring people should not be corrupted by unlawful games "such as *cards, dice, domino, shuffleboard, what's o'clock, four corners, tales Mississippi, draughts, Sibley table, bumble puppy, ringing at the bell,* or any other alluring game: nor shall he permit *boxing, badger-baiting, cock-fighting.*"[5]

Despard was imprisoned at the last moment of light for the traditional games—blood sports, amusements, boundaryless football, pastimes, and play—before night befell Blake's darkening green. As an Irishman, he would have appreciated Thomas Moore's indifference to the religion of riotous sportsmen, as long as it opposed constituted authority: whereas the French fought for glory, the Spanish for religion, and the English for liberty, the Irish fought for *fun*. During play, the full range of liberty finds expression. We can

3. Atkins, *Book of Racquets.* The game of racquets originated in King's Bench and the Fleet. See "Muscular Society," *London Society* 8 (1865): 412.
4. Malcolmson, *Popular Recreations.*
5. Colquhoun, *Treatise on Indigence.*

easily imagine Despard finding both play and liberty in his years in King's Bench.

That the new game rackets is thought to have originated in a debtor's prison, and that its play requires a hard wall or two, makes it both a game of enclosure (when the ball bashes against the wall) and a game against enclosure (when the ball flies over it). This was the conclusion of the contemporary historian of sport Joseph Strutt, whose *Sports and Pastimes of the People of England* appeared in January 1801. Apprenticed to the same engraver who had taught William Blake, he was a conscientious antiquarian. He believed that "the character of the people" was better revealed in their sports than in their wars. "The general decay of those manly and spirited exercises which formerly were practiced in the vicinity of the metropolis, has not arisen from any want of inclination of the people, but from want of place proper to the purpose, such as in times past had been allotted to them are now covered with buildings, or shut up by enclosures." For want of commons, skittle or ninepins were now played only at drinking houses.[6] His chapter on ball games includes handball, tennis, cricket, football, golf, hurling, wind ball, stoolball, camp ball (played in open country), bandy ball, stow ball, pall-mall, club ball, and trapball but not—he publishes in January 1801—rackets.[7] It was a new game dependent on new circumstances, namely, enclosure. Later, a convict imprisoned in Cold Bath Fields learned a new meaning for *racket* as the flash title to any particular fraud, dodge, scheme, trick, or line of business—in fact, any game.

In the early twentieth century, a vigorous antiquarian debate took place concerning the origin of the game. Lord Aberdare edited the Lonsdale Library's 1933 publication *Squash, Rackets, Tennis, Fives, and Badminton,* which asserted the impossibility of finding "a single reference to rackets before 1800."[8] Robert Henderson of the New York Public Library responded with a note on spelling and a list of eleven published references and several images before 1800. The class prejudices of this discussion are evident. Aberdare cited John Armitage, who declared "It's foolish to suppose that the idea of the game originated in the minds of some poor debtors in . . . the Fleet Street Prison." Henderson also summarized its history. Rackets, he wrote, "began to be played in public houses and other nondescript places, and finally

6. *Sports and Pastimes*, xliv.
7. *Sports and Pastimes*, 84ff.
8. *Squash, Rackets, Tennis.*

FIGURE 16. "Fashionable Amusements. Two pugilists on a trade token struck by Thomas Spence.

was taken up by public schools, soon after the middle of the nineteenth century. The game was then enclosed within four walls, and attained respectability. Thus, while the game did not start in The Fleet, its development, if not its present existence as a game, is due to the fact that the prisoners detained there found it to be such a diverting pastime."[9] The issue was not the exact date or the precise location of rackets' origin but the social rank of the people whose play established it. Here there is no quarrel: prisoners and debtors, invented this game, and they did so in the era of massive enclosures.

Pierce Egan (1772–1849), the cockney compositor and historian of boxing, said the best rackets courts of the day were to be found in King's Bench and the Fleet, and that "all the early champions were either born or brought up in the debtor's gaols." The scene at King's Bench was one of gaiety and dash. Oppressed or colonized people found a means of recognition. It was multicultural: "Tawny Sam" was all finesse and delicacy, and Mr. Carney was "a wonderful all-round athlete from Ireland," "a *crack* player." "There is no game, perhaps, not even cricket itself," Egan wrote, "which combines so well skill with so much bustle."[10] The racket player is always on the move—

9. Henderson, *How Old?*; see also Noel, "Historical Sketch," 743.
10. Noel, "Historical Sketch," 743; Egan, *Table-Talk Book,* 228.

standing still is entirely out of the question—and the same might be said of the career of Edward Despard.

From the number of one-eyed players (Egan mentions several), we conclude that play was dangerous. In fact, it ruined the fighting career of Jemmy Belcher, "The Heroic Champion of England." The case was this: Belcher, who came from a family of prizefighters, was remarkable for both his strength and his art, but he was chiefly admired for possessing that combination of wind and heart called "bottom." His was never surpassed. His disposition was placid, but the quickness of his fists was unparalleled, severely felt but scarcely seen. Belcher "danced." An anonymous witness observed of Belcher, "in springing backward and forwards his celerity was truly astonishing. He fought a series of notable "turn ups," or "set tos," against other "heroes" at the turn of the century. He defeated Tom Jones in 1799 at Old Oak Common (Wormwood Scrubs). In May 1800, he demolished Jack Bartholomew on Finchley Common in seventeen bareknuckle rounds. On 22 December 1800, on Wimbledon Common, he fought and won against the Irish fighter Andrew Gamble, whose second was the Jewish former champion Mendoza, when London's "paddies" mobilized. "Belcher laughed at him throughout the fight." Surely, the derision was enjoyed in Westminster, where the Act of Union to obliterate independent Ireland was just being completed. In 1801 and 1802, he fought three battles against Joe Bourke, another Irishman and something of "a stranger to the fancy," winning them all. They hammered away at each other. After the August 1802 bout, Belcher knocked one of Bourke's teeth out and "gave him a prime leveller into the bargain." Bourke's face "was so disfigured, that scarcely any traces of a human being was left." Bourke "deviated from the path of Rectitude" (went to prison) but was freed after agreeing to enlist in a foot regiment.[11]

The following spring, a month after Despard, Macnamara, and the other conspirators hanged, Jem Belcher fought Jack Fearby on a commons seventeen miles from Newmarket. A constable and a clergyman attempted to end the battle, but the clamor was too great for their exhortations to be heard. At this fight too "Belcher at length put in a leveller."[12] Belcher wore yellow, and the "Belcher handkerchief" became the national fashion. For

11. "Famous Boxers," William L. Clemens Library, University of Michigan. This manuscript of more than five hundred pages complements Egan's *Boxiana,* often providing fuller, round-by-round descriptions, as well as odds for the "battles," from the end of the eighteenth century into the 1830s.

12. "Famous Boxers," 294.

Belcher, the turning point came at a game of rackets on 24 July 1803. Despard had been dead six months, and Robert Emmet was organizing insurrection in Ireland. Belcher lost his eye at the game, and while he kept on fighting, he never won again. He became a Soho publican and irritable.

In one sense, the sport was brutalizing. In another, it afforded the oppressed a place of recognition and the talented a reward, even if they were soon cheated of it. These fights were held on commons, where the magistrates had less influence. A punch knocking the opponent down was called a "leveller." Many prizefighters were butchers, while others were colliers, porters, nailers, paviors, sawyers, boatswains, and even weavers and dyers. These were artisans and laborers, who did the heavy lifting of the age and were possessed of strength, skill, and bottom. It was the sport of the poor, though its patrons were genteel. It was called both the "fancy" and the "science."

In April 1802, the police detained Belcher in the watchhouse. Bourke, we saw, was once jailed. Belcher's own end was spent in poverty and misery. He was confined in Horsemonger Lane Gaol for breaking the peace in a contest with Tom Cribb ("the Black Diamond"), one of his last. There he caught the cold that hastened his death. He went forty-one rounds with Cribb himself, by this time the champion of England. Belcher fought with bottom and gaiety against the former bellhanger and wharf-side porter. Cribb was trained by Captain Barclay, the famous pedestrian of the time, who in 1810 fought the African American Tom Molineaux, or "the Moor" as he was called in these sporting circles, at Tothill Fields, a disputed commons.

Let us not leave Belcher's story at this point of complete defeat but instead recall that he helped train the English champion Henry Pearce, also known as the "Game Chicken." In December 1805, Belcher challenged the Chicken, and they fought on a Nottinghamshire commons. By the twelfth round, Belcher was on the ropes, when the Chicken "exclaims most feelingly, 'I'll take no advantage of thee Jem—I'll not hit thee, No—lest I hurt thine other Eye!' Such a circumstance ought never to be forgotten. The spectators felt it at the time, by their universal plaudits—& it will live long in Humanity's memory."[13]

We tend to see these sports from a postwar perspective, after Napoleon had been defeated, and with him *liberté*, *égalité*, and *fraternité*. The militarist judgment of Pierce Egan is apt: "the alacrity of the TAR in serving his gun, the daring intrepidity of the BRITISH SOLDIER in mounting the Breach,

13. "Famous Boxers," 300.

producing those brilliant victories which have reflected so much honour on the English Nation may be traced to something like these sources."[14]

The secretary of war under Pitt was the conservative Norfolk squire William Windham, who defended traditional sports, especially boxing (as a schoolboy, he was thrown out of Eton for fighting), as useful both for promoting soldierly values and encouraging the exertions of "the efficient part of the community for labour." Boxing was an antidote to "the dangerous enthusiasm which was analogous to Jacobinism." Speaking in Parliament in May 1802, he expressed doubt that Jacobin ideas had made any progress among the poor and illiterate or whether "a single sportsman had distinguished himself in the Corresponding Society."[15]

In 1819, William Hazlitt described John Cavanagh, the Irish housepainter from Saint Giles-in-the-Fields, a great fives player (another racket sport). According to Hazlitt, Cavanagh was superior to Wordsworth's epics or Coleridge's lyrics because he was without affectation or trifling. His only peer was John Davis, a rackets man who "did not seem to follow the ball, but the ball seemed to follow him." He maintained that the motto "Who enters here, forgets himself, his country, and his friends" should be inscribed over the entrance to King's Bench Prison, where the best open-ground player of his time was imprisoned. Sport, an ideal of human grace, power, and beauty, provided transcendence; it could be an escape or, as Hazlitt put it, a "forgetting" from the oppressions of debt, misery, and hunger.[16] These possibilities were widespread as long as common lands were available.

In 1819, when the revolution was finished and its important dreams of equality destroyed, Hazlitt could say, "It may be said that there are things of more importance than striking a ball against a wall. There are things indeed which make more noise and do as little good, such as making war and peace, making speeches and answering them, making verses and blotting them; making money and throwing it away." While rackets was popular in King's Bench when Despard entered it, we do not know for a fact that he played the game. As he was freshly arrived from a British enclave in Mesoamerica, it would be surprising if he had not witnessed or heard of the ball game now known as *ulama,* which closely resembles rackets. Given his avid interest in

14. Egan, *Boxiana,* v.

15. Amyot, *Speeches,* 24 May 1802, 1:353, 346. Was he to become responsible for the adage that "the battle of Waterloo was won on the playing fields of Eton"?

16. Hazlitt's obituary appeared in the *Examiner* (1819). It was later included in "The Indian Jugglers," in Egan's *Table-Talk Book.*

mankind's spiritual traditions, he may even have known that the Mayan origin myth, as documented in *Popol Vuh,* describes the game.[17]

Be that as it may, when Despard was released from his obligations and gained his freedom, or "locomotion," once again in 1794, war had begun, and the speeches, poetry, and monetary system were making world-changing noise. We can now take these in turn, beginning with the actual stone he aimed at Number Ten Downing Street. Strutt remarked that "throwing heavy weights and stones with the hand was much practiced in former times, and as this pastime required strength and muscular exertion it was a very proper exercise for military men."[18]

Two months before the Oakley Arms arrests in 1802, William Wordsworth, strolling across Westminster Bridge early on a "bright and glittering" morning, looked on "Ships, towers, domes, theatres and temples lie / Open unto the fields, and to the sky."[19] We need to imagine not only this scene but its social relations—Tothill Fields, St. George's Fields, Pancras Fields, Copenhagen Fields, Marylebone Fields. Indeed, an unbuilded commons surrounded and interpenetrated the town. These were the gathering places for mass meetings, sport, conviviality, and pasturage. They were not yet enclosed or imparked. In the future London became a closed city of shops, shut doors, no trespassing signs, squares with locked gardens, and fog.

A Parliamentary Select Committee on Public Walks and Places of Exercise heard the following testimony in 1833: "I have witnessed dissatisfaction at being expelled from field to field, and being deprived of all play places." Hundreds used to play cricket every summer night in the fields in the back of the British Museum. Popular recreation was undergoing profound repression by evangelicals, landlords, and industrialists. Pugilism, pedestrianism, football, and dancing also suffered.[20] C. L. R. James wrote of cricket, "It was created by the yeoman farmer, the gamekeeper, the potter, the tinker, the Nottinghamshire coal-miner, the Yorkshire factory hand. These artisans made it, men of hand and eye."[21] James describes the game in the terms of Wordsworth's preface to *Lyrical Ballads.* The cricketer maintains human

17. Hazlitt, "Indian Jugglers"; Fox, *Ball.*

18. Strutt, *Sports and Pastimes,* 66–67.

19. "Composed upon Westminster Bridge, September 3, 1802," lines 6–7 in Wordsworth, *William Wordsworth,* 82.

20. Malcolmson, *Popular Recreation,* 110–11. See also Hammond and Hammond, *Age of Chartists,* 114, 118.

21. *Beyond a Boundary,* 221.

beauty and dignity against the "savage torpor" of urban, uniform occupation. E. P. Thompson once praised C. L. R. James for "his delight and curiosity in all the manifestations of life." "The clue to everything lies in his proper appreciation of the game of cricket." These men loved cricket but the game is not possible without a field, and so we are back to the commons.

As a boy, Jeremy Bentham boarded at the Westminster School between 1755 and 1760. He wrote his former headmaster for help in building a panopticon on Tothill Fields. The land was "in the state of Waste which might be subject to the rights of common." The parishioners of St. Margaret's and St. James's, enjoyed common of pasture. It was a cricket ground from "time immemorial" for the boys of Westminster School. Bentham appealed to the Westminster scholars, offering to find them a new pitch so that he could build his prison. "Whatever benefit they reap from the use of that dreary and ill-looking expanse, in the way of sport and exercise, is subject to the perpetual intrusion of *mean dangerous* and *unwelcome* company, of all sorts."[22] Sir Francis Burdett, Catherine's colleague, also boarded at the Westminster School, until he was expelled in 1786 for refusing to submit to the headmaster and inform against his fellow students, who had smashed windows in their boardinghouse.[23] Catherine and Burdett defeated Bentham, and to this day cricket is being played, rather than people imprisoned, on Tothill Fields.

One of Spence's political halfpennies from the midnineties depicts on one side a "Westminster scholar" wearing academic robes and a scholarly bonnet and on the other side a "Bridewell boy" wearing trousers, or sansculotte. The class division was already there. The Westminster scholars began to refer to the former commoners as "Scis," short for Volscis, the people whose conquest in 304 BCE, as the boys would have learned in Latin classes, initiated the expansion of Rome. They may have wondered who would be the Spartacus of Tothill Fields.

"Dear Sir," wrote Patrick Colquhoun from the police office in Queen Square to the home secretary on 17 September 1802, "for the two Sundays last past I find that great multitudes, chiefly Irish, have assembled in Tothill Fields to the amount of several thousands & have employed themselves in playing at a game called *Hurley:* attempts have been made by our Constables to disperse them but the multitude was so great that they bid them defiance." All Westminster magistrates and constables were ordered out, along with a

22. Forshall, *Westminster School*, 284–85.
23. Forshall, *Westminster School,* 199.

"picquet of 50 horse to be in readiness at the tiltyards to move towards Tothill Fields on the shortest notice."[24]

Burdett and Bentham fought over Tothill Fields. The *Morning Chronicle* (30 July 1802) hailed Burdett's victory in the Westminster election as a "spontaneous and honest expression of indignation against the system of solitary confinement." Burdett and Catherine prevailed against the panopticon. As a viable historical event, rather than as a philosophical concept, the panopticon had been defeated by June 1803, when Prime Minister Addington informed Bentham that he was unwilling to finance it.[25] However, even though Bentham's panopticon had been denied Tothill Fields still ceased to be a commons of play. In 1810, the dean of Westminster and former head of the school "paid a man with a horse and plough to drive a furrow around ten acres and the following year gates and rails were erected."[26]

24. NA, HO 42/66.
25. Semple, *Bentham's Prison,* 3, 16.
26. Communication between the author and Elizabeth Wells, archivist, Westminster School, 24 April 2013.

THIRTY-TWO

Catherine Despard Confronts the Penitentiary

CATHERINE VISITED HER HUSBAND IN THREE PRISONS that we know of: Cold Bath Fields, the Tower, and Horsemonger Lane Gaol. He was incarcerated between 1798 to 1799 in Cold Bath Fields, in the Tower in 1802, and in Horsemonger Lane for his trial and execution in 1803. In these years, he was also imprisoned in Shrewsbury, in Tothill Fields, and in Newgate, though we do not have documentary evidence that Catherine visited him in those places. For the others we have documents.

Despard departed life from the prison at Horsemonger Lane, and that is where she worked with him in the composition of his last speech, their testament to posterity. She visited him in the Tower of London, for centuries the prison for prisoners of state, and there she also helped him with writing, this time his will. But it was in the penitentiary in Clerkenwell known as Cold Bath Fields that her writing was most immediately efficacious and deeply challenging to Power. This struggle, her opposition to the carceral state and the carceral economy at their birth, is her most important legacy.

Cold Bath Fields opened in 1794. It was a new penitentiary, where constant discipline and solitary confinement were the rule. The chairman of the Middlesex Bench of Justices, William Mainwaring, supervised its construction. He was active in the Society for the Preservation of Liberty and the Protection of Property against Republicans and Levellers, which printed one of his law-and-order speeches: "Equality in the sense in which it is now attempted to be inculcated into the minds of the people by crafty and designing men is, in the nature of things, impossible."[1] The penitentiary was

---

1. Ignatieff, *Just Measure of Pain*, 136.

designed to enforce "the nature of things," indeed it helped *create* that so-called nature of things.

According to the romantic poet, Samuel Coleridge, this penitentiary was hell on earth: "As he went through Cold Bath Fields he saw / A solitary cell; / And the Devil was pleased, for it gave him a hint / For improving his prisons in Hell."[2] According to the political colloquialism of plebeian London Cold Bath Fields prison was called the "Bastille," shortened to "'Steel," a bit of cockney wit unknown to members of Parliament (it had to be explained to them) but known to any hackney coachman. As late as the 1850s, all other penitentiaries and workhouses were called the 'Steel. Even Francis Place referred to it as the Bastille in his records of expenditure on prisoner relief.[3] In *Caleb Williams,* William Godwin put it this way: "'Thank God,' exclaims the Englishman, 'we have no Bastile! Thank God, with us no man can be punished without a crime!' Unthinking wretch! Is that a country of liberty, where thousands languish in dungeons and fetters? Go, go, ignorant fool! And visit the scenes of our prisons! Witness their unwholesomeness, their filth, the tyranny of their governors, the misery of their inmates!—After that, show me the man shameless enough to triumph, and say, England has no Bastile!" Seventy to eighty political prisoners were held in the 'Steel, including sailors from the Nore mutiny, Irish republicans, parliamentary reformers, and Manchester democrats. The Irish Rebellion of 1798 was led by the United Irishmen, with fraternal allies among democrats and reformers in Scotland, England, and France. Confronted with this situation, the government responded in Ireland with war and terror; in Scotland with exile or transportation; and in England with selective terror tactics, such as hanging, a massive prison-building program, installation of a rationalized secret service of spies and provocateurs, a centralized municipal police force, and, finally, an ideological and cultural offensive of paid journalists and subsidized newspapers.

The historian of prisons in this era finds that "in the 20 years between 1775 and 1795 a wholesale rebuilding of the country's gaols and bridewells was accomplished." Forty-five were erected.[4] A new moral geography was made of security, which required enclosure; of salubrity, which required exposure; and of reformation, which required compartmentalization. The 'Steel imprisoned the unfortunate and the disobedient, such as a "disorderly woman, one

2. "The Devil's Thoughts," lines 33–36.
3. Francis Place Papers, BL, Add. MSS 27817 f.200, Francis Place Collection.
4. R. Evans, *Fabrication of Virtue.*

of those unfortunate creatures who walk the streets" or a boy "confined there for disobedience to his master."[5] If the plantation and the factory were the pillars of the Atlantic carceral economy, then its auxiliaries in the carceral state were the ship and the prison. The penitentiary and the cotton plantation, indeed the textile factory too, were institutions created at the time, and with many interrelations. The modern penitentiary was conceived to produce disciplined bodies of docile, deferential labor, providing "examples" to others.

William Godwin criticized John Howard, who proposed to "reform" the old prisons with solitary confinement and hard labor. Godwin learned that in the 'Steel, prisoners were made to "labor" five hours a day "trundling a wheel-barrow round in a circle," a cruelty made the worse for its "impudent uselessness."[6] Godwin compared the prisoner in England to the Negro in the West Indies.

In 1798 the Irish rebellion had begun aiming at independence and a republic. It provided the context for the suspension of habeas corpus in England and the imprisonment of fourscore London radicals and reformers. Despard was among them, having been imprisoned on 12 March 1798 (the same date as the raid on the Leinster leadership of the United Irishmen in Dublin). He was released and then reimprisoned on 22 April as part of the nationwide sweeps in Manchester, Birmingham, and Leicester. This effectively put an end to the London Corresponding Society (LCS). Neither a rising in England nor an invasion from France occurred to aid the Irish Rebellion, which was squashed at the cost of thirty thousand lives and untold exiles into factory life in England.

These arrests were part of an international crackdown. The secretary of the LCS, Thomas Evans, was also arrested. He had recently written an "Address to the Irish Nation." The United Englishmen, modeled on the United Irishman, was formed in April 1797. It had eighty societies in the north, mainly in Lancashire, and was strong among the textile workers, particularly spinners. By the winter of 1797–98 they were arming. In London, the United Britons, which included Despard, was formed and became part of a three-kingdom struggle. This was mediated by James Coigly, who helped put the coalition together.

5. "Debate in the Commons on the Habeas Corpus Suspension Act," 21 December 1798, in vol. 34 of Cobbett, *Parliamentary History of England*, 112.
6. *Enquiry concerning Political Justice*, 676, 679.

Coigly was a Catholic priest from county Armagh and a devout United Irishman A life-long revolutionary, he was in Paris for the demolition of the Bastille. He assisted in the formation of the United Scotsman. He was an emissary to the disaffected textile workers of Lancashire. He helped transform the Manchester Corresponding Society into the oath-bound United Englishmen. In London, Coigly met at Furnival's Inn with members of the LCS, several times with Despard in February 1798. Here with Evans and the Irish brothers John and Benjamin Binns, Despard and Coigly discussed "a regular plan of insurrection" or "whether we can make a hubbub." Despard said fifteen hundred men could take London "but that not less than 50,000 could keep it but that ought not to stop us."[7] With Despard in solitary confinement, James Coigly was hanged on 7 June 1798. His last address was to the people of Ireland, and he concluded with the militantly antislavery "behold the scourge of war, and all its evils, shall not be removed until the shackles of bondmen and slaves are broken."[8] There are some moments in history that are forks in the road. This had been one of them.

On the day Coigly was hanged, "An Irishman" addressed his fellow countrymen in England: "Is her prosperity become indifferent to you because the oppression of her Government has forced you to seek for bread in a foreign Country? ... The poor from the oppression of the rich are deprived of the means of providing subsistence and driven by hard necessity to seek support in a Country where they are upbraided with their poverty and obliged to labour almost unceasingly." He concludes with the admonishment "Associate with each other in a 'Bond of Brotherhood and Union,' be bold, be courageous, act firmly, act like Irishmen."[9] William Sampson, a native of county Derry, wrote from America of Ireland that "the nation became one general prison."[10]

The attorney general warned, "There were artful men in that prison, and some of them had shown they ill deserved the lenity that was shown to them; some of them had a great number of O'Connor's pamphlets ready for circulation."[11] The "artful men" depended on the art of their couriers, such as Catherine Despard and Janet Evans, to bring in this literature. Francis Place remembers that "all sorts of provisions sent to them were searched, yet paper,

7. Keogh, *Patriot Priest*, 68, 69.
8. John Fenwick, "Observations on the Trial of James Coigly, for High Treason," in Howell, *Complete Collection*, 23:176.
9. NA, HO 42/43, 7 June 1798.
10. *Memoirs*, 48.
11. *Parliamentary History of England*, 34:129.

pens, and ink were conveyed to them." And he explained one of the methods: "in large quills carefully pushed into the meat close to the bones."[12] From this small detail, we can imagine Catherine's work—the trip to the butcher to get a joint of meat; the trip to the stationer's to obtain quills with barrels of requisite length and diameter for the rolled papers; the fletching, boiling, hardening, and sharpening of the quills; the insertion of the papers into the quills and the quills into the roast; the cooking of the meat over a coal fire that was not so hot as to ruin the papers inside the quills. Finally, her coach ride across London from Berkeley Square to Clerkenwell to insert warming words into the English Bastille.

Papers had been discovered concealed in the rooms of the state prisoners in late March 1799, said Richard Ford, the chief magistrate of London. "Some few of the papers were found upon the persons of some of the prisoners, but the greater Part was concealed up the Chimney."[13] Richard Ford considered these communications improper and seditious. Ideas of colonial liberation were preserved inside a chimney, for that is where Arthur O'Connor's book, a classic of the literature of national liberation, was hidden in the 'Steel.

Arthur O'Connor (1763–1852) was a leader of the United Irishmen, on whose behalf he negotiated with France in 1795 and 1796. He believed that "there were 200,000 men in London so wretched that in rising in the morning they were not sure to find dinner in the day. He was arrested and imprisoned in Dublin Castle, where in six months he wrote *The State of Ireland*, which was distributed in February 1798. He, along with Coigly, was arrested in England en route to France and charged with treason. Interrogated by the Privy Council, including the prime minister, the home secretary, and the lord chancellor, he was sent to the 'Steel. We know little of his experience there apart from this, as he later wrote, "Of all the furies I ever met the wife of the gaoler was the greatest."[14] His book was hidden up a chimney, becoming part of the clandestine prison library, as the attorney general revealed in parliamentary debate. It belongs on the shelf reserved for the literature of colonial liberation, alongside Fanon, Connolly, Cabral, Nehru, James, Biko, and Toer. It is also prison literature.

Addressing England, O'Connor wrote, "O Ignorance! Thou guardian of bastilles! Thou parent of famine! Thou creator of slaves, and supporter of

12. *Autobiography of Francis Place*, 181.
13. *Report from the Committee Appointed to Enquire into the State of His Majesty's Prison in Cold Bath Fields*, 49.
14. Conner, *Arthur O'Connor*, 115.

despots, thou author of every mischief and every ill! How long must we bear thy accursed dominion?" The Irish people were the "worse housed, worse clad, worse fed" of any people in Europe. "Your corn, your cattle, your butter, your leather, your yarn," all the produce of the land is exported. He praised Irish hospitality, the absolute axiom of the commons. He opposed mechanization, monopoly, high grain prices, and primogeniture. He castigated British imperialism for its crimes. not only in Ireland, but "in every quarter of the globe, pillaging, starving, and slaughtering the unoffending inhabitants of the East Indies; lashing the wretches they have doomed to slavery in the West Indies." As his modern editor writes, "The only logical antidote to the pathologies of the state of Ireland was a democratic, socially egalitarian republic. O'Connor wrote "Redress means restoration of plunder and restoration of rights."[15]

As these movements began to include more workers, the expression of material demands also emerged. According to the dynamic of revolution, the leading reformers appealed to ever-broadening parts of the people—its demands becoming more relevant to their conditions. And since their condition was characterized by want, revolutionaries began to add subsistence to their project. This happened in France, in San Domingue, in Ireland, and in England. The Friends of Universal Emancipation resolved, in the first place, "that as the earth abounds even to profusion with every thing necessary to produce human felicity, and no inherent mark of appropriation to favour of any man or class of men appearing in any portion thereof, it is reasonable to infer that the whole is the property of the whole people, that justice requires, because the happiness of the human race depends on an universal participation of the bounties of nature"; and, in the second place, "that society is a state the best calculated for carrying into effect this design of nature whilst its laws and institutions quadrate therewith, securing equally to all and every individual the means of a rational and happy enjoyment of life, founded on reciprocal dependence and mutual industry."[16] Here is a definition of the commons based not on penury but enjoyment. The 'Steel, however, was the opposite, a horrible place.

The weaver John Herron was arrested on board the man-of-war the *Robert* on 12 June 1798, from where he was brought to town and taken to Cold Bath Fields "loaded with heavy Irons and put into a dark Cell; in which dark Cell

15. James Livesey, in O'Connor, *State of Ireland,* 22, 32, 35, 48, 55.
16. NA, PC 1/3117, pt. 3.

the Excrement of the unhappy person who had been confined there before, remained, and produced a Stench, that was almost suffocating." There he remained for eight days. He was one of the habeas corpus prisoners.[17] He was kept on bread and water in a stone cell with no fireplace and an iron-grated window. The governor of the prison, Thomas Aris, caused him, almost lifeless with his legs bleeding, to be dragged through the streets to Bow Street.

John Smith, a poor bookseller, a democrat with the LCS, and a husband with four children, was accused of conspiring to assassinate the king. He was shut away in Newgate for a year before he was acquitted and released. He and his wife ran a bookshop, provocatively called "the Pop Gun," after a jury acquitted four LCS members of attempting to assassinate the king with a poisonous arrow shot from an air gun. There they sold a pamphlet titled *A Summary of the Duties of Citizenship,* which explained that government required three instruments: 1) soldiers ("soldiers are by profession slaughterers"), 2) clergymen ("they hallow with the sanction of Divinity, state robbery"), and 3) lawyers ("lawyers thrive on misery . . . they are tyrants of property"). The attorney general slapped an indictment of seditious libel on Smith. He was sentenced to hard labor for two years on bread and water in the 'Steel. Repression was merciless.

Immediately after his arrest, Ned wasn't allowed to see his wife except through an iron gate. After 1 November, he was able to see her in the porter's lodge, but only for a few minutes in the presence of turnkeys and others.[18] Later they were permitted to sit on a pile of bricks together. She sent him fruit, cheese, and biscuits. From April to November, he was imprisoned in solitary confinement. The walls of his stone cell dripped from the damp; rain and snow blew in through the unglazed window; and he had no chair, no desk, no bedstead, no knife, fork, or spoon. He had to use the chamber pot as a washbasin. His left side was paralyzed by rheumatism, and he developed severe chilblains on the heels of his feet. He subsisted on a diet of bread and water and slept on planks.

Sir Francis Burdett, MP (1770–1844) was married to an heir of the Coutts banking fortune; he was the only radical member of Parliament, and he financially supported the political prisoners. He helped look after Catherine when her husband was executed, making sure she got to Ireland to the hospitality of Valentine Lawless, Lord Cloncurry. Burdett maintained contacts with both

17. NA, KB 1/31, pt. 1, April 1801.
18. Patterson, *Sir Francis Burdett,* 1:68.

radical London and Irish republicans. The governor, Aris, noticing that Burdett conversed with the prisoners committed for sedition and mutiny, kept him under surveillance.[19] Burdett received from the Manchester political prisoners further information about the other prisoners. They were "confined in solitary cells measuring only eight feet by six, where they could not obtain anything like a bed without paying a shilling for it; where they were left without fire or candle, exposed to cold weather in a narrow space where the wet continued to flow down the walls, a situation in which they had been compelled to linger for seven months; that far different treatment had been promised them by the privy council."[20] Aris told Wickham "that the indulgence which had been given him ... had been shamefully abused; that Letters and Papers had been carried in and out, and I think he said, one of the Wives of the Prisoners had behaved very violently, and collected a Mob about the Prison."

Janet, née Galloway, was the wife of Thomas Evans, chairman of the LCS. Her brother, Alexander Galloway, an officer in the LCS, was also active in Westminster democratic politics. She was arrested, and afterward gave birth to stillborn twins. She supported her husband, looked after their children, shared his work as a colorist in the book trade, and was an active correspondent in the revolutionary movement. She participated in a demonstration outside the prison.[21] She and Elizabeth Bone (whose husband John Bone was also taken prisoner during the April arrests) were banished from the prison after they were caught communicating with the mutineers.

Thomas Evans spent sixteen months in Newgate Prison. He was an advocate of the "agrarian republic" of Moses, which assumed that the territory of a nation was the people's farm. Christianity was the embodiment, he believed, of "the broadest republican principles." To him, Moses, Jesus, and Alfred the Great were saviors of the commons. "I have lived long enough to witness the effect of enclosure after enclosure, and tax after tax; expelling the cottager from gleaning the open fields, from his right of the common, from his cottage, his hovel, once his own, robbing him of his little store, his pig, his fowls, his fuel; thereby reducing him to a pauper, a slave."[22]

Leadership of the efforts to support the prisoners was contested and played out in several ways—demonstrations outside the prison walls, cam-

19. *Report from the Committee Appointed to Enquire into the State of His Majesty's Prison in Cold Bath Fields.*

20. Conner, *Colonel Despard,* 192–93

21. McCalman, *Radical Underworld,* 16.

22. T. Evans, *Christian Policy,* 17.

paigns in the press, debate in Parliament, petitions to the government. The LCS organized a relief committee, whose operation reflected prior political divisions within the radical movement. Money was at the root of them.

In 1794, Francis Place visited Newgate, and the story he told might as well be a parable of political economy.

> One Sunday in particular I was there, when several respectable women were also there, relatives of those I went to see. When the time came for leaving the Prison arrived we came in a body of 9 or ten persons into a large yard which we had to cross—into this yard a number of felons were admitted, and they were in such a condition that we were obliged to request the jailer to compel them to tie up their rags so as [to] conceal their bodies which were most indecently exposed—and as I have no doubt intentional to alarm the women, and extort money from the men. When they had made themselves somewhat decent we came into the yard, and were pressed upon and almost husseled by the felons whose Irons and voices demanding money made a frightful noise and alarmed the women. I who understood these matters had collected all the halfpence I could—and by throwing a few at a time over the heads of the felons set them scrambling swearing and all but fighting whilst the women and the rest made their way as quickly as possible across the yard.[23]

Place appears to be describing a more or less permanent fault line of the London working class, one that separated the industrious from the idle, the craftsperson from the vagabond, the rough from the respectable, the honorable from the dishonorable. It was reflected in the Poor Laws that distinguished the deserving from the undeserving poor. By the 1790s, the fault line threatened to erupt with new forces from the expanding world proletariat—commoners dispossessed by Enclosure Acts, Irish people fleeing terror, the population of kidnapped transatlantic Africans, the defeated Highlanders of Scotland. This proletariat could no longer be disciplined just by the threat of hanging.

Four years later, in 1798, with the suspension of habeas corpus and mass arrests, Francis Place called a meeting and appointed himself secretary of a committee to support the prisoners. Some of whom were lodged in Newgate and could easily receive visitors, while others, including Despard, were immured with "incorrigible felons" in the 'Steel and were at first unable to have visitors. Although he says he cannot fathom the government's reasoning for consigning some prisoners to Newgate and others to the "Bastille," he

23. BL, Add. MSS 27826, f.186, Francis Place Collection.

himself politically opposed those, such as the United Englishmen, whose object was "to produce a revolution," an absurd and ridiculous project worthy only of Bedlam, in his opinion.[24]

Place worked with William Frend, Thomas Hardy, and Francis Burdett in weekly subscriptions of money. Prisoners received twelve shillings weekly, their wives eight shillings, and each child four shillings. "The wives and other female relatives . . . came to me Saturdays to receive their weekly allowances." It was excessively hot that summer. Place's wife moved her work into the front room with its open window, and Place made the disbursements in the kitchen. But when the prisoners' wives went into the front room, annoying his wife, Place "turned them all out." They neither forgave nor forgot the offence. The ill will was picked up by the men in prison, who soon remonstrated that the surplus subscription funds be given directly to them. More was at issue than temporary annoyance on a hot day. Place had made clear that he thought "revolution," advocated by some of the prisoners, was absurd and ridiculous.

After Place and his family removed from Holborn to Charing Cross in April 1799, he devoted himself full time to the business of his trade and the hiring of new employees. He also ceased doing relief work for the prisoners. April 1799 was also when his brother-in-law, Matthew Stimson, was found guilty of stealing a two-pound banknote during a highway robbery and sentenced to death. He was "a great favorite among the thieves," prisoner turn-keys, and those who felt that a pardon could be easily obtained. To prevent this, Place went to Ford the magistrate and arranged for the sentence to be lessened to transportation for life, thus avoiding the possibility of a pardon. Place's social ascent in a time of counterrevolution was accomplished on the basis of new conditions of moneymaking and family politics.

Sir Francis Burdett, MP, accompanied Catherine on her visits to Despard. Once he left three guineas for the "mutineers." The wooden walls of the ship and the stone walls of the prison concealed two sites of communication. The mutineers brought their wit and high spirits to Cold Bath Fields Prison. "*Let go the anchor;* upon which they all let go the *shank painters* (strings that fasten the irons to their middle), and the irons fall with a heavy noise upon the stone pavement."[25] This provided a rough music of protest. Similar to rattling the cages in today's prisons, it could shake the nerves of the most hardened guards. Soon after the imprisonment of the thirty-three mutineers, a

24. *Autobiography of Francis Place* 181–86.
25. Bannantine, *Memoirs.*

riot erupted and seven of the mutineers escaped over the prison walls. Despard was removed to one of their cells.[26]

Catherine fearlessly ventured into the recesses of the secret state, prodding it with the sharp point of her pen. She wrote directly to the home secretary, the duke of Portland, a future prime minister (1758–1809) and close ally of Prime Minister William Pitt; to William Wickham (1761–1840), the founder of the British Secret Service and "superintendent of aliens" from a place in the Home Office called "the Inner Office"; and to Richard Ford (1758–1806), the London stipendiary magistrate in Shadwell and Bow Street and former colleague of Wickham. She assailed the pyramid of power from top to bottom.[27]

Kate Despard's writings to the press and among the radical societies began almost immediately with Edward's arrest in April. In May 1798, Kate wrote the home secretary requesting a copy of the charges against him, despite the suspension of habeas corpus:

> I take the liberty of requesting to know of you if there [are] any order [orders] from his Grace the Duke of Portland, for the usual allowance of State Prisoners to be given to Colonel Despard, who is confined in the House of Corrections in Cold Bath Fields, five weeks Sunday without the common necessaries of life. When he was first taken to that Prison, he had one of the upper apartments given him, which he found very airy; but since his commitment he has been removed to the ground floor with not so much as a Chair to sit on or a Table to take his vitals [victuals] of; where he finds the Morning and Evening very could [cold] and not so much as a Fier [fire] to warm himself; and where he is deprived of Books Pen ink, and not even allowed to see me but for a few moments, and that among felons and People of the worst of crimes. In consequence of I wrote to his Grace the Duke of Portland this day is a week to request his Grace will be pleased to direct sum [some] change to be made in respect to his treatment, but as I did not mention my address; I presume is the cause of my not receiving an answer. I entreat Sir that you will be so obliging as to lett [let]me know wheather [whether] any thing is dun [done] or will be dun [done] to alleviat [alleviate] his distresses for in short he is treated more like a Vagabond, than a Gentleman or a State Prisoner.[28]

On 21 December, a member of Parliament named Courtney, speaking on Despard's behalf in the House of Commons, read aloud from a letter from Mrs. Catherine Despard:

26. NA, HO 42/70, "Humble Petition."
27. Sparrow, "Alien Office, 1792–1806."
28. NA, HO 42/43 f.292.

I think it necessary to state that he was confined near seven months in a dark cell, without fire or candle, chair, table, knife, fork, a glazed window, or even a book. I made severall applications in person to Mr Wickham, and by letter to the Duke of Portland, all to no purpose. The 20th of last month he was removed into a room with fire, but not until his feet were ulcerated by the frost. For the truth of this statement I appeal to the Hon R Lawless and John Reeves, Esq., who visited him in prison, and at whose intercession he was removed. The jailer will bear witness that he never made any complaint of his treatment, however severe.[29]

A visitor named Valentine Lawless recounted that "we found the colonel, who had served many years in tropical climates, imprisoned in a stone cell, six feet by eight, furnished with a truckle bed and a small table. There was no chair, no fireplace, no window. Scanty light was admitted into this miserable abode through a barred unglazed aperture over the door, which opened directly into a paved yard, at the time covered with snow."[30]

A government MP, one Burdon, defended the 'Steel's regime, claiming that Despard was comfortable. In September, he would not accept surgery for his chilblains. As soon as his complaints were known, he was removed to a room, where "he had fire, candles, and every accommodation he could fairly expect." He had "frequent interviews with his wife." This was stated in Parliament. The walls of the cells were not wet, said Burdon.[31]

William Wilberforce also spoke in Parliament in defense of Despard's imprisonment and suspension of habeas corpus. A respectable clergyman told him "that he had seen the food intended from the prisoners, which consisted of as good legs of mutton and pieces of beef as he had ever seen at his own table." Wilberforce then went on to offer to Despard's friends the advice of "that great and good man Lord Hale," who, when asked how he felt in sentencing a man to death, replied "that he felt for the situation of the prisoner but he felt likewise for the country." In his ambivalence, Wilberforce reminds us of Mr. Facing-both-ways, the allegorical character in Bunyan's *Pilgrim's Progress* who lived in the town of Fair Speech.

Knowledge of Catherine's campaigns to the press, to Parliament, and to government came to Despard's awareness behind the prison walls, and he

---

29. Fitz-Patrick, *Life, Times, and Contemporaries,* 168.
30. Lawless, *Personal Recollections,* 45.
31. *Parliamentary History of England,* vol. 34, 129.

petitioned Parliament defending her.[32] Francis Burdett affirmed that "the Colonel's petition clearly and unequivocally contradicted the whole of Burdon's statement in the House and also that of the Attorney General."[33] In February 1799, he submitted a petition to Parliament authenticating his wife's assertions, confirming her many letters to Wickham, denying that he ever contradicted her statements, and insisting once again that in his solitary commitment he was denied book and paper and was not permitted to speak with her except in a tiny space in the Porter's Lodge, in the presence of a turnkey. A severely censored version of Despard's petition is printed in Hansard's *Parliamentary History*. Burdett, fortunately, kept the original, which can be found among his papers.[34] Rather than dispute the actual conditions of prison or the behavior of its notorious governor, the authorities instead impugned Catherine's testimony on the grounds of its language.

The attorney general who doubted Catherine's literacy was Sir John Scott. As a member of Parliament in the House of Commons, on Saint Stephen's Day 1798 (26 December), he participated in the debate on whether to continue the suspension of habeas corpus. He said "that the letter was not of the writing of Mrs. Despard. Perhaps she did not see the whole drift of it. It was a well-written letter, and for a certain purpose well adapted: and the fair sex would pardon him, if he said it was a little beyond their style in general." It is certainly a literate letter, conversant with modes of address and the formulae of petition, but the meanings of *literacy* were refined to a high degree. Catherine's proud voice comes through, as does her desperation and pain at the separation from her husband. Her strong sense of herself emerges, as she enumerates the deprivations that the colonel suffers—no chair, no table, no fire, no books, no writing materials. Finally, he is deprived of her.

Sir Francis Burdett copied her letters verbatim. "Though they may contain some errors that might reasonably be expected in the style of a woman brought up in a foreign country," they were "sufficiently expressive of the severe treatment her Husband experienced." Burdett copied her letters to prove "that she is not so illiterate as Mr. Canning would have us believe." George Canning (1770–1827), future paymaster of the forces, was at this time

32. Though he did correct her dates. The amelioration of his conditions began on 25, not 20, November, as she had said.

33. *Parliamentary History*, MS "English History," c. 295, fol. 143, Burdett Papers.

34. *Parliamentary History*, December 1798–March 1800, 34:515; MS "English History," c. 296, fols. 9–11, Henry Burdett Papers.

FIGURE 17. *Citizens Visiting the Bastille.* Etching by James Gillray, 1799.

an MP, a speaker on behalf of the prime minister, a skilled essayist, and a principal writer for the *Anti-Jacobin,* where he lavished wit and ridicule on the principles of reform and revolution.[35] If Wilberforce were Mr. Facing-both-ways, Canning was Mr. Smooth-man. But not even he could silence her.

The Jamaican writer Michelle Cliffe, considering the affliction of speech-lessness, noted that at worst, it leads to an inability to act or to an implosion of the will, at best it finds release only in chatter or giggles. Self-denial and the inability to reveal oneself nullify the person.[36] It is a condition, Cliffe thought, that is often invested in the powerless by the powerful. We see its failure to take hold in Catherine Despard, though not for want of trying.

Something similar happened to Olaudah Equiano. His autobiography was the first, firsthand account of the slave trade by an African and former slave. It was published by Joseph Johnson, the publisher of Mary Wollstonecraft, Thomas Paine, and William Blake, among others. The white power structure denied that he was the author of his own autobiography, and in so doing undermined the truthfulness of the atrocities he described, thus maintaining the racist myth of African illiteracy and intellectual incapacity. The advanced view of the 1790s was that civilization had begun in Africa. Since this view was promulgated mainly by French scientists, racist supporters of the West Indian lobby in England instinctively opposed it. Equiano died in 1797. The nine editions of his autobiography in the 1790s remained an immensely important resource for abolitionists.[37]

Between 1793 and 1818, Parliament refused to admit petitions that did not meet those standards of grammar and spelling it considered the linguistic signs of decency and decorum. Such standards, however, actually acted as a filter excluding heterodox opinion. In 1793, William Wilberforce, for example, dismissed petitions for an extended parliamentary franchise on these grounds. English spelling was notoriously difficult, partly because it maintained its etymologies in Greek, Latin, and Anglo-Saxon, and schooling in these languages was largely reserved for the upper class. This explains Thomas Spence's interest in spelling reform. When he began his studies, he found

35. MS "English History," c. 295, Henry Burdett Papers.

36. Cliff, "Notes on Powerlessness."

37. Even a favorable review in the *Monthly Review,* quoted in Vincent Carretta's edition of the *Autobiography,* found "it not improbable that some English writer has assisted him" Gates, *Signifying Monkey,* 154. See also Fryer, *Staying Power,* 111, for attacks by other newspapers supported by the West Indian lobby.

that politics and language were disordered: "But both of these I reduced to order: the one by a New Alphabet, and the other by a New Constitution."[38]

Thomas Spence fought against the difficult, unphonetic English spelling in his *Grand Repository of the English Language* (1775). The purpose of phonetic spelling was to emancipate writing from weird spelling, which preserved only the influence of dead languages available in elite education. And it influenced the radicals of the 1790s. For instance, Francis Place praised it, and in 1794, from Newgate itself, James Henry Lawrence published a book that expresses the influence of Spence's orthography even in its title: *An Essay on the Nair System of Gallantry and Inheritance; Shewing Its Superiority over Marriage, as Insuring an Indubitable Genuinness ov Birth, and Being More Favorable Tu Population, the Rights ov Women, and the Active Disposition ov Men* (1794). The book proposed "the abolishment ov this impolitic and vexatious institution," marriage. Patriarchal inheritance, it argued, reduces the woman to the character of an ignorant fool: "As long as marriage continues a profession, love will continue a trade. The eighteenth-century discussion of the Agrarian Law, or equal partition of property, was based on the policies of the brothers Tiberius and Gaius Gracchus, the plebeian tribunes of ancient Rome. James Henry Lawrence asked, "Were not the Gracchuses indebted tu the good education which they had received from their mother, Cornelia, for the pre-eminence which they enjoyed among their fellow citizens?" Encounters in the colonial world, Kerala in southern India, led to the recovery of an all-but-forgotten history in the imperial world, the association of women and the commons. Both the emancipation of women and phonetic spelling leveled hierarchy. In the lower class, Lawrence writes, "wun will find boath sexes much more on a level." Certainly Ned and Kate were "on a level."[39]

Catherine Despard made a striking figure in society. She accessed the highest military officers, was the subject of debate by the attorney general, was discussed in Parliament, and was accepted in person by the home secretary. A black woman in a white man's world, she was held at arm's length. While she was not mentioned by name, unless to defame her, she nevertheless stirred the minds of a metropolis whose population was growing from the riches of slaving, sugar, and cotton and whose leaders eagerly sought to protect and augment these ill-gotten riches by waging war or preparing for it.

38. O. Smith, *Politics of Language,* 30.
39. Lawrence, *Essay,* 37.

On 19 April 1799, Pitt addressed Parliament to request his government be given "the power of transferring from the metropolis to any part of the kingdom the persons detained for treasonable and seditious practices."[40] Despard was forty-seven years old and Spence just a year older when they were imprisoned in the 'Steel. Spence was confined in Cold Bath Fields in 1798.[41] He may have known Despard. He was confined for twelve months, after June 1801, in Shrewsbury prison, but since Despard had only recently been released, their paths did not cross directly at the penitentiary chapel, mess, or yard. In their persons, they formed a contrast: a big man and a short man, the son of a planter and the son of a netmaker, an Irishman and an Englishman. The Irish soldier and the English communist crossed paths in institutions designed to suppress revolution, the commons, and talk! Perhaps Spence's ideas reached Despard secreted in a hollow quill or chimney.

In August 1799, Despard was moved to Shrewsbury Prison, where he remained until spring 1801.[42] At Shrewsbury, all prisoners, male and female, were cleaned and put in blue-and-yellow-striped woolen uniforms made up of a short jacket, waistcoat, and cap. This was before classification by gender and offense. The uniforms were part of the prison-building program. Thomas Telford, the Scottish civil engineer, whose numerous bridges, roads, and buildings earned him the title "colossus of roads," built the new Shrewsbury Prison, which opened in 1793. The architect of commercial infrastructure was also the architect of a corresponding disciplinary infrastructure.

Catherine wrote to the home secretary, the undersecretary of state, and the chief magistrate. She wrote to the newspapers. She went to the wives of the other political prisoners. She educated the leader of the government's opposition about conditions. She exposed the horrid tyrant Aris, who ran the prison. She initiated and sustained what we would call a prisoners' rights movement. And in a way, it succeeded. In 1801, Despard was released. In light of Kate's legacy from her mother it is quite possible that it was the wealth of slaves which made this freedom possible.[43]

In summer 1802, Burdett ran a successful campaign in Westminster for a seat in the House of Commons, defeating his rival, William Mainwaring, the magistrate who was responsible for Cold Bath Fields Prison to begin with.

40. Conner, *Arthur O'Connor*, 197.
41. Chase, "Spence, Thomas," 236–45.
42. M. Jay, *Unfortunate Colonel Despard*, 264.
43. Erin Trahey, "Amongst My Kinswomen: Legacies of Free Women of Color in Jamaica," *William and Mary Quarterly* (April 2019).

That summer, the scot and lot electors of Westminster, which even as the most democratic borough in the country was still limited to twelve thousand, shouted "Burdett and No Bastille" all the way to victory.[44] A contemporary wrote that it was "impossible to describe the enthusiasm of the multitude. . . . The people were, to a man, on his side." This was the first of his Westminster campaigns, which provided him with the base that made him "the outstanding advocate of Parliamentary reform."[45] It was not banking money that elevated Burdett but the persistent campaign of Catherine Despard. "The story of 19th century Radicalism commences with these two men," wrote Thompson—the parliamentary reformer in Burdett and the working-class revolutionist in Despard.[46] Inasmuch as Catherine supported Despard and inasmuch as it was she who exposed the scandal of his imprisonment to Burdett, whose career depended on bringing the scandal to the (voting) public, she was among those who commenced the story of nineteenth-century radicalism. The government must have thought something similar because, if we are to believe Lord Minto, government denied her a pension because she had supported Ned's speech at the gallows.[47]

We can detect Catherine Despard's presence—despite the developing racism, despite the defeat of Irish hopes, despite the clampdown on political dissent by the gag orders and press persecutions—in the imaginations of the artists. It is there in Thelwall's *The Daughter of Adoption; A Tale of Modern Times* (1801), with its description of "mulatto women," who "in defiance of all the disadvantages of complexion, and the opprobrium of 'relations on the coast,' eclipsed at once the more delicate charms and boasted accomplishments both of European ladies, and the native whites." We can detect her presence in Maria Edgeworth's "The Grateful Negro," published in March 1802, in which plantation arson and rebellion originates with an obeah woman. And in her novel *Belinda,* published the year before, in which an interracial marriage takes place between Juba, an African servant, and an English farmgirl. Erasmus Darwin's *The Temple of Nature; Or, the Origin of Society,* begun in 1800 and published in 1803, avoids mentioning her, though not her associates on prison visits: "So Howard, Moira, Burdett, sought the

44. Patterson, *Sir Francis Burdett.*

45. Dinwiddy, "Sir Francis Burdett," 17. Thompson records his importance in exposing the scandals at the prison but does not mention Catherine Despard, Jane Evans, or the wives of the other prisoners. See *The Making of the English Working Class,* 174.

46. E. P. Thompson, *Making,* 175.

47. Minto, *Life and Letters,* 3:273–74.

cells, / Where want, or woe, or guilt in darkness dwells." Among Wordsworth's great 1802 sonnets describing the transition from the generous hopes of the 1790s to the selfish fears that followed is "September 1, 1802," which says of a white-robed, languid, Negro woman crossing the Channel from Paris that "her eyes retained their tropic fire." He does not say, but perhaps her eyes burned with anger over Toussaint L'Ouverture's imprisonment in the frigid Jura Mountains. Catherine's presence is there in the poet and novelist Amelia Opie, the Norwich abolitionist and friend of Godwin and Wollstonecraft, whose 1802 novel *Adeline Mowbray* contains a plotline similar to the actual lives of Ned and Kate during the 1790s: a mixed-race woman and her "tawny" son are saved from destitution after her husband is imprisoned for debt. Even in the 'Steel, we find those who defied enclosure and affirmed the common— Spence, O'Conner, Thomas Evans, the mutineers of the fleet, and the radicals from the Manchester cotton districts.

J

———

TWO STORIES

THIRTY-THREE

"The Whole Business of Man"

WILLIAM BLAKE (1757–1826) AND NED DESPARD (1751–1803) were approximately the same age. Though they came from different countries and had different class relationships in British society, they were both radicals, capable of extreme daring in thought or deed, implacably hostile to the forces of greed and cruelty governing society, and possessed of spiritual interests expressed in vision or in action. There is no direct evidence that they knew each other, though Erin, or Ireland, was to play an important prophetic part in Blake's mythological reconstruction of the history of Britain. It is one of the themes in his tremendous epics *Milton* and *Jerusalem,* written after three years in Felpham. Despard's plot was an important and daring element, among other things, in the continuation of the Irish Rebellion.

The coevality of time comes from an extraordinary letter that Blake wrote to one of his patrons in November 1802, less than a week after Despard's arrest at the Oakley Arms. The coincidence of space arises from the fact that Oakley Street, the scene of Despard's arrest, is the continuation of Hercules Road, where William and Catherine Blake lived between 1791 and 1800. This was south of the river Thames in the parish of Lambeth, whose governance in the 1790s was highly volatile. In 1792, Blake the enthusiast for the French Revolution donned the bonnet rouge, the cap of liberty and equality, and defiantly walked about the streets of Lambeth.[1]

Since "the commons" was being destroyed by enclosure of land, conquest of the lands of Native Americans, mechanization of production into factories, and prison construction, revolutionaries of the time worth their salt would have seen this too and responded according to their lights. William

---

1. Worrall, *Radical Culture*, 20–21; Phillips, "Lambeth and the Terror," 152–54.

Blake, the visionary poet and engraver, the craftsman and metalworker, did so in a discourse of his own, a rewriting of the Bible, a deep history of Britain, and a thorough acquaintance with Enlightenment thinkers. The transformation of the land of the Angles (England) into private property was step one in a fall. As private property, the land could be bought and sold as a commodity. This was step two. As a commodity, the land could and did become capital, a means of exploiting those who worked on it as agriculturalists or under it as miners. This was step three in the fall of England. To Blake, this enclosure was akin to the expulsion from paradise. While he was vividly aware of war, enclosure, conquest, mechanization, and prison, he understood that the original cause of human degradation was the loss of the commons. His notion of the commons included law, love, education, childhood, religion, spirit, and art.

The concept of the commons is not part of canonical interpretations of Blake for the simple reason that it was not a category of alternative political economy to Blake. He also did not use it to refer to the array of common rights of town and country. Yet the commons infuses all his work, as it combines his notion of realized humanity in psychological, spiritual, and mundane life. In 1821, toward the end of his life, Blake summarized his life's work: "The whole Business of Man Is / The Arts & All Things in Common" ("Laocoon," lines 105–6). In 1827, the last year of his life, Blake again referred to the commons, this time to mock a new translation of the Lord's Prayer. Dr. Thornton treats God as Caesar Augustus, a combination of king and priest, who creates nothing that can't be weighed, measured, and taxed. "Grant unto me, and the whole world, day by day, an abundant supply of spiritual and corporeal food," he prayed. To Blake, money and law were two aspects of Caesar, for which he substituted, "Give us the Bread that is our due & Right by taking away Money or a Price or Tax upon what is Common to all in thy Kingdom."[2]

Blake's poetic responses to war and dearth were politically private because he did not, could not, publish them. The realized imagination was his goal, and with it the radical transformation of the totality of human existence.[3] Despard's mental strivings have to be inferred from his experiences in Ireland, Jamaica, Honduras, Nicaragua, and London. The revolutionary must also be a visionary, though unlike the poet the revolutionary is an activ-

2. Erdman, *Blake: Prophet against Empire,* 668.
3. Kovel, "Blake."

ist agent of transformation. Both worked underground in the sense that Despard had to secretly recruit people to a revolutionary project, and Blake had to find the antinomian springs of a counter-Enlightenment that was both subversive and apocalyptic.

Blake's removal on 18 September 1800 to Felpham on the Sussex coast came after the London food riots, which had begun four days earlier. That night, the crowds surrounding a baker's shop in Shadwell were dispersed by the Wapping, Limehouse, and Ratcliffe Volunteers. "Terrible the distress." A handbill was posted declaring "Bread Will be Sixpence the Quartern If the People Will Assemble at the Corn Market on Monday." Inflammatory leaflets were stuck up on public places. Bakers' shops were attacked, and on the day the Blakes left, a handbill addressed to "Starved Fellow Creatures" called for an armed gathering in Saint George's Fields, with the exhortation "Rouse to Glory Ye Slumbering Britons." "We Want Bread & Bread We Will Have." Their targets included the Bank, the royal palace at Saint James, and Prime Minister Pitt and his colleagues. "The Aristocrats are your mortal foes— plunge your daggers in their hearts."

Fellow countrymen

How long will ye quietly and cowardly suffer yourselves to be imposed upon, and half starved by a set of mercenary slaves and Government hirelings? Can you still suffer them to proceed in their extensive monopolies, while your children are crying for bread? No! let them exist not a day longer. We are the sovereignty; rise then from your lethargy. Be at the Corn Market on Monday.[4]

The government responded to the crisis by implementing a policy of retrenchment, at first with mean-minded suggestions and then by compelling people to eat less. It also enforced radical dietary changes, with maize, rice, soup, or gruel, if not swill, being substituted for the English wheat loaf. The Brown Bread Act of 1801, which prohibited the white wheaten loaf, was not a success.[5]

Blake packed up everything in sixteen boxes for the seventy-mile journey to a cottage on the coast, down the road from his prosperous patron Hayley, who could feed the village by day and night. Yet he had written, in anticipation of his departure, "rending the manacles of Londons Dungeon dark I have rent the black net & escap'd." London he wrote, is "dropping with human gore ... Lo! I have left it! ... Pale, Ghastly pale: stands the City in

4. Worrall, *Radical Culture*, 43–47.
5. Wells, *Wretched Faces*.

fear."[6] Looking to the future, he concluded a letter to Hayley on a hopeful note: "My fingers Emit sparks of fire with Expectation of my future labours." Owing to the coincidence of time and place with Despard and his conspirators, we can take Blake's words as applying to the resistance the radicals offered against the place and ghastly fear. The sparks of fire might have literal meanings in the minds of the revolutionaries.

The simple tools of the plow, loom, hammer and chisel were mechanized and transformed to make weapons of war:

> And all the arts of life they chang'd into the arts of death.
> The hour glass contemn'd because its simple workmanship
> Was the workmanship of the plowman, & the water wheel
> That raises water into Cisterns, broken & burn'd in fire
> Because its workmanship as like the workmanship of the shepherd
> And in their stead intricate wheels invented, Wheel without wheel,
> To perplex youth in their outgoings & to bind to labours
> Of day & night the myriads of Eternity, that they might file
> And polish brass & iron hour after hour, laborious workmanship,
> Kept ignorant of the use that they might spend the days of wisdom
> In sorrowful drudgery to obtain a scanty pittance of bread.[7]

It is not just war and hunger that Blake denounces; it is child labor, and the dehumanized, alienated, endless, indoor labor of manufactures. The machine is replacing the hand, and so the word *manufactory* was shortened to factory (*manus* L. for hand). The monotonous, continuous labor of machine tending was not industrious labor, which historically had meant ingenious, resourceful, craftlike labor. Blake and his generation did not know the victors would call the suffering they were imposing the Industrial Revolution, which not only altered the mode of production but reversed the meaning of *industry*.

In June 1802, Parliament passed the first Factory Act (42 George III, c. 73). Its provisions should be read literally, or "satanically." It had a promising title, "An Act for the Preservation of the Health and Morals of Apprentices and Others Employed in Cotton and Other Mills, and Cotton and Other Factories." Its provisions were simple, and in mandating what must change, Parliament described the actuality of what was: that the factory walls be washed twice a year; that there be windows to supply fresh air; that appren-

6. Erdman, *Blake,* 709; Phillips, "Lambeth and the Terror."
7. *Valla,* 7b, *Poetry and Prose,* 327.

tices be supplied twice a year with shoes and a suit of clothes; that not more than two sleep in a bed; that females be separated from males in the sleeping apartments; that instruction in reading, arithmetic, and Christianity be offered; that night work be forbidden in most cases; and that twelve hours be the maximum duration of daily labor.

In response to the counterrevolution, Wordsworth zoomed in on local English places and customs. Blake's response was the opposite. He zoomed out to America, Asia, Africa, the solar system, the cosmos:

> First Trades & Commerce, ships & armed vessels he builded laborious
> To swim the deep; & on the land, children are sold to trades
> Of dire necessity, still laboring day & night till all
> Their life extinct they took the spectre form in dark despair;
> And slaves in myriads, in ship loads, burden the hoarse sounding deep,
> Rattling with clanking chains; the Universal Empire groans. (*Valla,* 7b)

Commerce is not separate from exploitation; the ships of commerce and child labor are combined in the slave ship. Blake is inveighing against the hypocrisy characteristic of the English ruling class, with its infamous smile:

> Compell the poor to live upon a Crust of bread by soft mild arts
> Smile when they frown when they smile & when a man looks pale
> With labour & abstinence say he looks healthy & happy
> And when his children sicken let them die there are enough
> Born even too many & our Earth will be overrun. (*Valla,* 7a)

"There are enough" alludes to Malthus, whose *Essay on Population* was published in 1802 in a second expanded revision.

The repressive, conservative mood of the time was enforced. In 1802, the Society for the Suppression of Vice was founded to "check the spread of open vice and immorality, and more especially to preserve the minds of the young from contamination and exposure to the corrupting influence of impure and licentious books, prints, and other publications." It had formerly been known as the Proclamation Society from the June 1787 Royal Proclamation for the Encouragement of Piety and Virtue.

Capital punishment and war are two aspects of man-made death, here put in a cosmic setting. "Albion" is a name for the British people both before and after their fall. Albion has succumbed to church and state and the egoistical reasoning of political economy:

. . . Albion groan'd on Tyburn's brook:
Albion gave his loud death groan. The Atlantic Mountains trembled.
Aloft the Moon fled with a cry: the Sun with streams of blood.
From Albion's Loins fled all Peoples and Nations of the Earth,
Fled with the noise of Slaughter, & the stars of heaven fled. (*Vala*, 2)

While still in Felpham, Blake sent a letter to Thomas Butts on 22 November 1802, less than one week after Despard and forty others were arrested at the Oakley Arms, just down the road from William and Catherine Blake. The letter is in rhyming couplets. It is an amazing letter. It begins with Blake's happiness in the blue sky, the mild sun, the shimmering light on the sea, strolling in cornfields. He recalls his dead father and brother, who appear in his path, and speaks of his double vision, an inward eye and an outward eye. The outward eye reminds him of his poverty, envy, old age, and fear. He is made anxious by the complexities of patronage. He speaks of his labors night and day. He and his wife eat little and drink less. They do not find happiness on earth, and the sun does not warm them, or even measure time and space. The inward eye frees him of fear and terror. The letter is one of powerful, defiant emotion, of wrath, joy, grief, and adherence to his visions, written in the serenity of simple couplets that reach this conclusion:

> Now I a fourfold vision see
> And a fourfold vision is given to me;
> Tis fourfold in my supreme delight
> And three fold in soft Beulah's night
> And twofold Always. May God us keep
> From single vision & Newton's sleep.[8]

The single vision is of private property, of enclosed earth, of manacled mind, of ego, of aggression, of aggrandizement, of crude empiricism. One vision is of the minute particulars, whereas another, found in soft Beulah's night, is the dream time of the unconscious. A third is his own vision of cosmic psychic forces in historic time. The reference to Beulah relates to the book of the prophet Isaiah, where Beulah means land that is "married"—a happy place of unity between people and earth. But it is more. It refers also to Iolo Morganwg, the Welsh stonemason and Druidic Jacobin, whose recently published history of Wales influenced not only Blake's conception of a bardic past but many Welsh migrants to America, who in searching for Beulah land

8. *Poetry and Prose*, 861–62.

believed the Native Americans were lost Welsh. One of these was Morgan John Rhys—the Welsh freethinker, veteran of the siege of the Bastille, advocate for the abolition of slavery, and friend of the Iroquois—who helped found the Pennsylvania town of Beulah in 1797.[9] Blake's visions mixed biblical prophecy and contemporary revolutionary projects. Blake wrote the following in a letter to Butts in November 1802:

> Los flame'd in my path, & the Sun was hot
> With the bows of my Mind & the Arrows of Thought –
> My bowstring fierce with Ardour breathes,
> My arrows glow in their golden sheaves.

The great lyric "Jerusalem" was composed in the cottage by the sea in Felpham. "Bring me my Bow of burning gold: / Bring me my Arrows of desire" (lines 9–10). This and the earlier version to Butts are both about the mental strife, the intellectual war, or ideological struggle that must take place. Bows and arrows of course may be and once were weapons of war. They were on Blake's mind as Despard and the forty others were arrested at the Oakley Arms.

By the end of 1802, Blake was unwell and depressed. He could not support himself but had to work for others. By early 1803, he was determined to return to London, which he did in the autumn. The days were over when he and his wife, Catherine, could take off their clothes and read *Paradise Lost* to each other while naked in the garden. A different time, a different place, and an inebriated soldier could swagger into his garden and accuse him of treason, as happened in August 1803. The dates of Blake's arrest (summer 1803) and acquittal (winter 1804) parallel the discovery of Emmet's rising in Ireland and Haiti's independence.

Despard's proposed actions and Blake's private visions originated in the same time and in the same place. Although they were virtually neighbors, there were no commons where they could meet.

9. Williams, *Search for Beulah Land.*

THIRTY-FOUR

The Red Cap of Liberty

LIBERTAS AMERICANA IS THE NAME of the medal Augustin Dupré struck in 1783, at the suggestion of Benjamin Franklin, the American ambassador in Paris. It portrays one of the most powerful images of the Atlantic revolutions, an image of tremendous vitality and energy. It shows in profile the head of a young woman looking left, her abundant hair streaming behind her, as if blown by a strong wind. Some of it has curled around to her front and is pressed on her sternum. The hair flows fully free of cover, artifice, wig, crown, diadem, hat, cap, or pomatum. It is the opposite of eighteenth-century aristocratic headdress. Behind her sculpted head, as if resting on her right shoulder, is a staff on whose tip is firmly placed the liberty cap. More than independence is suggested. One can easily perceive why she is compared to a maenad as well as the relationship of this Liberty to Dionysus.[1]

The wild LIBERTAS became widely know and entered the iconology of American coinage. The coin carried an image of energy and freedom. The figure of liberty as a device on coinage has at least since Roman times expressed the liberty of exchange necessary to commodity production. Coins also expressed sovereignty. Brutus, the tyrannicide, issued one with the *pilleus,* the name of the cap. One coin depicted the cap between the daggers used to assassinate Caesar. The freed slave wore it during the ceremony of manumission.

The Red Cap of Liberty made its appearance in the early months of the French Revolution, when it was adopted by the militant plebeians of Paris. During the revolution, the bonnet rouge was similar to trousers in being a class symbol of the sansculottes, as distinct from the bourgeoisie. The sanscu-

1. Korshak, "Liberty Cap," 53.

FIGURE 18. "Libertas Americana." Medal struck by Augustin Dupré, 1776.

lottes were marked by this as well as by strong language, and intimate address or *tutoiement*. They made the combination of class hostility and positive egalitarianism an integral part of the assemblies, clubs, and societies of the Parisian sections. By the end of 1792, the bonnet symbolized the political power of the sansculottes rather than the revolutionary bourgeoisie. Robespierre rejected it.[2]

The sansculottes made Louis XVI wear the cap after they invaded the Tuileries on 20 June 1792. Kropotkin's description is low-key: "the King took off his hat, and allowed a woolen cap to be put on his head; the crowd also made him drink a glass of wine to the health of the nation." Carlyle, however, indirectly associates it with racialized slavery: "So stands Majesty in Red woolen Cap, black Sansculottism weltering around him, far and wide, aimless, with inarticulate dissonance."[3] The stocking cap of the French

2. Harris, "Red Cap of Liberty."

3. Kropotkin, *Great French Revolution,* 259; Carlyle, *French Revolution,* 465; Lefebvre, *French Revolution,* 230.

FIGURE 19. Four sansculottes wearing the Red Cap of Liberty and triumphantly carrying away a model of the Bastille. Jean-Baptiste Lesueur, *Modèle de la Bastille*, ca. 1790.

workman and the Phrygian Cap of Liberty were deliberately mixed during the revolution. In the contest of symbols, covering the head with the republican cap replaced the royalist crown. Indeed the "battle over the bonnets" in October 1793 pitted the *républicaines* of the Club of Revolutionary Women against the Jacobin men, who feared that the women's demand for the red cap would be followed by a demand for pistols.

The sexual energy of these customs was associated with the Roman Saturnalia and the world turned upside down, when masters served slaves and slaves *capere pileum*, "took the cap," of the freedman.[4] Joel Barlow kept a notebook in 1796–97 containing notes to a "Genealogy of the Tree of Liberty." Barlow was a translator (along with Thomas Jefferson) of Volney's *Ruins of Empires.* He traced the origin of the Liberty Tree to the myth of Osiris, the Egyptian sun god, whose genitals were thrown into the river Nile after a furious conflict with Typhon. The fecundating power of the Nile was the source of life and vegetation, so Isis, his wife, gathered what she could of his body. To commemorate his tragic death and resurrection, a solemn feast

4. Nourse, *Campania Foelix,* 195.

FIGURE 20. "The Tree of Liberty." Trade token struck by
Thomas Spence.

was instituted in which a phalluslike symbol was carried in procession. This
fable was extended to other countries, where Osiris was given other names:
in Phoenica, Adonis; in Phrygia, Atys; in Persia, Mythra; and in Arabia and
India, Bacchus. The god acquired the name of Eleutheros, or Freedom, and
according to Barlow the phallus became the emblem of Libertas. "The first
civil or political use that was made of it was by the Romans when they gave
liberty to a slave. They put a Red Cap upon his head, which he wore ever after,
to denote that he was a Freed Man."[5] Further, Barlow notes that the liberty
cap had precisely the same origin: "The Liberty Cap is the head of the Penis."

Empire and commerce grew with a veritable explosion of money. Telling
money was telling liberty, and this was especially true for the small tradesmen and artisans, who dealt in small coin, for it was the copper coinage that
retained the Cap of Liberty. There was a shortage of this money. It could not
meet the needs of the people. Thomas Spence struck a halfpenny coin in 1795,
one side of which showed a skinny man chained in prison "Before the
Revolution." On the obverse side was a seated Britannia holding a staff and
gazing at a cap of liberty that appeared to have just fallen off the tip of her

5. "Notebook, c. 1796–97," bMS.Am1448 (13), Houghton Library, Harvard
University, Cambridge, Massachusetts.

staff. Conservative opinion called the people "the swinish multitude," so Spence struck another copper coin called "Pig's Meat," that showed a pig trampling on crown, miter, and scepter. A liberty cap is at the zenith of the obverse side.[6]

Edward Gosling, an informant for the government and minion to Patrick Colquhoun, reported that the manual and platoon exercise in some of the divisions of the London Corresponding Society in April 1794, "the figures were in caps and pantaloons and worship said the caps were to be coloured Red."[7] William Blake "courageously donned the famous symbol of liberty and equality—the bonnet rouge—in open day, and philosophically walked in the streets with the same on his head."[8]

After the counterrevolution began to develop in England, the bonnet rouge became a symbol in the cartoons of Thomas Rowlandson, James Gillray, and George Cruikshank of the revolutionary forces, invariably portrayed as dirty, lower class, and unpatriotic. Gillray published a vicious print on 20 April 1798 called *The London Corresponding Society*. Six men sitting around a candlelit table in a cellar eagerly strain forward as they listen to a red-capped member reading aloud about the state arrests. The names of O'Connor, Binns, and Evans are legible; presumably Despard's name is farther down on the list. Two portraits hang on the wall, of Horne Tooke and Tom Paine, both wearing the Red Cap of Liberty. These dirty, unshaven men are city plebeians. The physiognomy of the men is distinctly simian, a warning of the strategy of visual virulence in the nineteenth-century racialization of the Celt and the Negro. The bonnet rouge has gone underground, joining the creatures of the lower depths.

The most powerful cartoon of the era was sarcastically titled *A Free Born Englishman!* and dated 15 December 1819. It shows an emaciated weeping man in leg irons and wearing ragged clothes, with his hands tied behind his back and his lips pierced shut with a huge lock. His wife and children are starving. In the background is a prison. Under his bare feet are the Bill of Rights and the Magna Carta. The bonnet rouge lies in the mud. The documents and symbols of liberty are no less violated than the people. It is an adaptation of an 1813 print that was itself derived from one of 1795.[9]

6. These are in the Ulster Museum, Belfast. See the catalogue of the exhibition, Maguire, *Up in Arms*, 76–77.

7. London Corresponding Society, *Selections from the Papers*, 149.

8. Gilchrist, *Life of William Blake*.

9. Gilchrist, *Life of William Blake*, 184.

On 2 April 1792, George Washington signed the congressional bill establishing coinage and the Mint. Coins were prescribed to display a device, "Upon one side . . . there shall be an impression emblematic of liberty."[10] There were different heads of Lady Liberty—capped, classic, wild hair, braided hair, crushed cap. Inspired by Dupré's medal, Joseph Wright designed the large liberty cap penny of 1793–96. Wright's Liberty lost the strand of hair at her throat, and while her hair remains unbound and flowing, it does not wave at the same high angle. She is less active, and the bonnet is softer.[11] Using a symbol of manumission as a national symbol at a time when slavery production and unpaid labor were being expanded, owing to the development of the cotton gin and plantation, put the Americans in a hypocritical position. The contradiction was resolved, as concerns the design of the coinage, by omitting the cap and staff, which was duly done in 1792 for the ten-cent piece and penny. In September 1793, the Cap of Liberty was introduced supported on a wand projected behind the head. In June 1796, the cap was omitted from the one-cent piece, and in June 1800, from the half-cent piece. The first silver coin was struck in 1794, but not until 1807 was Lady Liberty adorned with a cap, "not intended as I learn from the Officers of the Mint, to represent the cap of Liberty, nor approaching it in form, but taken from life, and considered a model in good taste of the fashion of the time."[12]

John Reich, a German engraver and indentured servant, sought a position in the Philadelphia Mint in 1801 but was not hired until 1807. He designed a buxom Liberty with her name inscribed on her cap, misnamed a turban and initially taken for the *pilleus,* or Phrygian, liberty cap. Breen writes, "Much controversy has developed to little purpose over whether the mobcap Reich placed on Ms. Liberty's head was intended to represent the *pilleus,* or Phrygian liberty cap." Robert Scot designed a neck-up Liberty facing right and wearing a soft cap, also mistaken for *pilleus.* "The head on them was, from the first, ornamented with a cap head dress; not the Liberty cap in form, but probably conforming to the fashionable dress of the day."[13]

On February 14, 1825, the director of the Mint wrote to Thomas Jefferson. As new dies were about to be made, he sought the answer to an unsettled

10. Stack, *United States Type Coins,* 2.
11. No US coin has been so intensely studied. The members of the Early American Coppers Club are described as among the most dedicated specialists in the world. See William H. Sheldon, *Penny Whimsy: A Revision of Early American Cents* (New York: Dover, 1990).
12. Breen, *Walter Breen's Complete Encyclopedia,* 518–19.
13. Breen, *Walter Breen's Complete Encyclopedia,* 518–19.

question. What device is emblematic of liberty? "Was the cap of Liberty adopted or alluded to as the fit emblem by any act of the confederation, or of any of the states, or by popular usage, during the revolution, or previously to 1792, so that this device may be supposed to have been intended?" Jefferson replied that the Cap of Liberty was not proper headwear for a goddess, as we were never slaves, and that he did not recall any common impression (emblem) of liberty before 1792. Of course, there were many.

In Ireland, the Cap of Liberty was displayed on the flags of several corps of the Irish Volunteers.[14] In 1790, Grattan was accompanied to the hustings in the general election by a well-dressed black boy carrying the Cap of Liberty.[15] The United Irishmen had as their device an Irish harp surmounted by a Cap of Liberty. This was the device on Napper Tandy's proclamation of September 1798, as it had been on the proclamation by Lazare Hoche to the French Army, destined to operate the Irish revolution by means of the Bantry Bay expedition of Christmas 1796.

The Cap of Liberty became increasingly popular during the 1790s. The First National Battalion had for its device a harp surmounted by a Cap of Liberty, not a crown. Lord Charlemont was aghast, saying "No Egyptian hierophant could have invented a hieroglyphic more aptly significant of a republic than the taking the crown from the harp and replacing it by a cap of Liberty." Only after June 1792 could the red cap signify a republic; before that date it signified liberty, or the liberation of slaves, as did the Phrygian cap. The United Irishmen brought the two meanings together.

The publication of *Paddy's Resource* in 1795 was an important step in the cultural politics of the United Irishmen.[16] It's frontispiece shows a female figure. Her left arm rests on the harp and her right arm carries a staff with the bonnet rouge on top. The top of the page describes the harp below as "Tun'd to Freedom," and the bottom of the page declaims, "Irishmen Unite—Tear off your Chains and let MILLIONS BE FREE." Wolfe Tone wished to form Irish prisoners of war in France into a corps to accompany the Bantry Bay expedition of 1796. He wanted their uniform to include the harp and Cap of Liberty. A Cap of Liberty two feet long was discovered in Lord Edward Fitzgerald's lodging when he was arrested on 19 May 1798. Emmet designed a flag and a seal for his rebellion. The flag displays a gold harp with winged

14. Hayes-McCoy, *History of Irish Flags*, 89–121.
15. Geoghegan, *Robert Emmet*, 54.
16. Whelan, *Fellowship of Freedom*, 37.

maiden, a pike through the harp strings with the Cap of Liberty on top, and a scroll with "Erin go bragh" below. His seal of the United Irish shows a harp, a pike staff, and a liberty cap, with "Equality" scrolled on top and on the bottom referring to the harp, "It is new strung and shall be heard."

The Cap of Liberty provided a rallying point in visual organization, indicating advance and retreat, letting people know in distant parts of the crowd, above the drums and slogans and the shouts and cries, how fared the battle. It could be a trophy. A row broke out in Stockport in February 1819, when some cavalry attempted to seize a Cap of Liberty, and the radicals beat them off. The episode was the primary cause of the legendary August 1819 Peterloo Massacre at St. Peter's Field, where nine men and two women were killed. The crowd attempted to defend the banners and Caps of Liberty made by the female reformers, who had carried them many miles to the meeting. Factory children carried the Red Cap of Liberty.[17] It was "the pre-eminent symbol of class confrontation," Epstein writes.[18] In November 1819, Parliament passed the Six Acts to suppress popular insurgency, which included a provision outlawing the red cap from public display.

Turner crossed the English Channel in turbulent weather in July 1802—this was the year of peace.[19] Hundreds of Irish underwent this experience in the company of strangers—the spray and spume, the rolling and pitching. At the start of 1803, Turner took his place at the Royal Academy Council, which George III founded in 1768. In 1803, he exhibited *Calais Pier*. Because the king objected to the number of democrats in it, he did not attend the exhibition. The crisis and confusion, the shudder, the storms of land and sea, became an image of social and spiritual crisis. Turner advised, "Always take advantage of an accident." The voyage stayed with him, and he turned to it again in 1827, for a painting called *"Now for the Painter," Passengers Going on Board,* which is now in the Manchester City Museum of Art, not far from the site of Peterloo. In the painting, the tide is full, and the vessel is caught between two swells. There is a sense of both departure and arrival. In the center of the picture is he helmsman, his right hand on the rudder and his left arm raised to receive the painter from the crowded ferry. He wears the bonnet rouge. There appear to be eight sailors aboard the two craft—eight on the ferry and two on the one-masted broad boat. A mother and child and

17. Walmsley, *Peterloo.*
18. Thompson, *Persons and Polemics*, 185; Epstein, "Understanding the Cap."
19. Lindsay, *J.M.W. Turner*, 78, 84.

attending maid with a trunk and large corked jug are midships. The mother carries the infant in her arms. Both of them are further protected from the sting of the salty breeze by an "oriental" wrap. The painting feels allegorical, especially when it is pointed out that at the center of the frieze of busy sailors and watching passengers aboard the ferry is Turner himself, his arm outstretched, with hat in hand, in a beckoning gesture. Turner was not a political or allegorical painter per se. The characteristics that predominate, sky and sea, wind and wave, elemental motion, inevitable turbulence, surround the little scene of cooperation among nationals traditionally and recently at war.

The geographic matrix for understanding Despard cannot be restricted to one nation, or political entity—Ireland, England, France, Haiti, or America. It was the same with the bonnet rouge, which had meanings from several overlapping political and cultural regions. "The mnemonic force of the cap of liberty was multivocal," writes James Epstein.[20] In times of repression, it served as a symbol within cultural expression, as in Turner's painting or in a curious bit of lore from the Irish neighborhood where Despard was born.

Despard is not remembered much in Ireland, yet the causes for which he died—justice, liberty, "the human race"—had an underground existence in county Laois, in the figures of the cottiers, workers, and spalpeens who resisted the disastrous conditions of land tenure and agricultural appropriation that prevailed after the Union. The terror of defeat in the Rebellion of 1798 was followed by the extreme hardships of dearth and shortages of 1817 and 1822; the Tithe War of 1831, and the looming starvations of the potato blight. The underlying conditions that produced revolutionaries like Despard did not go away. Others had to fight them. Two of them were Despard's countrymen John Keegan and James Fintan Lawlor.

We met John Keegan, a neighbor of Despard, in chapter 11. He was born in Closh (or Clash) near Shanahoe, county Laois, in 1809, and died in the cholera sheds of Kilmainham in 1849. "I am an Irish peasant, born and reared in an Irish cabin, and educated in an Irish hedge-school," he wrote in the introduction to his 1839 *Legends and Tales of the Queen's County Peasantry*. Keegan recorded the self-activity of the peasantry "from below," describing the enchanted landscape, the land of spirits and fairies—as insubstantial in appearance as the surplus value of the commercial banking houses, and yet with violence in waiting, again as with surplus value. He was clerk to the county Queen relief committee during the famine, before going to Dublin in

20. Epstein, "Understanding the Cap."

1847. In 1839, he told a story to the new generation of young Ireland. His story of the river Nore is called "The Boccough Ruadh: A Tradition of Poorman's Bridge."[21] The seven-arched bridge is still standing, and the story of its name is still being told, for instance, by Peter Welsh, the current farmer of Donore.

It seems that a hundred years ago Neale O'Shea had a cabin near the ford. "Ever willing to relieve a fellow-creature," when an old sailor from Ulster, who had been crippled fighting the French comes along, O'Shea gives him charity. The old sailor wears a red woolen cap. He finds a flat rock by the river ford, not far from the Despard house, and there the red-capped *boccough* makes his home. He guides travelers across the river "from the crow of the cock to the vesper song of the wood-thrush," becoming well known to the villagers. After forty years, he dies. The son of his benefactor, Neale O'Shea, dreams the first of a series of nightmares, waking with the scream, "the *Boccough!* the *Boccough!*" The ghost causes as much noise and trouble "as if the devil or Captain Rock was about the place." He dreams that the red cap contains a fortune. So the boy digs up the *boccough*'s grave and there finds three hundred pounds in gold guineas. His mother advises him to give the money to the priest, but the priest refuses to touch it, urging him to give it to the landlord and magistrate. Accordingly he does so, and the grand jury of the nearest assize town orders that the money be used to build a bridge.[22]

As is the case with all good stories, we might read several meanings into it. Is it an allegory of capitalist improvement? John Feehan refers to the eighteenth century as "the golden age of bridge-building" in county Laois.[23] The bridges were essential to wheeled traffic and trade. Whether he thought this was good or bad, Keegan does not say; he accepts it as inevitable. The people's wealth, accumulated through years of small acts of service and charity, was appropriated by landlord and magistrate for commercial infrastructure. The social order of cottier, priest, and traveler was a pedestrian culture. The bridge, which carried provisions out of the district and conveyed troops into the area, was by no means a socially neutral improvement.

At night, "the figure of a wan and decrepit old man with his head enveloped in a red nightcap, may be seen wandering about Poorman's Bridge, or walking quite 'natural' over the glassy waters of the transparent Nore."[24] The haunting of the *boccough* was thus a reminder that capitalist improvement

21. Keegan, *Legends and Poems*, and *John Keegan: Selected Works*.
22. Keegan, *Legends and Poems*, 197.
23. John Feehan, *Laois*, 424.
24. Keegan, *Legends and Poems*

FIGURE 21. The Poorman's Bridge over the river Nore. Photo by the author.

was not inevitable, irreversible, or progressive. It was accompanied by hob-goblins of one sort or another. *Boccough* means *lame.* The mysterious arrival of a crippled veteran haunting the bridge is an archetypal event (the fisher king). An old sailor guiding folks across a river is equally evocative of trans-formation, the crossing from one state to another.

The *boccough* wears the bonnet rouge. At a time when men blushed to speak of '98, its memory was preserved in such stories. After Thermidor, the bonnet rouge, Archibald Hamilton Rowan tells us—and he was there!—was the first symbol of the revolution to be disgraced, trampled on in the theaters and public places.[25] The beggar was from the north, the historical origin of the United Irishmen, and had fought in the French Revolutionary wars. He was thus a veteran of world-shaking events, and he wore the insignia of radi-calism. A person crossing the river Nore could receive a political education delivered by a sailor and a sansculotte.

Edward Despard's other countryman was James Fintan Lawlor, born in Tinakill, Abbeyleix, in 1807. Tinakill is a couple of miles to the north of Coolrain. Keegan's mother lived "in the house of a respectable farmer, Mr.

25. *Autobiography,* 238.

Fintan Lawlor of Scotchrath."[26] Such a fierce and uncompromising pen was held by an asthmatic, tubercular, body with a malformed spine.[27] Lalor was influenced by William Connor, the natural son of Arthur Condorcet O'Connor, and he was influenced by the tenants and the class "resembling the Proletarii of the Roman Empire [which was] increasing with fearful rapidity." Many, he wrote, migrated to factories in England. We know from reading Keegan that the peasantry paid attention to Lalor, and he paid attention to them, the tillers of the earth of Tinakill. From them he learned, "The earth, together with all it spontaneously produces, is the free and common property of all mankind."[28]

Unblushingly, he declared himself heir to the constitutional project of '98 in the first article he wrote in June 1848 for the *Irish Felon*. The project was land and freedom; the means a rent strike, refusal of eviction, passive resistance, "to barricade the island, to break up the roads, to break down the bridges—and, should need be, and favourable occasion offer, surely we may venture to try the steel. For a revolution is beginning which will leave Ireland without a people, unless it be met and conquered by a revolution which will leave it without landlords."[29]

The masthead of the Chartist newspaper the *Red Republican,* the one-penny weekly edited by Bronterre O'Brien's student, showed a Red Cap of Liberty on top of the people's weapon, a pike. Helen Macfarlane, of Burnley, Lancashire, published her translation of *The Communist Manifesto* in the *Red Republican*. "A frightful hobgoblin stalks throughout Europe. We are haunted by a ghost, the ghost of Communism." Hobgoblin and ghost remind us of the *buccough ruadh* and the commons. The famine in Ireland and the near genocide of its people could not kill the idea of the commons. Its memory persisted even where dearth and death prevailed against it. Janet Zandy, an oral historian of the working class writes that memory is "a catalyst for engagement with the present and future."[30] But, she warns, "the whole story is always out of reach."[31]

26. See J. Canon O'Hanlon's introductory notes to Keegan, *Legends and Poems*, xix.
27. Buckley, *James Fintan Lalor.*
28. Lawlor, *Irish Felon*, 24 June 1848
29. Lawlor, *Irish Felon,* 8 July 1848.
30. Zandy, *Liberating Memory*, 4.
31. Zandy, "What We Hold," 249.

THIRTY-FIVE

The Red-Crested Bird
and Black Duck

"THE DISH WITH ONE SPOON" is a rhetorical figure of the Haudenosaunee expressing the unity of the five nations of the Iroquois Confederacy with the commons of the Great Lakes.[1] The same region produced the warrior leader Tecumseh, who also struggled for confederation in the name of the "commons." In 1789, the indigenous people of Connecticut lamented, "The times are turned upside down. . . . They had no contention about their lands, for they lay in common; and they had but one large dish, and could all eat together in peace and love."[2] It is a lament heard over and over again.

Jefferson, at the head of the party of Republicans, was swept into the White House in 1800. He allied with the Indian haters and secessionists of the western frontier, who were in the midst of the forty-year war (1772–1812) to take the Indian lands of the Old Northwest.[3] In 1801, he outlined his dream of a white continent that could not contemplate "either blot or mixture on that surface." Jefferson was an implacable enemy of Toussaint L'Ouverture and the Haitian slave struggle.

The years 1802–3 were decisive in the formulation of his Indian policy— trade monopolized at federal factories, inevitable ties of indebtedness, surreptitious alcohol dealing, the depletion of forest resources, introduction of patriarchal agriculture, land cessions, forced removal if incorporation was resisted, and acquisition of the whole northern continent. A recent scholar concluded, "The Jeffersonian vision of the destiny of the Americas had no

1. The Mohawk, Oneida, Onondaga, Cayuga, and Seneca Nations were the original five members of the Iroquois Confederacy. The Tuscarora joined in 1722.

2. Quaquaquid and Ashpo, *Petition*. See also Boal, Stone, Watts, and Winslow, *West of Eden*.

3. White, *Middle Ground*.

place for Indians as Indians."[4] Duplicitous, subtle, implacable, a secret land speculator, a ruthless zealot with the appearance of benevolence, the smile of this chief of the long knives boded ill.

American deists campaigned for freedom of conscience, abolition of slavery, emancipation of women, universal education, and the end of economic privilege. Deism "solicits the acquaintance of peasants and mechanics, and draws whole nations to its standards."[5] Elihu Palmer wrote, in 1801, "Reason, righteous and immortal reason, with the argument of the printing types in one hand, and the keen argument of the sword in the other, must attack the thrones and the hierarchies of the world, and level them with the dust of the earth; then the emancipated slave must be raised by the power of science into the character of an enlightened citizen."[6]

Before 1798, the United Irish were curious about the American Indians; afterward, as exiles, they had opportunity to learn from them. *The Temple of Reason* was first edited by Dennis Driscoll, an Irish exile of the Rebellion of '98.[7] The editor after April 1802 was John Lithgow. Taking a leaf from the book of Thomas Spence, whose *Spensonia* advocated a system of common ownership of land and resources, Lithgow named his political romance *Lithconia,* subtitled *Equality: A Political Romance.* It was published in *The Temple of Reason* in seven numbers, from 15 May into the summer of 1802. The editors dedicated it to Dr. James Reynolds of county Tyrone, the United Irish émigré, who on the occasion of George Washington leaving office said, there "ought to be a jubilee," meaning the release from debts, the return of land, and the abolition of slavery.

Disregarding the prevailing orthodoxy, Lithgow inverted the stadialist fairy tale. "The Lithconians are not a people that are progressing from a state of nature, to what is vulgarly called civilization; on the contrary, they are progressing from civil society to a state of nature, if they have not already arrived at that state." Love, friendship, and wealth are attainable for all. Prostitution is removed by the abolition of private property and the patrilinear lines of descent: "Here the laws do not make the trembling female swear to the father of her child." Dancing on the green commences every day at four o'clock. Music is the principal branch of liberal education. A printing press is open to all in every district. There is no money in the country, the lands are

4. Wallace, *Jefferson and the Indians*, 11.
5. Walters, *American Deists*; Hall, *Modern Infidelity.*
6. Palmer, *Principles of Nature.*
7. Wilson, *United Irishmen*, 115.

in common, and only a few hours of labor are required. "No such words as *mine* and *thine* are ever heard." No markets, no shopkeepers, no debtors, no creditors, no lawyers, no elections, no theft.

The Temple of Reason folded on 19 February 1803, three days before Despard suffered his last and a day after Jefferson privately wrote his extraordinary letter to Benjamin Hawkins about the Indians, "I have little doubt but that your reflections must have led you to view the various ways in which their history may terminate." The best that the Indians could do was to sell their land and become US citizens. The chiefs could get rich, the men would take the plough, women would give up the hoe, exceptional souls might go to college, and the whiskey keg would be full for the rest.[8] The hanging and decapitation of Despard, the closing of *The Temple of Reason,* and the termination of Indian history (as imagined by President Jefferson) were serious setbacks to proletarian insurrection, American utopian socialist discussion, and Native American resistance.

The Poor Man's Catechism in Ireland (1798) called for a return of the common land, and John Burk wrote *The Cry of the Poor for Bread* for the return of land. Such voices were silenced in Ireland after 1798 but not in America, where in 1803 the Iroquois leader Joseph Brant wrote, "We have no law but that written on the heart of every rational creature by the immediate finger of the great Spirit of the universe himself. We have no prisons—we have no pompous parade of courts.... We have no robbery under the color of law—daring wickedness here is never suffered to triumph over helpless innocence—the estates of widows and orphans are never devoured by enterprising sharpers."[9]

Tecumseh spoke eloquently, and his words were translated in an English diction with origins in the seventeenth century: "You wish to prevent the Indians from doing as we wish them, to unite and let them consider their lands as the common property of the whole," as militants had argued for three decades. "Since my residence at Tippecanoe, we have endeavored to level all distinctions, to destroy village chiefs by whom all mischiefs are done. It is they who sell the land to the Americans." "The way, the only way to stop this evil is for the red men to unite in claiming a common and equal right in the land, as it was at first, and should be now—for it was never divided, but belongs to all. No tribe has the right to sell, even to each other, much less to

8. Jefferson, *Political Writings.*
9. Stone, *Life of Joseph Brant-Thayendanegea,* 481.

strangers ... *Sell a country! Why not sell the air, the great sea, as well as the earth?* Did not the Great Spirit make them all for the use of his children?"[10]

Women determined whether hostages were an acceptable alternative to war. The village republics contained runaway slaves, too. Thus the first article of the 1785 Treaty of Fort McIntosh provided that the Indian sachems provide three hostages until prisoners, *white and black,* had been returned to the United States. The Indian confederacy of 1786 met at Brownstown, where Brant enunciated his principle of Indian unity and common land as a "dish with one spoon."

In May 1802, John Dunne spoke at the Royal Irish Academy, on Dawson Street, Dublin.[11] He was a son of a native of Lurgan, county Armagh, who became a dissenting minister at Cooke Street, Dublin. He was a classmate of William Drennan, a graduate of Glasgow University, a leading member of the bar, and a member of the Irish House of Commons for Randalstown, county Antrim from 1783–97.[12] Let Archibald Hamilton Rowan introduce him further: "Disgusted by the turbulent and sanguinary scenes of civilized life at a time when his professional reputation would have seated him on the bench, he was led by a romantic wish to become acquainted with men in the savage state. Accordingly he crossed the Atlantic, and for a time conformed to the manners and customs of an Indian tribe."[13]

A year earlier, the first Parliament of the "United Kingdom" met. Dunne spoke to Irishmen who had their independence taken away (the Act of Union had gone into effect a year earlier, in January 1801), and the bid for freedom was launched in 1798. Gaelic antiquaries were assisted by Anglo-Irish liberals of the Royal Irish Academy, which had encouraged Celtic studies since its founding in 1785. They used the remote past to achieve social and civic parity; it proved that they were at least on the same footing as the conquerors.[14] Ledwich argued in the second edition of *Antiquities of Ireland* (1803) that the association of Gaelic, Catholic, and radical political views was dangerous.

William Blake sang in "A Song of Liberty" (line 3) that "shadows of Prophecy shiver along by the lakes and the rivers and mutter across the Ocean." Dunne knew "from a thousand sources" that the Indians hunted

10. Esarey, *Messages and Letters*, vol. 1, 459. Joseph Barron was the translator. Sugden, *Tecumseh,* 204; Dowd, *Meitheal,* 140.

11. Dunne, "Notices."

12. C.J. Woods, *Dictionary of Irish Biography,* Royal Irish Academy.

13. Rowan, *Autobiography,* 137.

14. MacDonagh, *States of Mind.*

and fought and sported. But did they also exercise memory, invention, and fancy? Did they laugh and weep at fictitious tales? Did they conjure up "the forms of imaginary beings to divert and instruct them"? He obtained the friendship of Little Turtle, who adopted him "according to their custom, in the place of a deceased friend, by whose name I was distinguished." Lord Edward Fitzgerald, the military commander of the United Irish, received the Seneca name Eghnidal in Detroit in June 1789. Similarly, John Dunne now possessed a dual identity. "I wish I could make the Indians here speak," he lamented to the academicians. Their discourses are forcible, feeling, and expressive in tone. "The Indian lyre is unstrung." "How then can I exhibit examples of Indian speech?"[15]

The Indians were degenerating and wasting away; in a half century they would be extinguished. Dunne hoped their stories "may furnish an additional motive to treat them with humanity." "It is a part of the destiny of an unlettered people, to write their memorials with the pen of a stranger. They have no alternative, imperfect representation, or blank oblivion.—But of whom are we speaking? Who are these evanescent tribes? And in what class of created beings is posterity to place them?" He does not answer the questions; he imagines their answers. Ask the Abenaki, and he will say he is *the man of the land;* the Illinois will respond, he is a *real man;* Algonquin speakers will say they are *doubly men.* The Spaniards will say *barbarian,* the Canadian will say *savage.* Ask the wise men of Europe, who, though they have never even seen the smoke of an Indian village, will "dogmatize and write volumes upon their nature, powers and capacities, physical moral, and intellectual; these men will tell you they are *an inferior race of men."* "To what opinion shall we hold? What constitutes a man? What energies entitle him to rank high in his species?" Dunne answers his own questions with the story of the red-crested bird and black duck, told to him by none other than Little Turtle, the chief responsible for defeating the United States in its first battles.[16]

Dunne repeats the story as an allegory of England and Ireland. A man separated himself from "the society of his fellows, and took up his abode in a desart place, in a remote part of the wilderness." He hunted by day, and in the evening he imparted a portion of food to his brother, whom he had imprisoned in a gloomy cave. "This unfortunate brother, from having his hair of a fiery red, infectious to the touch, was known among the men of his nation by

15. Dunne, "Notices." 107.
16. Dunne, "Notices," 106.

the name of the red man." The younger brother is the figure of dispossession in societies, such as Europe, where primogeniture prevails. The infectious red hair symbolizes ethnic origin and the Jacobin revolutionary, who wore the bonnet rouge, or red Phrygian Cap of Liberty.

After many winters, the hunter grew lonely. He went to a village and approached a wigwam on its perimeter, where he found a widow, whom he presented with some deer meat for dinner. The next day, he hunted and brought her a whole deer, which he invited her to share with the villagers. The villagers were given to understand "in whispers by the women that a great hunter whom she was bound to conceal, who appeared to come from some distant country, was the providore of her bounty."[17]

Let the solitary hunter stand for the isolated individualist, the Yankee, the capitalist, the inventor. At the same time, the Indians had two things to sell— furs and land—each of which became their undoing. Furs were traded for alcohol; land was bribed away. The Indians provided Thomas Malthus in 1798 with his example of the population thesis that "misery is the check that represses the superior power of population and keeps its effects equal to the means of subsistence." Women, children, and the old are the first to suffer, he argued, in this "rudest state of mankind," or "the first state of mankind," where hunting is "the only mode of acquiring food."[18] By 1803, this was no longer possible. The actual conditions of the forest hunt in the lands watered by the Ohio, Monogohela, and Wabash Rivers were of diminishing game and severe competition among hunters, red and white. In fact, in 1798 the Indians of the Ohio were in an advanced political economic relationship with imperial Europe, involving considerable commodity trade, capital-intensive agriculture, massive alcoholism, and racial separation.

To return to Little Turtle's tale as told to Dunne: the hunter expressed his desire for a wife, and the chief's brother granted his wish to form an alliance with his sister. They married; they feasted; and "thus the moons rolled away," until he returned to take her away, to "the seat of solitude." Again he passed the days hunting. She noticed that after dinner he tiptoed away, carrying the tongues and marrow of the animals he had killed. Not many days passed before her worry grew, and against his commands she stole away to the spot where she had seen him descend into the cavernous prison. His brother heard "the sound of her feet upon the hollow ground, roused the half torpid senses

17. Dunne, "Notices," 109.
18. See chapter 3 of Malthus's *An Essay on the Principle of Population* (1798).

of the subterraneous inhabitant and drew forth his groans." She recognized her brother. "She learnt his story, she wept over his sufferings, she administered to his wants, her conversation like a charm gave him new existence." She induced him to clamber out into the sunshine. Her humanity engaged, she separated the clotted knots of his hair and removed the clammy concretions on his forehead. An alliance, in effect, was made between the dispossessed younger brother, the figure of the Jacobin or the United Irishman, and the woman seeking her own subsistence and longing for her own community of women's labor.

When her husband observed her hands stained with red, she sank in despair, to be roused when he held by its long red hair the severed head of a brother. The air resounded with her screams. He fled into the moonlit forest, coming at length to an ancient oak hollowed by lightning, into which he hurled the head with its fiery tresses. Then with wolfish yelps, he began to transmogrify, "adding to his nature what alone was wanting, the shape and figure of a wolf." *Homo homini lupus.* She lost the source of her food. His productivity still depended on murder and oppression. "Some human beings must suffer from want," Malthus concluded. "All cannot share alike the bounties of nature."

"Murder," to quote Richard White, "gradually became the dominant American Indian policy." Whiskey was the poor man's medium of exchange, solace, capital investment, and drug to deal to his enemies. John Heckewelder, the Moravian missionary, wrote, "When the object is to murder Indians, strong liquor is the main article required; for when you have them dead drunk, you may do to them as you please."

Meanwhile, the woman passed her days in near lifeless despair. She heard a distant sound. She listened, she was aroused, she recognized the voice of her brother calling. He was telling her where to find berries. She ascended the tree and with a cord of twisted bark drew forth the head. She placed it in her bosom, and it became her counselor, providing subsistence by felling deer or caribou with a glance of his eye. "The storm was now passed over, and a better world seemed to open through the separated clouds. The wants of hunger supplied, the fears of danger banished." She only missed "the cheerful buzz of the village, the labors of the field sweetened by the converse of her companions." This was the collective labor of the commons, practiced in the Great Lakes, Ireland, England alike, before enclosures, clearance, or conquest. The absence of the market, the entirely incidental character of private tenures, the communal work with hoes and digging sticks were suggested in this picture of women among the Seneca people.[19]

The red man attempted to deflect her attention: "Did he show her the beauties of the wilderness, she was blind; did he warn her of the dangers of the frequented village, he spoke to the winds." He relented on condition that she hide his head. So clasping "the friendly head still closer to her bosom; and associating it with her heart" she made her way to a village. There she joined a numerous assembly of women gambling. Enticed by the passion of play, the inevitable followed: her cloak opened and the head dropped from her bosom down a hill into a river below. As she chased after it, she saw the head transform itself into a rare bird, whose dusky plumage was surmounted by a tufted crown of red feathers, while she herself was transformed into a black duck.

"What constitutes a man? What energies entitle him to rank high in his species?" Who are these evanescent tribes? And in what class of created beings is posterity to place them?"[20] It is a story of mutilation and of organic, interspecies reproduction. In the context of diminished territory for game, considerable corn production, and strategic reliance on European trading items, it is unpersuasive to pass off the story as one belonging to a society of hunters and gatherers, though certainly the nativist revivals (Neolin in the 1760s, Handsome Lake in 1802, Tenskwatawa in 1809) resisted the fur trade.

Unrestrained gambling corrupts. Commodity exchange and the appeal to fortune subverted the community that the woman had hungered for. But the magic of the story is one of transformation and continuity: the Jacobin sans-culottes and his nurturing female sister persisted despite commodification, despite decapitation. The possibility of insurrection remained, and survival, even in famine, was possible. Little Turtle and his people knew famine and defeat (Battle of Fallen Timbers, 1794), and the listeners to Dunne's story remembered the Irish famine of 1800–1801, the assassination of Lord Edward Fitzgerald, and the defeat of the Wexford Republic of 1798. We have listened to a story among the defeated.

Whose story was this? Little Turtle, the Miami chief, spoke to John Dunne, the jurist of Armagh, while William Wells interpreted. When we learn that Wells was captured in 1784 as a thirteen-year-old boy by the Miami Indians, who raised him and named him Apeconit, meaning "wild carrot"

19. Wallace, *Jefferson and the Indians*, 24.
20. Dunne, "Notices," 106.

on account of his red hair, we realize there is another story here than the one Dunne is telling in Dublin. Further, when we learn that William Wells married Manwangopath, or Sweet Breeze, the daughter of Little Turtle, the storyteller himself, it is clear that the story of the red-crested bird and black duck is also a complex story of a multiethnic family from the border country.[21] John Dunne was thus present at an intimate family gathering. Little Turtle's family was a political one. In October 1791, he defeated General Harmar twice. Then in November 1791, with the sound of war whoops ringing in their ears like a thousand bells, the governor of the Northwest Territory, General Arthur St. Clair, and his army of the Federal Government of the United States succumbed to Little Turtle and the braves who followed him. The battlefield casualties were found with earth placed in their mouths, a revenge against enclosures. In that way the warriors of Little Turtle tried to satisfy the land hunger of the Long Knives.

This battle stunned Gilbert Imlay, the Kentucky adventurer who became Mary Wollstonecraft's husband. He wrote, "Though we (or rather the federal troops) have been defeated several times, yet we shall soon establish a permanent security against savage invasion and massacre; for, though we have not acted entirely like Hercules, who destroyed the serpents while an infant in his cradle, still, I presume we shall do it in our approach to maturity." He advocated "extinction" of the Indians or enclosure in reservation. Settler victory was inevitable owing to "the power of our increasing numbers," itself the result of "the fecundity of our women."[22] And yet Hercules could not prevent the recurrence of struggle in new forms represented by the many-headed Hydra.

In January 1802, Little Turtle addressed President Jefferson, with Wells serving as translator. The volume of rum into the region, essential lubrication to the land cessions, doubled between 1800 and 1803.[23] "Father, When our White Brethren came to this land, our forefathers were numerous, and happy, but since their intercourse with the white people, and owing to the introduction of this fatal poison, we have become less numerous and happy." "Father, the introduction of this poison has been prohibited in our camps, but not the towns, where many of our hunters, for this poison, dispose of not only their furs, &c., but frequently of their guns and blankets and return to their families destitute."[24]

21. Hutton, "William Wells."
22. Imlay, *Topographical Description*, 246.
23. White, *Middle Ground*, 479.
24. Hill, *John Johnston*, 17.

Wells, Turtle, and Dunne understood one another. As Lord Edward Fitzgerald learned something from Joseph Brant about "the dish with one spoon"—a unified Ireland of Catholic and Protestant—so about ten years later did John Dunne bring back to Dublin something about survival and transformation in a period of traumatic catastrophe.

The red-crested bird and black duck might have evolutionist, scholarly interpretations, but they would not be part of a dialogue: the Indians were defeated at Fallen Timbers (August 1794), their land was taken at the Treaty of Greenville (August 1795), and their stories now were groundless. At this hour of defeat, a Princeton deist struck a stadialist note against the commons, writing that "in the history of the progress of nations from barbarism to civility ... the establishment of private property [has] entered into the foundation on which the superstructure of civil society has been erected."[25] To an Irish audience, in the throes of the loss of political independence, widespread famine, recurring pestilence, and repression of spirit, the story had a totally different meaning. An older cultural form like the animal tale gathered a magical political realism as an allegory of survival by transformation. The tale was told in May 1802 in Dublin, and Ned was beheaded in February 1803 in London, where Kate took care of his body. United Irish people at the latter may have thought of the former, a red-crested bird and a black duck.

25. Wood, *Thoughts*, 23.

THIRTY-SIX

What Is the Human Race?

AT THE BEGINNING of *Red Round Globe Hot Burning*, I described how the quest for Catharine Despard led me to Ireland and a search for her grave. My quest was in some ways like hers. The purpose of my search for her body was not for closure, the enemy of the commons, but for memory and its two daughters, imagination and inspiration.

Let us imagine ourselves in Horsemonger Lane Gaol with Ned and Kate that Sunday night before the Monday dawn when Ned and comrades were to be "launched into eternity." During these last hours, we find them composing—the finishing touches?—his address from the gallows. The address was quoted at the beginning of this book, and its rhetorics, its tricolons, its Jacobin abstractions noted. But now we have been with them through thick and thin—in and out of commons in Ireland, England, Jamaica, Nicaragua, and Honduras, and throughout the commoning of prison and field, city and country. We have seen with them the enclosure of land (real estate) and hand (manufactory), and how war and conquest, money and machine, closed their lives and those of the people. Let us imagine what they were thinking that last night, this couple, this African American woman from a growing slave empire, this Irish renegade, this soldier from a country whose revolutionary bid for independence had just been crushed in mass carnage.

It is the breadth of the freedom struggle that gives depth of meaning to Ned's coauthored address from the gallows. They were not skilled in rhetoric, and they were certainly not sophists. Now, however, we can go beneath the verbal surfaces of the speech. What would Ned and Kate have discussed as they reviewed their own experiences as a man and a woman contemplating the future of humanity? Their rhetorical triads no more exhaust their meanings than does the Holy Trinity exhaust the spirit that moves mountains.

Citizens, I hope and trust, notwithstanding my fate, and the fate of those who no doubt will soon follow me, that the principles of freedom, of humanity, and of justice, will finally triumph over falsehood, tyranny and delusion, and every principle inimical to the interests of the human race.

At this point, just as listeners were pondering whether the triads were deliberately placed as contradictions (freedom against falsehood, humanity against tyranny, justice against delusion) and were reflecting on the phrase "the interests of the human race," the sheriff interrupted and threatened immediate execution. Why now, at the mention of the human race and its common interests? What did Ned and Kate mean by "the interests of the human race"? We can conjecture or speculate. Conjecture has been a procedure in this book, namely, to bring into relationship with Ned and Kate the historical forces that determined the context of their lives. These included the texts, scientific and otherwise, of the period in which they lived. But they would not have reduced the question to biology, and said that the human race was the sum of the species *homo sapiens*.

Though frowned on by historians, speculation is essential when documentary evidence is slight. As a procedure, speculation must recall the speculum, an instrument no less powerful that the telescope. But instead of enhancing vision of the outer cosmos, the speculum enables optical knowledge of the birth canal and the uterus. It can become a means of overcoming that dualism that separates the internal psyche from the external world. To speculate is to gain knowledge of the soul. The meaning of Ned and Kate's lives, of their comradeship, and hence their conception of "the human race," cannot be separated from the world around them. To Ned and Kate, those interests were inseparable from commoning as a form of social reproduction. The two were joined. The human race cannot be separated from its surrounding ecology. The attempt to do so—to separate psyche from earth, to tear them asunder in the production of Cartesian dualism, and to transform humans as "slaves" or "labor power"—is what propelled Ned and Kate to action on behalf of the human race and to give birth to the commoner from the womb of history.

We can list the variety of subsistence commons as a means of summarizing Despard's experiences. He was born in Ireland, where the clachan was the significant social unit and the rundale a characteristic form of collective landholding. He worked with soldiers from Scotland, who had been violently dispossessed from the Highlands and a type of commoning called runrig. As a young man, he could scarcely have avoided hearing the European discussion of the consciously communist preservation efforts by the Jesuits in Paraná and the *tupambaé*. He formed a life partnership with an African American woman, whose cultural and social heritage included the commons of the West African village. His brothers were soldiers in North America, where the Iroquois Confederacy sought to preserve its commoning of agriculture by the doctrine of a dish with one spoon. He worked for years in Jamaica, where the provision grounds held autonomously by the plantation slaves were worked in common and were subject to periodic redistribution. He visited the Midlands of England as a member of a recruiting party and thus would have been familiar with two decisive forces—the statutory enclosure of common lands and the struggle to retain the "moral economy" as a bulwark against dearth or famine. His military ventures in Nicaragua depended on subsistence gained from commoning techniques, such as the law of two haves, observed by the Miskito and other indigenous people. He lived in Honduras (now Belize) at a time when the Mayan *milpa,* or common land, remained the basis of ordinary subsistence. As superintendent, he distributed land by lottery. He was in London when Fletcher Christian wrote of the absence of private property among the Tahitian islanders. "The gentle character of the Guanches was the fashionable topic, as we in our times, land the Arcadian innocence of the inhabitants of Otaheite." The mutiny on the *Bounty* arose from the crew's opposition to the division between Captain Bligh's "oeconomy," his money economy, and their customs of the sea.[1] In Tahiti, this division opened into a cruel gulf between the two civilizations: "To the Europeans theft was a violation of legal ownership.... To the Tahitians it was a skillful affirmation of communal resources."[2] (The goose again.) Despard's associates in London in the years before his insurrectionary attempt included sailors and dockers, who, their wages being desperately in arrears, formed material relations that paralleled customary trade usages. In Haiti, the *lakou* and the *coumbite* (village cooperative labor) became all the more essential in wartime conditions.

What did these formations share? One theme was an objective antiperistasis to global commodity production, including opposition to the plantation monoculture of sugar, tobacco, or caffeine. Another form was the demand for a moral economy that allowed for regulation of subsistence goods

---

1. Humboldt, *Personal Narrative,* 121–22; Dening, *Mr Bligh's Bad Language.*
2. Holmes, *Age of Wonder,* 16, 17. In Tahiti, the exchange between a Stone Age and an Iron Age culture, not to put to fine a point of it, was one nail = one fuck.

like the bread grains (wheat). As important was opposition to the values associated with commodity production—proprietorship, individualism, cupidity, avarice, representation, cruelty. The second theme was opposition to proletarianization, and the loss of subsistence powers. It touched everything: criminalization, enclosure, slaving, conquest, taxation, kidnapping, war, disease, and famine. It changed the face of the earth, mountain, woods, field, and marsh. The term *landscape* scratches only the surface of the mutuality in earthly production, reproduction, and consumption. To sum up. The loss of commons included a manifold of practices from the country, from the "barbarian" and "semibarbarian" nations (Marx), from customary trade practices, and from urban "criminality." Where or how could these practices be compared? How might the various commons have become subject to synthesis? Paradoxically, one such place was in prison.

It is likely that Despard personally knew Thomas Spence, the English expounder of common property. Surely he knew his ideas. The energies of the French Revolution reached both a conclusion and a beginning in the 1795 conspiracy of Gracchus Babeuf that began the European communist tradition. Gracchus Babeuf, its French advocate of communism, belonged to the Conspiracy of Equals. The London Corresponding Society published *The Moral and Political Magazine,* whose leading article in June 1796 was a translation of Babeuf's letter from prison. Babeuf edited *Le tribun du people.* He composed the song "Dying of Hunger, Dying of Cold." Babeuf came to his communism through experience with the commons and the expropriation of common rights. "The most degrading and monstrous inequality insolently weighs upon the human race," its manifesto stated. "The common good" was "community of property." They looked forward to the disappearance of the "revolting distinctions between rich and poor, great and small, master and servants, rulers and ruled." There is one sun, said the manifesto, and one air. Why should there not be one nourishment, one education? "Neither gold nor silver will ever again be brought into the Republic." He spoke of the sacred nature of the conspiracy, of the grandeur of its soul, of its boldness and beauty.

On the day Despard delivered the last words and suffered his last breath, Alexander Humboldt sailed north on the Pacific Ocean, crossing the equator and leaving behind one continent, with its mountains and volcanoes. The Atlantic mountains shook. A few years earlier, in 1799, Alexander von Humboldt (1769–1859), the Prussian aristocrat, inspector of mines, and friend of Goethe, sailed west to explore Spanish America. Five years later, he returned to Europe with sixty thousand plant specimens, as well as the guano that, as he demonstrated, made excellent fertilizer—globalizing the cycle of life from excrement to food. He was particularly interested in volcanoes and the relation between what is beneath and what is above the surface of the earth. As a result of his work in the Andes Mountains, he drafted his *Naturgemälde* in the summer of 1802, which graphically correlated observations of plant species with altitude, precipitation, and temperature.[3] Humboldt related different organic forms of life to specific ecological characteristics. It was Humboldt who began to study, as part of the earth system, volcanic subterranean events and their relation to those above ground. These did not correspond to the delineations of private property, but they did relate to varieties of human commons. The same can be said of Ned and Kate. They too sought to "recognize the general connections that link organic beings"— spalpeen, pleb, sailor, plantation slave, soldier, servant. Ned and Kate also sought causal unity beneath the surface of the directly visible.

Speculating now about Catherine and reproduction, I want to link her struggles supporting her husband in prison with the movement to abolish slavery. The lessons at the 'Steel in 1798 were not lost on the authorities in 1803. A week before Edward was executed, the attorney general and the home secretary discussed "the subject of Col. Despard's writing in prison." It was "extensive and voluminous." The attorney general recommended that it be stopped. "With respect to seizing the papers in Mrs Despard's possession the opinion which would be formed of that measure would depend entirely upon what was found." "I cannot think him so rash & absurd as to trust so far to our delicacy as to transmit anything by his Wife." He concluded by forbidding Ned to send papers out of prison either to his wife or anyone else.[4]

The popular campaign in England against slavery and the slave trade collapsed in 1792 and would not revive for a generation, though the parliamentary campaign achieved victory in 1807.[5] In her 1798 *The Wrongs of Woman; Or, Maria*, Mary Wollstonecraft asked, "Was not the world a vast prison, and women born slaves?". Conditions of reproduction among the Atlantic mountains were about to change fundamentally. "The growth of the Southern economy was tied directly to the productivity of the capitalized womb, a term we use to refer to the way enslaved women's bodies functioned as the essential

3. Wulf, *Invention of Nature*, 92.
4. NA, HO 42/70, 15 February 1803.
5. Clare Midgley, *Women against Slavery*, 40.

production engine of the slave-breeding economy, which in turn fueled a global economy that processed slave-grown cotton into mass produced cloth."[6]

The abolitionist movement was a revolutionary movement, according to Herbert Aptheker.[7] Its modern chronicler, Manisha Sinha, defined abolition as follows: "Abolition was a radical, interracial movement, one which addressed the entrenched problems of exploitation and disenfranchisement in a liberal democracy and anticipated debates over race, labor, and empire." She put the slave's struggle at the heart of the movement and showed that the women were not only its foot soldiers but its leaders and orators. She might have broadened her definition to include prison.[8] "The entrenched problems of exploitation and disenfranchisement" cannot be dealt with without consideration of the prison, which was essential to their entrenchment. As the historian of abolitionists omits the prison, so the historian of prisons omits slavery. Yet the two systems are back-to-back in history, economics, and life.[9]

The utilitarian philosopher Jeremy Bentham proposed a panopticon, or an architecture based on wheel and spokes, which could isolate individuals in solitary while maintaining complete surveillance. Bentham believed that "labor of the hardest and most servile kind" made the best punishment. Political society depended on government, government depended on punishment, and punishment depended on labor. The panopticon was "a mill for grinding rogues honest and idle men industrious."[10] He advised that heads be shaved; that labor be fourteen hours a day, with a fifteenth spent on the treadmill; and that laborers sleep seven hours in cells measuring six by nine feet. William Cobbett called him "the beggar-whipper general" for his cruelty and "everlasting babbler," because he could not stop talking about it. Bentham's panopticon was generalizable to schools, asylums, and orphanages—and to all the disciplinary institutions of modernity.[11] He conceived of the human race as a steam engine.

The panopticon was defeated by a combination of forces, and Mrs. Despard was among them., She lobbied Parliament, penned letters to the

6. Sublette and Sublette, *American Slave Coast,* 24.
7. Aptheker, *Abolitionism.*
8. Sinha, *Slave's Cause.*
9. Ignatieff, *Just Measure of Pain.*
10. Semple, *Bentham's Prison,* 27, 107, 157.
11. Foucault, *Discipline and Punish.*

newspapers, petitioned the home secretary, worked with the wives of the other prisoners, visited Edward, and challenged directly the governor of the 'Steel. Otherwise, in 1803, the boys who played cricket on the Tothill Fields commons prevented its enclosure and sale as the site for Bentham's panopticon.[12]

It may be difficult to see Catharine as an abolitionist, even though she opposed the societies based on African slavery and racist subordination that she came from. She now lived far from the slave plantation, in London, Upper Berkeley Street, in a cosmopolitan city where hierarchy was at least not in the first instance based on race but on money and land. She had become an Irish revolutionary, instrumental as a courier and messenger. She was becoming a fierce opponent of the prison, whether the "corrupt" house of correction or the "reformed" penitentiary. Neither Ireland nor prison was to her an abstract "cause" but the life and breath of her husband, partner, and comrade. These evolutions in her own history corresponded to the vigorous expansion of slavery, colonial occupation, and prison construction. They occurred in the midst of the bloodiest slave rebellion in history. The five-year period from 1798 to 1803 witnessed the rise of Napoleon and the demise of the Republic in Europe, but it also saw the emergence in San Domingue of an independent Republic of Haiti, which sent a message threatening slave regimes everywhere. The term *abolition* will signify an array of causes, of prison, of patriarchy, of capital punishment, and of slavery.

Catherine was a person of color. The descriptions—black, Negro, creole—varied but the white line was clear. She belonged to people with African roots, who had fought for freedom on the other side of the Atlantic, and who also had led the fight against the prison in London. The African Americans Benjamin Bowsey and John Glover had led the storming of Newgate in June 1780, during those riots that terrified the ruling class and its spokespeople then and have continued to do so ever since. These persons embodied the struggle against enslavement and against imprisonment. Francis Burdett said that, "She was brought up in the West Indies but her father was a most respectable clergyman of the established church."[13] She was a product of African American Christianity, which emphasized exodus from slavery. Invoking Isaiah's prophetic words (42:1–9), she was called in righteousness, taken by the hand, to be a light to the nations, to open the eyes that are blind,

12. This story is told more fully in my *Stop, Thief!*
13. Patterson, *Sir Francis Burdett*, 1:68.

to bring out the prisoners from the dungeon, and from the prison those who sit in darkness.

William Lloyd Garrison, the towering American abolitionist, wrote that women were "the life of the cause." Similar to the chattel slave, women were oppressed in the tyrannies of patriarchy, which restricted them politically, economically, and culturally and reduced them to property. Many of the abolitionists were also prison reformers, such as the suffragist Elizabeth Pease (1807–97), and Lydia Maria Child (1802–80), who also fought for Native Americans. Elizabeth Heyrick (1769–1831) sympathized with slave rebellions, opposed war and capital punishment, and condemned prison conditions. She wrote, "Truth and justice, make their best way in the world, when they appear in bold simple majesty."[14] Words that apply to Ned and Kate.

"We ask for full, free, instantaneous, total, unconditional emancipation and freedom for the enslaved Negroes," declared the Hibernia Negro's Friend Society. A leading director was the Cork physician Edward Henry Orpen, also a proponent of the Irish language and the founder of the Dublin school for the hearing impaired. He escaped the famine by immigrating to Port Elizabeth, South Africa, where he continued good works.

Karl Polanyi describes these years as "the institutional separation of society into an economic and political sphere." He writes, "Labor is only another name for human activity which goes with life itself." Further, "Labor is the technical term used for human beings," and "the organization of labor is only another word for the forms of life of the common people" (not to mention childbirth!).[15] Life does not involve only work, said Polanyi. E. P. Thompson characterized the nub of this "great transformation" as "the making of the English working class."

What is the wage? It is a quantity of money. The money provides social power and may be exchanged for commodities, or the products of the labors of others. Karl Marx called the wage irrational for two reasons. First, it conceals the dynamic of exploitation itself, or the production of surplus value within the labor process. The central drama of capitalism is secret. Second, it excludes from social valorization those who work without any monetary compensation at all, notably the plantation slave and the domestic housewife. In these ways the wage form organizes both the exploitation of the worker

14. Quoted in Hochschild, *Bury the Chain*, 320; Heyrick, *Immediate, Not Gradual Abolition*, 4.

15. Polanyi, *Great Transformation*, 71–75.

and the composition of the working class as a whole. The wage concealed two principal kinds of people exploited by Atlantic capital—namely, unpaid slaves and unpaid women. The former produced the most dynamic global commodities (first sugar, then cotton), and the latter produced those who produced them.

Expropriation from the commons was a precondition of proletarian exploitation and modern work. Enclosure of the commons was a precondition of the formation of the land market in real estate. Those who owned the land no longer worked it, and those who had worked it no longer owned it. A culmination of these two processes took place during the long 1790s, that is, the enclosure and conquest of land and the production of people who could be exploited. Enclosure meant that the latter not only did not own land but also no longer had access to it. More slaves were traded, more land enclosed, more country conquered, more factory hands made during this long decade than ever before.

At the time Ned and Kate conspired for "the human race," two sciences were named for the first time—biology and geology. Ivan Illich made several observations about life. "First, life, as a substantive notion, makes its appearance around 1801." It is an arresting thing to say, particularly for us, since Despard was released from prison in March 1801! Illich's starting point was semantic. This was the year Jean Baptiste Lamarck coined the term *biology,* which he adopted from the German naturalist Gottfried Renhld Treveranus. *Biology* became the name of the science of life, plants, and animals, including humans. Before this time, the Hebrew and Greek names for life came from words whose cognates were "blood" and "soul." Lamarck and Illich were not referring to systematic classification, collection, investigation, and experimentation. Lamarck was reacting against mere classification and mechanistic interpretations of life. Illich related "life" to the ideology of possessive individualism; it was now talked about as property.[16] In this reading, "man" is individual, isolated, needy, competitive, and factitious. "Man" becomes *Homo economicus.* A redefinition of the meaning of "life" coincided with a new composition of global labor power.

Also in the 1790s, *geology,* a seventeenth-century term, acquired its meaning as the science of the earth's crust and strata, which was developed in John Hutton's 1795 *Theory of the Earth.* The materiality of the world became a machine, far removed from animating conceptions, such as "Mother Earth"

16. Illich, *In the Mirror,* 227.

or "creation" or the unique powers, energies, and substances of each location. As a machine, it might accompany labor power and turn a profit!

Biology as the science of life became separated from geology, the science of the earth. This is the parallel I see with the proletariat—this is a living factor of production, and the owners of the means of production or capitalists, usually an inert factor of production. The labor theory of value depends on both commodities—labor power and constant capital. When combined in the value of what it produces, labor power has contributed new value and the constant capital has transferred old value. Biology and geology became separate subjects. Their separation paralleled the expropriation of living labor from the world that gave it meaning, as well as life (their means of production). These sciences became necessary to the technical organizing of work, and hence to the organizing of the class relation between workers and owners.

In 1795, J. F. Blumenbach (1752–1840) published *On the Natural Variety of Mankind* (1795). It was a seminal work of racial anthropology that replaced the geographic classification of the races of *homo sapiens* with a hierarchical classification. It put the white race at the summit as the most beautiful and primeval. Stephen Jay Gould believed that "the shift from a geographic to a hierarchical ordering of human diversity marks a fateful transition in the history of Western science."[17]

The transition was fateful, and not only to science. It also marked a major step in the scientific construction of "race," at a contentious historical moment when the racial regime of the plantation was being challenged by the slaves of San Domingue, and plantation slavery was looking to expand over the entire continent of North America. Indeed, coeval with Blumenbach's hierarchy of races was the Louisiana Purchase, the independence of Haiti, the increase of the pushing system of whip-induced productivity, and the transition from the sugar plantation on the islands to the cotton plantation on the mainland. The latter produced the raw material that was shipped by sailors and unloaded by lumpers to supply the Lancashire factories, where it was consumed by the labor power of the Irish, the women, and the children to make cotton cloth and surplus value: voilà civilization!

What science had to offer was the prospect of abstract universals serving the same ends, namely, the accumulation of capital ("industrial revolution"), the accumulation of surplus value ("rise of the middle class"), the accumulation of

17. Gould, *Mismeasure of Man*, 405.

labor power ("population explosion"), and the accumulation of raw materials ("nature"). Biological reasoning and geological reasoning were mechanical, systematic, and quantitative. They were also state sponsored. They were separated from both the vernacular knowledge of working people and the working wisdom of the commons, both sacred and profane.

Ireland was central to both capitalism and colonialism. The drive to conquest, the ceaseless accumulation, the periodic famine, the immigration and exile, the racist domination, the exploitation of labor, and the expropriation of land occurred first in Ireland, so close to England. Ireland's proverbial wisdom provides a key to the era. Irish stories often end with the warning: "there are three things to be wary of—the hoof of a horse, the horn of a bull, and the smile of an Englishman." The hoof provided the traction of power, when material life—transport, ploughing, carriage—depended on horsepower. The bull's horn belonged to the animal whose power of fertilization was the basis of the cattle ranching that began to replace the subsistence commons. Meanwhile, conquest and enclosure were accompanied by a hypocritical ethos of doing good or making "improvements." Hence, "the smile."

The smile turned to a sneer with the first number of the *Edinburgh Review,* which appeared in October 1802, one month before the raid at the Oakley Arms. Its editors and Despard took opposite approaches to the French Revolution: Despard led "the criticism of arms," while the lead article of the *Edinburgh Review* developed the "slashing" style (as they called it) of "the arm of criticism." Its editors smiled with complacence. The interval of the Peace of Amiens permitted a consolidation of the new knowledge that accompanied the growth of money, commerce, and wealth.[18] Middlebrow opinion and high finance accompanied each other in its pages as "public opinion"; the effect, according to Lord Cockburn, was "electrical."[19]

The *Edinburgh Review* opposed the commons. The first article of the first number began with an attack on Rousseau, whose 1755 *Discourse of the Origin of Inequality* (part 2) began with an attack on enclosures: "The first man who, having enclosed a piece of land, bethought himself of saying 'this is mine' and found people simple enough to believe him was the true founder of civil society." The *Discourse* concluded by observing that "the privileged few gorge themselves with superfluities while the starving multitude are in want of the

18. Cobbett's *Political Register* appeared a few months earlier, as did the evangelical magazine the *Christian Observer.*

19. *Edinburgh Review,* no. 1 (October 1802), 216

bare necessities of life" which Despard died trying to prevent. Rousseau's "brilliant absurdities" were pernicious.[20] Together with Mably and Condorcet, he "unsettled all the foundations of political duty, and taught citizens of every existing community that they were enslaved and had the power to be free."[21] Rousseau's ideas, according to the *Edinburgh Review,* were the result of a disordered imagination. The *Review* contained articles on the expropriation of the Scottish highlands, on the monopolies of grain producers, on Hutton's geological theory of the earth ("the continents are crumbling fast into the sea" owing to "the agency of both fire and water"), on Godwin's theory of universal benevolence ("a dazzling phantom"), on the Romantic poets, on the effects on political economy of paper credit, and on the Haitian revolt and the crisis of the sugar colonies.[22]

Napoleon's son-in-law General Leclerc, along with forty thousand troops, arrived in Haiti early in 1802 to restore slavery. "Since terror is the sole resource left to me, I employ it," he said, before succumbing to yellow fever in November 1802. Recalling Tacky's Jamaican revolt (1762) the *Review* shrank in horror against the danger of a "negro commonwealth" or "savage republic." "The negroes are truly the Jacobins of the West India islands—they are the anarchists, the terrorists, the domestic enemy." James Stephens called for the parliamentary abolition of the slave *trade* and an alliance with France for the restoration of the slave *system.*[23] Piety and profit, the smile again.

Francis Horner wrote the review of Henry Thornton's *Inquiry into the Nature and Effects of the Paper Credit of Great Britain.*[24] Horner explained that "England . . . [was] the native country of political economy." The Bank of England had taken on the functions of sovereignty. Thornton was the "father of central banking." According to F. A. Hayek, the twentieth-century conservative economist, the book marked "a new epoch in the development of monetary theory." Paper money would put the unemployed to work and force the laborer "by necessity to consume fewer articles, though he may exercise

20. Rousseau, *Social Contract,* 76, 105.

21. Francis Jeffrey, review of *De L'Influence attribuée au Philosophes, aux Francs-Maçons, et au Illuminés sur la Revolution de France,* by J. J. Mounier, *Edinburgh Review,* no. 1 (October 1802): 18.

22. [Sydney Smith], review of *Spital Sermon,* by Dr. Parr, *Edinburgh Review,* no. 2 (October 1802): 18–24; review of *Illustrations of the Huttonian Theory of the Earth,* by John Playfair, *Edinburgh Review,* no. 26 (October 1802): 201–16.

23. Review of *The Crisis of the Sugar Colonies* (1802), by [James Stephens], *Edinburgh Review,* no. 27 (October 1802): 216–37.

24. *Edinburgh Review,* no. 25 (October 1802): 172–201.

the same industry." It encouraged the "machinery of manufactures." As treasurer of the Bible Society and the Missionary Society, Thornton led "the party of the saints." This powerful banker subsidized the mass conservative propaganda of Hannah More's cheap repository tracts. The banker smiled.

The class bigotry of the *Review* was direct—"poverty makes men ridiculous." The emotions of the refined and enlightened—love, grief, indignation—are different from those of "a clown, a tradesman, or a market-wench." Instead of praising civilization, the Lake poets "are filled with horror and compassion at the sight of poor men spending their blood in the quarrels of princes, and brutifying their sublime capabilities in the drudgery of unremitting labour." The words are truthful, the tone is nasty. After accurately noting that the poets "have an unconquerable antipathy to prisons, gibbets, and houses of correction, as engines of oppression, and instruments of atrocious injustice," the *Review* expresses its disgust toward such a sentiment with the sneering, "If it be natural for a poor man to murder and rob, in order to make himself comfortable, it is no less natural for a rich man to gormandize and domineer, in order to have the full use of his riches."[25]

Also in 1802, *Lyrical Ballads* went into its third edition. The poets omitted the two prison poems that had appeared in the 1798 edition. Their concern was not aesthetic—they were not bad poems,—but political. The poets deliberately withheld sympathy from prisoners, and withdrew from the prisoners' struggle, lest their literary opportunities be compromised within the commercial and politicized environment of London publishing. In 1802, William Wordsworth (1770–1850) revised and published "Preface to the *Lyrical Ballads*," a manifesto of Romantic poetry. It proposed first of all "to choose incidents and situations from common life, and to relate or describe them, throughout, as far as was possible, in a selection of language really used by men. . . . Low and rustic life was generally chosen." His poems were apparently products of investigation, of talking with individuals– a convict, a beggar, a shepherd, a peddler, a young woman, an Indian. His poetic program offered more than an oral history of individuals. The public was depraved owing to the "accumulation of men in cities" and the uniformity of their occupations. The result was the blunting of the mind and the "savage torpor" that leads humans to abandon their agency to make and change history.[26] To

---

25. *Edinburgh Review,* no. 1 (October 1802), 66, 71, 72.

26. Johnston, *Hidden Wordsworth,* 501. This preface becomes "the most influential document of literary theory in English."

summarize, the program required investigation of the working class, a critique of capitalism, and, in place of redemption for the working class through collective action, the nearly divine testimony by the poet. The "Preface" thus has two aspects—the descriptive project of history from below and the prophetic duty of the inspired individual. But what about the prisoners? They were expunged.

Catharine Despard's hand in composing her husband's last words, spoken from the gallows, and her attentions to his funeral in London cost her the widow's pension she was owed for her husband's many years of military service. A relationship exists between the decent burial of the revolutionary fighter and the subsequent memories of the revolutionary principles themselves. I compare her ministrations to her husband's corpse and the memory of his life to those of four other women in that era of revolution—Irish, Haitian, English, and maritime.

First is Anne Devlin, whose cousin was a bandit and brother a rebel. She met Robert Emmet in 1803, when he returned to Ireland from France to begin preparations for the insurrection for an independent Irish republic. She became his courier and housekeeper in their clandestine life. She was jailed after the revolt failed and while he awaited hanging. In Kilmainham jail yard, he played rackets under intense surveillance. Under the guise of retrieving a loose ball, he managed to reach Anne in another part of the yard and whisper to her that she should betray him and save her own life. Moments later, while pretending to remove a stone from her shoe and drawing up her stocking, she found occasion to reply sotto voce that she never would. "You are the most incorrigible person I ever met with," Major Sirr, the leading police authority in Dublin of the English overlords, told her. After being temporarily released on 20 September 1803, so that she could witness the pigs and dogs lapping up Emmet's blood from the paving stones, she was taken back to her stone-cold cell. She never recovered.[27]

Second we have Défilé, who was sutler and peddler of provisions to the troops of Dessalines. Remembering the 1780 Tupac Amaru rebellion in the Andes, he called his army of liberation "Incas of the Sun." Dessalines replaced Toussaint after he died in the Swiss Alps a few weeks after Despard suffered. Dessalines, born in 1758, was Despard's peer and contemporary. He led the successful fight for Haitian independence in January 1804. Two years later, he was viciously killed and mutilated in the postindependence struggle for land.

27. Cullen, *Anne Devlin Jail Journal,* 67.

He advocated for a broader ownership of land, even for those born outside of wedlock. Défilé sewed his mutilated body parts back together for burial. Her devotions helped preserve the oral history of the agrarian ideal.[28]

Third is Susan Thistlewood, the wife of Arthur Thistlewood, a leader of the 1820 Cato Street conspiracy to assassinate the English cabinet while they were at dinner. Arthur had joined a regiment in 1792 and was sent to the West Indies, where his uncle, a violent Jamaican planter and notorious sexual predator, lived. Arthur left in disgust, becoming a grenadier with the French revolutionaries at the battle of Zurich and then joining the Spenceans in London. William Davidson, a former slave in Jamaica, was a fellow conspirator. Susan's stays were removed and her body searched when she visited her husband on death row. She always wore her long hair unbound and combed out on these occasions. After the conspirators were hanged and decapitated, she led the new widows in petitioning Lord Sidmouth, the home secretary, for the restoration and internment of "the mangled remains of their late and unfortunate husbands, that they, your petitioners, may shed a silent tear over their mutilated remains." He refused.[29]

Walt Whitman tells the story of our fourth example.[30] In 1837, the American poet was in a London police office with a guide, who drew his attention to an aged, shabbily dressed woman applying for parish assistance. "Look closely at her," he whispered, "that woman's life has been indirectly involved with the welfare of nations." She "shook with terror the foundation of the throne itself." The woman was Anna, widow of Richard Parker, the "president of the fleet" after it mutinied in 1797. Aided by other women, she one night scaled the walls of the cemetery, where her husband's corpse had been interred after he was hanged. She carried it to London hidden in a dung cart and placed the coffin at the Hoop and Horseshoe public house, where the devotees of his cause could pay their last respects. The authorities became alarmed and tried to steal it back, which she prevented by sneaking the coffin from one place to another. By this time, thousands of weavers, Jews, Irish, Jacobins, and the flotsam and jetsam of London's maritime communities were assembled in murmuring insistence and potential explosiveness. Parker was buried in Whitechapel Church, which four centuries earlier had been the headquarters of Wat Tyler, a leader of the Peasants' Revolt.

28. Dayan, "Haiti, History."
29. Wilkinson, *Authentic History,* 73, 391–92.
30. Walt Whitman, "Richard Parker's Widow," *Aristidean* (April 1845), 111–14.

I want to say that "history begins with the body." If the authorities can destroy or hide the corpse, then memory of its life might also be destroyed or forgotten. More was involved than fair measure, and perhaps less than total peace, during the great mutiny of 1797, but its principles were remembered. The principles inherent in the Despard conspiracy were carried on, and his funeral and burial surely helped. Emmet's death was atrocious but, famously, his grave is unknown. In Haiti, the project of land for all the tillers did not die with Dessalines, owing partly to the oral history concerning the integrity of his corpse. Direct attack and destruction of the rulers could not establish the broad project of democracy, emancipation, and the commons that the Cato Street conspirators hoped to achieve.

Among the growing divisions of race, gender, and class the question arose, What is the human race? Even to ask the question is to reassert the power of human agency or freedom. And to link us with an old, simple project. What an effort it was to establish the race of Rome! said its poet Virgil. Hegel modified this, What a huge endeavor to know the mind! *Tantæ molis erat, se ipsam cognoscere mentem.* Kate helps us remember that Despard had a body as well as a mind, so we might want to modify Virgil yet again: What a great task to make the human race!

The story of Despard and the commons did not come to an end with his execution in 1803. Destruction of the commons and state-organized death continued on to the antipodes as nineteenth-century imperialism advanced. Henry Despard, the nephew or grandnephew of Edward Marcus Despard, commanded a British force in New Zealand. In July 1846, in a fit of uncontrolled anger, he launched an attack of his six hundred infantry and marines against the pa, or stockade, of the indigenous Maori. One third of his men perished in the failed attempt. Hone Heke, the leader of the Maori, wrote the governor, "You are a foreigner, we are strangers to each other. We do not understand your thinking, and you do not understand ours. God has given this land to us. It cannot be cut into strips like whale blubber."[31]

31. Vaggioli, *History of New Zealand*, 128.

WORKS CITED

Archival Materials

Barlow, Joel. "Notebook, c. 1796–97." bMS.Am1448 (13). Houghton Library, Harvard University.

Boulton and Watt Collection. Birmingham Central Reference Library, Birmingham, United Kingdom.

Burdett, Henry. Papers. Bodleian Library, University of Oxford.

Collis and Ward. Despard Estate. 2/463/26. National Archives of Ireland, Dublin.

Coote, Eyre. Papers. William L. Clements Library, University of Michigan, Ann Arbor.

Despard, E. M. Appendix to the Narrative of Publick Transactions in the Bay of Honduras 1784–1790. CO 123/11. National Archives, London.

Despard, Elizabeth. "Recollections on the Despard Family." 1841. Mr. and Mrs. M. H. Despard Collection.

Despard, Jane. "Memoranda Connected with the Despard Family from Recollections." 1838. Mr. and Mrs. M. H. Despard Collection.

"Famous Boxers." MS. William L. Clements Library, University of Michigan, Ann Arbor.

Hogan, Garrath. *A Book of Maps, Earl of Mountrath's Estate* (1740). National Library of Ireland, Dublin.

Honduras Bay Letter Books, 1787–1790. CO 123/5–9. National Archives, London.

"Humble Petition." HO 42/70. National Archives, London.

Kemble, Stephen. Papers. Vol. 1. William Clements Library, University of Michigan, Ann Arbor.

Lease for Three Lives from John Despard of Cordstown to William Despard of Killaghy (1714). National Archives of Ireland, Dublin.

London Metropolitan Archive. ACC/1437/5. City of London.

"Narrative of Sir Alexander Leith, Lieut. Col. 88th Regiment." Germain MSS. William L. Clements Library, University of Michigan, Ann Arbor.

Place, Francis. Collection. British Library, London.

Rebellion Papers (1790–1807). National Archives of Ireland, Dublin.

Registry of Deeds. Henrietta Street, Dublin.

Shelburne MSS. William L. Clements Library, University of Michigan, Ann Arbor.

Treasury Solicitor's Papers. National Archives, London.

Wellcome Medical Library. London.

Wentworth Woodhouse Collection. Sheffield Archives. Sheffield Reference Library, Yorkshire.

PRIMARY SOURCES

Amyot, Thomas. *Speeches in Parliament of the Right Honourable William Windham*. 3 vols. London, 1912.

Ancient Irish Prophecies. Cork, 1800.

Atkins, J. R. *Book of Racquets*. London, 1872.

An Authentic Narrative of the Life of Colonel Despard. London, 1803.

Badham, Charles. *Observations on the Inflammatory Affections of the Mucous Membrane of the Bronchiæ*. London, 1808.

Bage, Robert. *Man as He Is Not; or, Hermsprong*. London, 1810.

Bannantine, James. *Memoirs of Edward Marcus Despard*. London, 1799.

———. *New Joe Miller; Or, the Tickler, Containing Five Hundred Good Things*. London, 1800.

Barrett, John. *An Enquiry into the Origin of the Constellations That Compose the Zodiac*. Dublin, 1800.

Barrington, Jonah. *Personal Sketches in His Own Time*. 2 vols. New York, 1853.

Beddoes, Thomas. *Essay on the Causes, Early Signs, and Prevention of Pulmonary Consumption: For the Use of Parents and Preceptors*. London, 1799.

Binns, John. *Recollections of the Life of John Binns*. London, 1854.

Blake, William. *The Complete Poetry and Prose of William Blake*. Edited by David Erdman. Berkeley: University of California Press, 1982.

———. *The Poetry and Prose of William Blake*. Edited by Geoffrey Keynes. London: Nonesuch, 1967.

———. *Visions of the Daughters of Albion*. London, 1793,

Blincoe, Robert. *A Memoir*. London, 1828.

Bollan, William. *Britannia Libera*. London, 1772.

Burdon, John Alder. *Archives of British Honduras*. 3 vols. London, 1931.

Burke, Edmund. *A Philosophical Enquiry into the Origin of Our Ideas of the Sublime and Beautiful*. London, 1756.

———. *Thoughts and Details on Scarcity*. London, 1795.

Borrow, George. *Lavengro*. London, 1851.

Bristow, James. *Narrative of Suffering of James Bristow of Bengal Artillery*. London, 1794.

Bryson, Andrew. *Andrew Bryson's Ordeal: An Epilogue of the 1798 Rebellion*. Edited by Michael Durey. Cork, 1998.

Callender, James. *The Political Progress of Britain*. London, 1792.

Campbell, Archibald. *A Memoir Relative to the Island of Jamaica*. London, 1782.

Campbell, John. *Lives of the Chief Justice of England: From the Norman Conquest till the Death of Lord Mansfield*. 3 vols. London: John Murray, 1849.

Carlyle, Thomas. *The French Revolution: A History*. New York: Modern Library, 2002. First published 1837.

Castlereagh, Stewart. *Memoirs and Correspondence*. Edited by Charles Vane. 2 vols. London, 1850.

Chaigneau, William. *The History of Jack Connor*. London, 1752.

Claeys, Gregory, ed. *The Political Writings of the 1790s*. 8 vols. London: Pickering and Chatto, 1995.

Cobbett, William. *Cottage Economy*. Oxford: Oxford University Press, 1979. First published 1822.

———. *The Parliamentary History of England*. London, 1806–20.

Colquhoun, Patrick. *A Treatise on the Commerce and Police of the River Thames*. London, 1800.

———. *A Treatise on Indigence*. London, 1806.

———. *A Treatise on the Police of the Metropolis*. London, 1795.

Coote, Charles. *General View of the Agriculture and Manufactures of the Queen's County*. Dublin, 1807.

Coram, Robert. *Political Enquiries*. London, 1791.

Cotterel, James. *Survey of Kilcross and Clewen*. London, 1812.

Cringle, Tom. *Tom Cringle's Log*. Vol. 1. London 1833.

Cugoano, Quobna Ottobah. *Thoughts and Sentiments on the Evil of Slavery and Other Writings*. Edited by Vincent Carretta. New York: Penguin, 1999.

Curr, John. *The Coal Viewer's and Engine Builder's Practical Companion*. London, 1797.

Curry, John. *A Candid Enquiry . . . by the People Called Whiteboys or Levellers*. London, 1767.

Curtis, William. *Flora Londinensis*. 2 vols. London, 1777, 1778.

Dalmar, Antoine. *Histoire de la révolution de Saint-Domingue*. London, 1814.

Dancer, Thomas. *A Brief History of the Late Expedition against Fort San Juan So Far as It Relates to the Diseases of the Troops*. Kingston, 1781.

Darwin, Erasmus. *The Botanic Garden*. London, 1798.

———. *The Economy of Vegetation*. London, 1791.

———. *Phytologia, or the Philosophy of Agriculture and Gardening*. London, 1800.

The Debtor and Creditor's Assistant; Or, a Key to the King's Bench and Fleet Prisons. London, 1793.

Defoe, Daniel. *A Tour through the Whole Island of Great Britain*. 2 vols. London: Everyman, 1962.

Dialogue between a Labourer and a Gentleman: A Familiar Letter from John Bull to His Countrymen. London, 1793.

Drennan, William. *Letters to Orellana, an Irish Helot.* London, 1784.

Dunne, John. "Notices Relative to Some of the Native Tribes of North America." *Transactions of the Royal Irish Academy.* Vol. 9. Dublin, 1803.

Eagan, Pierce. *Boxiana; Or, Sketches of Ancient and Modern Pugilism.* London 1829.

———. *Table-Talk Book of Sports and Mirror of Life: Embracing the Turf, the Chase, the Ring, and the Stage.* London, 1836.

Edgeworth, Maria. *Castle Rackrent.* Project Gutenberg. n.p. London: Macmillan, 1895.

Edwards, Bryan. *The History Civil and Commercial of the British Colonies in the West Indies.* 4 vols. London, 1801.

Elyot, Thomas. *The Book Called the Governor.* London, 1531.

Emmet, Thomas Addis. *Memoir of Thomas Addis Emmet and Robert Emmet.* 2 vols. New York: Emmet Press, 1915.

Equiano, Olaudah. *The Interesting Narrative of the Life of Olaudah Equiano.* Edited by Vincent Carretta. London: Penguin, 1995.

Evans, Thomas. *Christian Policy, the Salvation of the Empire.* 2nd ed. London, 1816.

Evelyn, John Evelyn. *Fumifugium, or, The Inconveniencie of the Aer and Smoak of London Dissipated.* London, 1661.

Farington, Joseph. *The Farington Diary.* Edited by James Geig. 2 vols. London: Hutchinson, 1923.

Ferguson, Adam. *An Essay on the History of Civil Society.* London, 1767.

Fitz-Patrick, William J. *The Life, Times, and Contemporaries of Lord Cloncurry.* Dublin, 1855.

Frend, William. *Peace and Union Recommended to the Associated Bodies of Republicans and Anti-republicans.* London, 1793.

———. *What Shall the Rich Do to Be Safe?* London, 1797.

Fullarton, William. *A Statement, Letters, and Documents Respecting the Affairs of Trinidad.* London, 1804.

Godwin, William. *Caleb Williams.* London, 1794.

———. *Enquiry concerning Political Justice.* London, 1793.

Grimshaw, William. *Incidents Recalled: Or, Sketches from Memory.* Philadelphia, 1848.

Grose, Francis. *The Antiquities of Ireland.* Vol. 1. London, 1791.

Gwynn, E. J. *The Metrical Dindshenchas.* Dublin: Irish Academy, 1903–35.

Hall, Robert. *Modern Infidelity Considered with Respect to Its Influence on Society.* Charlestown, MA, 1801.

Harriot, John. *Struggles through Life, Exemplified in the Various Travels and Adventures in Europe, Asia, Africa, and America.* 2 vols. Philadelphia, 1809.

Hazlitt, William. *Selected Essays.* Edited by Jon Cook. Oxford: Oxford University Press, 2009.

———. *William Hazlitt: Selected Writings.* Edited by Alexander Ireland. London, 1889.

Hegel, Georg Wilhelm Friedrich. *Hegel's Lectures on the History of Philosophy.* Translated by E. S. Haldane and Frances H. Simson. London: Routledge, 1955.

Heyrick, Elizabeth. *Immediate, Not Gradual Abolition.* London, 1824.

Hone, William. *The Every Day Book.* London, 1827.

House of Commons. *Report from the Committee Appointed to Enquire into the Practices and Effects of Imprisonment for Debt.* April 1792.

———. *Report from the Committee Appointed to Enquire into the State of His Majesty's Prison in Cold Bath Fields.* Clerkenwell, 19 April 1799.

Howard, John. *The State of Prisons in England and Wales.* London, 1776.

Howell, T. B. *A Complete Collection of State Trials.* London, 1820.

Humboldt, Alexander von. *Personal Narrative of Travels to the Equinoctial Regions of America.* London, 1805

Hume, David. *Enquiry concerning Human Understanding.* Edited by P. H. Nidditct. London: Oxford University Press, 1975.

Hunt, Henry. *Memoirs of Henry Hunt Written by Himself in His Majesty's Jail at Ilchester.* London, 1820.

Hutton, James. *The Theory of the Earth.* 2. vols. London, 1796.

Imlay, Gilbert. *A Topographical Description of the Western Territory of North America.* London, 1792.

Invasion! A Familiar Letter from John Bull to His Countrymen, on the Report of an Invasion. London, 1803.

Jefferson, Thomas. *The Papers of Thomas Jefferson.* Edited by Barbara B. Oberg. Vol. 34, *1 May to 31 July 1801.* Princeton, NJ: Princeton University Press, 2007.

———. *The Political Writings of Thomas Jefferson.* Edited by Joyce Appleby and Terence Ball. Cambridge: Cambridge University Press, 2012.

Kemble, Stephen. *Documents and Correspondence, 1780.* Collections of the New York Historical Society. Vol. 17. New York, 1884.

Lawless, Valentine Browne. *Personal Recollections.* Dublin, 1849.

Lawlor, Fintan. *The Irish Felon.* In *The Field Day Anthology of Irish Writing,* edited by Seamus Deane, Andrew Carpenter, and Jonathan Williams. Vol. 2. Derry: Field Day Publications, 1991. First published 1848.

Lawrence, James Henry. *An Essay on the Nair System of Gallantry and Inheritance.* In *Newgate in Revolution: An Anthology of Radical Prison Literature in the Age of Revolution,* edited by Michael T. Davis, Iain McCalman, and Christina Parolin. London: Continuum, 2005. Originally published 1794.

Leadbetter, Mary. *The Annals of Ballitore.* London, 1862.

Ledwich, Edward. *Antiquities of Ireland.* 2nd ed. Dublin, 1804.

Lendy, A. F. *Treatise on Fortification.* London, 1862.

Letter Addressed to Munster Peasantry. Pamphlet. London, 1786.

Letters Containing Information Relative to the Antiquities of the Queen's County. 2 vols. London, 1838.

Locke, John. *Two Treatises of Government.* New York: Hafner, 1956.

London Corresponding Society. *Selections from the Papers of the London Corresponding Society, 1792–1799.* Edited by Mary Thale. London: Cambridge University Press, 1983.

Long, Edward. *The History of Jamaica.* 3 vols. London, 1774.

Ludlow, Edmund. *Memoirs, 1625–1672.* Oxford: Clarendon Press, 1894.

Malthus, Thomas. *An Essay on the Principle of Population.* London, 1798.

Mayhew, Henry. *London Life and London Labour.* Vol. 2. New York: Dover, 1968.

M'Callum, Pierre F. *Travels in Trinidad during the Months of February, March and April 1803.* Liverpool, 1805.

McAuliffe, E. J. *An Irish Genealogical Source: The Roll of the Quaker School at Ballitore County Kildare.* Dublin: Irish Academic Press, 1984.

Memoirs of the Life of Colonel E.M. Despard, Now Under Sentence of Death for High Treason. 3rd ed. London, 1803.

Middleton, John. *View of the Agriculture of Middlesex.* London, 1798.

Minto, Gilbert Elliot. *Life and Letters of Sir Gilbert Elliot, First Earl of Minto.* 3 vols. London, 1874.

Moore, Thomas. *Memoirs of Captain Rock.* Dublin: Field Day, 2008.

———. *The Poetical Works of Thomas Moore.* Boston: Little Brown, 1856.

More, Hannah. *Village Politics: Addressed to all the Mechanics, Journeymen, and Day Labourers in Great Britain.* London, 1793.

More, Thomas. *Utopia.* London: J. M. Dent, 1923.

Moreton, J. B. *Manners and Customs in the West India Islands.* London, 1790.

Morley, Henry. *Memoirs of Bartholomew Fair.* London: Chapman and Hall, 1859.

Moseley, Benjamin. *A Treatise on Tropical Diseases; on Military Operations; and on the Climate of the West Indies.* 2nd ed. London, 1789.

Nourse, Timothy. *Campania Foelix.* London, 1700.

Observations on Woollen Machinery. Leeds, 1803.

O'Connor, Arthur. *The State of Ireland.* Edited by James Livesey. Dublin: Lilliput Press, 1998.

O'Connor, Feargus. *The Employer and the Employed: The Chambers Philosophy Refuted.* London, 1844.

Oswald, John. *The Cry of Nature.* Edited by Jason Hribal. London, 2002.

———. *The Government of the People; Or, A Sketch of a Constitution for the Universal Common-Wealth.* London, 1793.

———. *De La Marche Universelle of the Human Spirit toward Social Perfection.* London, 1792.

———. *Review of the Constitution of Great Britain.* London, 1791.

Paine, Thomas. *Rights of Man.* London: Penguin, 1969.

Palmer, Elihu. *Principles of Nature; Or, a Development of the Moral Causes of Happiness and Misery among the Human Species.* London, 1801.

Petty, William. *Political Arithmetick.* London, 1690.

Pigott, Charles. *A Political Dictionary Explaining the True Meaning of Words.* London, 1795.

Pinel, Philippe. *Medico-philosophical Treatise on Mental Alienation.* London, 1800.

Pinkard, George. *Notes on the West Indians.* London, 1816.

Place, Francis. *The Autobiography of Francis Place.* Edited by Mary Thrale. Cambridge: Cambridge University Press, 1972.

Porter, David. *Considerations on the Present State of Chimney Sweepers*. London, 1792.

Postlethwayt, Malachy. *Universal Dictionary of Trade and Commerce*. London, 1766.

Priestley, J. *A Historical Account of Inland Navigation and Railroads*. London, 1831.

The Proceedings of the Peace and Gaol Delivery at Old Bailey. London: Sessions House.

Pyne, W. H. *The Microcosm of London*. London, 1809.

Rae, John. *The Life of Adam Smith*. New York: Cosimo, 2006.

Rainsford, Marcus. *An Historical Account of the Black Empire of Hayti: Comprehending a View of the Principal Transactions in the Revolution of Saint Domingo with Its Ancient and Modern State*. London, 1805.

Rawson, James. *Statistical Survey of the Co. Kildare*. London, 1807.

Reeves, John. *Thoughts on English Government*. London, 1795.

Reflections on the Pernicious Custom of Recruiting by Crimps. London, 1795.

Robinson, William. *The History and Antiquities of Enfield*. 2 vols. London, 1823.

———. *The History of the Reign of the Emperor Charles the Fifth*. London, 1769.

Rousseau, Jean Jacques. *Discourse on Inequality*. London, 1754.

———. *The Social Contract and Discourses*. Translated by G. D. H. Cole. London: J. M. Dent and Sons, 1973.

Rowan, Archibald Hamilton. *The Autobiography of Archibald Hamilton Rowan*. Edited by William H. Drummond. Shannon: Irish University Press, 1972.

Rule, Henry. *Fortification*. London, 1851.

Ruskin, John. *The Stones of Florence*. New York: Hill and Wang, 1960.

Saint-Simon, Henri. *Selected Writings on Science, Industry, and Social Organization*. Edited by Keith Taylor. London: Croom Helm, 1975.

Sampson, William. *Memoirs of William Sampson*. New York, 1907.

Seacole, Mary. *Wonderful Adventures of Mrs. Seacole in Many Lands*. Edited by William L. Andrews. Oxford: Oxford University Press, 1988.

Smith, Adam. *The Wealth of Nations*. 2 vols. London: Everyman, 1977. First published 1776.

Spence, Thomas. *Pig's Meat: The Selected Writings of Thomas Spence, Radical and Pioneer Land Reformer*. Edited by G. I. Gallop. London: Spokesman, 1982.

———. *The Rights of Infants*. London, 1797.

Stanhope, Philip Henry. *Life of Pitt*. Vol. 2. London, 1861.

Stedman, John Gabriel. *Narrative of a Five Years Expedition against the Revolted Negroes of Surinam*. Edited by Richard Price and Sally Price. Baltimore: Johns Hopkins University Press, 1988.

Stephen, James. *The Crisis of the Sugar Colonies*. London, 1802.

Stranger, Charles. *Remarks on the Necessity and Means of Suppressing Contagious Fever in the Metropolis*. London, 1802.

Strutt, Joseph. *The Sports and Pastimes of the People of England*. London, 1801.

Tighe, William. *Statistical Observations Relative to the County of Kilkenny*. 2 vols. Dublin, 1800, 1801.

Tone, William T. W. *The Life of Wolfe Tone Compiled and Arranged by William Theobald Wolfe Tone.* Edited by Thomas Bartlett. Dublin: Lilliput Press, 1998.

Tooke, John Horne. *The Diversions of Purley.* London, 1805.

Townsend, Joseph. *Dissertation on the Poor Laws.* London, 1786.

Trant, Dominick. *Considerations on the Present Disturbances in the Province of Munster.* Dublin, 1787.

The Trial of Edward Marcus Despard, Esquire, for High Treason at the Session House, Newington, Surrey, On Monday the Seventh of February 1803. Transcribed by Joseph Gurney and William Brodie Gurney. London: Gurney, 1803.

A Twelvemonth's Residence in the West Indies during the Transition from Slavery to Apprenticeship. 2 vols. London, 1835.

Ure, Andrew. *The Philosophy of Manufactures.* London, 1835.

Vaggioli, Dom Felice. *History of New Zealand and Its Inhabitants.* Translated by John Crockett. Denedin, NZ: University of Otago Press, 2000.

Vaux, James Hardy. *The Memoirs of James Hardy Vaux Including His Vocabulary of the Flash Language.* Edited by Noel McLachlan. London: Heinemann, 1964.

Vincent, Dr. *Short Hints upon Levelling.* London: Association for Preserving Liberty and Property against Republicans and Levellers, 1792.

Volney, C. F. *The Ruins; Or, Meditation on the Revolutions of Empires.* Baltimore: Black Classic Press, 1991.

———. *Travels through Egypt and Syria.* 2 vols. New York, 1798.

Wakefield, Gilbert. *Reply to the Bishop of Llandaff.* London, 1798.

Wedderburn, Robert. *The Horrors of Slavery and Other Writings by Robert Wedderburn.* Edited by Iain McCalman. (New York: Markus Wiener, 1991.

———. *Truth Self Supported; Or, a Refutation of Certain Doctrinal Errors.* London: W. Glindon, 1802.

Wesley, John. *The Works.* Vols. 3 and 4. New York: Waugh, 1835.

White, Charles. *An Account of the Regular Gradation in Man.* London, 1799.

Wilkinson, George Theodore. *An Authentic History of the Cato-Street Conspiracy.* London, 1820.

Winterbotham, W. *An Historical, Geographical, Commercial, and Philosophical View of the United States of America.* 2 vols. London, 1796.

Wilson, James. *Collected Works of James Wilson.* Edited by Kermit L. Hall and Mark David Hall. Vol. 1. Indianapolis: Liberty Fund, 2007.

Winstanley, Gerrard. *The True Levellers Standard Advanced* (1649). In *The Works,* edited by George Sabine. Ithaca, NY: Cornell University Press, 1941.

———. *The Works.* Edited by George Sabine. Ithaca, NY: Cornell University Press, 1941.

Wollstonecraft, Mary. *Collected Letters of Mary Wollstonecraft.* Edited by Ralph M. Wardle. Ithaca, NY: Cornell University Press, 1979.

Wood, Silas. *Thoughts on the State of the American Indians.* New York, 1794.

Young, Arthur, *General View of the Agriculture of the County of Norfolk.* London, 1804.

Secondary literature is divided into eight overlapping categories: general, poetry, Ireland, Haiti and slavery, indigenous, United Kingdom, United States, and prison.

General

Ariès, Phillipe. *Centuries of Childhood*. Translated by Robert Baldick. London: Knopf, 1962.

Bellamy, Joyce M., and John Saville. *Dictionary of Labour Biography*. London: Macmillan, 1987.

Bollier, David. *Silent Theft: The Private Plunder of Our Common Wealth*. New York: Routledge, 2002.

———. *Think Like a Commoner: A Short Introduction to the Life of the Commons*. British Columbia: New Society, 2014.

Bollier, David, Silke Helfrich, and Heinrich Böll Foundation, eds. *The Wealth of the Commons: A World beyond Market and State*. Amherst, MA: Levellers Press, 2012.

Caffentzis, George C. "On the Scottish Origin of 'Civilization.'" In *Enduring Western Civilization: The Construction of the Concept of Western Civilization and Its "Others,"* edited by Silvia Federici. Westport, CT: Praeger, 1995.

Clausewitz, Carl von. *On War*. Edited and translated by Michael Howard and Peter Paret. Princeton, NJ: Princeton University Press, 1976.

Cliff, Michelle. "Notes on Powerlessness." *Sinister Wisdom* 5 (Winter 1978).

De Angelis, Massimo. *Omnia Sunt Communia: On the Commons and the Transformations to Postcapitalism*. London: Zed Books, 2017.

Dening, Greg. *Mr. Bligh's Bad Language: Passion, Power, and Theatre on the Bounty*. Cambridge: Cambridge University Press, 1992.

Elias, Norber. *The Civilizing Process: The Development of Manners*. Translated by Edmund Jephcott. New York: Urizen Books, 1978.

Engels, Frederick. *Socialism: Utopian and Scientific with the Essay on the Mark*. Translated by Edward Aveling. New York: International, 1994.

Esteva, Gustavo, and Madhu Suri Prakash, *Grassroots Post-Modernism*. New York: St. Martin's Press, 1997.

Fabian, Johannes. *Time and the Other: How Anthropology Makes Its Object*. New York: Columbia University Press, 1983.

Federici, Silvia. *Caliban and the Witch: Women, the Body, and Primitive Accumulation*. New York: Autonomedia, 2004.

———. *Re-enchanting the Commons: Feminism and the Politics of the Commons*. Oakland: PM Press, 2018.

Foucault, Michel Foucault. *Discipline and Punish: The Birth of the Prison*. Translated by Alan Sheridan. New York: Vintage, 1990.

Fox, John Fox. *The Ball: Discovering the Object of the Game*. New York: Harper, 2012.

Giedion, Siegfried. *Mechanization Takes Command: A Contribution to Anonymous History*. New York: W. W. Norton, 1969.

Gould, Stephen Jay. *The Mismeasure of Man*. Rev. and expanded. New York: Norton, 1996.

Graeber, David. *Debt: The First 5,000 Years*. New York: Melville House, 2011.

Hill, Christopher. *The World Turned Upside Down: Radical Ideas during the English Revolution*. London: Temple Smith, 1972.

Hobsbawm, Eric. *The Age of Revolution: Europe, 1789–1848*. London: Wiedenfeld, 1962.

Hulme, Peter. *Colonial Encounters: Europe and the Native Caribbean, 1492–1797*. London: Routledge, 1986.

Hyde, Lewis. *Common as Air: Revolution, Art, and Ownership*. New York: Farrar, Straus and Giroux, 2010.

———. *The Gift: Creativity and the Artist in the Modern World*. New York: Vintage, 2007.

Illich, Ivan. *In the Mirror of the Past: Lectures and Addresses, 1978–1990*. New York: Marion Boyars, 1992.

Klein, Naomi. "Reclaiming the Commons." *New Left Review* 9 (May–June 2001).

Kropotkin, P. *The Great French Revolution*. Translated by N. F. Dryhurst. London: Heinemann, 1909; New York: Schocken Books, 1971. Citations are to the 1971 edition.

Lefebvre, George. *The Coming of the French Revolution*. Translated by R. R. Palmer. Princeton, NJ: Princeton University Press, 1967.

———. *The French Revolution from Its origins to 1793*. Translated by Paul Beik. New York: Cambridge University Press, 1962.

Linebaugh, Peter. "'A Dish with One Spoon': American Experience and the Transformation of Three Officers of the Crown." In *1798: A Bicentenary Perspective*, edited by Thomas Bartlett, David Dickson, Dáire Keogh, and Kevin Whelan. Dublin: Four Courts Press, 2003.

———. *Stop, Thief!* Oakland: PM Press, 2016.

Linebaugh, Peter, and Marcus Rediker. *The Many-Headed Hydra: Sailors, Slaves, Commoners, and the Hidden History of the Revolutionary Atlantic*. Boston: Beacon Press, 2000.

Linklater, Andro. *Owning the Earth: The Transforming History of Land Ownership*. New York: Bloomsbury, 2013.

Mantoux, Paul. *The Industrial Revolution of the Eighteenth Century: An Outline of the Beginnings of the Modern Factory System in England*. Translated by Marjorie Vernon. 2nd ed. London: Jonathan Cape, 1961.

Marx, Karl. *The Ethnological Notebooks*. With an introduction by Lawrence Krader. Assen: Van Gorcum, 1972.

McCalman, Iain. *Radical Underworld: Prophets, Revolutionaries, and Pornographers in London 1795–1840*. Cambridge: Cambridge University Press, 1988.

Michelet, Jules. *History of the French Revolution*. Translated by Charles Cocks. London, 1847.

Mies, Maria, and Veronika Bennholdt-Thomsen. *The Subsistence Perspective: Beyond the Globalised Economy*. London: Zed Books, 1999.

Moriarty, Christopher. *Eels: A Natural and Unnatural History*. London: David and Charles, 1978.

Novak, M. E. *Daniel Defoe: Life and Ideas*. Oxford: Oxford University Press, 2001.

Ostrom, Elinor. *Governing the Commons: The Evolution of Institutions for Collective Action*. Cambridge: Cambridge University Press, 1990.

Palmer, R. R. *The Age of Democratic Revolutions: A Political History of Europe and America, 1760–1800*. Princeton, NJ: Princeton University Press, 1959.

Patel, Raj. *The Value of Nothing: How to Reshape Market Society and Redefine Democracy*. New York: Picador, 2009.

Polanyi, Karl. *The Great Transformation: The Political and Economic Origins of Our Time*. Boston: Beacon Press, 1957.

Pomeranz, Kenneth. *The Great Divergence: China, Europe, and the Making of the Modern World Economy*. Princeton, NJ: Princeton University Press, 2000.

Poovey, Mary. *A History of the Modern Fact*. Chicago: University of Chicago Press, 1998.

Rayner, Alan. "Conflicting Flows: The Dynamics of Mycelial Territoriality." *McIlvainea: Journal of the North American Mycological Association* 10 (1991).

Reid, Herbert, and Betsy Taylor. *Recovering the Commons: Democracy, Place and Global Justice*. Urbana: University of Illinois Press, 2010.

Rose, R. B. "The 'Red Scare' of the 1790s: The French Revolution and the 'Agrarian Law.'" *Past and Present,* no. 103 (May 1984).

Schmidt, Johannes. "The Breeding Places of the Eel." *Philosophical Transactions of the Royal Society of London,* ser. B, 211 (1923): 179–208.

Scott, James C. *Against the Grain: A Deep History of the Earliest States*. New Haven, CT: Yale University Press, 2017.

Shiva, Vandana. *The Violence of the Green Revolution*. London: Zed Books, 1991.

Solnit, Rebecca. *A Paradise Built in Hell, The Extraordinary Communities That Arise in Disaster*. New York: Viking, 2009.

Steffen, Will, Jacques Grinevald, Paul Crutzen, and John McNeill. "The Anthropocene: Conceptual and Historical Perspectives." *Philosophical Transactions of the Royal Society* 369 (2011).

Taussig, Michael T. *The Devil and Commodity Fetishism*. Chapel Hill: University of North Carolina Press, 1980.

Weinreb, Ben, and Christopher Hibbert, eds. *The London Encyclopedia*. London: Macmillan, 1983.

Wulf, Andrea. *The Invention of Nature: Alexander Humboldt's New World*. New York: Knopf, 2015.

Zalasiewica, Jan, Alejandro Cearreta, Paul Crutzen, Erle Ellis, Michael Ellis, Jacques Grinevald, John McNeill, Clément Poirier, Simon Price, Dan Richter, Mary Scholes, Will Steffen, Davor Vidas, Colin Waters, Mark Williams, Alexander P. Wolfe. "Response to Austin and Holbrook on 'Is the Anthropocene an

Issue of Stratigraphy or Pop Culture?'" *Geological Society of America Groundwork* 22 (October 2012).

Zandy, Janet. *Liberating Memory: Our Work and Our Working-Class Consciousness.* New Brunswick, NJ: Rutgers University Press, 1995.

———. *What We Hold in Common: An Introduction to Working-Class Studies.* New York: Feminist Press, 2001.

Poetry

Cardenal, Ernesto. *With Walker in Nicaragua, 1949–1954.* Middletown, CT: Wesleyan University Press, 1984.

Césaire, Aimé. *The Collected Poetry of Aimé Césaire.* Translated by Clayton Eshleman and Annette Smith. Berkeley: University of California Press, 1983.

Clare, John. *The Poetry of John Clare.* Cambridge: Cambridge University Press, 1972.

———. *The Prose of John Clare.* Edited by J. W. Tibble and Anne Tibble. London: Routledge and Keegan Paul, 1951.

———. "Remembrances." In *Major Works.* Oxford: Oxford University Press, 1984.

Coleridge, Samuel Taylor, *Specimens of the Table Talk of the Late Samuel Taylor Coleridge.* London, 1835.

Erdman, David. *Blake: Prophet against Empire.* 3rd ed. Princeton, NJ: Princeton University Press, 1977.

Gilchrist, Alexander. *The Life of William Blake.* Revised by Ruthven Todd. London: J. M. Dent and Sons, 1945.

Goldsmith, Oliver. *The Collected Works of Oliver Goldsmith.* Edited by Arthur Friedman. Vol. 4. Oxford: Oxford University Press, 1966.

Holmes, Richard. *Coleridge: Early Visions.* London: Hodden and Stoughton, 1989.

Johnston, Kenneth R. *The Hidden Wordsworth.* New York: Norton, 2001.

Keegan, John. *Legends and Poems.* Edited by Canon O'Hanlon. Dublin: Sealy, Bryers, and Walker, 1907.

———. *Selected Works.* Edited by Tony Delany. Co. Kilkenny: Galway Press, 1997.

Kovel, Joel. "Blake and the Radical Spirit." Lecture at the Tate Gallery, London, October 1991.

Linebaugh, Peter. "*London*'s London: Working-Class Composition in William Blake's Poem." In *River of Fire: Commons, Crisis & the Imagination,* edited by Cal Winslow. Arlington, MA: Pumping Station, 2016.

Martí, José. *José Martí Reader: Writings on the Americas.* Edited by Deborah Shnookal and Mirta Muñiz. Melbourne: Ocean Press, 1999.

O'Rahilly, Egan. *The Poems of Egan O'Rahilly.* Edited by Patrick S. Dinneen. London: Irish Texts Society, 1900.

Thelwall, John. *Incle and Yarico: Two Plays by John Thelwall.* Edited by Frank Felsenstein and Michael Srivener. Teaneck, NJ: Fairleigh Dickinson University, 2006.

———. *The Peripatetic*. Edited with an introduction by Judith Thompson. Detroit: Wayne State University Press, 2001.

———. *Poems, Chiefly Written in Retirement*. Oxford: Woodstock Books, 1989.

———. *Poems Written in Close Confinement in the Tower and Newgate*. London, 1795.

———. *Poems . . . Written in the Tower and Newgate*. London, 1795.

Thompson, E. P. *Witness against the Beast: William Blake and the Moral Law*. New York: New Press, 1993.

Wordsworth, William. *The Prelude: The Four Texts*. Edited by Jonathan Wordsworth. London: Penguin, 1995. First published 1805. Citations are to the 1995 edition.

———. *William Wordsworth*. Edited by Stephen Logan. London: J. M. Dent, 1998.

Wordsworth, William, and Dorothy Wordsworth. *The Letters of William and Dorothy Wordsworth*. Vol. 3, *The Later Years Part I: 1821–1828*. 2nd ed. Revised by Mary Moorman. Oxford: Clarendon Press, 1978–93.

IRELAND

Aalen, F. H., Kevin Whelan, and Matthew Stout, eds. *Atlas of the Irish Rural Landscape*. 2nd ed. Cork: Cork University Press, 2011.

Andrews, J. H. "The Struggle for Ireland's Public Commons." In *Rural Ireland 1600–1900: Modernisation and Change*, edited by Patrick O'Flanagan, Paul Ferguson, and Kevin Whelan. Cork: Cork University Press, 1987.

Bartlett, Thomas, David Dickson, Dáire Keogh, and Kevin Whelan, eds. *1798—A Bicentenary Perspective*. Dublin: Four Courts Press, 2003.

Beaumont, Daniel Matthew. "The Gentry of the King's and Queen's Counties: Protestant Landed Society, 1690–1760." 2 vols., PhD diss., Trinity College, 1999.

Bigger, Francis Joseph. *William Orr, the Northern Leaders of '98*. Facsimile of the first edition. Dublin: Belfast Linenhall Library, 1998. First published 1906.

Bourke, Angela. *The Burning of Bridget Cleary*. London: Penguin, 1999.

Bowen, Elizabeth. *Bowen's Court*. New York: Knopf, 1942.

Bric, Maurice J. "The Whiteboy Movement in Tipperary, 1760–80." In *Tipperary: History and Society*, edited by William Nolan. Dublin: Geography, 1985.

Buckley, David. *James Fintan Lalor: Radical*. Cork: Cork University Press, 1990.

Burtchaell, Jack, and Daniel Dowling. "Social and Economic Conflict in Co. Kilkenny, 1600–1800." In *Kilkenny: History and Society*, edited by William Nolan and Kevin Whelan. Dublin: Geography, 1990.

Carroll, Denis. *The Man from God Knows Where: Thomas Russell, 1767–1803*. Dublin: Tartan, 1995.

Cassidy, Daniel. *How the Irish Invented Slang: The Secret Language of the Crossroads*. Oakland, CA: AK Press, 2007.

Clifford, Brendan. *Prison Adverts and Potatoe Diggings*. Belfast: Athol Books, 1992.

Conner, Clifford D. *Arthur O'Connor: The Most Important Irish Revolutionary You May Never Have Heard Of*. New York: Universe, 2009.

———. *Colonel Despard: The Life and Times of an Anglo-Irish Rebel.* Conshohocken, PA: Combined, 2000.

Connolly, James. *Labour in Irish History.* Dublin: New Books, 1983.

Corkery, Daniel. *The Hidden Ireland: A Study of Gaelic Munster in the Eighteenth Century.* Dublin: M. H. Gill and Son, 1924.

Crawford, E. Margaret, ed. *Famine: The Irish Experience 900–1900, Subsistence Crises and Famines in Ireland.* Edinburgh: John Donald, 1989.

———. "William Wilde's Table of Irish Famines 900–1850. In *The Irish Experience 900–1900, Subsistence Crises and Famines in Ireland,* edited by E. Margaret Crawford. Edinburgh: John Donald, 1989.

Cullen, Luke. *The Anne Devlin Jail Journal.* Edited by John J. Finegan. Cork: Mercer Press, 1968.

———. "Economic Development, 1750–1800." In *A New History of Ireland.* Vol. 4, *18th Century Ireland, 1691–1800.* London: Oxford University Press, 1986.

Cullen, Seamus, and Hermann Geissel, eds. *Fugitive Warfare: 1798 in North Kildare.* Kilcock, Kildare: Lord Edward Fitzgerald 1798 Committee, 1998.

Curtin, Nancy J. *The United Irishmen: Popular Politics in Ulster and Dublin, 1791–1798.* London: Oxford University Press, 1994.

Deane, Seamus, Andrew Carpenter, and Jonathan Williams, eds. *The Field Day Anthology of Irish Writing.* 3 vols. Derry: Field Day, 1991.

Delany, Ruth. *The Grand Canal of Ireland.* Dublin: Lilliput Press, 1995.

Dickson, David. "The Gap in Famines: A Useful Myth?" In *Famine: The Irish Experience 900–1900, Subsistence Crises and Famines in Ireland,* edited by E. Margaret Crawford. Edinburgh: John Donald, 1989.

Donnelly, James S. Jr. "The Whiteboy Movement, 1761–5." *Irish Historical Studies* 21, no. 81 (March 1978).

Drennan, William. "The Intended Defence." In *The Field Day Anthology of Irish Writing,* edited by Seamus Deane. 3 vols. Derry: Field Day, 1991.

Elliott, Marianne. "The 'Despard Conspiracy' Reconsidered." *Past and Present* 75 (1977).

Evans, E. Estyn. *Irish Heritage: The Landscape, the People, and Their Work.* Dundalk, Ireland: Dundalgan Press, 1942.

———. *The Personality of Ireland.* London: Cambridge University Press, 1995.

Feehan, John. *The Landscape of Slieve Bloom: A Study of Its Natural and Human Heritage.* Dublin: Blackwater, 1979.

———. *Laois: An Environmental History.* Ballykilcavan, Ireland: Ballykilcavan Press, 1983.

Ffolliott, Rosemary. "The Registry of Deeds for Genealogical Purposes." In I*rish Genealogy: A Record Finder,* edited by Donal Begley. Dublin: Irish Books and Media, 1983.

Froude, J. A. *The English in Ireland in the 18th Century.* Vol. 2. New York: Scribner, Armstrong, 1874.

Geoghegan, Patrick. *Robert Emmet: A Life.* Dublin: Gill and Macmillan, 2002.

Gibbons, Luke. *Edmund Burke and Ireland: Aesthetics, Politics and the Colonial Sublime*. Cambridge: Cambridge University Press, 2003.

Gorster, John. *The Life and Times of Oliver Goldsmith*. 2 vols. London, 1877.

Hayes-McCoy, G. A. *A History of Irish Flags*. Dublin: Academy Press, 1979.

Keegan, John. *Legends and Tales of the Queen's County Peasantry*. Edited by John O'Hanlon. Dublin, 1839.

Kelly, James. *"That Damn'd Thing Called Honour": Duelling in Ireland 1570–1860*. Cork: Cork University Press, 1995.

Kelly, Martin J. "History of Lyons Estate." In *Newcastle Lyons—A Parish of the Pale*, edited by Peter O'Sullivan. Dublin: Geography, 1986.

Larcom, Thomas, ed. *The History of the Survey of Ireland, Commonly Called the Down Survey, A.D., 1655–6*. Dublin: Irish Archaeological Society, 1850.

Lawless, Jo Murphy. "Images of 'Poor' Women in the Writings of Irish Men Midwives." In *Women in Early Modern Ireland*, edited by Margaret MacCurtin and Mary O'Dowd. Edinburgh: Edinburgh University Press, 1991.

Lewis, Samuel. *A Topographical Dictionary of Ireland*. 2 vols. London: S. Lewis, 1887.

Little, Nigel. *Transoceanic Radical: William Duane: National Identity and Empire, 1760–1835*. London: Pickering and Chatto, 2008.

Lloyd, David. *Irish Times: Temporalities of Modernity*. Dublin: University of Notre Dame; Dublin: Field Day, 2008.

Loeber, Rolf. "Preliminaries to the Massachusetts Bay Colony: The Irish Ventures of Emanuel Downing and John Winthrop, Sr." In *"A Miracle of Learning": Essays in Honour of William O'Sullivan*. Edited by T. Barnard, D. Ó Cróinin, and K. Simms. London: Routledge, 1998.

Lyons Demesne: A Georgian Treasure Restored to the Nation. Limited ed. Belfast: Nicholson and Bass, 1999.

Lysaght, Patricia. "Fairylore from the Midlands of Ireland." In *The Good People: New Fairylore Essays*, edited by Peter Narváez. Lexington: University of Kentucky Press, 1997.

MacDonagh, Oliver. *States of Mind: A Study in Anglo-Irish Conflict, 1780–1980*. London: Allen and Unwin, 1983.

Madden, R. R. *The United Irishmen, Their Lives and Times*. 3rd ser. 2nd ed. London: Catholic, 1960.

Maddock, Fidelma. "The Cot Fishermen of the River Nore." In *Kilkenny: History and Society*, edited by William Nolan and Kevin Whelan. Dublin: Geography, 1990.

Maguire, W. A., ed. *Up in Arms: The 1798 Rebellion in Ireland, a Bicentenary Exhibition*. Belfast: Ulster Museum, 1998.

Ó Buachalla, Breandán. "From Jacobite to Jacobin." In *1798: A Bicentenary Perspective*, ed. Thomas Bartlett, David Dickson, Dáire Keogh, and Kevin Whelan. Dublin: Four Courts Press, 1998.

O'Donnell, Ruan, ed. *Insurgent Wicklow 1798: The Story as Written by Luke Cullen, O.D.C.* Wicklow: Kestrel Books, 1998.

O'Dowd, Anne. *Meitheal: A Study of Co-operative Labour in Rural Ireland*. Dublin: Baile Atha Cliath, 1981.

Oman, Charles. *The Unfortunate Colonel Despard and Other Studies.* London: Longmans, 1922.

O'Sullivan, Peter, ed. *Newcastle Lyons—A Parish of the Pale.* Dublin: Geography, 1986.

Plummer, Alfred. *Bronterre: A Political Biography of Bronterre O'Brien 1804–1864.* Toronto: University of Toronto Press, 1971.

Quinn, James. *Soul on Fire: A Life of Thomas Russell.* Dublin: Irish Academic Press, 2002.

Russell, Thomas. *An Address to the People of Ireland.* Dublin, 1796.

Salaman, Redcliffe N. *The History and Social Influence of the Potato.* Edited by J. G. Hawkes. Rev. ed. Cambridge: Cambridge University Press, 1985.

Scally, Robert James. *The End of Hidden Ireland: Rebellion, Famine, and Emigration.* Oxford: Oxford University Press, 1995.

Smyth, James. *The Men of No Property: Irish Radicals and Popular Politics in the Late 18th Century.* New York: St Martin's, 1992.

Súilleabháin, Seán Ó. *A Handbook of Irish Folklore.* Dublin: Folklore of Ireland Society, 1942.

Thuente, Mary Helen. *The Harp Re-strung: The United Irishmen and the Rise of Irish Literary Nationalism.* Syracuse: Syracuse University Publications in Continuing Education, 1994.

Tillyard, Stella Tillyard. *Citizen Lord: Edward Fitzgerald, 1763–1798.* New York: Vintage, 1998.

Whelan, Kevin. "Events and Personalities in the History of Newcastle, 1600–1850." In *Newcastle Lyons—A Parish of the Pale,* edited by Peter O'Sullivan. Dublin: Geography, 1986.

———. *Fellowship of Freedom: The United Irishmen and 1798.* Cork: Cork University Press, 1998.

———. *The Tree of Liberty: Radicalism, Catholicism and the Construction of Irish Identity, 1760–1830.* Cork: Cork University Press, 1996.

Woodham-Smith, Cecil. *The Great Hunger: Ireland 1845–1849.* London: Penguin, 1962.

Young, Arthur. *Tour in Ireland (1776–1779).* Belfast: Blackstaff Press, 1983.

Haiti and Slavery

Aptheker, Herbert. *Abolitionism: A Revolutionary Movement.* Boston: Hall, 1989.

———. *American Negro Slave Revolts.* New York: Columbia University Press, 1993.

Blackburn, Robin. *The Making of New World Slavery: From the Baroque to the Modern, 1492–1800.* London: Verso, 1997.

———. *The Overthrow of Colonial Slavery, 1776–1848.* London: Verso, 1988.

Boulenger, Jacques. "The King of Gonaives." In *Negro: An Anthology 1931–1933,* edited by Nancy Cunard. London: Wishart, 1934.

Braithwaite, E. K. *The Development of Creole Society in Jamaica, 1770–1820*. Oxford: Oxford University Press, 1971.

Buck-Morss, Susan. *Hegel, Haiti, and Universal History*. Pittsburgh: University of Pittsburgh Press, 2009.

Bush, Barbara. *Slave Women in Caribbean Society, 1650–1838*. Kingston: Heinemann, 1990.

Cunard, Nancy. *Negro: An Anthology 1931–1933*. London: Laurence and Wishart, 1934.

Dayan, Joan. "Haiti, History, and the Gods." In *After Colonialism: Imperial Histories and Postcolonial Developments,* edited by Gyan Prakash. Princeton, NJ: Princeton University Press, 1995.

Dubois, Laurent. *Avengers of the New World: The Story of the Haitian Revolution*. Cambridge: Harvard University Press, 2004.

———. *Haiti: The Aftershocks of History*. New York: Holt, 2012.

Epstein, James. *Scandal of Colonial Rule: Power and Subversion in the British Atlantic during the Age of Revolution*. Cambridge: Cambridge University Press, 2011.

Gates, Henry Lewis. *The Signifying Monkey*. Oxford: Oxford University Press, 1988.

Geggus, David. *Haitian Revolutionary Studies*. Bloomington: Indiana University Press, 2002.

Girard, Philippe R. *The Slaves Who Defeated Napoleon: Toussaint Louverture and the Haitian War of Independence, 1801–1804*. Tuscaloosa: University of Alabama Press, 2011.

Hall, Douglas. *In Miserable Slavery: Thomas Thistlewood in Jamaica, 1750–86*. London: Macmillan, 1989.

Harding, Vincent. *There Is a River: The Black Struggle for Freedom in America*. New York: Vintage, 1983.

Hochschild, Adam. *Bury the Chains: Prophets and Rebels in the Fight to Free an Empire's Slave*. Boston: Houghton Mifflin, 2005.

James, C. L. R. "The Atlantic Slave Trade." *The Future in the Present: Selected Writings*. Westport, CT: Lawrence Hill, 1977.

———. *Beyond a Boundary*. Durham, NC: Duke University Press, 1993.

———. *The Black Jacobins: Toussaint L'Ouverture and the San Domingo Revolution*. 2nd rev. ed. New York: Vintage, 1989.

Kaisary, Philip. "Hercules, the Hydra, and the 1801 Constitution of Toussaint Louverture." *Atlantic Studies* 12, no. 4 (2015).

Kiple, Kenneth F. *The Caribbean Slave: A Biological History*. Cambridge: Cambridge University Press, 1984.

McClelland, James E. *Colonialism and Science: Saint Domingue in the Old Regime*. Chicago: University of Chicago Press, 2010.

Millás, José Carlos. *Hurricanes of the Caribbean and Adjacent Regions, 1492–1800*. Miami: Academy of the Arts and Sciences of the Americas, 1968.

Rediker, Marcus. *The Slave Ship: A Human History.* New York: Viking, 2007.

Roumain, Jacques. *Masters of the Dew.* Translated by Langston Hughes and Mercer Cook. New York: Reynal and Hitchcock, 1947.

Scott, Julius Sherrard. *The Common Wind: Currents of Afro-American Communication in the Era of the Haitian Revolution.* London: Verso, 2018.

Sinha, Manisha. *The Slave's Cause: A History of Abolition.* New Haven, CT: Yale University Press, 2016.

Indigenous

Arvigo, Rosita. *Panti Maya Medicine Trail Field Guide.* San Ignacio, Cayo, Belize: Ix Chel Tropical Research, 1992.

Ashcraft, Norman. *Colonialism and Underdevelopment: Process of Political Economic Change in British Honduras.* New York: Teachers College Press, 1973.

Bell, Charles Napier. *Tangweera: Life and Adventures among Gentle Savages.* London: Arnold, 1899.

Bolland, O. Nigel. *The Formation of a Colonial Society: Belize from Conquest to Crown Colony.* Baltimore: Johns Hopkins University Press, 1977.

Brandon, William. *New Worlds for Old: Reports from the New World and Their Effect on the Development of Social Thought in Europe, 1500–1800.* Athens: Ohio University Press, 1986.

Caraman, Philip. *The Lost Paradise: An Account of the Jesuits of Paraguay, 1607–1768.* London: Sidgwick and Jackson, 1975.

Conzemius, Eduard. *Ethnographical Survey of the Miskito and Sumu Indians of Honduras and Nicaragua.* Smithsonian Institution Bureau of American Ethnology. Bulletin 106. Washington, DC: Government Printing Office, 1932.

Craig, Alan. "Logwood as a Factor in the Settlement of British Honduras." *Caribbean Studies* 9, no. 1 (1969).

Dozier, Craig L. *Nicaragua's Mosquito Shore: The Years of British and American Presence.* Birmingham: University of Alabama Press, 1985.

Ellingson, Ter. *The Myth of the Noble Savage.* Berkeley: University of California Press, 2001.

Esarey, Logan, ed. *Messages and Letters of William Henry Harrison.* New York: Arno, 1975.

Fairlie, Susan. "Dyestuffs in the Eighteenth Century." *Economic History Review,* 2nd ser., 17 (1965).

Finamore, Daniel. "Documentary Evidence of Frontier Settlement and Social Change in an Eighteenth-Century Caribbean Community." *Proceedings of the Thirteenth International Congress for Caribbean Archaeology.* Pt. 1. Willemstad, Curaçao: Institute of Archaeology and Anthropology of the Netherlands Antilles, 1991.

Ganson, Barbara. *The Guaraní under Spanish Rule in the Río de la Plata.* Stanford, CA: Stanford University Press, 2003.

Grandia, Liza. *Enclosed: Conservation, Cattle, and Commerce among the Q'eqchi' Maya Lowlanders*. Seattle: University of Washington Press, 2012.

Hamnett, Brian R. *Roots of Insurgency: Mexican Regions, 1750–1824*. Cambridge: Cambridge University Press, 1986.

Hill, Leonard U. *John Johnston and the Indians in the Land of the Three Miamis*. Piqua, OH: Piqua Press, 1957.

Hutton, Paul A. "William Wells: Frontier Scout and Indian Agent." *Indiana Magazine of History* 74 (1978).

Jones, Grant D. *Maya Resistance to Spanish Rule: Time and History on a Colonial Frontier*. Albuquerque: University of New Mexico Press, 1989.

Lewis, Oscar. *Tepoztlán Village in Mexico*. New York: Holt, Rinehart and Winston, 1960.

Millás, José Carlos. *Hurricanes of the Caribbean and Adjacent Regions, 1492–1800*. Miami: Academy of the Arts and Sciences of the Americas, 1968.

Morgan, Lewis Henry. *Houses and House-Life of the American Aborigines*. Washington, DC: Government Printing Office, 1881

———. "Montezuma's Dinner: An Essay on the Tribal Society of North American Indians." *North American Review* (April 1876). Reprinted. New York: Labor News, 1950.

Nash, June. *We Eat the Mines and the Mines Eat Us: Dependency and Exploitation in Bolivian Tin Mines*. New York: Columbia University Press, 1993.

Nietschmann, Bernard. *Between Lane and Water: The Subsistence Ecology of the Miskito Indians, Eastern Nicaragua*. London: Seminar Press, 1973.

Patch, Robert W. *Maya Revolt and Revolution in the Eighteenth Century*. New York: Sharpe, 2002.

Pocock, Tom. *Horatio Nelson*. New York: Knopf, 1988.

———. *The Young Nelson in the Americas*. London: Collins, 1980.

Quaquaquid, Henry, and Robert Ashpo. *Petition to the Connecticut State Assembly*. May 1789. Rept. in John W. DeForest, *The History of the Indians in Connecticut*. Hartford, 1852.

Reiter, Frederick J. *They Built Utopia: The Jesuit Missions in Paraguay, 1610–1768*. Potomac, MD: Scripta Humanistica, 1995.

Schiebinger, Londa. *Plants and Empire: Colonial Bioprospecting in the Atlantic World*. Cambridge, MA: Harvard University Press, 2004.

Stern, Steve J. "The Age of Andean Insurrection, 1742–1782: A Reappraisal." In *Resistance, Rebellion, and Consciousness in the Andean Peasant World, 18th to 20th Centuries*. Madison: University of Wisconsin Press, 1987.

Stone, William L. *Life of Joseph Brant-Thayendanega*. New York: George Dearborn, 1838.

Sugden, John. *Tecumseh: A Life*. Holt: New York, 1997.

Thompson, J. *Maya History and Religion*. Norman: University of Oklahoma Press, 1970.

Wainwright, Joel. *Decolonizing Development: Colonial Power and the Maya*. London: Blackwell, 2008.

Aberdare, Lord, ed. *Squash, Rackets, Tennis, Fives, and Badminton*. Lonsdale Library Series. London: Seeley Service, 1933.

Armstrong, Murray. *The Liberty Tree: The Stirring Story of Thomas Muir and Scotland's First Fight for Democracy*. Edinburgh: World Power Books, 2014.

Aspinall, A. *The Early English Trade Unions: Documents from the Home Office Papers in the Public Record Office*. London: Batchworth Press, 1949.

Avery, David. *The Irregular Common Fields of Edmonton*. Edmonton Historical Society, Occasional Papers, n.s., 9 (1964).

Baker, T. F. T., and R. B. Pugh, eds. *A History of the County of Middlesex*. Vol. 5. London: Victoria County History, 1976.

Brimblecombe, Peter. *The Big Smoke: A History of Air Pollution in London since Medieval Times*. London: Methuen, 1987.

Budleigh, J. K. *Trench Excavation and Support*. London: Thomas Telford, 1989.

Cazzola, Matilde. "'All Shall Be Happy by Land and Sea': Thomas Spence as an Atlantic Thinker." *Atlantic Studies* (Sept. 12, 2017).

Chandler, Dean, and A. Douglas Lacey. *The Rise of the Gas Industry in Britain*. London: British Gas Council, 1949.

Chase, Malcolm. *The People's Farm: English Radical Agrarianism, 1775–1840*. London: Breviary, 2010.

———. "Spence, Thomas." In vol. 8 of *Dictionary of Labour Biography*, edited by Joyce M. Bellamy and John Saville. London: Macmillan, 1987.

Coleman, Terry. *The Railway Navvies: A History of the Men Who Made the Railways*. London: Hutchinson, 1965.

Cookson, J. E. *The British Armed Nation, 1793–1815*. Oxford: Oxford University Press, 1997.

Crook, J. Mordaunt, and M. H. Port. *The History of the King's Works*. Vol. 6, *1782–1851*. London: HMSO, 1973.

Dinwiddy, J. R. "Sir Francis Burdett and Burdettite Radicalism." *History*, no. 65 (February 1980).

Dugan, James. *The Great Mutiny*. London: Deutsch, 1966.

Durey, Michael. *William Wickham, Master Spy*. London: Pickering and Chatto, 2009.

Ehrman, John. *The Younger Pitt: The Reluctant Transition*. London: Constable, 1983.

Epstein, James. "Politics of Colonial Sensation: The Trial of Thomas Picton and the Cause of Louisa Calderon." *American Historical Review* (June 2007).

———. "The Radical Underworld Goes Colonial: P. F. McCallum's Travels in Trinidad." In *Unrespectable Radicals? Popular Politics in the Age of Reform*, edited by Michael Davis and Paul Pickering. Aldershot, UK: Ashgate.

———. "Understanding the Cap of Liberty: Symbolic Practice and Social Conflict in Early 19th Century England. *Past and Present* 122 (February 1989).

Erdman, David V. *Commerce des Lumières: John Oswald and the British in Paris, 1790–1793*. Columbia: University of Missouri Press, 1986.

Forshall, Frederic H. *Westminster School: Past and Present*. London: Wyman, 1884.

Fryer, Peter. *Staying Power: The History of Black People in Britain*. London: Pluto Press, 1984.

Frykman, Niklas. "The Wooden World Turned Upside Down: Naval Mutinies in the Age of Atlantic Revolution." PhD diss., University of Pittsburgh, 2010.

Gilmour, Ian. *Riot, Risings and Revolution: Governance and Violence in Eighteenth Century England*. London: Pimlico, 1983.

Goodwin, Albert. *The Friends of Liberty*. Cambridge, MA: Harvard University Press, 1979.

Haarmann, A. W. "Notes." *Journal of the Society of Army Historical Research* 49 (Winter 1971).

Hammond, J. L., and Barbara Hammond. *Age of Chartists 1832–1854*. London: Longmans, 1930.

———. *The Skilled Labourer, 1760–1832*. London: Longmans, Green, 1919.

———*The Village Labourer: 1760–1832: A Study in the Government of England before the Reform Bill*. 4th ed. London: Longmans, 1927.

Hartley, Dorothy. *Food in England*. London: Macdonald, 1954.

Hay, Douglas. "The State and the Market: Lord Kenyon and Mr Waddington." *Past and Present* 162 (February 1999).

Hearnden, Arthur. *Red Robert: A Life of Robert Birley*. London: H. Hamilton, 1984.

Henderson, Robert W. *How Old Is the Game of Racquets?* New York: New York Public Library, 1936.

Hibbert, Christopher. *Nelson: A Personal Biography*. Boston: Addison Wesley, 1995.

Holmes, Richard. *The Age of Wonder: How the Romantic Generation Discovered the Beauty and Terror of Science*. New York: Pantheon Books, 2008.

Hone, Ann. *For the Cause of Truth: Radicalism in London, 1796–1821*. Oxford: Oxford University Press, 1982.

Jay, Mike. *The Unfortunate Colonel Despard: Hero and Traitor in Britain's First War on Terror*. London: Bantam Press, 2004.

Johnston, Kenneth R. *Unusual Suspects: Pitt's Reign of Alarm & the Lost Generation of the 1790s*. Oxford: Oxford University Press, 2013.

Kain, Roger J. P., John Chapman, and Richard Oliver. *The Enclosure Maps of England and Wales*. New York: Cambridge University Press, 2003.

Keown, John Keown. *Abortion, Doctors and Law*. Cambridge: Cambridge University Press, 1988.

Klingberg, F. J., and S. B. Hustvedt. *The Warning Drum: Broadsides of 1803*. Berkeley: University or California Press, 1944.

Layton, Edwin J. *Thomas Chippendale: A Review of His Life and Origin*. London: Hodder and Stoughton, 1928.

Lindsay, Jack. *J. M. W. Turner: His Life and Work*. London: Cory, Adams and Mackay, 1966.

Lloyd, Christopher. *The British Seaman: 1200–1860*. London: Paladin, 1968.

McCalman, Iain, ed. *An Oxford Companion to the Romantic Age: British Culture, 1776–1832*. Oxford: Oxford University Press, 1999.

———. *Radical Underworld: Prophets, Revolutionaries, and Pornographers in London 1795–1840*. Cambridge: Cambridge University Press, 1988.

Maidment, Brian. *Reading Popular Prints, 1790–1870*. Manchester: Manchester University Press, 2001.

Malcolmson, Robert W. *Popular Recreations in English Society, 1700–1850*. Cambridge: Cambridge University Press, 1973.

Matin, R. Montgomery. *History of the British Colonies*. Vol. 2, *Possessions in the West Indies*. London, 1834.

Midgley, Clare. *Women against Slavery: The British Campaigns, 1780–1870*. London: Routledge, 1992.

Moran, Richard. "The Origin of Insanity as a Special Verdict: The Trial for Treason of James Hadfield (1800)." *Law and Society Review* 19, no. 3 (1985).

Morley, Henry. *Memoirs of Bartholomew Fair*. London: Chapman and Hall, 1859.

Mossner, Ernest Campbell. *The Life of David Hume*. Oxford: Clarendon Press, 1980.

Neeson, J. M. *Commoners: Common Right, Enclosure, and Social Change in England, 1700–1820*. Cambridge: Cambridge University Press, 1993.

Noel, E. B. "An Historical Sketch of the Game of Rackets." *National Review* 72 (1919).

Pam, David. *A History of Enfield*. Vol. 1, *Before 1837*. Enfield: Enfield Preservation Society, 1990.

Patrick, J. Max. "William Covell and the Troubles at Enfield in 1659: A Sequel of the Digger Movement." *University of Toronto Quarterly* 14 (1944–45).

Patterson, M. W. Patterson. *Sir Francis Burdett and His Times 1770–1844*. 2 vols. London: Macmillan, 1931.

Phillips, Michael. "Lambeth and the Terror." In *William Blake,* edited by Robin Hamlyn and Michael Phillips. London: Tate Gallery, 2000.

Pickard, Tom. *Ballad of Jamie Allen*. Chicago: Flood Editions, 2007.

Pinchbeck, Ivy. *Women Workers and the Industrial Revolution, 1750–1850*. 3rd ed. London: Virago, 1981.

Ponting, Kenneth G. *The Woollen Industry of South-West England: An Industrial, Economic and Technical Survey*. New York: Augustus Kelley, 1971.

Porter, Roy. *London: A Social History*. Cambridge, MA: Harvard University Press, 1994.

Rackham, Oliver. *The History of the Countryside*. London: Weidenfeld and Nicolson, 1986.

Randall, Adrian. *Before the Luddites: Custom, Community and Machinery in the English Woolen Industry, 1776–1809*. Cambridge: Cambridge University Press, 1991.

Repcheck, Jack. *The Man Who Found Time: James Hutton and the Discovery of the Earth's Antiquity*. Cambridge, MA: Perseus Books, 2003.

Rosen, Barbara, ed. *Witchcraft in England, 1558–1618*. Amherst: University of Massachusetts Press, 1991.

Smith, Olivia. *The Politics of Language, 1791–1819*. Oxford: Oxford University Press, 1984.

Sparrow, Elizabeth. "The Alien Office, 1792–1806." *Historical Journal* 33 (June 1990).

Steedman, Carolyn. *Labours Lost: Domestic Service and the Making of Modern England*. Cambridge: Cambridge University Press, 2009.

Stevenson, John. *Popular Disturbances in England, 1700–1870*. London: Longman, 1979.

Strange, K. H. *Climbing Boys: A Study of Sweeps' Apprentices, 1773–1875*. London: Allison and Busby, 1982.

Thompson, E. P. *Customs in Common*. London: Merlin Press, 1991.

———. *The Making of the English Working Class*. New York: Pantheon, 1963.

———. *The Romantics: England in a Revolutionary Age*. New York: New Press, 1997.

———. *Whigs and Hunters: The Origin of the Black Act*. London: Allen Lane, 1975.

Thompson, R. H. "The Dies of Thomas Spence." *British Numismatic Journal* 38 (1969–1970).

Tsurumi, Ryoji. "The Development of Mother Goose in Britain in the 19th Century." *Folklore* 101 (1990).

Ulrich, Nicole. "International Radicalism, Local Solidarities: The 1797 British Naval Mutinies in Southern African Waters." *International Review of Social History* 58 (2013).

Valenze, Deborah. *The First Industrial Woman*. Oxford: Oxford University Press, 1995.

Walmsley, Robert. *Peterloo: The Case Reopened*. Manchester: Manchester University Press, 1969.

Wells, Roger. *Insurrection: The British Experience, 1795–1803*. Gloucester: Alan Sutton, 1986.

———. *Wretched Faces: Famine in Wartime England, 1763–1803*. Gloucester: Alan Sutton, 1988.

Williams, Gwyn A. *The Search for Beulah Land: The Welsh and the Atlantic Revolution*. New York: Holmes and Meier, 1980.

Winchester, Simon. *The Map That Changed the World: William Smith and the Birth of Modern Geology*. New York: HarperCollins, 2001.

Worrall, David. *Radical Culture: Discourse, Resistance and Surveillance, 1790–1820*. Detroit: Wayne State University Press, 1992.

United States

Baptist, Edward. *The Half Has Never Been Told: Slavery and the Making of American Capitalism*. New York: Basic Books, 2014.

Beckert, Sven. *Empire of Cotton: A Global History*. New York: Vintage, 2014.

Boal, Iain, Janferie Stone, Michael Watts, and Cal Winslow, eds. *West of Eden: Communes and Utopia in Northern California.* Oakland: PM Press, 2012.

Breen, Walter H. *Walter Breen's Complete Encyclopedia of U.S. and Colonial Coins.* New York: Doubleday, 1988.

Chinard, Gilbert. *Volney et l'Amerique.* Baltimore: Johns Hopkins University Press, 1923.

Cotlar, Seth. *Tom Paine's America: The Rise and Fall of Transatlantic Radicalism in the Early Republic.* Charlottesville: University of Virginia Press, 2011.

Durey, Michael. *Transatlantic Radicals and the Early American Republic.* Lawrence: University of Kansas Press, 1997.

———. *"With the Hammer of Truth": James Thomson Callender and America's Early National Heroes.* Charlottesville: University of Virginia Press, 1990.

Federici, Silvia. "Feminism and the Politics of the Commons in an Era of Primitive Accumulation." In *Uses of a Whirlwind: Movement, Movements, and Contemporary Radical Currents in the United States,* edited by Craig Hughes, Stevie Peace, Kevin Van Meter, and the Team Colors Collective. Edinburgh: AK Press, 2010.

Forman, James. *The Making of Black Revolutionaries.* Seattle: University of Washington Press, 1985.

Genesio, Jerry. *Portland Neck: The Hanging of Thomas Bird.* Portland, ME: CreateSpace, 2010.

Harris, Jennifer. "The Red Cap of Liberty: A Study of Dress Worn by French Revolutionary Partisans, 1789–94." *Eighteenth-Century Studies* 14, no. 3 (Spring 1981).

Korshak, Yvonne. "The Liberty Cap as a Revolutionary Symbol in America and France." *Smithsonian Studies in American Art* 1 (Fall 1987).

Lewis, Jan Ellen, and Peter S. Onuf, eds. *Sally Hemings & Thomas Jefferson: History, Memory, and Civic Culture.* Charlottesville: University of Virginia Press, 1999.

Linklater, Andro. *Measuring America: How the United States Was Shaped by the Greatest Land Sale in History.* London: Penguin, 2002.

Mann, Bruce H. *Republic of Debtors: Bankruptcy in the Age of American Independence.* Cambridge, MA: Harvard University Press, 2002.

Sheldon, William H. *Penny Whimsy: A Revision of Early American Cents.* New York: Dover, 1990.

Stack, Norman. *United States Type Coins: An Illustrated History of the Federal Coinage.* New York: Stack's, 1986.

Sublette, Ned, Constance Sublette. *The American Slave Coast: A History of the Slave-Breeding Industry.* Chicago: Lawrence Hill, 2016.

Twomey, Richard J. *Jacobins and Jeffersonians: Anglo-American Radicalism in the United States, 1790–1820.* New York: Garland, 1989.

Wallace, Anthony F. C. *Jefferson and the Indians: The Tragic Fate of the First Americans.* Cambridge, MA: Harvard University Press, 1999.

Walters, Kerry S. *The American Deists: Voices of Reason and Dissent in the Early Republic.* Lawrence: University of Kansas Press, 1992.

Way, Peter. *Common Labour: Workers and the Digging of North American Canals, 1780–1860.* New York: Cambridge University Press, 1993.

White, Richard. *The Middle Ground: Indians, Empires, and Republics in the Great Lakes Region 1650–1815.* Cambridge: Cambridge University Press, 1991.

Williams, Gwyn A. *The Search for Beulah Land: The Welsh and the Atlantic Revolution.* New York: Holmes and Meier, 1980.

Wills, Garry. *"Negro President": Jefferson and the Slave Power.* Boston: Houghton Mifflin, 2003.

Wilson, David A. *United Irishmen, United States: Immigrant Radicals in the Early Republic.* Dublin: Four Courts, 1998.

Wulf, Andrea. *The Invention of Nature: Alexander Humboldt's New World.* New York: Knopf, 2015.

Prison

Davis, Michael T., Iain McCalman, and Christina Parolin, eds. *Newgate in Revolution: An Anthology of Radical Prison Literature in the Age of Revolution.* London: Continuum, 2005.

Evans, Robin. *The Fabrication of Virtue: English Prison Architecture 1750–1840.* Cambridge: Cambridge University Press, 1982.

Gatrell, V. A. C. *The Hanging Tree: Execution and the English People, 1770–1868.* Oxford: Oxford University Press, 1994.

Hay, Douglas. "The Laws of God and the Laws of Man: Lord George Gordon and the Death Penalty." In *Protest and Survival: Essays for E. P. Thompson,* edited by R. W. Malcolmson and John Rule. London: Merlin Press, 1993.

Ignatieff, Michael. *A Just Measure of Pain: The Penitentiary in the Industrial Revolution 1750–1850.* New York: Pantheon, 1978.

Innes, Joanna. "The King's Bench Prison in the Later Eighteenth Century: Law, Authority and Order in a London Debtor's Prison." In *An Ungovernable People: The English and Their Law in the 17th and 18th Centuries,* edited by John Brewer and John Styles. London: Hutchinson, 1980.

Linebaugh, Peter. *The London Hanged.* 2nd ed. New York: Verso, 2003.

Lloyd, Thomas. "Impositions and Abuses in the Management of the Jail of Newgate." In *Newgate in Revolution: An Anthology of Radical Prison Literature in the Age of Revolution,* edited by Michael T. Davis, Iain McCalman, and Christina Parolin. London: Continuum, 2005.

Semple, Janet. *Bentham's Prison: A Study of the Panopticon Penitentiary.* Oxford: Oxford University Press, 1993.

Teeters, Negley K. *The Cradle of the Penitentiary: The Walnut Street Jail at Philadelphia, 1773–1835.* Philadelphia: Pennsylvania Prison Society, 1955.

Vaux, James Hardy. *The Memoirs of James Hardy Vaux Including His Vocabulary of the Flash Language.* Edited by Noel McLachlan. London: Heinemann, 1964. First published 1812.

INDEX

abolition. *See* slave revolts and abolition movements

abortion, 299

"The Acts of the Parliament of Clan Thomas" (Ó Rathaille), 125

Adair, James, 59

Adam (biblical), 276

Address of the London Corresponding Society, 272

"Address to the Irish Nation" (Evans), 357

Address to the People of Ireland (Coigly), 203

An Address to the People of Ireland (Russell), 59

Adeline Mowbray (Opie), 373

"The African's Complaint on Board a Slave Ship" (Russell), 202

Age of Reason (Paine), 40

agrarian commons. *See* subsistence commons

Agrarian Justice (Paine), 268

Agrarian Law, 10, 129, 261–63

alehouses. *See* public houses

Alien and Sedition Acts (1798), 212n4

allegiance. *See also fraternité*, as triad concept; Oakley Oath

American commons, 11

American Indian culture and social values: common laws of, 57, 59, 274, 275–76, 342–43, 398–99; Dunne and, 399–404; Jefferson on, 396–97, 398

American War of Independence, 127, 139, 146

Anglo-Irish Ascendancy, 9, 62, 96

Anthropocene, as term, 7, 8, 11, 70. *See also* geology; industrial revolution

antinomianism, 144–45, 151, 220, 322–23

Aptheker, Herbert, 411

Archer, William, 239

area-slum, 319

An Argument on Behalf of the Catholics of Ireland (Tone), 56–58

Armitage, John, 347

Armstrong, Benjamin, 62

Arvigo, Rosita, 174

Association for the Protection of Liberty and Property from Republicans and Levellers, 270, 271

Atlantic slave trade. *See* slavery

atmospheric science, 295

Auburn, Ireland, 128. *See also* "Deserted Village" (Goldsmith)

Babeuf, Gracchus, 79, 262, 409

back-slum, 319

Badham, Charles, 321

Bage, Robert, 274

ballooning, 183

Bankruptcy Law (1800), 337

Bannantine, James, 45, 49, 98, 173, 209

Barbados, 100, 151, 270

Barlett, James, 165

Barlow, Joel, 194, 386

Barrett, John, 195

Barrington, Jonah, 100, 101–2, 114, 131

Bastille. *See* Cold Bath Fields Prison

bastille, as term, 38, 85, 337, 356

Cugoano, Ottobah, 213, 217, 218, 220
Curry, John, 130
Curtis, William, 266–67

Darwin, Erasmus, 74, 321, 372–73
The Daughter of Adoption (Thelwall), 188, 372
David, Jacques-Louis, 4
Davies, John, 96
Declaration (Covel), 256
Defenders revolt (1795), 30, 127
Defense Act (1803), 228
Défilé, 419–20
De Graves, Samuel, 315
De la legislation (Mably), 262
demographics of proletariat, 46–47
Descourtilz, Michel, 174
"Deserted Village" (Goldsmith), 43, 84, 128
Despard, Andrew (Ned's brother), 101, 102
Despard, Cateret (Ned's brother), 100
Despard, Catherine (Ned's sister), 100
Despard, Catherine "Kate": overview of life of, 2–6, 14, 408; death and grave of, 19n1, 21, 31; denial of widow's pension for, 419; descriptions of, 209; Haitian life and escape of, 19–20; influence of, 371–73; inheritance of, 153; meeting Ned, 138–39, 150–51; Ned's gallows speech and, 35–37, 39, 355, 406–7; petitions and writings of, 354, 365–67, 370, 411–12; poem for, 43; revolutionary acts of—term, 30; son of, 5, 12, 209, 214, 218; visiting Ned in prison, 338, 355, 358–59, 366, 406
Despard, Edward Marcus "Ned": overview of life of, 2–6, 407–8; at 1795 riots, 234–35; 1802 Oakley Arms arrest and trial of, 154–55, 270, 283, 286–91; early life and family of, 37–38, 93–94, 100–103; execution of, 5, 6, 19, 41–42, 218; final pleas and gallows speech of, 35–37, 39, 355, 406–7, 410; Francis Place on, 82; Honduras and Belize administrative work of, 137, 155, 165, 168–75; imprisonment of, 38, 317, 327–28, 340, 346–47; Jamaican military service of, 137, 146–50, 154; meeting Kate, 138–39, 150–51; military service of, 133–34, 137; *Narrative of the Public Transactions in the Bay*

of Honduras, 327; Nicaragua expedition of, 155–64; property of, *95*, 96–97, *99*, 104, 108–9, 108n17, 114–15; son of, 5, 12, 209, 214, 218; work of, 38
Despard, Elizabeth (Ned's sister), 93, 94, 99–100, 101, 209
Despard, George (Ned's cousin), 106
Despard, Green (Ned's brother), 102
Despard, Henry (Ned's nephew or grand-nephew), 421
Despard, Jane (Ned's niece), 100, 116, 209, 218
Despard, Jane (Ned's sister), 93, 102, 103
Despard, Jane Walsh (Ned's mother), 100
Despard, John (Ned's brother), 101, 102
Despard, John Edward (Kate and Ned's son), 5, 12, 209, 214, 218
Despard, Lambert, 104
Despard, Letitia (Croasdaile), 100
Despard, Philip, 100, 122
Despard, Richard, 104
Despard, William (Ned's brother), 100
Despard, William (Ned's father), 109
Despard, William (Ned's grandfather), 99
Dessalines, Jean-Jacques, 181, 419–20
Devlin, Anne, 20, 419
Dickens, Charles, 330
Dictionary (Johnson), 10, 297
Discourse of the Origin of Inequality (Rousseau), 416–17
diseases, 122, 185, 320–22
division of labor theory, 74, 75, 314
Dixon, Charles, 159
Dolben, William, 259
Dowling, Daniel, 126
Doyle, James, 116
Drennan, William, 56, 58, 275
Driscol, Denis, 202, 276, 397
Dublin Evening Post, 41
Dublin Society. *See* United Irishmen
Duffin, Patrick W., 333–34
Dundas, Henry, 204, 226
Dunne, John, 399–405
Dupré, Augustin, 384
Dwyer, Michael, 27

"The Echoing Green" (Blake), 345
Edgeworth, Maria, 113–14, 246, 372

Hazlitt, William, 328, 351
Heckewelder, John, 59, 402
Hegel, G. W. F., 79, 198, 421
hell as metaphor for revolutionary underground, 87–88
Helliker, Thomas, 50–51
helots, 56, 63
Hemings, Sally, 137–38, 211–12
Henderson, Robert, 347–48
Henry VIII, 8
Herron, John, 360
Heyrick, Elizabeth, 413
Hirst, Thomas, 293–94
historical conjecture, 137–38
historical determinism, 76
historical stages—or stadialism, 75
History of Jamaica (Long), 211
Hodgson, Robert, 160
Hodgson, William, 231
Hollow Sword Blade Company, 98–99
Holmes, Richard, 295
Honduras, 137, 155, 165–75, 215
Hono Heke, 421
Hope, James, 63
Horner, Francis, 417
Horse Guards Parade, 292–93
Horsemonger Lane Gaol, 327, 350, 355
hotchpot, as term, 105, 107
Houghton, Mary, 48, 268
Howard, John, 329, 357
Howard, Luke, 295
Howe, George, 233
Hulme, Peter, 159
human oppression, 197, 399–402, 404, 415–16. *See also* slavery
human race, as concept, 5, 7, 407, 421
Humboldt, Alexander von, 409–10
Hume, David, 117
hunger. *See* famine
Hunt, Henry, 337–38
Hutton, James, 71, 76, 414–15
Hyde, Lewis, 83

ideal commons, 10
Illich, Ivan, 414
illness, 320–21
Illustrations of the Huttonian Theory of the Earth (Playfair), 71

Imlay, Gilbert, 404
Impositions and Abuses in the Management of the Jail of Newgate (Lloyd), 336
Inchbald, Elizabeth, 273–74
industrial revolution, 3, 7, 50–51, 70, 74–75, 301–2, 415–16. *See also* Anthropocene
infrastructure and forced labor, 23, 133, 147–50. *See also* slavery
Innes, Joanna, 332
Inquiry into the Nature and Effects of the Paper Credit of Great Britain (Horner), 417
Insolvency Acts, 332
International Commission on Stratigraphy of the International Union of Geological Sciences, 7
Ireland: 1798, Irish Rebellion, 19, 56, 83, 317–18, 356–64; 1803, Emmet's revolt, 5–6, 30–31, 63; 1831, Tithe War, 392; abolition movement in, 201–3; canals of, 20, 21, 22–23; commons laws of, 105–7, 115; as a commonwealth, 2, 55; conquest history of, 94, 97; Laois, 14, 93, 97–98; townlands of, 107–8
Irish Felon, 395
Irish language, 318–19
Irish Rebellion (1798), 19, 56, 83, 317–18, 356–64
Irish republican party, 283
Irish revolt led by Emmet (1803), 5–6, 30–31, 63
iron industry, 314
Irons, John, 257
Iroquois Confederacy, 342–43, 398–99
Isaiah (biblical), 265, 412

Jamaica, 137, 139, 146–53, 270. *See also* Tacky's Revolt (1760)
James, C. L. R., 149, 352–53
Jefferson, Thomas, 396; on American Indians, 396–97, 398; description of black people by, 210–11; on master and slave, 211–12; *Notes on the State of Virginia,* 211; presidential election of, 3, 70, 185, 192; relationship with Sally Hemings, 137–38, 211; Volney's *Ruins* translation by, 12, 41, 193–94

proletariat, demographics of, 46–47

property. *See* private property

Prosser, Gabriel, 52–53

prostitution, 205, 217, 222, 296–97, 397

Pryer, Thomas, 341

public houses, 283–86, 296, 318

Q'eqchi', 169. *See also* Mayan communities

Quota Acts (1795), 228

racial supremacy, 54, 210–11, 215–16, 297, 415. *See also* slavery

racket, as term, 347

rackets, 345–48, 350, 351, 419

Rainborough, Thomas, 263, 264

Rainsford, Marcus, 180, 186–87, 195–96, 198, 203

rape, 59, 152, 211, 216, 220

Rawley, William, 310

Rayner, Alan, 80

Recollections (Lawless), 20

Red Cap of Liberty, 384–97

Red Republican, 395

"red round globe hot burning," as phrase, 1–2, 11

Reeves, John, 270–71

Reflections on the Revolution in France (Burke), 262–63

Regent's Canal (England), 73

Reich, John, 389

A Relation of the Cruelties and Barbarous Murthers Committed by Some Foot-Souldiers and Others, 255

religion, 40, 41–42, 194

Reply to the Bishop of Llandaff (Wakefield), 342

res communa, 55

res plebeia, 55

res publica, 55

The Restorer of Society to its Natural State (Spence), 288

Reynolds, James, 276

Rhys, Jean, 138

Rhys, Morgan John, 202, 383

Richardson, Mary, 302

rickets, 320

The Rights of Infants (Spence), 268, 269

Rights of Man (Paine), 38, 48, 57, 229, 263

The Rights of Nature against Usurpation of Establishments (Thelwall), 188

roads. *See* infrastructure and forced labor

Robins, James, 241

Rochambeau, Vicomte de, 20, 180, 181, 183

Rochford, Rowland, 146–47

rose metaphor, 25

Ross, Hercules, 158

Rotter, James, 307–8

Roumain, Jacques, 208

Rourke, Felix, 27, 29

Rousseau, Jean Jacques, 9, 416–17

Rowan, Hamilton, 29, 394, 399

Rowlandson, Thomas, 345

Royal Canal (Ireland), 22

Royal Gazette, 270

Royal Gunpowder Works, 259–60

Royal Navy, 51

The Ruins of Empire (Volney), 12, 22, 37, 40–41, 193–97, 273

rules of proportionality, 148–49

rum, 159, 306

rundale, 112–13

Ruskin, John, 148

Russell, Thomas, 59, 60–61, 141–43

Rutland, John, 305–6

R. v. Fletcher, 298–99, 300

Salmon, Elizabeth, 48, 268

salop, 266–67

Sampson, William, 358

San Domingue revolt. *See* Haitian Revolution (1791–1803)

sansculottes, 385, *386*

saoirse, 127

Sargasso Sea, 138

Saunders, Henry Martin, 235

Scally, Robert, 28

scarcity, 157

Schmidt, Johannes, 138

scientific socialism, 8, 37, 76, 78

Scot, Robert, 389

Scotland, 2, 55, 71, 283

Scott, James C., 10

Scott, John, 367

Scully, Morris, 306

Seacole, Mary, 151

Seditious Meetings Act (1795), 82